Fashion Law Journal's

A Practical Guide to

Fashion Law

From Brand Planning to Setup, Brand Protection, Compliances, Business of Fashion, Supply-Chain, Workforce, Sustainability, Culture, Tech in Fashion & More.

Legal Desire Media and Publications

Anuj Kumar
Cindy K. Sotomayor

Law in this book is as amended upto December, 2021
The book focuses on Law relating to Indian Jurisdiction along with references to laws in various countries.

Price: INR.1000/-

ISBN: 978-0-578-38003-2

Edition: First, Feb'22

Published by:
Legal Desire Media and Publications
C-110/2, Ramnagar Kanker Khera
Meerut Cantonment, Uttar Pradesh – 250001
India

All Disputes will be subjected to Meerut Jurisdiction

Website: legaldesire.com
Email: office@legaldesire.com

Contributing Authors:

Anuj Kumar, Apoorva Mehta, Annalucia Fasson Llosa, Cindy K. Sotomayor, Letícia Lôbo, Chitra Sahay, Khushi Kundu, Ananya Bali, Snehal Khemka, Vanshika, Ambreen Imam, Anushka Indurkar, Tanya Sinha, Sonal Sinha, Shivani Singh, Yashika Nagpal, Muskan Mahajan, Apurbaa Dutta, Namah Bose, Garima Ranka, Varuna Sharma, Srushti Kedarpawar, Yukta Karnavat, Aastha Chahal, Lavanya Bhakuni, Lipika Sharma, Mannat Sardana, Srishti Raichandani, Nur Tandon, Ijas Muhammad, Srijaa Grover, Sujata Porwal, Shubhangi Baranwal & Aprajita Sharma.

Edited by:
Anuj Kumar

Asst. Editor:
Apoorva Mehta

Student Editors:
Riya Sahijwani
Navya Shukla
Saloni Thapa

About Fashion Law Journal

Fashion Law Journal is a venture of Legal Desire Media, A leading publisher of legal insights for the last 8 years. With Fashion Law Journal, the organise aims to provide quality insights in field of Fashion Law by way of publishing insights in digital and print format. The organisation assists fashion brands in understanding the legalities in field, compliances and helping startup fashion brands availing govt schemes. The organisation also runs regular training, masterclass, and courses in Fashion Law. Fashion Law Journal is a valuable resource for legal issues involving the fashion industry. Fashion Law Journal is a professional network for the fashion community. FLJ provides expert, timely and relevant insights about all things fashion! You'll find in-depth articles covering everything you need to know related to the law and fashion industry, legal issues regarding the fashion industry, how to start a business in the fashion world, trends (and beyond), design & technology news as well as and around-the-world look at glamour. Fashion Law Journal is a professional network for the fashion community. Members of FLJ are industry lawyers, law firms, and advisors devoted to the corporate practices and hottest trends in fashion and luxury. We strive to help those who work in the fashion industry learn about all the ways they might encounter legal problems or encounter situations in which their rights might be at risk. We help you understand where your fashion business falls within the law, avoid pitfalls, and plan a more successful future. This book is an initiative to provide insights about fashion law.

Visit us at: fashionlawjournal.com

About Legal Desire

For the past 8 years, Legal Desire has been a publisher of legal insights and news. Legal Desire offers a thorough, in-depth, and panoramic perspective on today's complicated legal matters. Real-time and in-depth analysis of recent legal developments and dissemination of updates about firms, in-house counsels, corporations, legal institutions, and governments around the world. Quality research reports on a wide range of legal and policy issues. Our journalism team looks into the most major global and national topics, covering both historical milestones and current occurrences, through live blogging of judgments, news coverage, policy reports, analysis, opinion, interviews, data, video, podcasts, and a lot more. The organization exclusively works with lawyers and law firms to manage their business development and legal marketing so that they can focus on practice and we take care about generating leads for them. The organisation is engaged in exploring new fields of law for new opportunities and possibilities for adding new dimensions to legal fraternity.

Visit us at: legaldesire.com

Editor's Note

'A Practical Guide to Fashion Law' is a valuable resource for legal issues involving the fashion industry. A Manual for the Fashion Industry is an authoritative, technical and practical guide to legal matters that fashion professionals need to know about. Ranging from the business of fashion to the rights of stakeholders in the fashion industry, This Book is an invaluable resource for lawyers, fashion designers, fashion entrepreneurs, students as well as for business people and those who are interested in the fashion industry. This book also provides an excellent reference for all those with a general interest who want a comprehensive guide to the law of fashion.

With inputs from over 25+ Contributing authors across the globe, The book covers fashion and legal developments over the years, compliances involved, management issues, brand management, labor laws, international trade, sustainability ethics, fashion artificial intelligence and a lot more. This Book will help us to understand what Fashion Law is, its scope, history, various segments, a new revelation in the fields of fashion and law, and its concerned institutions. It also makes us familiarize ourselves with various laws in the field of fashion and different sections, acts and legislations across the world. The book also discusses the various challenges faced by fashion stakeholders during brand building and design production. Fashion law is not only about protecting intellectual properties but it also involves labor laws, supply chain issues, various compliances, agreements and rights of stakeholders in fashion. The book also provides various agreements templates relating to. Fashion Industry, Guide to brand setup, checklists and case studies.

Anuj Kumar
Founder & Editor-in-Chief,
Fashion Law Journal, Legal Desire
anuj@legaldesire.com

Contents of Book

Chapter 1. Introduction

1.1 What is Fashion?

An elementary definition of Fashion can be translated as *"style or styles of clothing and accessories worn by a group of people at a given time."*[1] However, fashion cannot be restricted to physical appearance. In the contemporary world, fashion has acquired diverse definitions. Fashion is viewed as a form of art and expression, an infinite space for creativity, experimentation, and innovation.

A thorough interpretation of the Fashion Industry opens a pandora of knowledge, questions, and ideas. The youth paints 'Fashion' as a form of self-expression. In the words of Coco Chanel, a Fashionista, *'Fashion is more than just a set of dresses. Fashion is in the air, on the sea, and on the street; fashion is about thoughts, how we work, and what is going on.'*[2] Therefore, fashion is a way of liberating oneself from the monotonous nature of life. According to the famous quote by Diana Vreeland, 'Fashion must be the most intoxicating release from the banality of the world'.[3]

Thus, the term 'Fashion' cannot be summarized in a small definition. Fashion extends to the air, sea, and everything that surrounds us, not just metaphorically. Fashion is derived from nature and therefore has an extended effect on nature.

1.2 Significance of Fashion

Fashion is significant. The economy, culture, and each and every one of us are all impacted. What you wear reveals more about who you really are – or strive to be – then anything. Although, fashion is mostly seen as frivolous, and fleeting business. Many people don't realize how important and far-reaching it is.

Clothing has the power to alter people's perceptions of you as well as your own. Various places of the world have different fashion trends. Fashion is, in truth, the very essence of our existence. Our emotions, as well as our preferences, have an impact on fashion. Fashion trends are influenced by how we all feel about the things around us.

---

1 John Major & Valerie Steele, *Fashion Industry*, ENCYCLOPEDIA BRITANNICA (Oct 23, 2020), https://www.britannica.com/art/fashion-industry.
2 Barry Samah A & Shelby Ying Hyde, *The Best Coco Chanel Quotes About Fashion, Love, and Success*, HARPERS BAZAR (JUL.7, 2021), https://www.harpersbazaar.com/fashion/designers/g32971271/best-coco-chanel-quotes/.
3 Lauren Fisher, *Diana Vreeland's Most Memorable Quotes*, HARPERS BAZAR (Jul.29, 2014), https://www.harpersbazaar.com/culture/features/a2964/diana-vreeland-best-quotes/

To begin with, fashion does not entail purchasing gleaming designer garments or lavish jewelry and make-up sets. Rather, it is an absolute term that denotes that various people have distinct perspectives on fashion. It is for this reason that elegance is so crucial. This not only improves your performance but also helps to determine your individuality. Without any further ado, here are some pointers to assist you to appreciate the significance of current fashion trends.

Fashion has a Long-Lasting Impact.

You may have heard that first impressions matter, which is why we attempt to provide the finest first impact possible. As a result, anytime you meet someone for the first time, the initial few seconds are critical. Furthermore, if you wear jewelry, accessories, or apparel, it is crucial if you want to make a positive impression on the people you encounter.

Fashion is a Way of Self-Expression.

We recognize the importance of art in our lives. You can express your inner creativity through art. When you use art to express yourself, it's called self-expression, it helps to generate fashion trends. In reality, the things we create with our imagination can make a stylish statement. Fashion, after all, is about discovering inner power or comfort. Your sense of style and taste can be shown in the things you wear.

Fashion Allows you to Express Yourself Creatively

To get your creative juices flowing, you don't have to be a fashion designer. All you have to do now is select high-end clothing and shoes to go with them. The argument is that inspiration is the source of creativity. Furthermore, fashion can assist you in gaining the better understanding creativity.

Fashion May Boost Your Self-Esteem

If you wish to boost your self-esteem, fashion can assist you. You can complete yourself with the help of fashion trends. You should feel at ease no matter what you're wearing.

Fashion Entertainment Industry

The most important part of the entertainment business is fashion. Everything that happens in the entertainment industry revolves on fashion. Fashion and the entertainment business are crucial to every television show and film.

Fashion has a history of portraying the sentiments and behaviour of society as a whole, it is a representation of joy, festivities, social characteristics, morals, and values prevailing at a particular time. The Victorian-era corsets are the best example of fashion reflecting societal nature. The tight-fitting corsets can be construed to resemble the male dominance/ patriarchy in ancient Europe. Besides, some colours represent a certain faction of the society. For example, the rainbow flag and clothing on the same lines, symbolizes the logo of the LGBTQ community. Modern-day fashion is extending its limit beyond representational value. The focus is shifting from 'Fast Fashion' to concepts like thrift shopping and sustainable fashion. It would be incorrect to state that Fashion is percolating into society since Fashion has always been a factor in the exponential growth and evolution of human beings. However, modern-day Fashion is expanding to immeasurable lengths thereby affecting the lives of each stratum of the society alike.

With the rapid expansion of Fashion, innumerable questions about the rights and duties of Fashion designers, Fashion models and protection of Fashion content come into foreplay. The Fashion industry and its rapid growth internationally pose a potential threat to the legal rights of the members associated with the industry, making it extremely fundamental to introduce a comprehensive legal framework in the industry. A vast majority of people throughout the globe interpret the growth of fashion as ephemeral and meaningless. However, the fashion industry has a wider impact. It is an industry that offers a global language to millions of people to interact and intermingle with the essence of diverse cultures in order to express and present themselves and thus, is labelled as one of the most innovative and imaginative industries.

Fashion is an important factor of economic growth for a nation and aids growth supplements through consumption and conformity principles. According to social philosophers, Fashion is a window into social change. Fashion is also interpreted to encapsulate the representative character of modernity and reflect on the symbolic significance and social values. As a result, it's difficult to imagine a social life that isn't influenced by fashion in any way.

1.3 The stakeholders in the Fashion Industry

To what concerns the fashion industry, the main – though not exclusive –stakeholders are:

- the workers engaged in the many fields of the Fashion Industry, such as manufacturing or advertising, fashion shows or stores, as well as logistics;
- fashion designers;
- fashion models;
- fashion photographers and bloggers
- celebrities, influencers, and those working in the movie industry;
- those the work on the company's overall logistics;
- shopping malls and retail stores;

- consumers.

Furthermore, at a time, those may be divided into six types:
1. employees;
2. owners and investors;
3. customers;
4. suppliers;
5. the community; and,
6. the government

Regarding the first type, it can be said that employees are ones with a direct interest in the company's welfare, not only because they rely on them for income, but because the success of a business is a direct reflection of their services.

In fashion, once analysed the entire supply chain, one might consider not only hired designers, models, photographers as well as the rest of the more creative employees, but also officers, such as the company's CEO and CFO, as well as lawyers and workers hired to tend to the production of fabric, to manufacturing items and advertising them. In truth, though often forgotten, workers of manual labor represent the vast majority of the Fashion Industry's employees.

With that in mind, it is imperative to point out not only how diverse the group integrating it can be, but just how significant the number of workers in the Fashion Industry is worldwide. Well, when it comes to the latter, according to the World Bank, over 3.3 billion people integrated the global workforce in 2020[4], that being said, though it is difficult to raise accurate data or a definitive number of textile and garment workers around the world, not only because each source uses different definitions but because the industry has a great percentage of informal workers, there is an estimative that there are "430 million workers in the industry involved in activities ranging from raw material production (cotton) to the cut-make-trim stage".[5] In other terms, the estimated number is that around one out of every eight workers worldwide are somehow contributing to the fashion industry.

---

4 ILO, *ILO Flagship Report World Employment and Social Outlook -Trends 2020*, INTERNATIONAL LABOUR ORGANISATION (2020), https://www.ilo.org/wcmsp5/groups/public/---dgreports/---dcomm/---publ/documents/publication/wcms_734455.pdf.
5 CO DATA, *Faces and Figures: Who Makes Our Clothes?*, CO DATA (May.22, 2018), https://www.commonobjective.co/article/faces-and-figures-who-makes-our-clothes.

The second group, on the other hand, is more restricted, including shareholders and debtholders, who would contribute to the company with financial returns as well as suffer from an eventual disappointing performance.

When it comes to customers, it is plain to see how those would be the Industry's consumers. As stakeholders, consumers are affected by the quality of the product while also being responsible for a company's utmost success or failure. As such, any person who consumes a fashion item is automatically one of Fashion's stakeholders.

With that in mind, it is suitable to point out how the value of the global fashion industry currently represents roughly 2 percent of the World's Gross Domestic Products, being of over three trillion dollars.[6] Be that as it may, the Covid-19 pandemic had initial devastating results on sales, impacting the fashion industry so harshly that companies were forced to quickly adapt to a virtual setting in order not to lose such an important section of its stakeholders. As such, one can argue that, though significant and grand, the managing of consumers' unstable demands is difficult, and should be one of the industry's main concerns.

The fourth group, referring to suppliers, includes those who would provide a product or service to a company, acting as an intermediary between the areas of manufacturing and retail, as a way to guarantee – among other things – that stock is of sufficient quality.

In terms of the fifth group, it is safe to say that having the community as a stakeholder is an inherent characteristic of any socially relevant industry. Moreover, having gone through the statistics of the fashion industry, there is no denying that it should consider the interests of society as a whole when opting for a course of action, for not only does it provide jobs for a vibrant percentage of people, but its actions may influence broad issues, such as the concerns towards human's rights and the environment. In truth, communities may be affected by a considerable number of aspects of the fashion industry and other industries alike, being benefited by economic development, while also risking its health, in occasions where the presence of a company may endanger the environment.

In closing, there is the government, whose actions might limit or endorse the fashion industry through the creation of laws or the judging of cases concerning the fashion business. Other than that, it is clear how, considered the effects of fashion on the fifth group, States might hope for the industry to thrive.

---

6 Fashion United, *Global Fashion industry statistics- international apparel*, FASHION UNITED, https://fashionunited.com/global-fashion-industry-statistics/.

1.4 What is Fashion Law?

Fashion Law is not a statutory law rather it's the accumulation of various kinds of law. Take the example of production of a garment, from the various stages of how that garment is manufactured, material is procured, produced and distributed. Every step involves different laws, from the artist thinking of a garment in his mind to the initiation of supply chain, warehouse, retailer, finally to the consumer. The entire process has various laws involved, culminating into what we call as Fashion Law. The term as such does not have a great impact around the word, all industries seem to think that fashion is all about intellectual property, whereas the fashion industry is more than just the design. Fashion is inherently dependent upon culture and Fashion law is an extensive term that covers a wide range of legal concerns, including law of contracts, arbitration, labour law, intellectual property law, and many more. Privacy, consumer preferences, and unbridled consumerism are all topics that it addresses. With technological improvements, the term "fashion" has expanded in today's fast-paced world; it has become a widely acknowledged standard to identify an individual based on how they dress, extending to the quality of "brands." As the adage goes, "dress for the job you want," emphasizing the need for appropriate attire. In the twenty-first century, fashion has expanded to include nanotechnology, e-commerce, custom-fit clothing, new materials, and wearable technology such as smartwatches, Fitbits, and smart clothing, among other things.[7] Fashion has been important all throughout history. Fashion has been a major subject of all the legal rules and regulations. But fashion law as a distinct legal field is still upcoming. In 2004, a group of French lawyers published "Droit du Luxe" in a legal magazine, which translates to law of luxury goods.[8] In 2006, a professor Susan Scafidi started the first course in Fashion Law at Fordham Law School.[9] The world's first academic centre, the Fashion Law Institute was launched in 2010.

1.5 Myths about Fashion Law

There exists myths about Fashion Law that this field of law talks only about the business of fashion, intellectual property, celebrities and brands. The field of Fashion Law is not limited to the shining side of Fashion Industry but it also deals with the rights and duties of stakeholders, workforce in fashion, cultural appropriation in fashion, privacy, e-commerce, legal issues in supply chain, and yes, now the field is evolving with coming up of concepts of Metaverse, NFTs, use of blockchain and AI in fashion industry. We need to understand that this industry provides a massive employment

---

7 Aleksandr Ometov et al, *A Survey on Wearable Technology: History, State-of-the-Art and Current Challenges*, 193 COMPUTER NETWORKS. 1, 1-36 (2021), https://www.sciencedirect.com/science/article/pii/S1389128621001651.
8 Diana Barbur, *Fashion law. Concept and Beginning in European Union and Romania*, 8 JURDICAL TRIBUNE 1, 7 (2018) http://www.tribunajuridica.eu/arhiva/An8vS/1.%20Flavia%20Barbur.pdf.
9 *Ibid 11*

across global and forms significant part of GDP of nations, so the legal issues in this industry can't be ignored or can't be limited to rights about few stakeholders or issues. When we say term 'Fashion Law' it means the law dealing with the stakeholders in Fashion without excluding any section.

1.6 History and Evolution of Fashion Law

Ever since the Middle Ages, rulers and politicians throughout the globe have been laying down laws and regulations about what clothes we can wear. Every day when we wake up and get dressed, we do end up feeling that we are perhaps only limited by our closet when in reality, there is an extensive interplay of restrictions and regulations, not visible at the surface level.

It in fact, all dates back to the sumptuary laws that were used from the Middle ages onwards to not only bolster a sense of national identity but also keep those belonging to the lower strata of society, in their place by "dictating the style and quality of clothing citizens of every rank could wear"[10]. For instance, during the period of Scottish uprisings, an Englishman caught wearing a kilt could actually get arrested and land in jail[11], as explained by Robson, a lecturer at City University, London.

Britain

In the past, sumptuary laws were used by English rulers to prevent the mixing of ethnic groups. For example, back in 16th century Ireland, Queen Elizabeth I passed laws "banning native Irish dress and requiring people to dress in "civil garments" in the English style"[12]. Travelling back as far as 4 centuries before, in 1297, Englishmen in Ireland were even banned from sporting Irish hairstyles.

Another example is, how in 1463, the English Parliament passed a law which prohibited men from "wearing short coats and gowns that did not cover "privy members and buttocks"[13].

Another such instance is the 1732 Hat Act enacted by the English parliament, which banned American made-headgear. The only word that springs in one's mind after reading about these situations is bizarre! Moving on, the rigid rules of mandatory corsets to be worn by British women continued to be in force, until quite recently in the context of recent history-the beginning of the 20th century to be precise.

---

10 Brian Wheeler, The secret history of fashion laws BBC News (2014), https://www.bbc.com/news/uk-politics-25127293 (last visited Sep 6, 2021).
11 *Id.*
12 *Id.*
13 *Id.*

France

It is important to talk about fashion trends because they actually played quite a crucial role in shaping the legal future of France, transgressing the aspects of aesthetics and glamour. One such trend that was followed was during the French Revolution. The distinctive costume of the typical sansculotte was the pantalon (long trousers) in place of the culotte (silk breeches) worn by the upper classes, as well as the carmagnole (short jacket) and the red cap of liberty. Jacques-René Hébert's popular newspaper, the Père Duchesne, did much to spread the image of the sansculotte: a woodcut on the front page of each issue showed a man in Revolutionary costume, holding a musket and smoking a pipe.[14]

The United States of America

The history of USA will forever be tainted with the blotch of slavery. Things were in fact so bad for slaves, that they were banned from "wearing good quality fabrics or accepting hand-me-downs from their masters"[15.] The obsession with clothing styles existed to such an extent that as per speculations, a national dress code was almost included in the US Constitution!

People thought that would be perhaps good for the "morals" of the nation (rather the lack thereof)!

Conformity that was playing on the minds of the US school boards in the 1960s also exemplifies this compulsion of wanting to regulate as many spheres as they could, of citizens. The rise of the British boy band, the Beatles, not only brought about a major upheaval in popular culture and fashion trends but also court battles with students in US courts, over the length of their hair[16.]

Other forms of rules included having measurements in place, as to how short a skirt can be, how low pants can be and then checking the same.

The Middle-east

Sharia law is a set of precepts, composed of the principles of Islam which is further subject to the interpretation of jurists, clerics and politicians.

---

14 Reign of Terror, https://www.britannica.com/event/Reign-of-Terror (last visited Sep 6, 2021).
15 Wheeler, *supra* note 10
16 Wheeler, *supra* note 10

What this means in the context of women's rights is that their clothing, among other things, stands subject to scrutiny of those in power. "The Quran states that a woman should not reveal her beauty to men beyond her family while some Islamic jurists have ruled that this requires women to cover their hair and according to others, their faces as well". At the same time, many Muslims all over the world ascribe to a more liberal interpretation and take it to simply mean that women should not dress provocatively and behave modestly in public[17.]

When the Taliban came to power in Afghanistan from 1996 to 2001(and now again in 2021) they ended up enforcing the most extreme of interpretations possible; forcing women to cover themselves from head to toe in public, barring them from education and work and even from leaving home without a male escort[18.]

Without an iota of doubt, one's heart goes out to the women living in such autocratic regimes, thinking about their plight and what all they have to endure. To be very honest one shudders at the very thought of braving such injustices.

Thus, we can see how throughout history, fashion and apparels have been subjected to legal regulation for a long time. Initially sumptuary laws limited people by prescribing who could and could not wear certain garments, which in the modern world has metamorphosed into laws grounded in moral policing along with others dealing with trade restrictions and intellectual property protection.

Fashion as a concept is no longer myopically understood simply as a factor in shaping social, cultural, and interpersonal relationships. Instead, Its Evolution can be read through multiple glasses. To begin with, Psychologists interpret fashion dynamics as the seeking of individuality and oneself and talk about elements of body positivity and confidence in fashion. Sociologists scrutinize structures of race, caste, and class competition and equate social conformity to dress norms. Economists analyze it from the concepts of wants, needs, and scarcity driven by consumer behavior. Aestheticians credit the creative and artistic components of beauty, and Historians offer evolutionary explanations for changes in design with time.

---

17 Lisa Beyer, What Sharia Law for Afghan Women under the Taliban Might Mean Bloomberg.com (2021), https://www.bloomberg.com/news/articles/2021-08-17/sharia-law-for-afghan-women-what-that-might-be-quicktake (last visited Sep 6, 2021).
18 *Id.*

Over time, fashion has not only contributed to people's perceptions, beliefs, and trends but also has acted as a means to voice one's opinion and showcase unity and strength. This can be cited with the example of Indian's boycotting British-made goods and adopting Khakis in an effort to be united and strong. Additionally, evolving fashion has also helped in questioning and calling out complex structures of oppression in history, such as the restriction of Victorian women to wear corsets as a means to maintain an ideal and fragile body. What's particularly interesting is that both khakis and corsets now act as clothing adapted by all genders of the community freely, expressively and progressively.

The 21st Century is witnessing the state of fashion theory as a loose but inclusive array of descriptive principles and propositions that are not formalized or specific of certain structures of concepts, variables, and relations but are instead more gender fluid and non-conforming. Fast fashion makes people experiment with new themes and elements and proclaim their identity without feeling the need to imitate preconceived and pre-existing stereotypes. Additionally, pop culture opens up more room for representation and acceptance when people see Harry Styles, Korean boy bands, or even Ranveer Singh wearing genderless clothes that best suit their identity. Further, with more and more companies like H&M and Calvin Klein adopting models of all shapes, sizes, and colours, it not only helps shatter age-old standards of beauty but also promotes diversity, normalizes normal bodies, and promulgates ideals of body confidence and body positivity.

However, the Evolution of fashion law has explicitly been slow, with the field resting on four pillars majorly; intellectual property, business and finance, international trade and government regulations, and consumer culture and civil rights. What's important to note is that with rampant globalization and consumerism, there is a growing spectrum of legal issues faced by various fashion companies like customs, consumer preferences, data rights, product safety regulations, manufacturing ethics, and models' right to privacy. Hence, there is a pressing need for fashion companies to have lawyers specialized in fashion to address these issues. It is time to be done away with calling lawyers specifically specialized in Intellectual Property rights, Trademark or Mergers and Acquisitions each time a legal necessity arises. This is a waste of time and money and an active hindrance to the growth of fashion law as an emerging concept. A fashion lawyer can understand, interpret, empathize with, and act on behalf of clients in a technical and specialized industry by understanding the quirky details in the constantly rising and changing fashion industry.

Chapter 2. Fashion Law

2.1 Fashion Lawyers & their significance

Whom do we call a Criminal Lawyer? A lawyer with expertise in field of Criminal Law having knowledge of laws relating to crimes. So, if we need to define, who is a Fashion Lawyer? Then answer will be:

Fashion lawyers perform a broad range of duties ranging from forming and dissolving business entities, advising on brand development, IP monetization, franchising, merchandising, adverting, protection to drafting, and negotiating contracts in arbitrating and litigating trademark, copyright, and other intellectual property issues, looking into export and import matters related to the Fashion Industry, like making necessary arrangements for securing Import and Export licenses, securing the rights of fashion designers, models, photographers, and other stakeholders. To become a successful fashion lawyer, one needs to have a thorough understanding of the fashion industry's legal issues, compliances, supply chain, legal issues of stakeholders and their solution.

Now as we read about the legal issues in this industry in next section we'll under the significance of hiring a Fashion Lawyer.

2.2 Legal Issues in Fashion Industry

When we come to terms with any of the billion- or trillion-dollar industries that have been growing tremendously over the years, we do come across the essential need of backing it up legally. The fashion industry is that trillion-dollar, versatile industry that legally needs to be protected tactfully to ensure its harmonious existence. The fashion industry gained recognition quite recently hence, the laws governing it yet need to stem out.

Fashion law or Apparel law as it may be called is one of the emerging areas in the legal field. Fashion has an array of situations where their Intellectual Property Rights can be misused. The basis of fashion is exclusivity and creativity which if not protected could lead to an unethical approach in the industry. Counterfeiting designs of fashion brands at a local level is one of the most wanted issues that needs to be curbed. Fashion is not only about creating a brand name and selling the products but to sell those products you need a model a lot of times and protecting the model's rights is another aspect that needs to be considered too. The rampant prevalence of knock-offs in the industry tells us that there is no one-step solution or protection to all answers in the industry.

It is rightly agreed that the copyright protects the creative tangent of a design however it does not help in attaining monopoly over the product. It is a deterrent factor for the majority of the designers who live on economies of scale as the protection of design expires too once reproduced 50 times. The garment industry is one of the most important strategic industries that contributed 7% to the industry output in 2018-19. The Indian textiles and apparel industry contributed 2% to the GDP, 12% to export earnings and held 5% of the global trade in textiles and apparel in 2018-19.

After farming, textile is the second largest industry, in terms of the number of workers employed in the industry. The textile industry is classified into 3 sectors: spinning, weaving, and finishing. It also provides direct employment to over 45 million people. Thus, the textile sector in India plays an important role in the country's economy, providing employment to a significant population in rural and urban areas. The garment industry is under a veil of secrecy, with an almost complete lack of transparency, leading employees to be exploited. Our second skin's labels have become synonymous with exploitation, abuse, and harassment.

'Conscious fashion' started as a response to the hidden atrocities in the fashion industry, which infused the clothes we wear with shame and guilt. As a result of this abuse, genuine activism emerged, calling for revolutionary improvements in the entire sourcing, production, and purchase chain. Recognizing these hidden exploitative practices is the first step toward change.

Promoting and implementing ethical standards in the garment industry needs coordinated efforts. The COVID-19 pandemic's unpredictability has added to the problem, as brands have cancelled orders, leaving the supply chain short on both orders and output. Migrant workers' misery, when they returned to their home states in difficult circumstances with little savings, served as a reminder of their subsistence living conditions for many years. It should be difficult to carry on with business as usual as a result of this. The window of opportunity will close soon, and governments, brands, and suppliers must act quickly.

I.Counterfeit

Counterfeit means to imitate something. Counterfeit goods are imitated copies of original products. Counterfeit goods are often created in order to benefit from the superior value of the imitated product. Fake company logos and brands can be found on counterfeit items. It results in patent infringement or trademark infringement in the case of goods. Counterfeit consumer goods are known for being of poor quality and even not working at all and can even contain toxic substances. Counterfeiting is the practice of producing low-quality goods and selling them under a brand name without the authorization of the brand owner. Counterfeit products are copies or duplicates of original products with high brand value in the market that are sold at substantially lower prices than the originals and are almost indistinguishable from the original design in certain aspects when viewed from a distance.

The issue of counterfeit product buying and selling poses a challenge to brand owners, retailers, and consumers. Counterfeit false products hamper companies' valuable and intangible assets, such as intellectual property and brand, by eroding equity, reputation, and market positioning. This erosion results in the loss of consumers' trust and confidence in the company.

Counterfeiting is not a new concern in India. Nehru Place and Palika Bazaar in New Delhi, Richie Street and Burma Bazaar in Chennai, Manish Market, Heera Panna, Lamington Road and Fort District in Mumbai, and Chandni Chowk in Kolkata are among the markets that need to be watched out for this high-volume trade, according to a study by the United States Trade Representative (USTR). In fact, India remains on the "Priority Watch list" of the United State Trade Representatives' "Special 301" Report 2020 for lack of sufficient measurable improvements to its IP framework.

II.   Piracy of design

The application of a design or its imitation to any article belonging to a class of articles in which the design has been registered for the purpose of sale or importation of those articles without the registered proprietor's written consent is known as design piracy. It is also piracy of the design to publish such articles or expose terms for sale with knowledge of the unauthorized application of the design to them. Piracy is provided in Section 22 of the Designs Act of 2000. If any person acts in violation of Section 22 of the Act, he will face the consequences, which include payment of damages and an order of injunction prohibiting him from repeating the infringement.

III.   Health and safety risks

Productivity and economic growth are dependent on a healthy and motivated workforce. Workers seek better working conditions and a safer working environment in exchange for their productive efforts.

Most workplaces have a variety of risks, which can be classified into the mechanical, physical, chemical, biological, ergonomic, and psychosocial categories. All of these factors are interconnected, and they can have an effect on both overall efficiency and the worker's personal wellbeing. Employees usually work in unsafe buildings with no ventilation, breathing in hazardous substances and inhaling fibre dust or blasted sand. On textile production facilities, accidents, explosions, injuries, and disease are all too common. Research from the Delhi capital region similarly reported a 10-12 hour working day as standard for 67% of workers employed in informal workshops, with 39% of all workers suffering from eye strain and 41% from exhaustion.

Most workplaces have a variety of risks, which can be classified into the mechanical, physical, chemical, biological, ergonomic, and psychosocial categories. All of these factors are interconnected, and they can have an effect on both overall efficiency and the worker's personal wellbeing.

TYPES OF HAZARDS

1. Physical hazards

Occupational hearing loss, postural defects, falls, accidents, and other issues commonly affect many Operators in the workplace. Hearing loss is one of the most common problems in a manufacturing unit with loud machines, such as industrial sewing machines or cutters; postural defects, such as cervical and bone shape shift, can occur if a person is required to sit or stand in an incorrect position for an extended period of time. Accidents and falls are also a frequent cause of workplace accidents and deaths in industries such as transportation, mining, etc.

2. Fire hazards

These are common in industries that deal with a lot of flammable materials, such as cotton, chemicals, and so on. The common causes of fire hazards are most industries lack fire and smoke alarm systems, inadequately maintained fire escapes or emergency staircases, etc.

3. Biological hazards

It can be caused by stuffy and dark rooms, suffocation due to bad ventilation, and unhygienic restroom conditions. Animal bites and stings, toxic plant problems, and animal-transmitted diseases are all examples of these.

4. Chemical hazards

When some chemicals are mixed with others, they may be harmful. Chemical hazards are common in the clothing and textile industries during the dyeing and printing phases. When handling chemicals in the garment industry, a worker should exercise caution. The worker must be aware of the specific guidelines that must be followed when handling a specific chemical.

5. Ergonomic hazard

Ergonomic concerns can be found in the majority of textile-related businesses in India. The majority of these units have a hazardous and dangerous working environment. Workers in these units face a variety of issues, including inadequate furniture, inadequate ventilation and lighting, and a lack of effective safety measures in the event of an emergency. The workers in such units are at risk for developing various occupational diseases. Musculoskeletal disorders like carpal tunnel syndrome, forearm tendinitis, bicipital tendinitis, lower back pain, epicondylitis, neck pain, shoulder pain, and osteoarthritis of the knees are some of the occupational diseases that have been observed among the workers on account of poor ergonomic conditions. These issues are more common in developing nations as compared to developed ones.

6.   Psychosocial hazards

This implies that the mental health and emotional well-being of an organization's Operators may not be normal. This may be caused by job insecurity, long working hours, a lack of motivation for work, irritation at not being able to produce a satisfactory product due to the pressures of quantitative production, workplace abuse, and a poor work-life balance.

The bulk of management is ignorant of health and safety, and another problem is that workers in the textile industry are uneducated and ignorant about OHS. Based on the RPN number, the hazards are prioritized. The RPN number is calculated by the multiplication of severity, probability and detectability.

RPN = Severity x probability x Delectability

The RPN is calculated for all of the hazards that are involved in the textile industry. The risk priority number may have a maximum value of 1000.

IV.   Low wages

Workers are paid below the minimum legal wage, paid below the legal rate for overtime, and required workers to work excessive and illegal overtime. Their monthly wage payments are sometimes late, causing difficulties paying rent and adding to their stress. If they are unable to meet the production level their wages are deducted. Overall excessive hours and low wages impact on workers' health, wellbeing and workplace safety, and can cause unforeseen indirect costs for garment factories in the form of accidents, injuries, absenteeism, lower productivity and high worker turnover.

Workers are often unable to afford appropriate housing, food, health and education for themselves and their families and fail to save for emergencies such as becoming unexpectedly ill or losing employment. Salaries that are too low make people vulnerable. The lack of a minimum wage magnifies problems such as maternity leave denial, poor sanitation, and workplace sexual abuse.

Paying a living wage is one of the concrete solutions to prevent this. Paying people a living wage, especially women, will have a significant impact on making the world more equitable, and it is a key component of a more "human economy."

V.   Wage theft and forced labour practices

Wage theft practices may be defined as institutional tactics used by firms to ensure that labor costs are kept as low as possible while reaping significant profits. Nonpayment, underpayment, and late payment of salaries to employees, as well as fraudulent deductions from wages, are also examples of wage theft.

Forced labour has been defined by ILO as '*all work or service which is exacted from any person under the menace of any penalty and for which the said person has not offered himself voluntarily*'.

In northern India, one in 10 people were trapped in forced labour. Almost 6% were in bonded labour, where a person is forced to work to pay off a debt. In the Indian garment industry, there are many institutional channels by which firms have instituted forced labor. There are-

1. Legal and institutional violations

Labour's bargaining power is reduced as a result of institutional abuses, rendering them vulnerable to debt bondage systems. These practices reveal that garment industry workers are often denied their right to equitable and decent working conditions, leaving them with unstable and insecure employment. Despite the fact that contract workers are legally entitled to Provident Funds and insurance benefits, there is no social security or other benefits. For some cases, social security payments are never deducted from workers' salaries, and in others, they are deducted but not deposited in workers' accounts.

2.   Excessive overtime work as a means of forced labour

Long hours of work, frequently 10-14 hours a day plus forced overtime, often result in injuries that go undiagnosed. Employees that are unable to keep up with production due to pain or discomfort are fired. Staff may be required to work 18 hours a day if there is pressure to fulfil large orders. There have been instances of employees being fined or even fired if they deny overtime.

3.   Union busting

Garment workers in most of these factories are not permitted to join unions to collectively protect their interests. Trade unions are often suppressed, and union organizers are physically threatened.

Workers complain that certain supervisors treat employees who help form unions unfairly or compel them to leave. Some say they have been beaten up by local gangsters who threaten workers outside of work and even at their homes. Many workers do not belong to any trade union or had a written contract, leaving them with no way of seeking redress for unfair or abusive treatment.

VI.   Work conditions

The garment industry has terrible working conditions. Garment workers are often forced to migrate from rural areas where they have little job security to dingy, small sweatshops where they are exposed to cruel and inhumane working conditions. They are not equipped with safety equipment needed to work with hazardous substances, in addition to long continuous working hours without breaks and earning half of the minimum wage. Many factory workers in India are paid so little that a month's salary will not cover the cost of a single item they produce. Other concerns, such as the gender pay gap and the use of child labor in the clothing industry, exacerbate fashion's problems. In the factories, we still have a problem of disorganization. When workers try to form labor unions, they are often threatened by management and forced to leave the factory.

VII.   Long working hours

Work hours in the industry are long, particularly during peak periods, when they could be as high as 15 to 16 hours a day. Long hours of work, frequently long plus forced overtime, often result in injuries that go undiagnosed. Employees that are unable to keep up with production due to pain or discomfort are fired. Staff may be required to work 18 hours a day if there is pressure to fulfil large orders. There have been instances of employees being fined or even fired if they deny overtime. Being forced to work excessive hours means they do not get sufficient rest, nor do they have time to spend with or raise their children or enjoy their freedom for recreation. This also prevents a worker benefiting from freedom of association, as the worker does not have the time or energy to participate in trade union activities which means they can't advocate for better standards and conditions.

VIII.   Fast fashion

The promise of cheap, disposable, trendy clothing drives the fast fashion industry. Fast fashion has irreversible and severe negative environmental consequences, such as water pollution, increased usage of hazardous chemicals, and massive textile waste production. Textile dyeing is also the world's second-largest polluter of clean water, after agriculture. While cotton and polyester are the most commonly used fabrics in this industry, both have negative environmental consequences.

Cotton, a water-intensive crop, uses 16 percent of the world's insecticides to combat weeds and pests. Furthermore, several brightly colored fashion accessories contain lead-based paint and dyes, which can cause nerve damage and kidney failure. By 2030, the fashion industry's $CO2$ emissions are expected to have increased by more than 60% to nearly 2.8 billion tons per year, based on current production rates.

The balance between the environment, the economy, and ethics is referred to as sustainability. We must recognize that "sustainability" is not a trend or a marketing tool; it is a serious issue that must be approached with sincerity.

IX.   Animal abuse

For thousands of years, humans have used leather, wool, and fur, and each year, billions of animals are brutally slaughtered for the clothing industry. Animal products are widely used in the industry, but the process and repercussions of this usage are seldom addressed. The fashion industry's animal cruelty is divided into two parts: one tortures the animal directly by objectifying it for its hair, skin, or hide, while the other abuses animals by polluting their environment and disturbing their food chains. The processes involved in fashion manufacturing make it difficult for these animals to survive in the wild and free in both cases.

Animal rights advocates have expressed outrage about the mass manufacturing of fur and leather products, which has resulted in a barbaric system of farming, trapping, and skinning. Animals are often made to walk for days on end without rest, food, or water. Despite their dehydration, they are thrashed or injured in order to keep them walking. Many of them die before they enter the factory. When the animals arrive, they are held in small enclosures where they can be castrated, dehorned, or branded without anaesthesia. The slaughterhouses are then an unavoidable reality for them. They are still alive as they are hung upside down and forced to bleed to death until their flesh is carved away. After that, it's treated with highly hazardous chemicals.

Animals used for clothes undergo electrocution, gassing, strangulation, mutilated, poisoning, and a variety of other atrocities like being skinned or boiled alive only to get you the next skin bag, silk sari, wool scarf, fur hat, pair of leather shoes, or some other animal-based clothing product or accessory.

X.   Sweatshops

Workers are sometimes required to perform their duties under "sweatshop" conditions. Sweatshops employ a large number of women and children. Sweatshops are workplaces that have very bad, socially inappropriate, or unlawful working conditions. Work can be difficult, risky, climatically challenged, or underpaid. They work long days every day, often without even a weekly break, and overtime is frequently unpaid. Many of them are not working on a regular contract. Workers face a lot of work insecurity. Workers are constantly on the verge of being dismissed. Small mistakes in work, failure to meet deadlines, being late to work by even a few minutes, and talking back when yelled at are all grounds for dismissal.

XI.   Sub-contracting

Many major apparel brands and companies do not have complete control of their supply chains, which enables unethical labor practices (including sweatshops, trafficking and servitude). The brand subcontracts output to non-affiliated manufacturing companies in developing countries. As a result, there is no legal requirement for these fashion brands to have adequate working conditions. Furthermore, since unauthorized subcontractors are not registered, they operate outside of government control and supervision, resulting in deteriorating work environments with widespread workplace violence. Producing goods by themselves not only does it legally bind these brands to have secure working environments, but it also exposes them to liability lawsuits if anything goes wrong. There is a strong desire. There is an urgent need for brands to take responsibility for the blood, sweat and tears that are poured into their products.

XII.   Discrimination (employment and occupation)

The women and men who make our clothes are impoverished. Though retailers such as Kmart, Cotton On, Just Group, and H&M are growing, workers are often living in slum-like housing and barely meeting ends. Women garment workers are often subjected to verbal and physical abuse as well as sexual harassment at work, in addition to earning less than men. Workers are sometimes paid less than the minimum wage. Also, lack of paid leave, in spite of being entitled to the same under the law

According to a report by the International Labour Organization (ILO), a significant proportion of clothing, footwear, and textiles workers in seven Asian garment-exporting countries are paying less than the minimum wage. Women were found to be more likely than men to be paid less than the minimum wage, and workers with less education were also found to be more likely to be paid less than the minimum wage.

Many garment workers face issues such as sexual harassment in the workplace, a lack of professional growth, childcare, and hygiene and sanitation facilities. Pregnant women are discriminated against in a variety of ways at various stages of the employment process, including during recruiting, promotion, and dismissal. Factory managers often fail to provide adequate accommodations for pregnant women, such as more frequent bathroom breaks or lighter work with no pay loss.

XIII.   Child labour

Fast fashion has sparked a race to the bottom, forcing businesses to seek out ever-cheaper labor. The fast fashion industry has built its empire on the blood and bones of many impoverished children and women. According to a UNICEF report, the garment industry employs 170 million children. Hands that should be carrying books and pens are sewing, stitching and dyeing garments for 12 hours a day to meet global market demand for fast fashion. This is the truth for 11% of the world's children.

Child labor is a particular problem in the apparel industry because much of the supply chain necessitates low-skilled labor, and certain tasks are better suited to children than to adults. Employers prefer to hire children for cotton picking because their tiny fingers do not damage the crop. Children are seen as obedient employees that go unnoticed, rendering them easy to manage. Employers are able to get away with it because the apparel supply chain is highly complex, making it difficult for businesses to control every stage of production. As a result, it is possible to hire children without major brands or customers knowing.

These children are forced to work long hours and may experience fatigue, heat stroke, and malnutrition as a result of their labor. Harsh chemicals can cause tremors, fatigue, blurred vision, severe dizziness, depression, and even paralysis or death in children. Children have been found working without protective equipment in ginning, inhaling toxic air and developing respiratory problems. The impact of physical labor and long hours on a child's body (even non-hazardous work deemed safe for an adult) can lead to health issues that will affect their adult years, limit their earning potential, and increase the chance that their children will have to start working early.

XIV.   Overseas manufacturing delays

Brands nowadays outsourced production to low-cost countries like China, India, etc. LCCs will be able to deliver lower production costs as a result of lower labor costs and possibly less environmental and workforce regulations. However, there are disadvantages attached to it too. These are-

- Language barriers and time zone variations, inadequate communication, training constraints, and a lack of on-site technical support.
- The cost of transporting products from LCCs to their final destinations, especially if air transportation is needed, can be very high as it includes all transportation costs, including freight, duties, and insurance etc.

XV.   **Lost or damaged shipments**

For apparel companies that outsource their production and use drop shipping on a regular basis, shipping damage and lost shipments combine to create ongoing headaches.

XVI.   **Labelling Requirements**

A mark not only establishes an apparel and brand name, but it also provides instructions about how to care for the garment after it has been purchased. Thus, it shall include all the requirements provided by Legal Metrology (Packaged Commodities) Rules, 2011. The labelling requirement of garments shall include-

  a) Name/ Description of the product,
  b) Size: Internationally recognizable size indicators- S, M, L, XL etc. as well as details in metric notation in terms of cm or m as the case may be.
  c) MRP
  d) Name, address and Customer care No. of manufacturer

XVII.   **Cyber squatting**

Whether it is Chanel, Louis Vuitton or Adidas, the biggest brands are becoming targets of cyber squatters, in fact, the bigger the brand the higher the risk. The fashion industry is phased with the rising issue of cyber squatters. According to WIPO, fashion, banking, finance, and IT make up almost one-third of all the cybersquatting disputes handled by WIPO's Arbitration and Mediation center back in 2017. Since then, the issue has grown steadily each year. Now with the Covid-19 pandemic, there has been a surge in cybercrimes, this can be seen in the prominent increase in the number of cases against cybersquatting.

Cyber-squatting is the unauthorized use and registration of domain names that are identical or deceivingly similar to trademarks, service mark, a particular company's name or even personal names. To put it simply, let us take a look at a domain name; 'louisvuittonbag.site.' From the first look, it looks like a genuine page handled and authorized by Louis Vuitton, however, in reality, this is one of the 120 domain names and websites that were report by the brand for infringement of its trademark in 2018. In this digital age, where every company wants to build their brand, domain names have become analogous to trademarks. However, the major issue faced here is that there are numerous TLDs (Top-Level Domains, these are the words that follow the 'dot' in any domain name) and under these combinations, any domain name can be registered. For example, a web page for H&M maybe www.hm.com or www.hm.net or even www.hmindia.com

The domain registration process works on the principle of "first come, first serve". As a result, if an individual registers a domain name that is similar to a trademark, someone else who uses a similar mark will be refused registration of a domain name that is similar to that trademark.

Cyber-squatting is the practice of registering a domain name that is likely to be wanted by another individual, business, or organization in the hopes of selling it for a profit on the Internet. It entails the registration of trademarks and trade names as domain names by third parties that do not have any ownership rights in the domain names. Such trade-marks belonging to third parties are registered with the common law by cyber-squatters or bad faith imitators.

There is no law in India that directly addresses dispute settlement in the context of cybersquatting or other domain name disputes. The new Information Technology Act makes no provision for cyber-squatters to be punished.

TYPES OF CYBER SQUATTING

a) **Typo Squatting-** It entails registering a domain name that is confusingly identical to a well-known trademark by deliberately misspelling the original trademark. These cyber-squatters bet on users misspelling the original trademark and being directed to their webpage site as a result.

b) **Name Jacking-** This is the act of registering a domain name with its own goodwill that reflects endorsement by the individual whose name appears in the domain name. These cyber-squatters use the traffic to divert and target individuals whose name the domain is registered in.

c) **Identity theft-** It is carried out by using online applications to track the expiration dates of well-known domain names, then registering them in the monitors' names as soon as the previous registration expires. This is intended to deceive visitors of the previous website who believe it still belongs to the true owner.

d) **Domain Name Squatting-** It refers to the act of registering a domain that has already been registered in order to extort money from the trademark's original holders.

Louis Vuitton Malletier Vs Defendants

In the case, Louis Vuitton sued for the infringement of its trademark in Florida, there are about 120 domain names and websites that have been highlighted in the case that have reproduced counterfeited versions of the Louis Vuitton trademarks. There were about 200 Chinese retailers who were selling knock-off goods online in the USA. The brand demand that these counterfeited sites should be canceled and permanently delisted from all search engines. The court ruled in favor of the luxury retailer and compensation worth $23 million was given.

Titan Industries Ltd v Prashanth Koorapati & Others

This is the first case decided by an Indian court which deals with the protection of domain names. The plaintiff had registered 'Tanishq' as a trademark in 23 countries to produce and sell jewelry and timepieces. The defendant filed an application for the domain name 'tanishq.com,' and Tanishq objected to this unauthorized use of its trademark as a domain name.

Tanishq argued that the consumers were very likely to believe that the defendant is in some way affiliate with Tanishq which will lead to unjust enrichment to the defendant while Tanishq will suffer a financial loss. The similarity in the same would confuse the people at large and the Delhi High Court found in favor of the Tanishq and granted an ex-parte ad-interim injunction restraining the defendant from using the trade name "Tanishq" or any other name that is deceptively similar.

2.3 Legalities in a Fashion Runway Show

A fashion show is associated with dazzling models, catwalks, elegant and sophisticated clothing. It serves as a wonderful platform for fashion businesses. Fashion shows target not only the client but also fashion journalists and clothing manufacturers and it is the only way for a designer's work to get noticed.

Buyers from all over the country travel to fashion shows in order to purchase clothing in quantity for their stores. Designers, on the other hand, have the best chance to show off their amazing work on stage. The ideal method to exhibit their designer's garments is on the catwalk, where the models' bodies are well-sculpted and kept. On the catwalk, clothes appear even more alluring in the midst of dazzling surroundings. However, only a few people comprehend the amount of legal work that must be done in order for their business to run properly. Let us look at the legalities involved to organize a fashion show.

1. Trademark registration

Trademark registration plays a vital role in organizing a fashion show. Registration has its benefits: It helps to protect the public from confusion and deception by identifying the origin of a particular product and safeguards the goodwill attached to the goods or services of the trademark. Section 2(1)(zb) of the Trademarks act, 1999 defines "trademark" as "a mark capable of being represented graphically and which is capable of distinguishing the goods and services of one person from those of others and may include the shape of goods, their packaging, and combination of colors." On the other hand, Section 2(1)(m) of the same Act lays what is included in a mark: "a device, brand, heading, label, ticket, name, signature, word, letter, numeral, shape of goods, packaging or combination of colors."

The term "mark" is defined in a broad sense. It may also comprise other items that are within the scope of the general and straightforward meaning. The Supreme Court stated that the definition of trademark is very wide and laid down three essentials of trademarks:

- It should be a mark
- It should be capable of being represented graphically and
- It should be capable of distinguishing the goods & services of one person from those of others.

Fashion shows/week can be registered under Trademark Class 41 which covers: Organizing and presenting fashion shows, cultural events, education, training, entertainment, and sporting and cultural activities using the appropriate approved forms found in Schedule II of the Trade Marks Rules 2002.

2. **Event Venue**

To organize a fashion show, it is really important to acquire a permit to use the premises or a showroom. The municipal authority of the event location issues the license for the premises. The organizers must apply for the license in advance, following the regulations and standards set forth by the relevant Authority. The procedure for obtaining a license varies in every state since the governing Acts differ; for example, the Mumbai Municipal Corporation Act, 1888 specifies the requirements in Mumbai.

3. **Music License**

Music has always played a significant role in conveying emotions and experiences to the general audience, and fashion shows are no exception. The presence of music, regardless of genre, encourages the models while also assisting them in re-creating themselves in the setting and improving their performance. And it also creates a rhythm and a pace for them. If a fashion house utilizes music made by another entity, the fashion house must get authorization for each of the following rights:

- notes and lyrics;

- song recording;
- public performance;
- recording.

All rights are not often controlled by the same entity, which makes music a genuine issue. Understanding the legal consequences of playing music during and after a runway show is critical, as music is an essential element of many fashion presentations. The process of obtaining permission for the approval, validation, and protection of musical works is known as obtaining a music license. Business units that organize fashion shows are not permitted to play music in the studio for commercial purposes without first obtaining a music license. Any entity that plays pre-recorded music in their establishments must get a music license under the Copyright Act of 1957.

Section 2(p) of the Copyright Act, 1957 defines musical work as, "a work consisting of music and includes any graphical notation of such work but does not include any words or any action intended to be sung, spoken, or performed with music."

The Copyright Society for Sound Recording, which is administered by Phonographic Performance Limited (PPL), grants music licenses to entities who wish to play music on their premises. Music owners, lyricists, composers, and publishers are all represented by the Indian Performing Right Society (IPRS). The IPRS is also authorized to issue licenses for the use of music and literary works under Section 33 of the Copyright Act of 1957. As the owner of copyrights through assignment deeds completed with its members, who are the owners and have assigned the rights to the society, IPRS undertakes the business of issuing licenses under section 30 of the Copyright Act.

4. Agreements with every service provider

Organizing a fashion show can be time-consuming and complicated, and agreements play an important role in keeping track of each contributor's responsibilities. A contract is a legally enforceable agreement that allows two people to form a legal relationship. A contract is defined under Section 2(h) of the Indian Contract Act, 1872 as "An agreement enforceable by law." Agreements with each service provider aid in adhering to the limits and restrictions that might be imposed.

A contract is an important element of the event planning process since it protects all parties involved. It precisely outlines the event's intended features as well as what may be expected. Contracts also assist to avoid misunderstandings regarding expectations and event plans. They can also spell out the ramifications of any mistakes made and the measures that will be taken as a result. Types of agreements that organizers need to enter into for a fashion show are:

- Manufacturing Agreement
- Consignment Agreement
- Agreements with Models
- Independent contractor Agreement
- License Agreement for event space
- Sales representative Agreement
- Sponsorship Agreement
- Media partnership Agreements
- Apparel manufacturing Agreement
- Franchise Agreement
- Advertising and promotional Agreement
- Employment Agreement
- Outsourcing Agreement

However, Fashion Models are exploited frequently in the name of contracts, for instance; agencies withhold payments owed to models without their knowledge because they keep models in the dark about how much they are paid for their job. They are compelled to sign contracts that bind them to their agencies and provide them exclusive rights to negotiate modelling assignments for them at their own will, without informing the model. Moreover, models are required to check in with their agents many times each day, and nearly every element of the models' lives are monitored by their agents.

5. Images Rights

In India, photographs are protected as creative works under Section 2(c) of the Copyright Act 1957. However, if one wants to utilize copyrighted pictures in a runway show, one will need to get permission from the artist beforehand.

Using the work usually entails either licensing the photograph through a third-party website or directly contacting the artist. Copyright can also be transferred from one person to another. This is usually accomplished by a document signed by the copyright owner or an authorized agent.

6. Labour rights

Majority of the individuals contributing in the successful working of a fashion show are an independent contractor, who is not hired employees of any business unit but an individual who is contracted for a particular project. The terms and conditions of an agreement between an employer and an independent contractor regulate their relationship.

When an employer pays a salary to an employee, he or she must withhold tax. An employee's pay may contain perks and allowances to which he or she is entitled, which is advantageous to the employee from a tax standpoint. However, in the case of independent contractors, the employer is required to withhold the required taxes; however, the amount paid may not be in the form of a wage, but rather as professional fees for services rendered. Employees and independent contractors will be required to submit their income tax returns as required by law in each of these situations. The principal employer's responsibilities under the agreement are controlled and governed by the provisions of the Contract Labour (Regulation and Abolition) Act, 1970, in the event of a contractor's inability to execute an employer's responsibilities to the extent of the primary employer's obligations.

2.4 Dispute Resolution in Fashion

A question that is often posed in front of various fashion designers, their labels and even big fashion brands is how to resolve any dispute. Like any other layman, they seek legal counsel but what is missing from their understanding is the knowledge of ADR and its multiple forms in which it offers dispute resolution. Alternative Dispute Resolution is a process that is quite different from the traditional approach used to resolve disputes, i.e., litigation. Different types of ADR Mechanisms are:

Negotiation: An approach wherein parties resolve the disputes by themselves and their legal counsel without any third-party intervention.

Conciliation: An approach wherein disputes are aimed to resolve with the help of a conciliator who meets with parties separately. Based on that, the conciliator proposes a settlement that the parties may or may not agree to.

Mediation: An approach wherein the mediator facilitates the process of dispute resolution and help parties reach an agreement on their own which is beneficial for both.

Arbitration: An approach wherein an arbitrator or a tribunal of arbitrator plays a judge's role while resolving a dispute in front of them. Their interference in the matter is direct except that the proceedings are not in a court. They hold power to call witnesses or examine the evidence provided by the legal counsel. The award which they render has a binding nature, and parties cannot ignore it.

All mechanisms listed above are fast-paced and cost-efficient. They do not take years like judicial trials and court proceedings before delivering a judgement. They are quite beneficial because they not only help parties to prepare their settlements but also help in maintaining cordial relations between them. Another pertinent point that must be kept in mind is that every ADR mechanism is consensual, which makes the entire purpose of dispute resolution more effective in its essence.

Multiple types of disputes can be found in the fashion industry, largely depending on what kind of segment the dispute has arisen. It can range from the very beginning, when the creator is at its creative stage, to the very end when the product has been finalised and is out in the market. As per World Intellectual Property Organisation (WIPO) Mediation and Arbitration Centre[19], here is a list of potential areas of dispute:

- advertising

- agency agreements

- brand management

- copyright and related rights

- distribution agreements

- event management

- franchising agreements

- image rights

- industrial design rights

- internet retail and e-commerce

- IP infringements

- licensing agreements

- manufacturing agreements

- marketing agreements

- patents

- product development

---

19 WIPO, Arbitration and Mediation for Fashion, WIPO, https://www.wipo.int/amc/en/center/specific-sectors/fashion/

- software

- sponsorship agreements

- trademark

It also lists down the potential parties which are involved in the disputes

- agents

- designers

- distributors

- event organisers

- fashion houses

- inventors

- non-profit foundations

- manufacturers

- model agencies

- service providers

- sponsors

- retailers

- television and media companies

However, the protection of ideas and the original content which a designer draws from a source of inspiration is always in dispute. These usually come within the ambit of Intellectual Property Rights. These are given to persons over the creations of their minds. In the fashion industry, industrial design rights are for the protection of a particular design; it must be registered, or else one can be subjected to the case of counterfeiting. Such disputes can involve complex legal issues.

Other definite types of disputes can arise in the compliance part as a designer creates every fashion creation for commercial purposes, which inevitably brings out the business side of the fashion industry. Like all other businesses, even fashion brands or a single designer will be subjected to legal issues relating to contract, delivery, manufacturing, brand compliances, including licensing, labour laws, outsourcing, environmental protection, etc., to name a few.

Some disputes also arise in the marketing and promotion area, especially relating to the brand endorsement[20] and advertisements done by celebrities or by lifestyle/fashion influencers online as per the latest trends. Disagreements between them and the brand may lead to any form of dispute.

Cybersquatting refers to online ransom where someone misuses a domain name with the intent to make a profit from other's trademark goodwill.[21] Often the domain names are similar, which can easily confuse the not so aware consumers. In a 2018 report by the WIPO arbitration and mediation centre, famous brands such as Fendi, YSL, & Givenchy have sought ADR mechanisms to resolve this issue on a fast track basis.

Need to resolve such disputes

As we can see, even the cybersquatting issue, which is usually within the ambit of criminal law and is an offence, is resolved by ADR mechanisms as per parties wish. This is because the fashion industry is very fast-paced. It is so versatile and dynamic that it is constantly evolving and changing with time. It is difficult for a brand or a designer to move ahead if any kind of issue remains unresolved. This industry demands a quick response as most of the brands fall under the fast fashion category, where the aim is to manufacture quality trendy products in a short period. If taking the road towards litigation, there will be plenty of time bumps and an increase in legal expenses as the disputes may last up to many months and years before being resolved. Not only that, in the fashion industry, many cross border disputes arise as it spread and dealt across all over the world, so often we've found our clothes designed somewhere else and manufactured somewhere else, and if at all any dispute arises between two parties who do not share the same jurisdiction, court litigation itself becomes almost impossible, and the only way to resolve such disputes is through international mediation or International arbitration. Some other advantages which are associated with ADR are listed below.[22]

Party Autonomy is given the utmost importance to ensure that both the parties are satisfied with the agreed settlement and business can be carried forward without any remaining issues. It is also used when selecting an arbitrator having expertise in the subject matter.

20 Abey Thomas, ADR in India's Fashion Industry, DE LEX DOCTRUM, https://delexdoctorum.com/?p=6822
21 The Fashion Law, Fashion Brands continue to be among the most attractive target for Cybersquatters, THE FASHION LAW, April, 05, 2019 https://www.thefashionlaw.com/fashion-brands-continue-to-be-amongst-most-vulnerable-to-cybersquatters/
22 Heike Wollgast, Chiara Accornero, Ida Palombella, Federica Caretta, Managing Risks and Disputes in the Fashion Industry, WIPO MAGAZINE, March 2021 https://www.wipo.int/wipo_magazine/en/2021/01/article_0008.html

A single procedure is involved that makes sure that all the disputes are covered even if they do not belong to a single jurisdiction.

Confidentiality helps the parties focus on their advantages arising from the dispute without any fear of public scrutiny, which can hamper their public reputation.

They also help preserve business relationships and make sure they can continue their alliances for future collaborations where both of them will benefit.

As we all know by now, time and cost savings are fundamental reasons parties prefer to adopt the ADR process.

Some setbacks during the resolution process

Like any other good thing, even ADR mechanisms carry some limitations and setbacks. Although in the fashion industry, one may not give weightage to this as they do not limit the ultimate goal of resolving disputes except in some cases where parties can't afford to be flexible. One of the biggest setbacks in ADR for the fashion industry's related dispute is limiting the discovery process, which is essential for trademark disputes. It may reduce the scope and cost allocated for such discoveries, which otherwise are allowed in the traditional litigation approach. One thing which also needs to be kept in mind is that it is not necessary that a solution may arise even if the parties become flexible on their end and what once was considered an investment may turn into a waste of resources. Sometimes parties do not have a choice but to resort to the mandatory arbitration clauses inserted in a contract if any kind of dispute arises between them. Unless both the parties waive this clause, they must go through the process laid down in the clause. Often arbitration clauses are hybrid, i.e. they include various mechanisms of ADR within a clause an example would be med-arb-med or neg-arb-med, etc. where parties can try mediation or negotiation first for some disputes and later they can seek remedy for the remaining issues via arbitration and even then if some disputes are left those can again be resolved in negotiation or mediation whichever the parties may prefer. When it comes to arbitration, the only setback is that once an award is rendered, it is binding in nature, so it may happen that sometimes a party do not benefit from it simply because the other party won. Moreover, arbitration awards are only limited to monetary issues; they cannot issue an injunction and compel a party to act or not to act in a certain way.

All these aspects must be kept in mind, and it is totally on parties to decide whether they are ready to take such risks if they arise.

Indian Scenario

India has a history of the textile industry from before independence. This is because India has been a land that is quite rich for extracting different types of raw materials used for making cloth or any fashion product. Even for sustainable fashion, the materials required, such as jute, cotton, and bamboo, is widely available in India. Besides that, with the advent of globalisation and relaxed foreign investment policies, India became a hub of all things fashion. Imported brands made their presence and got a huge profit from targeting upper-class people. Many Indian designers also started to target a specific group and sell their products with an exclusive label. However, trends have flipped as we see many fast fashion brands have made their presence within the middle-class people. They aim to maximise sales by reducing the price at an affordable rate. Even after this, a large population in India still can't afford and access such brands, and it's only because of this we've seen multiple counterfeit practices take place which infringes a lot of rights of such brands such as Adidas and Nike, to name a few. Apart from that, new fashion brand companies continue to grow and make their presence in the Indian market, leading to more disputes for which ADR is an excellent choice. Here is a list of some legislations in India which protect fashion designs.

The Copyright Protection Act, 1957 aims to protect any original literary, musical, dramatic and artistic work. It only provides an exception for fair use and compulsory license.

The Patents Act,1970 protects the inventions which can be integrated with a product. Fashion designers can only claim a patent for a particular invention they've made, be it any procedure for making a product or maybe the product itself.

The Design Act, 2000 is the one that protects every original design a designer makes, be it two dimensions or three dimensions in nature.

The Trademarks Act, 1999 protect the brand name mostly. They protect the name, product shape, graphics, letters, even words and colour combination. Fashion companies mostly prefer trademark law within IPR as it covers most of the things for them via registration.

International Scenario

Internationally, fashion has always been moving from different continents; styles and trends have been shared across the globe. However, this certainly calls for newer challenges and cross border trade, and transactions have increased. This is why stakeholders from the fashion and luxury industry seek an efficient way of resolving disputes. World Intellectual Property Organisation (WIPO) is the one-stop destination for adopting ADR mechanisms for any dispute resolution. WIPO

ADR Services for Fashion Disputes include the WIPO arbitration and mediation centre**23**, which aims to provide guidelines and procedures for cost and time effective mediation and arbitration. Established in 1994, it is an independent body of WIPO and a leading global centre for resolving internet domain name disputes. A few examples are cases where a mediation process for distribution dispute for luxury goods was resolved; in this case, the dispute was between a European watchmaking company and a US-based distributor company. Also, with the help of arbitration, a trademark coexisting of a luxury good was resolved where a trademark specialist arbitrator was appointed. As per his award, the Asian company in dispute with a European company claimed remedy. WIPO also offers a Fashion Panel of Neutrals which includes top-class experts in mediation and arbitration. Parties can select mediators or arbitrators as per their requirements. Apart from this, WIPO actively advocates and provides guidance and pieces of training to practitioners who are interested.

CONCLUSION

It Is safe to say that the fashion industry is driven by trends, which do not stay for a long time. Fashion designers and brands need to up their game almost every season to keep up with such trends. Whether it's a creation of a new trend or a reemergence of a past trend, with so much creativity around, disputes are bound to happen. In addition to this, after the pandemic, there is a rise in the usage of e-commerce retailing, and new disputes are already at our doorsteps.

Even today there is a lack of understanding of IPR in some of the offbeat fashion countries especially India which circles back to the need for codified law to regulate this trillion-dollar industry. It has become extremely essential to draft and implement a distinctive law for this industry. It can be done either by amending the existing laws and moulding them according to the current fashion law needs or introducing new legislation, covering all the overlooked aspects.

Much needs to be addressed like the Intellectual Property, Business finance, and commercial laws, international trade, counterfeiting and fashion law litigation, civil rights, consumer culture, privacy, technology, Labour Laws for factories, Antitrust and competition law, modelling rights, etc.
The obligation is being acknowledged extensively to sync the laws of the fashion industry to make fashion lawyers receptive about their duties and responsibilities, as to bring awareness among consumers about their choices, by developing segregated programs. There is an immense need for everyone to acknowledge themselves with the legal issues facing the fashion industry varying from merchandising, distribution, franchising agreements to labour laws and intellectual property.

---

23 Chiara Accornero, Resolving Fashion and Luxury Dispute through WIPO Mediation and Arbitration, TAILORED, https://tailored.gr/portfolio_page/resolving-fashion-and-luxury-disputes-through-wipo-mediation-and-arbitration/

Multiple law schools are focusing to cater to the fashion law industry by adding their curriculum in their courses, which includes the World's First Fashion Law Institute, Fordham Law School, and coveted programs offered by Milano Fashion Institute, etc.

It is an undeniable fact that fashion law affects the economy as well as society. For now, the designers might have taken shelter under copyright and trademarks laws, but that is not enough. Keeping in mind, as previously mentioned, the wide ambit of this multifaceted industry, it undoubtedly requires more legal attention and awareness in order to keep flourishing and making it a better, safer, fashion haven.

Furthermore, organizing a fashion runway show may be exhausting, but it is necessary to guarantee that all legal requirements are met and that all licenses and permissions are procured in advance in order to conduct the show successfully on the day of the event.

The fashion business has a dynamic nature and influences everyone's life. As a result, drafting and enforcing formal and stringent rules for this business is very essential. Because fashion designs and designers are not legally recognized, the legal protection provided by the Indian legal system is inadequate. It is necessary to incorporate them into the legal provisions in order to safeguard their rights against violation.

Chapter 3. Fashion Law and Business

The business of Fashion & Luxury necessitates a thorough understanding of the legal framework that governs the firms' key internal activities, as well as their supply chain, relationships with clients and other third parties. There are various compliances involved when it comes to starting a new brand or establishing a brand.

3.1 Supply Chain and Legal Issues

Supply Chain Management (SCM) is a crucial element in the proactive fashion market to derive maximum consumer satisfaction. Manufacturers, suppliers, shipping/logistics, residential and retailing operations along with consumer service fulfilment are all a part of the supply chain, either wholly or in part. The core objective of the retail market is to retain acute awareness of the shifting changes in customers fashion preferences by exploring innovative designs to suit all clients at reasonable pricing. As a result, the prominence of the supply chain (management) emerged.

Supply chains in the fashion industry create tangible goods along with a confluence of duration, location, and performance of a brand's product and its services. The supply chain in fashion comprises numerous phases of work, the first being the cultivation of raw materials for the creation of materials that will be used for production. These materials are therefore collected for the textiles process, where they are stitched into cloth, which is then coloured and cut to make outfits. When the clothes are created, they are delivered to retail store outlets where customers can shop them.

Businesses in the fashion industry require a lot of labour due to the consumers increasing demands and it employs millions of labourers worldwide. This industry consumes vast quantities of water, chemical products, and fuel, and is amongst the most contaminating industries in general. The fashion supply chain process encompasses the manufacturing and delivery of commercial products, which incorporates key processes between fabric procurement to manufacturing.

Here are several of the supply issues faced in the fashion industry:

1. **Delay in delivery**

Ever since the outbreak of the Corona Virus, supply chain interruption incidents have posed a significant threat to the global market. A warehouse is used by distributors for storage, satisfaction, and delivery of products. Every single one of the services provided seems to have its own set of specialized procedures. Shipping issues may occur when the administration fails to have innovative warehousing strategies.

A professional supply management team is required to make sure that the products arrive and depart on time, the stock is precise, as well as the delivery process is fast and effective. A brand's inventory is not necessarily stored in warehouses. Deliveries could also be disrupted through transportation facilities such as cross-docking if packages are mishandled or carriers are late.

2. The difference in the material quality of the product as agreed during the manufacturing agreement

A manufacturing and purchasing agreement are signed between the brand owner and the manufacturer where the owner clearly mentions in the agreement about the type of material, he/she prefers for their product manufacturing and for the manufacturer to strictly abide by these standards and norms. The agreement will have specifications regarding the size, shape, colour, design, pattern etc. all mentioned explicitly to avoid having to deal with poor quality products. In some cases, the manufacturers end up deviating from the norms specified in the agreed agreement and end up manufacturing a product that doesn't fit the standard of the brand/company.

Disruptions from manufacturers are unavoidable. Blunders such as pollutants or inadequate sales forecasting can quickly hinder manufacturing. Manufacturers are susceptible to a plethora of global factors that can have an effect on the production requirements. Such faults frequently cause a rippling effect in the supply chain process, impacting all subsequent logistic operations.

3. Transportation and Logistics

To fulfil an order is entirely up to the transporters and shipping companies. Both suppliers and customers depend on cooperative shipment management to reduce frequent logistic problems in the last dispatch. Shipping chaos, like manufacturing and warehouse disruptions, is unavoidable. On top of that unpredictable factors like climate, traffic, and mechanics, interruptions can also be caused by a lack of supply chain management, timekeeping, communication and strategic planning.

The very first challenge is to specify the major shipping services, such as packing, offloading, transportation, storing into a warehouse, trying to take a space to store, to lift, distributing, inspecting, and so forth. Interruptions arise as a consequence of the said procedures being inefficient and halted. Disruptions are likely to emerge across the supply chain if partners decide to not follow a proper plan.

4. Lack of transparency across the chain is a major issue

There is an unlawful hiring of workers at the apparel manufacturing stage, as well as a paucity of transparency from outfit to fabric. Initially, supply chains were not structured to be transparent. Hence, transparency can generate the following difficulties:

- Businesses may be concerned that revealing excessive details may hamper their competition or subject them to scrutiny.

- It is possible that comprehensive data on main supply chain partners or procedures would not be provided. If it was accessible, it could be unethical or fraudulent.

- Investing in transparency alone does not meet the short-term ROI demands.

Transparency in the fashion industry's supply chains is becoming increasingly important to consumers. Even while organizations are dedicated to ending labour exploitation in their supply chains, initiatives to resolve the issues are frequently ineffective. A few brand owners publish details from raw material to final product's transparency, but that's not necessarily the accepted norm. This is indeed a demand for businesses to be a little more proactive in resolving the plethora of issues in their supply chain operations, specifically by branding their items with certification marks. Through the use of certification marks, it would contribute to building their business' brand and reputation and customer loyalty, leading to higher brand recognition.

5. Labour issues and violations

The fashion industry typically overworks, underpays, and places its workers in deplorable working conditions. Exploitation, penitentiary work, and child labour are all vital aspects of the fashion supply chain. Forced labour happens when workers are coerced to work under duress, such as violence and intimidation or expulsion, and are compensated hardly anything. Women, children, immigrants, and indigenous people are especially vulnerable to forced labour atrocities. Labourers among all age groups and sexes may be compelled to work in factories, which are typically defined as organizations that hire workers for low rates, insanely long work hours, and in appalling environments.

Therefore, unless a manufacturer complies with domestic labour laws, labourers would not be paid the minimum wage or be compensated for extra hours. Women who are pregnant as well as those who refuse to work late are some of the most frequently terminated. Manufacturing companies are indeed a critical concern since they may be found to be ineffective to provide a healthy environment to work and fail to fulfil structural requirements, subjecting labourers to possible hazards. In spite of the efforts that are mostly undertaken by or in partnership with the ILO over the last 20 years, labourers rights continue to remain a major problem.

6. Environment

Owing to the paucity of regulation or subsidies, there seems to be a surprisingly low level of acceptance on protecting the environment in the fashion industry-These are some of the solutions to addressing the heinous exploitation of labourers, waterways, and, eventually, the earth's sustainability. Toxic sludge, water contamination, habitat destruction, deforestation, long-term harm to ecosystems, harmful air emissions, carbon emissions, and fuel use are all causes of environmental repercussions from supply chains.

There is indeed a significant necessity to incorporate eco-friendly alternatives into supply-chain management. The supply chain expenditures have an effect on the environment since delivering goods more effectively can diminish your carbon footprint. Businesses nowadays are developing sustainability plans to benefit the environment by lowering miles travelled, manufacturing costs, recycling waste, and unnecessary expenditures. Shipping companies engage with their partners to explain their sustainability ideas and objectives.

7. Planning & Risk Management

Supply chain management refers to how a company manages the production of their products, comprising all procedures associated with changing raw resources used by the company to complete products or services offered by the organisation. It deals with the planning and supervision of sources, purchasing, and transition procedures, along with logistics and distribution responsibilities. Supplier risk management particularly includes issues about a vendor's facilities and equipment and also legal requirements. Supply chain risk management (SCRM) is the method for detecting, evaluating, and reducing supply chain risks in a business. Applying international supply chain risk management techniques can assist a business in operating more successfully, lowering expenses, and improving customer satisfaction.

A company may also be susceptible to supply chain financial risk if anything arises that jeopardises a supplier's financial stability, including insolvency. Furthermore, a brand's name and reputation may be compromised if a distributor participates in illegal actions, such as bribing, child labour, or any other unethical practice which may impact negatively on the business and its products. The online presence of a supplier might potentially affect your business' image. Minimizing such threats is critical, and several companies tackle this issue by broadening their sources.

8. Gender equity

Several attempts to tackle gender disparity go in vain as they do not focus or provide answers to gender-related issues in a comprehensive way. Women are significantly recruited in the supply chain across the world, with varying levels of processing based on the fashion business. Women workers are particularly vulnerable to violations of human rights and unjust gender-based discrimination. Gender discrimination displays itself in a multitude of ways, involving prohibitions mostly on the field of job a woman can do, limited exposure to worker's rights, and wage discrepancies.

9. Cost Control

Throughout the fashion industry, inflexibility costs are extremely high due to the industry's unique constraints. These are expenditures incurred as a result of inaccurate sales forecasting, product scarcity, excessive inventory, and expired goods. Managerial, financial, and research expenditures can all be extra charges. Material handling and stockpiling must be completely handled as part of a bigger supply chain management in order to bring down expenses.

Businesses can cut back on expenses by concentrating on their procedures, such as managing workspace, reducing damage, conserving packing, and so on. Enabling multi-client services is one way to save storage. This permits expenditures to be divided among various organisations and allows you to only pay for the space you actually utilise. It also implies that you won't have to recruit your personal staff.

10. Increase in freight prices due to the pandemic

Increased shipping costs are fuelling inflation, which is diminishing a larger portion of customers' salaries and increasing costs for businesses. A surge in demand earlier this year prompted supply networks to become unreliable when manufacturers and retailers struggled for products. Businesses are anticipating even steeper rises in freight and logistics expenses next year after supply-chain costs skyrocketed during the Covid-19 outbreak. Several firms are suffering from escalating transportation costs to deliver their products. Considering freight rates are a factor of each and every level of the supply chain, these rising prices have rippled across the market.

11. Changing consumer attitudes

Consumers are an important part of the supply chain management process as their demands, beliefs, and views influence the supplier's decisions that the purchaser makes. Research on consumer behaviour is significant as it helps companies perceive what factors impact customers' shopping choices. Studying how a consumer chooses a product enables businesses to bridge a market gap and recognize which items are essential and which are redundant. Consumers already have incredible accessibility to data in all of these categories and, as a result, have an immense impact on supply chain management. Hence, the customer is the most prominent person in the supply chain, because their demands and judgments dictate the company's actions.

Suppliers, logistics, and companies are all modifying their business models as a result of the clients they serve. For example, if a consumer buys a defective product and reports, the company that sold the product to the retailer must track the defective product via its supply chain to rectify the conflict. Tracking these defects is simple for a representative of the supply chain management team, and driven by consumer demands, several organizations nowadays are recruiting supply chain management or entire teams to tackle any challenges that develop in order to cope with them expeditiously.

12. The pandemic sparked the problem and a reduction in shipping.

Businesses that depend on labour-intensive procedures where the employees have to work frequently together have been hampered by this pandemic due to social distancing regulations. For eg: Transportation routes are susceptible to play havoc with if drivers become injured or fall sick. It is indeed hard to foresee where even the worst interruptions might occur, although certain supply chains have already been impacted. The pandemic has caused a shortage of labour and management issues in the supply chain process. Hence the businesses and logistic services have been hit with the worse consequences of the Covid-19 pandemic resulting in the loss of business and consumer dissatisfactions.

13. Customer Service

The management of the supply chain is mainly focused on the demands of the consumer. Providing accurate quality and the number of products required as per the demand appropriate costs. One of the most important aspects of logistics and supply chain management is client satisfaction. Consumers derive a sense of the product and the company that sells it via customer service. Although some businesses believe that customer care has little to do with supply chains, this couldn't be farther from the facts. In practice, the supply chain is not accomplished until the product delivers to the consumer. Therefore, the company hears from the consumer through customer support. Customer care is acquainted with all of the customer's problems and requirements. This feedback from the consumer may be used to enhance supply chain management.

14. Supplier Relationship

The core issues that supplier relationship managers face on a daily basis are guaranteeing product reliability, monitoring risk, encouraging corporate social responsibility, achieving regulatory standards, and allocating resources. Effective supply chain management groups are dedicated to providing services to customers to achieve a competitive edge overwork management to help businesses accomplish success via customer satisfaction.

Achieving the requirements of a supplier relationship management necessitates the use of a digital platform that enables your team and your overall supply network to function as a single, unified group, reducing or eliminating the need for disorganised manual supplier relationship management processes and providing a precise picture of developments, responsibilities, and due dates throughout all retail partners, individuals, and mechanisms.

15. Inventory issues

Even though it is improbable that luxury stores will have empty shelves for the next festive season, customers might feel that their options are very limited. Businesses obtained lower inventory than they had asked due to the minimal options. Hence, businesses and customers are dissatisfied, and sales have dropped. Excess inventory or shortage of inventory of products occurs as a result of an inadequate inventory system. Overstocking, particularly when demand is low, may result in losses due to deterioration, damage or the product being out of season. Understocking can have a negative impact on a company's business model and future production.

16. Payment issues

The COVID-19 pandemic has undoubtedly had an effect on the profitability of global markets. Delay in payments was a challenge long before any of the worldwide pandemic, although money is one of the most important shock absorbers for unpredictability, and many purchasers are utilising outstanding debts as an investment plan to acquire influence over suppliers within their supply chain in order to save their own money. Current regulations procedures in certain parts of the world are aiming to put an end to this, even though it does not happen everywhere. Suppliers are suffering as a result of delayed payment. Ineffective internal systems, which might lead to billing deadlines being missed or overlooked, are a frequent cause of overdue payments. Typically, a company's financial issues occur as a result of business owners simply not having enough time or capability to keep up with bills.

Suppliers may cut relations with your company if you habitually delay their payments. This can result in a gap in your supply chain that is harder to fill, resulting in a decreased product or service line, upset consumers, and fewer revenues. Delayed payments could soon add up, resulting in you spending more than you would otherwise for the products or services are given. An expense you won't be capable of passing on to your customers. Overdue/delayed payments can easily eat into your cash reserves, leaving you with very little room to expand your company's progress. Each year, up to 50,000 businesses collapse owing to financial problems. It also reduces your company's resiliency, making it more difficult to withstand unexpected setbacks.

This concludes the supply chain issues in the fashion industry. If you take care of the above-mentioned issues and work to develop a proper supply chain management, your business is bound to succeed.

3.2 Setting up a Fashion Brand

To set up your fashion brand from scratch it is extremely imperative that you adhere to these "8 steps" to always have a legal remedy against counterfeiters and have a smooth journey towards becoming a fashion brand owner/entrepreneur. The following 8 steps that are vital for setting up your fashion brand are as follows:

1. Brand Planning
2. Brand Set-Up
3. Brand Protection
4. Supply Chain
5. Employment
6. Marketing & Promotion
7. E-Commerce & Data Privacy
8. Business & Trade

Don't be afraid by looking at the list- we've got you covered with all the nitty-gritties required with simple and concise explanations along with examples.

STEP 1- <u>BRAND PLANNING:</u>

Brand planning includes- **Ideation stage, inspiration, product line, manufacturing/franchisee/white–label reseller.**

The ideation stage is your first step towards your product planning. You might have various ideas about the same (clothing, footwear, cosmetics brand) or you could also be inspired by any brand/competitors but you're not sure about your final product line so, in the ideation stage, you plan regarding what type of brand you want to set up so that it is easier for you to choose between your product line.

There are three types of fashion business:

I. **Manufacturing:-** The first type of fashion business is called manufacturing. If you're planning to have your manufacturing set up it means that you'll have your design as well as your manufacturing hub along with your workers. Here you're doing and managing everything by yourself.

II. **Franchisee:-** The second type of fashion business is called a franchisee. You can take up a franchisee of the already well-known fashion brand. For eg- You can take up the franchisee of well-known fashion brands like Zara, F21, H&M by opting for their franchisee plan.

III. **White-Label Reseller:-** The third type of fashion business is called the white–label reseller where you'll be having your designs which you will sell to the other brands. It's already a finalised product and you can put your brand's label on it. It means that you're starting your fashion label but the product is not manufactured by you. Here the manufacturer is different but you're putting your fashion label on the products thus coming up with your fashion label in the process.

Brand planning essentially includes a lot of research where you need to research/explore your product line as well as the sub-products of that line.

For eg- You are opting for a clothing product line so the sub-product lines will be T-shirts, crop tops, trousers, palazzos, jeans etc. Then you need to choose your brand type; whether you are opting for manufacturing, franchisee plan or white label reseller. This will be your initial stage and later you will have to come up with a final plan. To finalise your plan it is mandatory for you to research the competitor market analysis which will help you in the making of your finalised idea.

Note down your ideas on a rough sheet of paper and then focus on understanding the competitive market analysis-

- Who is your competitor?
- Who will be your target audience? and
- What products will work best for you?

COMPETITOR AND MARKET ANALYSIS:

Competitor and market analysis consists of finalising the following-

- **Product line,**
- **The target audience in the market,**
- **Budget/Capital and**
- **Competitor study**

If you finalise clothing as your product line then you need to mention the source of your inspiration behind your fashion brand and the competitors too. For eg- If you finalise ethnic wear then you can mention which brand inspired you to start your ethnic wear fashion brand and the competitors you have in the market. For ethnic wear, your competitors will be- Papa Don't Preach by Shubhika, Label Ritu Kumar, Abu Jani and Sandeep Khosla, Shantanu & Nikhil, Sabyasachi, Masaba, Manish Malhotra, Neeta Lulla, Falguni and Shane Peacock, Anju Modi, Anamika Khanna, Anita Dongre and Gaurav Gupta etc.

The target audience and market will be bifurcated so you need to know your budget thoroughly as well as your competitor's budget. This will help you to cross-check if you can match their budget and their supply chain expenses. You ought to know your initial budget and the supply chain process required to manufacture your final product. It is crucial that you conduct in-depth research on your competitors, their budget, why they're successful, the marketing methods they're opting for, their promotional strategy, their product line as well as their competitors, their sales method and how much market they're capturing as this will help you understand what you need to deal with when it comes to the marketing strategy and the expenses required for your fashion brand.

How to find the target audience for your fashion brand?

The target audience is divided into:

- Age group,
- Gender,
- Region,
- Consumption Behaviour (Understanding the consumer's culture)
- Cost
- Supply chain

Why is the supply chain so important to finalise your idea?

The supply chain helps you to make a final choice of whether you can manage the supply chain of your product. For eg- You're coming up with cosmetics as your product line so the procurement of raw material, manufacturing and machinery to create a final product will be different from the ones in the clothing line. It is mandatory that you know in detail about how your product is being manufactured to understand the supply chain required for your product, the ideas needed to make that product a reality, finances needed, workforce required, the set-up, machinery which will further decide the competitors in the market and the target audience of the brand.

This research will help you determine the finances required, legal compliances and the sales method that can be used for your brand's products.

STEP 2- BRAND SET UP:

A business plan is a crucial step when it comes to setting up a fashion brand.

What is a business plan?

It's a rough document that you can finalise later. In other words, it's like an initial brochure of your brand. All the preliminary research conducted must be mentioned in the business plan. The business plan includes the following-

- Brand name(unique)
- Brand description
- Products
- Competitors
- Target audience
- The target region of business
- Capital/investment
- Structure of company
- USP – unique selling proposition
- Sales method
- Marketing and promotion
- Targets

You need to fill in all these necessary details of your business plan so that you have a better understanding of your brand and can finally reach the step of setting up your fashion brand. The name of your brand ought to be unique so that you can register your brand's name and logo under the Trade Marks Act of your country. In the brand description, you must mention the type, look and feel of your product and the materials used to make the product. Bank loans, fashion investors and Govt. schemes can also be used for finances where you can avail of subsidised rates. Then you can choose the structure of the company for your brand. For eg- Partnership firm, Pvt. Ltd company, Sole Proprietorship, MSME etc. The sales method can either be offline (Retail stores) or online (E-Commerce website) or both depending on your choice of budget. Marketing and promotions can be done both online and offline. For online marketing methods, you can go for digital marketing including social media marketing, fashion influencer marketing, celebrity endorsements, Google advertisements. For offline marketing methods, you can go for fashion magazines, newspaper advertisements, hoardings on highways, malls, trains and posters above bus stops. The USP is the unique part of your brand- basically what sets your brand apart from the other competitors in the market. As per your product and budget, you need to decide the type of audience you will be targeting. For eg- If your brand is a luxury brand then your target will be limited only to the rich consumers who will be able to afford the price range of your brand. If your brand does not come under the luxury/bespoke category and is affordable for everyone then the choice of your target audience will be inclusive of all financial classes and not limited only to the rich class. The target region of business can be one country or worldwide depending on what you want. After completing your business plan the next step is the brand set up.

Brand set up – Brand set up includes-

- Legal structure,
- Permit/licence,
- Real estate,
- Banking and Taxation,
- Compliances,
- Government schemes

Firstly, you'll form a company and give it a legal structure- Partnership firm, Pvt Ltd company, MSME, Sole proprietorship firm as explained above. Another option that you can use is to make a legal entity of a Pvt Ltd. company and invite them as a director. The difference between MOA and AOA is- The MOA (Memorandum of Association) describes the powers and objects of the company while the AOA (Article of Association) defines its rules.

Then comes the significant stage of the permits and licenses of your brand. For eg- At the local, State, Union level depending on the Govt. structure of your country. The municipality will also give you a trade license and any specific department of the Govt will also give you a license for a particular product line. For eg- The textile sector trade license by the Department of Textile and other departments of the Govt for the jewellery and cosmetics trade license.

Other permits include- Gumasta license, Fire license, Import and Export license, GST, Compliances as per the Ministry of Textiles Govt. of India, IP license, Trade license, Shops and Establishment Act, PAN Card, CST/VAT, Service Tax, Professional Tax.

Real estate is vital for brand set-up as well as for the brand's registered office and workstation. For eg- You're coming up with a retail store, you need a place for manufacturing etc. If you're the owner of that manufacturing line then it's sorted and if you want to lease it then you can enter the lease agreement where you can have your workstation and office space ready.

Banking/Taxation- Making a bank account of the registered company where you'll make the transactions for the purchase of raw material or any other procurement as well as for sales. All the transactions required will be made through the registered company's bank account only. In taxation, you need to abide by whatever taxation method is followed in your country. For eg- GST in India. You have to apply for the registration of your brand on the https://eudyogaadhaar.org/ website. After your brand's registration application is accepted you will be granted the (legal structure of your company)/Udyam certificate. GSTIN also needs to be registered on the https://www.gst.gov.in/. Gumasta license should be obtained as well from the state of Maharashtra if it falls under the sale of your target region. Every state has their trade license. Gumasta license is only applicable for trade in the state of Maharashtra.

Compliance- Compliance is the necessary legal documentation that is required to run any organisation or business or trade.

Govt schemes – You need to be aware of the available Govt. schemes at the State or Union level as those schemes can support your brand maybe as an initial investment, the subsidy will be given on the purchase of any machinery required for the brand like the textile sector and various other schemes available especially for women entrepreneurs. You should take complete benefit of it for your brand.

STEP 3: Brand Protection- (IPR, Trademark, Trade dress, Copyright, Design, Patent)

Brand protection includes protecting the brand's designs and creativity. It is important to note that ideas are not protected under copyright. In the fashion industry, IPR laws are applicable. Under IP laws you can protect your creativity, your designs and your brand's trademark. It is mandatory that you register all your designs under the Designs Act of your respective country to have IP protection under the law. The following are important when it comes to the protection of your brand-

- Name of the company,
- trademark,
- trade dress,
- colour scheme,
- packaging,
- sound mark.

For example, McDonald's has the tagline "I am loving it" registered which is a sound mark and the sound of the "lion's roar" at the beginning of an MGM-produced film Corporation, that is protected under trademark. Pictorial representation of your brand's logo needs to be applied for registration under the Trade Mark Act of your respective country as well.

The main confusion exists between choosing copyright or design and it baffles many people as to which choice should be opted for when it comes to their brand's protection. Should they go for copyright or design protection?

So the answer to your dilemma above is- You have protection under both copyright and design but there are various differences involved for example: Under copyright, if you are coming up with a product and which will be replicated more than 50 times by your brand in the market then your copyright over your product ceases to exist as anything replicated for more than the prescribed number of times enters the public domain and you lose your sole ownership over the product.

Hence to avoid the above chaos where you have no options available for a legal remedy it's always preferable to go for design protection when you have such a product that's been replicated for more than 50 times to have various legal remedies and to have the upper hand in lawsuits against counterfeiters.

If it's a limited number of products that is less than 50 in the market then you can always go for copyright and have your copyright protection over that product. There are various countries where you have to register it separately. For example, in the US you have to register your designs and patents under copyright laws if you want to have protection under copyright. But in India it's not mandatory to register a copyright, you will always get copyright protection. You automatically have copyright protection whenever you write, draw or doodle something. When it comes to design you have to mandatorily apply for registration whether online or offline whatever the case may be in your respective country.

Creation must be useful and unique in order to be patented. The important criteria for patent protection are novelty and utility. In Patents, two types of patents can be applied for protection- Utility and Design Patent. For eg strapless bra and corset have been patented. Other examples of patented products in the fashion industry include Velcro, clasps and zippers. IP protection helps to raise the funds by way of-

- IP Monetisation
- IP Licensing and
- Franchising

Since the rise in the cheaper, more inexpensive knockoff/counterfeit products in the market today, designers must apply for patents to protect their product's originality.

Hence, it's extremely crucial to have your IP protected especially in the fashion industry so that you can always have legal protection and get compensation against counterfeiters.

STEP 4: SUPPLY CHAIN

A supply chain includes the following-

- Procurement of raw material and the agreement that needs to be entered into is the sales/supply agreement.
- Manufacturing/assembling and the agreement that needs to be entered into is the manufacturing agreement. For eg- If you own a manufacturing company it is sorted and if you have designed and want someone else to manufacture your product you need to enter

into a manufacturing agreement. Terms that should be included are quantity, quality, colour scheme, licensing. Since you are sharing your IP design with the manufacturer IP clause should be added as well which will restrict them to producing only the mentioned number of products in the agreement to be safe from the misuse of IP, counterfeiters and have a legal remedy if your designs are sold in the open market and to other competitors. You can also sue if the product is of poor quality.

- Labelling includes licensing agreement. There's a possibility that the labelling can be done by manufacturers. You can combine sales and manufacturing agreements together if the raw material and manufacturing company is one. IP clauses are mandatory in all these agreements to have the complete legal protection of your brand's IP.

- Packaging and delivery include logistics/distribution agreement. IP clauses are mandatory in these agreements to have the complete legal protection of your brand's IP.

Why are agreements important?

We have a legal right to sue them in case of any mishap. For eg- If a poor quality product is delivered to you which is different from your given prototype, in case of counterfeiting, if the manufacturer ended up producing a greater number of products than the number permitted, if the customer receives the wrong product and if there is a delay in delivery. In all these scenarios you can sue and get compensation. You're sharing your IP, the brand's logo and trademark so it's crucial that you need to have all these required agreements in the supply chain to have legal protection and to also save the misuse of your IP.

STEP 5: EMPLOYMENT- BUILDING YOUR TEAM

Hiring the workforce includes-

- Designers,
- Administrative/executive/marketing/business development,
- Other workforce,
- POSH (Prevention of Sexual Harassment at Workplace)

Why employment agreements are important in the fashion industry?

To protect your IP, your workforce will have access to your IP and design. They can take a photo of that design and sell it to someone else or post it somewhere so it's necessary that you have an IP clause in the employment agreement in order to restrict your employers from unfair IP use. It's obligatory for designers to have these agreements because when they create a design they are the rightful owner of the design in absence of any agreement that restricts them, so you can add a clause in their employment agreement that whatever designs they would be creating during the course of the employment, the IP rights will belong to the parent company- fashion brand. They're now restricted to sell those designs to someone else. Now they're not the rightful owner of that IP. The IP belongs to you even though they're the designers and creators. The IP is transferred by the way of that agreement because of the clause. Other workers can include the Office receptionist. IP clause needs to be mentioned in their employment agreement as well. The POSH clause is mandatory to be included in the employment agreement. Other compliances like labour laws and any other schemes for employment insurance need to be followed under the employment guidelines.

STEP 6: MARKETING AND PROMOTION

Let the world know about your brand

- **Offline print/outdoor**
- **Digital marketing**
- **Affiliate marketing**
- **Influencers**

Influencer agreements can include terms where they are not allowed to use filters while promoting your brand since it'll hamper the colour scheme of your fashion brand and its logo. Celebrity endorsement includes them being your brand ambassador and consists of the NDA and CDA and Exclusivity Clause. Social media agreement falls under the category of digital marketing. Website designers agreement should have an IP clause to protect your IP if the server of the website designer is hacked as IP can be stolen from their server during hacks and cyber-attacks. Affiliate marketing-means sharing some revenues with the person who is referring others to use to your product eg- Referral brands like Amway.

STEP 7: E-COMMERCE AND DATA PRIVACY

- E-commerce,
- Aggregators,
- Policies – return, refund, exchange, data privacy, etc.

In an E-commerce marketing strategy, you have options as to whether you want to come up with your website or start your online store, accept payments online, selling your products online. It also includes having your tracking system about logistics and the product you have, your catalogue online, listing all your products on the website with the pricing and charging customers by the way of payment getaway where you have a team working for you who are tracking all these things. A tie-up with a specific logistic company and delivery partners like DHL and FedEx is important too.

Other aggregators are also available in the market so when you are not opting for your e-commerce website or you have your e-commerce website plus you're also putting your products on the aggregator's website like Amazon, Flipkart and Myntra, you can list your products on these websites and create a Seller account there. It is important to know that whenever you create a seller account on Amazon always read the terms and conditions about IP and the sales and revenue percentage. It is very important for you to be aware of these terms and conditions in order to make an informed choice of the preferred website. You can also compare the terms and conditions and the revenue share and see which aggregator's website suits you more.

Policies- Return, refund and exchange policy need to be mentioned on the website.

Data privacy- GDPR guidelines are available in European countries. In data privacy, you ought to have a privacy policy on the website. If you're taking the email of your customer or any visitor of your website then it needs to be mentioned in the privacy policy. Whatever information you're retaining of a potential customer or regular customer, what are the reasons and what you will do with that information needs to be explained. Credit card information- whether the credit card information is safe or not or consent for cookies, browser information for the way of collecting cookies etc. should all be mentioned in the privacy policy. There are various softwares available like you can use Shopify to create a website and take your brand online.

STEP 8: BUSINESS AND TRADE

Sales- If you opt for e-commerce you can make sales through the online method and in the offline method you have options like newspaper ads, fashion magazines, hoardings on highways etc. You own a retail store or list your product in a third party store- eg Walmart, big bazaar, shoppers stop. You can list your products with them which is also an offline sales method.

Whenever you're sharing your IP with them, agreements come into the picture. This way they're not putting someone else's product under your brand's name. Sales give rise to legal issues and customer/consumer complaints. Another complaint can be that of Aggregators. You should always mention the return policy and refund policy in detail.

IP monetisation- It means earning from your IP via IP licensing. IP can be sold or licensed too by way of merchandising and franchising. Example of sharing the IP with another brand-H&M x Sabyasachi, Puma x BMW. Puma has done IP licensing with BMW. They collaborated to increase their sales. Percentage of profit will be shared with BMW as well due to licensing agreement with them and around per sale basis which can be negotiated in the terms.

Happy meals box merchandise in McD. Two brands coming together to make a new third product to increase their sales is called merchandising. It is available only for a limited period of time. Selling designs includes IP selling/transferring right to someone else to use your designs.

Franchising- If you have a retail store and it's making a good number of sales and now you feel the need to expand the brand in your country but you lack the required capital to invest in furniture and work, you can come up with a franchisee plan which is similar to the business plan as discussed earlier. In the franchise plan, you'll mention the minimum investment amount/ initial investment fees and then you can mention the revenue share % that will be shared between the parent store and the franchisee stores. Franchise agreements help you to control the following things- Look and feel of the store and even the furniture and the colour scheme, uniformity of the retail store. The franchise plan includes IP terms as well. Other things to be included in the franchise agreement- You can appoint an auditor so that they can visit any retail store to test the quality and to check whether they're complying with the terms or not and you can restrict them from selling any other products under your brand's name. Here you're expanding your brand without infusing your capital. You are raising funds from the market as franchise fees and they're driving sales by the mode of the franchise. You as a parent company can distribute the products as per their consumption and demand and then you can make sales.

Trying to expand your brand into other countries. Brand plan and competition analysis are required. Understanding the laws and consumption pattern of the country and population and target audience is required. Consult a Lawyer with skills in international trade with your target country or pay a visit to concerned country embassy or their official trade centre setup in your country to learn about the process of taking your brand to their country, learning about compliances, any special trade benefits etc.

3.3 Making Brand compliance ready

Compliance refers to adhering to legal or social obligations or regulations; in the fashion business, this means following industry-wide recognized standards, such as working conditions, garment quality, environmental implications, and human rights. Failure to comply might have far-reaching effects throughout the supply chain. The majority of brands are aware of this and aim to obey the rules.

Global buyers are focusing on buying from compliant garment factories, with many retailers such as H&M, C&A, Zara, and others requiring traceability to ensure that goods are produced ethically. The Government of India has also implemented a number of compliance standards, including labour compliance, social compliance, environmental compliance, and so on. As a result, adhering to recognized production standards has become one of the most important success elements for any garment manufacturing company aiming to serve global customers.

To avoid liability, sellers implement a "code of conduct" that requires overseas suppliers to follow their home country's health, safety, environmental, and labor laws. However, especially in developing countries, these are frequently little more than a set of sick and easily avoided guidelines. Despite this discrepancy, brands continue to believe in the strength of their codes and adhere to this approach. However, customers are rapidly catching on to this hypocrisy, and brands would be wise to address this omission.

In the fashion industry, transparency is vital in their purchasing decisions for consumers. While consumers' need for transparency is encouraging retailers to improve how they source products and communicate about their practices, it also provides an opportunity for forward-thinking companies to gain a competitive advantage by using transparency.

Lack of transparency in the supply chain is a critical supply chain risk that many businesses face. It can be extremely difficult for businesses to track the development of their products and connect with suppliers throughout the manufacturing process, particularly when the manufacturing is outsourced. Suppliers frequently postpone deliveries, causing logistical issues for businesses that are unaware of the situation. This lack of visibility has an influence on the operations as a whole, and the problem must be addressed.

Transparency is a strong instrument for increasing corporate accountability in global supply chains for garment workers' rights. Transparency can help identify global garment firms whose branded products are manufactured in sweatshops where employers violate workers' rights. Workers, consumers, labor advocates, and investors will be more confident of the garment firm if supply chain information is made public. It also sends a strong statement that the company does not fear being held accountable if labor rights violations are discovered in its supply chain. It lends credibility to a company's claim that it is concerned about labor practices at its suppliers' factories.

3.4 Fashion, Finance and Taxation

Fashion companies take a long time to establish brand recognition and break even. It takes an average of 5 years or more to reach breakeven. However, if a customer base has gained brand recognition, the revenue-driving prospects can be enormous. Fashion enterprises demand a lot of money to start out because you must invest in things that may or may not sell extensively and blindly.[24] New businesses have to do a macro variable analysis to assess the profitability of their business idea. The options for raising capital for establishing a fashion business may include fundraising, venture capital financing, business loans, etc. Most countries have government or commercial organizations that can help new companies start either by competing or by fulfilling specified criteria.[25] The Angel Investor approach is a more established and conventional way of acquiring funds. These are self-made millionaires who have backgrounds in entrepreneurship and business. However, It is difficult to secure such an investment.

Another highly efficient form of investment is 'factoring.' The procedure of "factoring" is well-known in the fashion business. In essence, it consists of a company that provides money to companies based on real orders they receive seasonally. Factoring works by passing over the order book to the factors after the purchasers have accepted the orders. They take a percentage of the total value and pay cash in exchange. They risk not collecting money until the things are delivered. Factors may not choose to write down some stockholders since they are too small or because they have a dreadful credit history in their verification procedure. Working with factors is an excellent way of supporting production while offering a much-needed assurance that buyers will pay. The money they charge is a small amount to pay for their peace of mind.

However, just like any other business model, along with finance and investments, a flourishing fashion business requires consideration towards taxation.

Taxation

The Fashion industry contributes a significant part to nation's GDP as outcome of tax collected from this industry by government for domestic sales, imports and exports. The pre and post effects of lockdown badly affected the fashion retail industry and have led to the loss of jobs for both skilled and unskilled employees. The overall slowdown in the economy has impacted the disposable income, directly impacting the industry and because of this, millions of jobs have been affected, and the retail industry has taken the strongest blow in its history.

Whether you sell clothing and apparel in New York, California, Texas, Florida (the four most populous states in the U.S.) or anywhere in between, handling sales tax is considerably less interesting than calculating per capita industrial tarp usage. Yet in the gloomy realm of dull but

---

24 Autumn Adeigbo. Raising Capital For Fashion Is Notoriously Difficult: Here's How She Raised Over $10M For Her Brand. Forbes. 2018. Raising Capital For Fashion Is Notoriously Difficult: Heres How She Raised Over $10M For Her Brand (forbes.com)

25 Allenby et al. *Economic Trends and Being Trendy: The Influence of Consumer Confidence on Retail Fashion Sales.* 14 Journal of Business & Economic statistics. 1996.

critical compliance-related tasks, sales tax management wields mighty powers. With the right tools, strong sales tax management can lead to streamlined processes, stronger financials, and cost savings. Handled incorrectly, sales tax can unravel the fabric of your bottom line with costly audit fines, penalties, and interest. In today's omni-channel commerce environment, transactions occur at stores, online, and over the phone. Most clothing and apparel sellers utilize POS, mobile, ERP, and ecommerce as a means to reach customers and expand market reach, and within each channel there are potentially nexus-creating elements that change the sales tax game entirely.

The Fashion brands needs to file their taxes as per the tax slab their productline attract according to the government. The brands need to maintain and keep record of sales, import, exports, earning from franchising, licensing etc. This age of technology makes this tough task easy by use of billing softwares and storing data in secure servers over cloud. Avoiding paying taxes will land brand in trouble, hire a Cost Accountant to file your taxes and who can also look for exemptions that your productline can have if there's any government scheme for the same.

3.5 Sustainability

For decades, the fashion industry has been under siege. Consumers who value sustainability and the environment are demanding greater transparency about the role textile production plays not only in environmental pollution but also in the often unethical labor conditions for workers, as well as the industry's promotion of fast-fashion throwaway culture. To meet escalating demands and create successful and long-term transformation, fashion brands will have to incorporate compliance. Compliance is the adherence to legal or social obligations or requirements; in fashion, that equates to conforming to recognized standards across the industry, including

- work conditions,

- garment quality,

- environmental impacts, and

- human rights.

Sustainable and ethical fashion is a method of sourcing, manufacturing, and designing clothing that optimizes the advantages to the fashion industry and society as a whole while minimizing the environmental effect. The ideologies of the two notions overlap, yet they both have slightly different concerns that are equally important to the future of fashion. In today's society, artisan coffee costs more than a T-shirt. This is the world of Fast Fashion, and it is a serious issue. Fast fashion, according to Merriam Webster, is "a strategy to the design, creation, and marketing of apparel fashions that stresses making fashion trends swiftly and affordably available to consumers." Fast Fashion's mainstays include H&M, forever 21, Primark, Zara, Urbanic, and Shein. While reducing consumption is certainly one option, it is not enough to erase fashion's unglamorous dark underbelly that lurks beneath all the satin and sequins. According to the Fair Fashion Center back in 2016, 150 million lives are touched by the global apparel industry daily. Most of these people do not receive a living wage and work in terrible conditions. To name but a few of the ethical violations:

- insufficient wages

- child labor

- modern slavery

- migrant exploitation

- gender discrimination (the majority of these workers are young females)

- verbal, sexual, and physical abuse

- forced overtime (on average, workers in Bangladesh work 60 hours per week while earning ⅓ as many wages as other Asian garment factories… and they often work over the legal limit of 60 hours a week)

- hazardous work conditions

The scope and unwavering quest for economic expansion in the fashion sector are mind-boggling. Capitalism keeps the engine chugging forward. On the producing side, it keeps people employed (however bleak that work maybe) and has enhanced many people's overall standard of living. This is partly due to the surge in population growth (more people = more clothes). However, it is also a result of overconsumption and unsustainable purchasing habits fostered by fast fashion. People all throughout the world are aiming to reach developed-country consumption levels. Every year, customers buy 60% more clothes, which last just half as long as they did 15 years ago. This unrestrained development corporate model has no consideration for the social and environmental consequences. Cotton accounts for roughly half of all textiles, according to the WWF. Cotton is the dirtiest crop, needing the most chemicals when cultivated conventionally: 25 percent of the world's insecticides and 18 percent of the world's pesticides. In fact, the cotton used to manufacture an ordinary t-shirt is farmed with 17 teaspoons of chemical pesticides and fertilizers. Toxic chemicals are not only employed in the production of fibres, but they are also widely used in the dyeing and processing of textiles. Heavy metals (such as nickel, lead, and chromium), phthalates (known carcinogens), and formaldehyde are among these substances. Most apparel has a poor end-of-life predicament, and rapid fashion surely does not promote a circular economy. Textiles have one of the lowest recycling rates of any reusable item, according to the EPA. Tons of fossil fuels are consumed in the production (petroleum-based fabrics), manufacturing (coal-powered processing), and distribution processes (gasoline which transports the majority of clothes halfway around the world). We can make a difference by using our purchasing power. Designers (and many others) have stated it before, but it bears repeating: every purchase we make is a vote for the types of items we want to see manufactured, and hence the type of world we want to live in.

We are essentially stating that by supporting ethical brands that generate sustainable products, we want more of those items. Fast fashion only exists because we continue to promote it. "If we want to see fashion become a force for good, we need to change the way we think about what we wear and why we wear it," writes Fashion Revolution. We need to appreciate our garments more. We must regard them as priceless relics and valued friends." Clothing swaps with friends are a terrific way to update your regular style without spending any money. It is a great way to be environmentally conscious while also having joy. There is a whole world of preloved and vintage apparel available to you. Giving pre-existing items a second life is a terrific way to please the inner stylist while also remaining environmentally conscious. You don't even have to leave your house or browse through countless racks that smell like a basement with so many fantastic online thrift stores.

If one has items they no longer wear, donate them to thrift stores or sell used clothes online for a little more cash. One man's last season trends are another man's aesthetic, as the saying goes. But, once again, donating is not a panacea, but rather a last resort. Composting cellulose-fibre clothes is a better solution with numerous environmental advantages, particularly for items that are too worn or have no resale/thrift value (like the majority of fast fashion pieces). If one must buy new, do so with a conscience. Examine all of the options and choose the highest quality one can afford. Simple quality checks, such as looking at the stitching, should be implemented. Avoid it if the seams are sloppy or the edges are unfinished. Most importantly, choose brands that value sustainability and ethics. Recognize that no brand is completely sustainable but try your very best to determine which brands are the real deal and making the most of an effect by doing more right than wrong.

Too frequently, brands start a sustainable development, CSR, or responsible consumption approach thinking they had a brilliant idea or a truly unique effort to create on these themes. This would allow them to properly understand what is most essential to their customers and lead them in the first place on what they should tackle and strive to be better at. Because, while planting trees is great and efficient, people may want to see advances in how materials are acquired or whether they are eco-designed to be readily repaired and reused. Becoming a more "sustainable" brand does not happen fast, nor is it a "one-shot" project. It's a lengthy procedure. Consumers have lost trust in businesses in recent years, and this is especially true when it comes to their communication on subjects such as sustainable development or health. To put it another way, they don't believe in corporate speeches anymore. In the food business, for example, too many consumers are unsure, due to a lack of openness, how goods are created, where components are sourced and at what cost, what influence they have on their health. That is why transparency, honesty, and gradually explaining (with facts and numbers in context) how things are done are critical.

Finally, a sustainability plan is one that is global, cross-departmental, and affects the business models of enterprises. As a result, businesses must be able to speak about their main business. Is a company known for producing high-tech equipment? So, how is this equipment created? Where? Who creates it? Under what circumstances? How much energy are you consuming? How much CO_2 is released into the atmosphere during transportation? What guarantees are there for traceability, durability, and repairability? Organizations must be able to communicate honestly and comprehensively about the actions taken in the products and services that comprise their core business. Of course, recycling cups at the office, encouraging employees to make eco-friendly gestures, and encouraging them to use public transit wherever possible are all vital goals. As a result, corporations are increasingly employing dialogue approaches to direct themselves: knowing what is right, what is wrong, where to go, and how to do things. These technologies, which have always powered marketing, are more important than ever in an era when consumers are more sensitive than ever, including on social and environmental problems.

Chapter 4. Fashion and Intellectual Property

Fashion is a popular industry that is constantly changing. Regardless of how dynamic the industry is, it is also a hotbed for intellectual property (IP) disputes. In the fashion world, a new creative idea can easily become the next big thing. But if that idea is protected by intellectual property rights, it can also lead to an infringement lawsuit. In this chapter, we will look at the rights associated with fashion industry and the rights that are afforded to fashion designers and content creators. We will also discuss the many factors that come into play when it comes to an IP dispute.

The intellectual right protection available in the realm of fashion industries for the design, photographs, content, fabric pattern can be categorized into patent, copyright and trademark. Disparate aspects of intellectual property rights such as patents, copyrights and trademarks serve different roles when it comes to the protection, such as patent protects inventions, copyright protects creative and artistic works and trademark protects the identity of the brand. Being one of the fastest growing industries of the country, some Indian brands and designers have earned global recognition as well.

The technological advancement has made it easy for the people to copy the exact design of any particular brand without the knowledge of the designer. Since globalization has made the world more closer and connected, the scope of vulnerability regarding the infringement of designs has also increased. The Internet and media platforms have unclogged the course of copying and pasting designs within hours of being telecasted on fashion ramps or runways. Earlier, the high-end and premium brands used to be diminutive, family owned businesses which are restricted to certain geographical boundaries, having an undivided clientele. The scope of infringement was very limited and the designers had no worry the protection of their intellectual property rights. But with globalization, there was an emergence of global economic network that made communicational exchange smooth mostly by advances in infrastructure, transportation and technology. The breeding interdependence of countries was resulted from integration of trade, finance, individuals and ideas which were part of one global market.

The heart of fashion lies in new and fresh designs. There is a galactic value of the intellectual capital of products in the fashion world, be it premium brands or petite designers. From the lawsuit that Puma filed against Forever 21 for selling lookalike versions of footwear from Rihanna's Fenty line for Puma to the shops in Chandni Chowk, Delhi selling replicas of designers like Sabyasachi and Manish Malhotra, there have been multiple cases of infringement across the globe. People might hesitate to go for the most coveted brands like Rolex, Dior, Balenciaga, Prada, Versace or Gucci but the street markets are growing prosperously by selling their fashion knockoffs. Counterfeit goods have existed as long as high-end fashion has been a coveted commodity. Before internet, gray market used to attract salespeople, and that further developed into a notorious place to buy knockoffs and other designer commodities. Salespeople contacted their consumers personally about the availability of products. The fashion counterfeit were sold in sort of underground way until the age of internet. In-person knockoff sale was easily traceable and they were subject of arrest by the police authorities. Whereas, online counterfeit fashion is not about someone on the street selling a fake Gucci bag, it could also be large corporations and celebrities stealing from independent artists and selling work almost identical to theirs with little to null repercussions. Social media serves a platform where the artists and designers can display their original work and gain recognition for it. One of the facts that should be concerned is the amount of fashion counterfeits is increasing with the passing time all over the world. The increasing demand of high-end brands by the people has stimulated the proliferation of imitators and counterfeiters in various regions. The globalization of marketing platforms, coupled with technologies like media and internet have diverted the original institutional boundaries and restructured the supply chains of the markets. Generally, any fashion entity be it a well known brand or individual designer, is rewarded with success due to their efficient mechanism, organizational hierarchy, baroque designs, daedal thoughts, fluent advertising, effective distribution system and veracious pricing strategies. The whole process goes in vein when counterfeiting comes into play. However, the designers lack to understand the exclusive rights that are being granted to them through intellectual property laws that can help them in saving their designs from getting copied. While fashion trends may come and go with a blink of the eye but the intellectual capital involved is of tremendous value, which should be protected at all costs.

4.1 TRADEMARK AND TRADE DRESS

Definition

A trademark is a word, phrase, symbol, configuration, device, the shape of goods, packaging, and combination of colors, or design that distinguishes one party's goods from those of others.

Section 2, Article 15, Clause 1 of the Agreement on Trade-Related Aspects of Intellectual Property Rights (TRIPS) defines a trademark as, *"Any sign, or any combination of signs, capable of distinguishing the goods or services of one undertaking from those of other undertakings, shall be capable of constituting a trademark*

According to section 2(1)(zb), a trademark means a *'mark which is capable of being represented graphically and capable of distinguishing the goods or services of* **one** *person from those of others, and may include the shape of goods or their packaging and combinations of colours.'*

There are three essentials of trademark-

i.It should be a Mark-

Section 2(1)(m) – "Mark" includes a device, brand, heading, label, ticket, name, signature, word, letter, numeral, shape of goods, packaging, or combination of colours or any combination thereof.

ii.The Mark is capable of being represented graphically

<u>Section 2(1)(k) of Trademark Rules, 2007</u> - *'Graphical representation is a representation of a trademark for goods or services represented or capable of being represented in paper form and include representation in digitized form.'*

This basic requirement for registration as a valid trademark simply means that the mark is able to be registered physically on the register and published in the Journal.

iii.Capable of distinguishing goods and services of one person from those of others-

In order for it to be distinctive or capable of distinguishing the goods, there may be certain intrinsic qualities or distinguishing features in the mark itself that make it so distinctive from the goods of others. As a result, the use of a mark that is incapable of distinguishing the goods of the trademark's owner does not qualify for trademark registration. This trademark requirement primarily states that a trademark must be distinguishable, i.e., it must not be devoid of a distinguishing character.

Scope of Trademark

I.Conventional Trademark

Following marks can be registered under the Trademark law-

a. Device

b. Brand

c. Heading

d. Label

e. Ticket

f. Name

g. Signature

h. Word, letter, and numerical

i. Shape of goods

j. Packaging

k. Combination of colors

l. Combination of different marks

What marks are not registrable as a trademark?

Section 9 of the Act provides that trademarks that lack distinctiveness and are likely to cause deception or confusion in the minds of the public or consumers are not registrable in India.

Other grounds-

a.   Trademarks that are likely to hurt religious sentiments of any community;

b.   Trademarks that comprise of any scandalous or obscene matter;

c.   Its use is prohibited under the Emblems and Names (Prevention of Improper Use) Act, 1950;

d.   The shape of goods which is purely functional or necessary to obtain technical results or which give substantial value to the goods.

II.   Non- Conventional Trademark

Words, logos, symbols, or a combination of these have traditionally been the subject matter of trademarks. Many techniques are used to attract the attention of consumers in today's era of aggressive marketing. This is where non-traditional trademarks are useful. Non-conventional or non-traditional trademarks are those that fall outside of the traditional trademark definition and include marks like shapes, sounds, smells, tastes, and textures, etc.

Although they are not expressly mentioned in the Act, non-conventional marks are included in the description of a trademark. Graphic representation of a mark is the *sine qua non* for trademark registration in India. The problem of graphical representation of non-traditional marks is a serious one. It is regarded as a significant barrier to the registration of non-traditional trademarks.

However, the position of Trade Marks Registry on the filing and acceptance of such unconventional applications is not clear. There is no guideline on how the application needs to be submitted, or on the examination procedure, that has been laid out by the Registry.

1. Smell Mark

One of the most powerful forms of human memory is smell. The manufacturers infuse their products with a pleasant fragrance. In order to register a smell mark, applicants must be able to visually represent the fragrance of the product and demonstrate that it is distinct from the product itself. It is difficult to write down a smell's chemical formula because it's presumed to represent the substance rather than the smell of that substance. Any written explanation of a smell must be so detailed that it cannot be confused with any other smell.

For example- The following has been successfully registered as a trademark-

- **Dutch** company's tennis balls with the scent of newly mown grass;

- **UK** registrations for tires with "a floral fragrance/smell reminiscent of roses" and darts with "the strong smell of bitter beer."

2.   Sound Marks

A sound mark is one in which the sound is used to identify the commercial origin of goods and services. Sound marks take on a distinct form and arrangement, when they serve as source indicators by associating the sound with a product or service in the listener's mind.

As per Rule 26(5) of the Trade Marks Rules, 2017, Sound trademarks can be registered *When an application for the registration of a trademark consists of a sound as a trademark, the reproduction of the same shall be submitted in the MP3 format not exceeding thirty seconds' length recorded on a medium which allows for easy and clearly audible replaying accompanied with a graphical representation of its notations.*

For example- Registered trademarks are-

- ICICI Bank for " *Dhin Chik Dhin Chik*"
- McDonald's "*I'm lovin' it*" jingle
- Yahoo's Yodle

3.   Taste Marks

Taste marks are easier to represent graphically since they can be used to denote the taste of the products using a written explanation of the taste. However, the issue is once again one of functionality. A trademark for the taste of pizza or pasta cannot be given because it inherently performs the purpose of making the dishes, i.e. adding flavor. As a result, we see chefs preparing dishes with the same ingredients and little or no variation.

The European Union Intellectual Property Office (EUIPO) and the United States Patent and Trademark Office (USPTO) received two applications for registration of taste marks, but both were rejected. Till date, no trademark is granted for taste anywhere in the world.

4.   Hologram Mark

Holography is a photographic technique that captures the light scattered by an object and displays it in a three-dimensional format. A hologram is a permanent record of the light reflecting off an object, similar to a photograph. A hologram, on the other hand, appears to be real and three-dimensional, and moves when you look at it, much like a real object. Its registration usually requires the use of a sequence of pictures or drawings to depict how the trade mark functions. India by far hasn't received any application for the registration of hologram mark.

5. Three- dimensional Mark

Rule 26(3) of the Trade Marks Rules, 2017, states that *'where the application contains a statement to the effect that the trademark is a three-dimensional trademark, the reproduction of the trademark shall consist of a two dimensional graphic or photographic reproduction as follows, namely:—*

(i) the reproduction furnished shall consist of three different view of the trademark;

(ii) where, the Registrar considers that it does not sufficiently show the particulars of the three dimensional trademarks, he may call upon the applicant to furnish within two months, up to five further different views of the trademark and a description by words of the trademark;

(iii) where the Registrar considers that the trademark referred to in clause (ii), still do not sufficiently show the particulars of the three dimensional trademark, he may call upon the applicant to furnish a specimen of the trademark.'

6. Well Known Marks

Section 2(1)(zg) of the Act defines well known mark as "*a mark which has become so to the substantial segment of the public which uses such goods or receives such services that the use of such mark in relation to other goods or services would be likely to be taken as indicating a connection in the course of trade or rendering of services between those goods or services and a person using the mark in relation to the first mentioned goods or services."*

A trademark owner can file an application in form TM-M with a request to the Registrar for the mark to be considered "well-known". In India, well-known trademarks are recognized based on their reputation, national, domestic, and cross-border basis.

7. Texture

Texture Marks, like scent marks, give the feel of a product by touch. They are difficult to register since there can be no representation of the texture's feel, such as fabrics, bottles, and so on. Non-Conventional Marks are the least common. It should be remembered that the texture of the product should not be attributed to its functional purpose. The touchmark must be distinct to the users; it cannot simply be an eye-catching or ornamental feature.

Touch marks that excite human touch senses are not claimed as commonly as other non-traditional trademarks, and as a result, touch marks are among the least celebrated and claimed of all non-traditional trademarks. No texture marks have come for registration before the Indian registry.

8.   Position Mark

A mark consisting of the way it is positioned or affixed to the product in a specific way. In the fashion industry, position marks are often used to provide protection. "The mark consists of three parallel equally-spaced stripes applied to footwear, the stripes placed on the footwear upper in the region between the laces and the sole," according to the adidas trademark description.

9.   Slogan as a TM

Slogans must be either:

- intrinsically distinctive and innovative, or
- have acquired sufficiently secondary meaning to automatically bring to mind a product or service to qualify as protectable marks. A slogan that is not intrinsically distinctive can only be covered by trademark law if it acquires secondary meaning. The more mundane a slogan is, the more secondary meaning the owner will need to show in order to gain protection from imitators. The owners of Excedrin, for example, had to show that the phrase "Extra Strength Pain Reliever" had created a clear secondary meaning.

10.   Trade Dress

Due to increased competition in the commercial industry, the importance placed on a product's trade dress has risen dramatically.

Trade Dress refers to a product's visual appearance, such as packaging, shape, and color combination that can be registered or protected by rivals in terms of their business and services. It aids consumers in recognizing the product and distinguishing it from others. The key purpose is to prevent the goods and services from being copied. It should be distinct from the goods of others. It should not cause confusion in the minds of consumers, as this could lead to unfair use of the commodity.

Section 2 (m) "mark" includes a device, brand, heading, label, ticket, name, signature, word, letter, numeral, shape of goods, packaging or combination of colors or any combination thereof;

Section 2 (q) "package" includes any case, box, container, covering, folder, receptacle, vessel, casket, bottle, wrapper, label, band, ticket, reel, frame, capsule, cap, lid, stopper and cork"

In India, there is no specific definition of trade dress under the Trademark Act 1999. In India, trade dress does not require formal registration and is connected to a company's reputation and goodwill built over time.

In the case of ***Christian Louboutin Sas v. Mr. Pawan Kumar & Ors.*** The designer's *red sole* was held to be a well-known trademark by the Delhi High Court. The Plaintiff claimed in this case that the shoe with the red sole clearly distinguishes Plaintiff's product from others. The plaintiff's 'RED SOLE' trademark became its signature. The trademark *"Red Sole"* is registered in many jurisdictions, including India, and it has a trans-border reputation due to several factors.

The Defendants in the case were local shoe dealers who manufactured and sold shoes with a red sole, infringing on the Plaintiff's trade mark. After considering the Plaintiff's material facts, the Court issued a permanent injunction prohibiting the Defendants from manufacturing, selling, or otherwise engaging with footwear bearing the Plaintiff's licensed trade mark for "Red Sole" and awarded damages to the Plaintiff. This is also the first time that a court in India has ruled a trade dress to be well-known status.

Obtaining Process of Trademark

The Trademarks Act of 1999 (India) protects trademark owners and makes those who infringe on their rights criminally liable. A trademark must be registered with the Trademark Registrar of the Registry of Trademarks, India, in order to be protected. The Controller General of Patents, Designs and Trademarks, Ministry of Commerce and Industry, Government of India, registers trademarks in India.

Following trademark registration, the applicant can use the 'R' symbol, and the trademark registration will be valid for a period of ten years. However, registered trademarks that are about to expire can easily be renewed by filing a trademark registration application for an additional ten years.

1. **Step 1: Trademark Search**

The entrepreneur or trademark professional must perform a trademark search of the trademark database before starting the trademark registration process. A trademark search will disclose whether or not a trademark that is identical or similar to one that has already been registered with the trademark registry. The trademark quest discloses all forms of trademarks, both registered and unregistered, that are available in the market. The search also determines if the applied trademark is in competition with other trademarks in the same class.

2. **Step 2: To file the trademark application**

After completing a trademark search, you can file an application for trademark registration with the Trademark Registrar. The trademark registration application must be completed in the prescribed manner and filed with the trademark registration fee. The trademark registration application is Form TM- A, which can be filed online via the official IP India website or in person at the Trade Marks Office, depending on the trademark's jurisdiction.

3. **Step 3: Examination of the trademark application**

After an extensive review of the trademark application in accordance with the provisions of the Trade Marks Act, the Examiner is required to issue a mandatory examination report following the filing of the trademark application. The authority's examination report may or may not reveal any objections, which may be absolute, relative, or procedural.

4.   Step 4: Entertaining any objections

Within four months of the mark's publication in the Trademark Journal, a notice to oppose the trademark must be submitted via Form TM- O. The Trademark Authority issues this examination report within 30 days of the filing of the registration application.

5.   Step 5: Counter-statement from the Applicant

Within 30 days of receiving the examination report, a reply must be filed asserting the arguments and evidence in opposition to any objections in order to waive them.

6.   Step 6: Publication

The trademark would be allowed for trademark journal publication if the Trademark Officer was satisfied with the trademark applicant's justifications. The trademark applicant has the right to appeal the Trademark Officer's decision to the Intellectual Property Appellate Board if the Trademark Officer is not satisfied with the justifications.

7.   Step 7: Trademark Registration

The final stage in the process is registration, which occurs after the application has conquered the objections and/or opposition to the trademark registration.

Furthermore, if no objections to the trademark's registration were raised during the four-month advertisement/publication period, the trademark is issued an auto-generated registration certificate within one week under the seal of the Trademark Office. After the registration is completed, it is valid for ten years, after which it must be renewed within a prescribed time period.

The trademark is considered a registered trademark of the owner once the trademark registration certificate is issued, giving the trademark owner exclusive use of the mark. Next to the logo or trademark, the ® symbol can be used.

Trademark Searching

The Comptroller General of Patent Designs and Trademarks is in charge of trademark registrations and registered trademarks in India. The Comptroller General operates an online trademark search database that can be used by both professionals and non-professionals to conduct trademark searches. The trademark database includes all trademark applications filed with the Indian Trademark Registrar, including trademarks that have been registered, applied for, objected to, and expired. A trademark search in the trademark database would provide useful results for the user's trademark search query.

At the Trademark Registry India, you can conduct a free online trademark search at https://ipindiaonline.gov.in/tmrpublicsearch/frmmain.aspx.

There are three different categories of trademark searches available-

a.   **Wordmark**- For similar representations of wordmark;

b.   **Vienna Code**- For similar artistic representations;

c.   **Phonetic**- For phonetically related words.

A.   Wordmark Search

To conduct a Wordmark search, choose *"Wordmar*k" as the search type and enter the proposed trademark's keyword(s) in the box marked *"Wordmark."*

There are 45 different trademark registration classes. According to the *Nice Classification*, Classes 1-34 deal with various goods, while Classes 35-45 deal with services. As a result, you will need to correct the class in the box to "CLASS." And the class(es) should be related to your trademark's services or products. You can only search the India trademark database using a single class at a time.

The wordmark search can be done with any prefix type, such as "Starts With", "Contains," or "Match With."

A keyword search in the "Starts With" option will return all trademarks that begin with the searched keyword. A search with a keyword in the "Contains," option, on the other hand, will display all trademarks that contain the searched keyword. For a search with a keyword in the "Match With" option, however, the result will only display trademarks that match the searched keyword.

B. Search Result

After you've entered all of the necessary information, click the 'Start Search' button to see the results of your search. The table will show the particulars of each trademark, such as the S.No., matching trademark(s), and images. To view all of the results, click the box in the left top corner or click the selection box shown in S.No. for the desired trademark. After checking the boxes, click "Report" to see a detailed report of all trademarks.

If there are no registered or applied trademarks that match the query if a trademark search shows "no matches found". Then you can proceed to file the trademark.

C. Phonetic Search

Except for the prefix method, the phonetic search will be the same as the above Wordmark search method. As a result, you will use the same procedure as before to conduct a phonetic search of the trademark.

D. Vienna code Search

The Vienna code search is primarily used to find similar device models, and you must enter the six-digit Vienna code in the box labelled "Vienna code" and select the appropriate class. Following the search, the result table will show all of the marks that contain the device.

Why conduct a Trademark search?

- TM search provides information and details about any existing brand name or trademark that is identical to yours.
- It gives you a list of prohibited marks (marks that can't be registered by a private individual) so you can see if your brand name or trademark is on the list.

Selecting a Strong Trademark

You want to choose a strong mark that communicates to the public that specific products and services come from your business and not from one of your rivals when choosing a trademark.

Businesses often choose names to describe their products or services, with generic or merely descriptive words thrown in for good measure. Consumer confusion, lost business, and the loss of one of your company's most important monetary assets, the trademark, may all result from this activity.

Depending on the mark chosen and how it is used, a trademark may be "strong" or "weak." Consider the line below to figure out which marks are the most effective. Every trademark falls somewhere along the following axis:

Choosing a "strong" mark will help you prevent many potential problems. What entrepreneurs and business owners should aim for is a name that will stick in the minds of their customers and become synonymous with their business.

1. Generic Terms

A generic term or phrase is so descriptive of the product or service for which it is associated that it will be incapable to act as a trademark. These are the names given to the goods or services to which they are applied. When used in their generic sense, they are incapable of obtaining secondary meaning and hence are not protectable as trademarks. Examples: JEAN for jeans.

2. Descriptive Trademarks

Those marks merely describe the services or goods for which the mark is used. These are also difficult to enforce unless the trademark owner can show that the mark has become distinctive, such as if it has been widely advertised to the point that customers can infer secondary meaning from the mark. Examples: AMERICAN APPAREL

3. Suggestive Marks

Those that suggest a quality or characteristic of the goods and services, rather than describing. But there is a greater chance that the trademark would conflict with the trademark rights of someone else. Examples: PAC SUN, NORTH FACE, and WRANGLER

4. Arbitrary Trademarks

Arbitrary Marks are those that are created up of existing words but have no connection in relation to the products or services. **Examples-** GAP, NIKE, FOSSIL, and GUESS

5. Fanciful Trademarks

Those marks are created solely for the purpose of functioning as a trademark and have no other meaning than that of a trademark. Sometimes these marks are made up of parts of other words, and other times they have no meaning or logic at all. These are thought to be the strongest form of mark. Example- EXXON, KODAK, and XEROX.

Trademark Infringement

Infringement of a trademark is a violation of the exclusive rights granted to the registered proprietor of the trademark to use the same. A trademark is deemed infringed when a non-permitted user uses an identical/similar/deceptively similar mark to the registered trademark without the permission of the trademark's registered proprietor. However, it is important to note that Indian trademark law, which is based on common law principles, protects a prior user's vested rights against a registered proprietor.

Infringement can be of two types- Direct Infringement and Indirect Infringement. Direct Infringement has been provided under Section 29 of the Act whereas there is no expressed provision related to Indirect Infringement.

Elements of an Infringement-

1. **Use by an unauthorized person-**

    This means that a trademark is only violated when it is used by anyone who is not authorized by the registered trademark holder. It is not considered an infringement if the logo is used with the permission of the registered trademark holder.

2. **Identical or similar goods-**

The trademark used by the unauthorized individual must be either identical to or deceptively similar to the registered trademark. The word "deceptively similar" simply means that the consumer can be confused by the marks and assume them for one another. It is sufficient to prove infringement if there is a chance of misrecognition of the marks.

3. **Registered trademark-**

Only trademarks that have been registered with India's trademark registry are protected by the Act. The common law of passing off is used to resolve conflicts when an unregistered mark is breached. It is a tort law that is applied when an individual or group of people suffers injury or harm to their goodwill as a result of the actions of another.

4. **Goods or services of the same class-**

In order to be considered a trademark infringement, the unauthorized use of the mark must be for the advertisement of products or services that are in the same class as the registered trademark.

In contrast to direct infringement, there is no clear provision in the Act dealing with indirect infringement. The common law principle underpins the concept and application of indirect infringement. It keeps not only the principal infringer liable but also anyone who aids or induces the direct offender to infringe. Indirect infringement can be divided into two categories:

Vicarious liability- Section 114:

If the person committing an offense under this Act is a company, the company as well as every person in charge of, and responsible to, the company for the conduct of its business at the time of the commission of the offense shall be deemed to be guilty of the offense and shall be liable to be proceeded against and punished accordingly.

Thus, anyone responsible for the company, not just the principal infringer, would be liable for indirect infringement, with the exception of those who behaved in good faith and without knowledge of the infringement.

Elements of vicarious liability-

a. When the person has control over the actions of the principal infringer,

b. When the person is aware of the infringement and contributes to it,

c. When the person wants to benefit financially from the infringement.

Contributory infringement-

Contributory infringement is composed of only three elements: -

a.   When the person is aware of the infringement,

b.   When the person contributes materially to the direct infringement,

c.   When the person persuades the principal infringer to commit the infringement

There is no exception in the case of contributory infringement since the contributory infringer has no chance of acting in good faith.

Remedies for Trademark Infringement

In India, trademark infringement is a cognizable offence, which ensures that the infringer will face both criminal and civil charges. The registration of a trademark is also not required by Indian law for the institution of civil or criminal proceedings. This is attributable to the common law concept of passing off, as previously stated. The following remedies can be awarded by the court in the case of trademark infringement:

1. Temporary injunction
2. Permanent injunction
3. Damages
4. Account of profits (damages in the amount of the profits gained from the infringement)
5. Destruction of goods using the infringing mark
6. Cost of legal proceedings

In the case of a criminal proceeding, the court will impose the following penalties:

1. Imprisonment for a minimum of six months and a maximum of three years.
2. A fine of not less than Rs 50,000 and up to Rs 2,00,000 can be imposed.

Can #Hashtags be protected as Trademark?

Social media has changed the way brands and businesses advertise their products and services. In a day and age where a Company's online presence greatly impacts its popularity and customer base brands have started to recognize the power of social media engagement. In 2006 Twitter introduced the concept of hashtag to the world of social media, it acted as a medium to hyperlink all posts that had the same # symbol allowing the users to view the information and images related to these hashtags together in an organized manner. Today almost all social media platforms have introduced hashtags and subsequently, hashtags have now evolved as a marketing tool.

With new trends coming up on social media every day, a business can gain massive traction and reach by jumping on the bandwagon, along with these trends come a series of hashtags that make the trends identifiable and searchable, for instance in 2020 #dalgonacoffee took social media by a frenzy, in 2021 the #dontrushchallege among others had gained popularity. There are certain evergreen hashtags like #OOTD, #throwbackthursday which social media users add to their pictures while sharing them on social media.

#HashtagForBrands

During New York Fashion Week 2016, which is one of the biggest and most awaited event in the fashion industry, designers launched custom hashtags such as #FentyXPuma, #YeezySeason3, #AllAccessKors, #TommyFall16 and #MyCalvins to display their latest fashion collections and to allow followers live and behind-the-scenes looks at their NYFW shows, triggering more than 561,000 mentions on social media in a single week.

GoPro uses #GoPro for creating value, promoting new products, and interacting with their customers. The hashtag has more than 48.2 million posts just on Instagram. Nike's #justdoit, #sayitwithpepsi by Pepsi and #CaughtOnDropCam by Google are some examples that show that brands have embraced hashtags and are using them as a medium to promote and distinguish their products.

However, can hashtags be registered as Intellectual property? Can you really stop others from using your hashtag?

There are many types of Intellectual Property recognized by the World Intellectual Property Organization like Copyright, Patents, Trademarks etc. Each of these types governs and protects different areas of work. In simple words, copyright offers protection to artistic works like music, paintings, films etc. whereas patents protect inventions and processes. Trademark on the other hand governs words, phrases, symbols, design or any combination of these that can be used to distinguish the product or services of one person from those of others.

Since hashtags are not ideas or inventions that would be subject to patent protection, and they are too short to qualify for copyright protection, a hashtag clearly fits best for protection under trademark law.

In India, the laws relating to trademarks are governed by the Trademark Act, 1999. According to Section 2(1) (zb) of the Act, a trademark is defined as a mark capable of being represented graphically and which is capable of distinguishing the goods or services of one person from those of others and may include the shape of goods, their packaging and combination of colours.

It is evident that a hashtag has the same two criteria for registration that any other trademark does, i.e.

- it should be capable of being represented graphically
- it should be capable of distinguishing goods and services of one person from another person.

A hashtag can be registered as a trademark only if it is distinctive and the hashtag is used in conjunction with the goods and services offered by you. The hashtag should be a "brand identifier" and should be associated with the business. Generic words that are used in daily communication are not generally given protection. Hashtags can be protected especially when you can demonstrate that it has become synonymous with you, or your content. For instance, when you hear the hashtag #kyaut, #scauzme you might associate it with well know influencer if you are familiar with her content because overtime the hashtag has become associated with her and hence in such a scenario the likeliness of getting protection is high as there is a certain reputation that has come to be associated with the catchphrase. Multinational companies like The Coca-Cola Company have successfully registered hashtags as trademarks these include #smilewwithacoke and #cokecanpics. Interestingly, no hashtags have been registered as trademarks in India.

The position in the US is slightly different and has evolved since the introduction of hashtags. The United States Patents and Trademarks Office acknowledges the # symbol to be registered as a trademark only if it functions as a source identifier of the applicant's goods or services.

For instance, in 2015, 1042 hashtag trademark applications were filled in the United States and the USPTO granted licenses to several trademarks like #EveryDayMadewell, #TheSelfie #HowDoYouKFC etc. but denied protection to #WORLDTRAVELER, #BETHEFAN due to its mere descriptiveness or discrepancy in the alignment of an acceptable specimen of use.

In *Fraternity Collection LLC v. Elise Fargnoli*, the US District Court has settled a trademark infringement case where it considered a hashtag as a trademark. The court found that there was trademark infringement and false advertising by the defendant, Elise Fargnoli. She had used the hashtag "#fratcollection" and "#fraternitycollection" on her Instagram account to promote a product that had earlier been designed for the plaintiff's competitor. The users on clicking the hashtag were directed to the same designs of another brand fraternity collections traffic was channelized to the products manufactured by its competitors. Even though the matter was eventually settled, the court held that there was trademark infringement and false advertising

In *Eksouzian v Albanese,* the issue was whether the use by one of the parties of the hashtags #Cloudpen and #Cloudpenz on Instagram breached the terms of a trademark settlement agreement. In this agreement, the party which using these hashtags had agreed to refrain from any trademark style use of the word "cloud" in conjunction with the words "pen" or "penz" The court, in this case, held that there was no breach of the agreement. The court ruled that a hashtag is a "descriptive device" and not a "source identifier".

Registering your hashtag as a trademark does not prevent other users from including it in their social media postings, it will not give you a monopoly over the use of the hashtag. However, it provides legal protection in the event when another company uses it to promote a competing product or service within the same industry as yours. It is evident that as brands strengthen their digital presence, registration of hashtags as trademarks and disputes arising out of their infringement will become more prevalent, it is important for brand owners to consider the use of hashtags in their branding strategy if the hashtag is worth promoting, ensure that it is worth protecting too.

4.2 COPYRIGHT

Copyright as the actual name shows is an Intellectual Property right given through a guideline to the originator of artistic, melodic, emotional, and imaginative works and originators of cinematograph motion pictures and sound chronicles. Truth be told, it's a bundle of rights including, entomb alia, privileges of generation, verbal trade to general society, variety, and interpretation of the work.

Copyright secures unique works. Copyright is not a flat outright of the proprietor. Positioning the owner's desire to confine his copyrighted works to those prepared to compensate for such access and the public's advantage in unreservedly utilising the copyrighted work remains a huge issue under Copyright law.[26] Original, literary, dramatic, musical, and artistic works are protected by copyright.[27] The Berne Convention for the Protection of Literary and Artistic Works, 1886, and the Universal Copyright Convention, the Geneva Act, 1952, are referenced in the Copyright Act of 1957. Copyright protection lasts for 60 years. In Zee Telefilms Ltd. v. Sundial Communication, Delhi High Court held that it becomes copyrightable when an idea is converted into a concept.[28]

---

26 Neha Wagle, *Copyright versus Designs: Kurukshetra of Indian Fashion Industry*, IPLEADERS (Nov. 26, 2019), https://blog.ipleaders.in/copyright-versus-designs/.
27 Copyright Act, 1957.
28 Zee Telefilms Ltd. v. Sundial Communication, 2003 (5) BomCR 404 (India).

Fashion Designs protected under the rules of the Copyright Act, 1957, when they fall under the scope of artistic works.[29] Fashion is an art of artistry, which artisans execute while designing dress, shoes and different frill. A painting, a sculpture, a drawing (including a diagram, map, chart, or plan), an engraving, or a photograph, whether or not such work has an artistic quality, a [work of architecture], and any other work of artistic craftsmanship are all considered creative works under the Copyright Laws.[30] As per Indian laws, fashion design is a unique artwork registered under the Design Act of 2000, but it does not receive protection under the Design Act of 2000; nonetheless, the design does receive protection under the Copyright Act of 2000.[31] From the registration date, the design protected under the Copyright for a term of ten years.

In *Rajesh Masrani v Tahliani Design*, The Delhi High Court's Division Bench looked into some of the issues raised.[32] Plaintiff claimed in the case that the designs it generated while producing clothing and accessories were artistic works under Section 2 (c) of the Copyright Act of 1957. The patterns printed and stitched on the fabric, as well as the completed outfits, were said to be creating masterpieces. The plaintiff also claimed copyright infringement in these diverse artistic works. The Court determined that because the creation was 'artistic' in nature, it could not be covered under the Design Act, 2000, and thus Section 15 (2) did not apply.[33]

In *Louis Vuitton Malletier v. Atul Jaggi & Anr*, Delhi High Court recognised the plaintiff's copyright in the 'Toile Monogram' pattern and the Murakami monograms of the plaintiff.[34]

In *Microfibres, Inc v. Girdhar & Co*, the question of whether the arrangement of motifs, flowers, leaves, and shapes that have been arranged in a particular manner would be applicable for Copyright as 'labour and skill' was raised.[35] The Court held that such work could not be included in the definition of "Artistic works" as provided under Section 2 (c) of the Copyright Act, 1957. [36]The shape, colour, pattern, and other characteristics of a product are referred to as design. The term "design" defines under sections 2 (d) and 4 of the Design Act, 2000. From the view of the fashion industry, the design act can't secure the complete articles of clothing; instead, it ensures design, shape, shading, an example of the product. The Copyright Act guarantees the enlisted designs,

---

29 *Ibid 23*
30 *Ibid 23*
31 *Ibid 23*
32 Rajesh Masrani v Tahliani Design 2008 SCC OnLine Del 1283 (India).
33 Rajesh Masrani v Tahliani Design 2008 SCC OnLine Del 1283 (India).
34 Louis Vuitton Malletier v. Atul Jaggi & Anr, 2010 CS(OS) 1419 of 2009 (India).
35 Microfibres Inc. v. Girdhar & Co. & Anr 2006 (32) PTC 157 Del (India).
36 Microfibres Inc. v. Girdhar & Co. & Anr 2006 (32) PTC 157 Del (India).

additionally ensure the privileges of the proprietor of the design.[37] The principal point of the demonstration is to shield the works from protection. The Act does not provide protection for unregistered designs, or no one can guarantee the harms of their unregistered design. Designs is basically the key of the fashion business to imagine their items on the lookout. Further, as per the Design Act 2000, one of the classifications of intellectual property rights is Industrial Design. So, the protection can only be given to the designs which are registered and follow the following conditions:

1. It should be novel and original.

2. It should apply to a helpful article.

3. It should be visible in a finished article.

4. It should be non-obvious.[38]

5. There should be no prior publication or disclosure of the design.

In ***Ritika Pvt. Ltd. v. Biba Apparels Pvt. Ltd.,*** The Court distinguished between designs eligible for copyright protection under the Copyright Act of 1957 and designs suitable for copyright protection under the Design Act of 2000.[39]

Copyright ensures insignificant protection of the privileges of creators over their manifestations, in this manner safeguarding and advantageous innovativeness. Inventiveness being the cornerstone of progress, no socialized society can have the assets to dismiss the basic prerequisite of empowering something very similar. The financial and social improvement of the general public is relying upon innovativeness. The well-being provided with the guide of utilizing copyright to the endeavours of scholars, specialists, planners, writers, artists, draftsmen and producers of sound accounts, cinematograph motion pictures, and PC programming, establish a climate helpful for innovativeness, which actuates them to make more noteworthy and inspires others to make.

4.3 DESIGN

I. Definition

An article in order to catch the attention of a buyer must be visually attractive since visual attraction enhances marketability. An industrial design to be protected must be aesthetic i.e. it should aim to

---

37 Neha Wagle, *Copyright versus Designs: Kurukshetra of Indian Fashion Industry*, IPLEADERS (Nov. 26, 2019), https://blog.ipleaders.in/copyright-versus-designs/.
38 The Design Act 2000.
39 Ritika Pvt. Ltd. v. Biba Apparels Pvt. Ltd. CS(OS) No. 182/2011 (India).

protect only the aesthetic or ornamental aspects of an article, not the technical or functional features. In a nutshell, an industrial design is a form of intellectual property that aims to protect the visual design of objects which are not purely utilitarian. Constituting the ornamental aspect of an article it may consist of 3D features like the shape of an article or 2D features like patterns, colour, or lines. The Indian Designs Act, 2000 providing a wholistic definition of a design defines it as, "design" means only the features of shape, configuration, pattern, ornament, or composition of lines or colours applied to any article whether in two dimensional or three dimensional or in both forms, by any industrial process or means, whether manual, mechanical or chemical, separate or combined, which in the finished article appeal to and are judged solely by the eye; but does not include any mode or principle of construction or anything which is in substance a mere mechanical device, and does not include any trade mark as defined under Trademark Act, 1999 (v) of sub-section (1) of section 2 of the Trade and Merchandise Marks Act, 1958 (43 of 1958) or property mark as defined in section 479 of the Indian Penal Code (45 of 1860) or any artistic work as defined in clause (c) of section 2 of the Copyright Act, 1957 (14 of 1957)."

II.   Scope

The outer appearance of an article makes it visually more appealing and attractive which acts as a value-adding aspect, and in turn, increases the marketability of that article. It is pertinent to note that industrial designs provide protection only for the visual/outer appearance of the article, and not for the structural or the utilitarian features the product consists of. This leads to an increasing need to protect your creation from third parties use, to prevent them from taking undue advantage of your rights in this highly competitive world. In the majority of the cases, the design itself becomes the identity of a brand for example; Coca-Cola's basic contour bottle, the contours of Apple's iPhone/iPad, the shape of the Volkswagen Beetle-the Mini Cooper, etc.

It is strongly believed that 'the first impression is the last impression', similarly in the case of a new product, the first impression is inadvertently made by its outer visual appearance, long before the user even explores its functionality. In this digital era of creativity, aesthetics, and presentation, the overall design and visual appearance of any new product are highly significant. Therefore, the ability to design a novel and creative appearance is a talent in itself. Designs can protect a wide range of articles and products ranging from fashion to automobiles, electronics to apparel, manufacturing parts to packaging, and even to graphical user interfaces like on-screen animations and images. When a product's design is protected, it prevents and stops illegitimate products from destroying the brand's efficacy, reputation, and safety. Additionally, the protection of industrial designs also encourages creativity in the manufacturing and industrial sectors, which further leads to an expansion in commercial activities.

An industrial design providing a wide range of scope bestows upon the owner of a registered design patent or an industrial design, an absolute right to restrict third parties from making, selling, or importing unauthorized articles bearing or embodying an industrial design which is a copy of the protected design when such acts are undertaken mainly for commercial purposes. With this exclusive right of protection, the registered owner of an industrial design can prevent and stop someone else who's benefiting from his hard work by copying or using his design without permission. If during this illegal and unethical process a person generates revenue, one can sue them for recovery of damages and earned revenue, apart from preventive rights, a design also accords the rightful owner of a registered industrial design an exclusive right to expose, publish articles for which design is registered already and the exclusive right to import for sale purposes only belongs to the registered industrial design.

III.   Obtaining process

Each country's government establishes a design patent or an IPR in design granting authority, who receives applications for the grant if design patents by creators. Hague Agreement Concerning the International Deposit of Industrial Designs (Hague System), a WIPO administered treaty provides for a mechanism for international registration of up to 100 industrial designs in 75 contracting parties concerning 92 countries through a single international application. The World Intellectual Property Organisation with over 90 countries as a member under 'The Hague System of International Registration of Industrial Designs' aims at providing the countries with a single-window facility for registration of designs internationally.

As per the USA, under the US Patent Law, currently, no protection is available for unregistered industrial designs. The patent-related designs must be procured timely by the proper filing of a design patent application at the USPTO, wherein after a design patent is granted by the USPTO subsequently. Similarly, a group of 40 member countries under the European Union (EU) as per the EPO convention can therein obtain Registered Community Design (RCD) from the EUIPO after an applicant has successfully registered the design patent application in their country subsequently obtaining national design registration.

Different countries around the world have their design registering and patenting process and norms for granting intellectual property rights. The protection period for an industrial design varies from country to country but generally ranges between 10 to 25 years for example design protection in the USA post 13th May 2015 is 15 years, the UK is 25 years while in India it is 10 years.

Some of the widely accepted pre-requisites for a design to qualify for protection consist of a design being:

1. novel and original

2. applicable to a functional article

3. visible on a finished article

4. non-obvious

5. no prior publication or disclosure of the design.

Rights for an industrial design are generally obtained through an application made either at the national or at the regional intellectual property office. There are also some countries wherein design rights are available through use. In order to qualify for the industrial design protection, one should comply with the definition of a design under the applicable national or international law, it should not be an identical design that has previously been available to the public or is quite similar to an already registered design. It should fulfil the criteria of being an original design i.e. Must have been independently created and should not be a true copy or an attempt to imitate any of the existing industrial design. All in all, having an individual character, the overall impression which a design aims to produce should be different from any other registered design.

However, an industrial design application can be rejected in these possible situations:

• If a design fails to meet the requirements of novelty, originality, or having an individual character;

• If a design is dictated exclusively by the technical function of an article or a product;

• If a design incorporates any protected official symbols or emblems for ex. a national flag;

• If a design is considered to be incongruous to public order or morality.

Industrial Designs under WIPO are registered in different function-oriented classes as per the *Locarno Agreement*. The agreement is herein used to classify goods for the registration of designs which further acts as an aid in design searches. After applying for registration, the application is therein examined by the International Bureau of WIPO for formal requirements after which the applicant is provided with an opportunity to correct certain existing irregularities in the application. Once the formal requirements have been met, it is officially recorded in the International Register and the details are later published electronically in the International Designs Bulletin on the online WIPO portal. If any Contracting Party considers that an industrial design that has been registered for protection but does not meet its domestic criteria for registration, it must notify the International Bureau that it refuses the registration of that industrial design.

Generally, the obtaining process of a design consists of the following steps:

A.   **Application**

The first step consists of submitting a duly completed application form by paying the required fees. Reproduction of the industrial design for which protection is sought is supposed to be included. In some countries, an elaborated written description of the industrial design along with an oath or declaration of inventorship from the creator might also be required.

B. Formal Examination

Subsequently, the office thoroughly examines the application making sure it complies with the administrative requirements or formalities such as the submission of the application fee or the completion of the form, etc.

C. Substantive Examination

In some countries, no search or examination is conducted prior to the registration of an industrial design, while in some countries a substantive examination is carried out wherein the design is checked against already registered/existing designs for novelty and originality.

D. Registration

Once it has been determined that no grounds for refusal exist, the design is officially registered by the issuance of a registration certificate. The duration of the protection of industrial designs generally varies from country to country, but it amounts to at least 10 years.

E. Grace Period

Some national laws allow for a grace period in order to process the registration of a design. This period usually ranges between six months to a year, counted from the date of disclosure of an industrial design to the public at large. If a product is marketed consisting of a design that has not been subject to a design application, it will lose its novelty and therefore will be ineligible for protection under the legislation. However, in some countries wherein a grace period is provided, an application may still be submitted within that prescribed period.

F. Renewal

Renewal of industrial design protection is usually subject to the payment of a renewal fee.

IV. Costs

The costs of protecting and industrial design vary significantly from country to country. They may generally include the application or registration fee which is paid to the IP office, the costs associated with services of an intellectual property agent, annual payment of renewal fees to maintain the exclusive right over a registered industrial design, and other documentation associated with filing-processing costs.

The International design applications under the Hague System are subject to the payment of 3 types of fees,

A.   **Basic Fee:** 397 Swiss francs for 1 design and 19 Swiss francs for each additional industrial design included in the same application

B.   **Publication Fee:** 17 Swiss francs for each reproduction and 150 Swiss francs for each page on which one or more reproductions are shown

C.   **Standard Designation Fee / Individual Designation Fee:** Applicable to each contracting party where protection is sought

V.   International Treaties and Conventions for the Protection of Designs

A.   Hague Agreement Concerning the International Registration of Industrial Designs

The Hague Agreement governs the registration of industrial designs internationally. Adopted in the year 1925, the Agreement effectively establishes an international system i.e. the Hague System, which allows protection of industrial designs in various countries and regions with bare minimal formalities. Currently, there are a total of 75 Contracting Parties.

The Hague System for international registration of industrial designs is based on the Hague Agreement Concerning the International Registration of Industrial Designs, constituted by 2 Acts:

- The Geneva Act (1999) was adopted on July 2, 1999, and entered into force on December 23, 2003, and

- The Hague Act (1960) was adopted on November 28, 1960, and entered into force on August 1, 1984.

Hague Agreement offers a possibility of obtaining protection for industrial designs in several Contracting Party Nations by a single international application filed with the International Bureau of the WIPO located in Geneva, Switzerland. Therefore, under this System, one international application replaces a series of applications that would otherwise have to be filed separately with different national offices i.e. filing an international application won't require any prior national application or any registration. It is administered by the International Bureau of WIPO which maintains an International Register by publishing the International Designs Bulletin (I.D.B).

The entitlement to file an application under the Agreement is only limited to either natural persons or legal entities having real and effective industrial/commercial establishment, or domicile, in at least one of the Contracting Party Nations to the Agreement, or being a national of one of these, or of a Member State of an inter-governmental organization which is a Contracting Party therein.

International registrations done under the Hague System are valid for an initial period of 5 years, which can further be renewed for one or more additional periods of 5 years, in respect of each designated Contracting Party, up to the expiry of a total term of protection allowed by the respective laws of the Contracting Parties. Hence, the maximum duration of protection which can be accorded in each designated Contracting Party Nation corresponds to the maximum duration provided for, by the law of that particular Contracting Party.

The Hague System arising from a need for simplicity and economy has proven to be highly advantageous. In effect, it enables design owners around the globe, originating from a Contracting Party to obtain industrial design protection with bare minimum formality and expense. Design owners are thereafter relieved from the need to apply separately to each of the Contracting Parties where they require protection, thereby avoiding multiple complexities arising from different procedures existing in various States. For example, the creators do not have to comply with filing massive documentation in various languages, nor keep a watch on the renewal deadlines for a whole series of national registrations, varying from one State to another. In addition, the system successfully avoids the need to pay fees in various currencies. Under the Hague System, a similar result can be obtained by filing a single application, bearing one language, accompanied by payment of a single set of fees in one currency. Subsequently, the management of the protection obtained is also considerably facilitated.

B. Paris Convention (Paris Convention for the Protection of Industrial Property, 1883)

Article 1(2) of the Paris Convention stipulates that *"the protection of industrial property has as its object patents, utility models, industrial designs, trademarks, service marks, trade names, an indication of source or appellations of origin, and the repression of unfair competition"*.

In Article 5, the Convention provides that *"industrial designs shall be protected in all the countries of the Union"*. However, the Convention not defining an industrial design leaves it to each country to decide how to protect their industrial design in consonance with their domestic laws. Furthermore, Article 5B of the Convention states that *"the protection of industrial designs shall not, under any circumstances, be subject to any forfeiture, either by reason of failure to work or by reason of the importation of articles corresponding to those which are protected"*. Hence, the Convention aims to prohibit countries of the Union from imposing any sanctions which forfeit the protection of industrial designs under domestic laws due to any failure to work or by the importation of an article incorporating a registered/protected industrial design.

C. Locarno Agreement (Locarno Agreement Establishing an International Classification for Industrial Designs, 1968)

Revised in 1979 in Stockholm, the agreement sets forth an international classification for design articles. It is composed of main classes, subclasses, and an alphabetical list of articles. However, such classification does not aim to bind the scope of protection granted by domestic design laws of the contracting party states.

D. TRIPS Agreement under the World Trade Organization Agreement (WTOA)

The TRIPS Agreement made it obligatory for its contracting parties to provide a high level of protection and enforcement mechanism over a wide variety of areas of IP like copyright, trademarks, geographical indications, industrial designs, patents, layout-designs of integrated circuits, protection of undisclosed information, and finally control of anti-competitive practices in the realm of contractual licenses. Section 4 part II of the TRIPS Agreement further sets forth regulations concerning "industrial designs".

Article 25 states that *"(1) Members shall provide for the protection of independently created industrial designs that are new or original. Members may provide that designs are not new or original if they do not significantly differ from known designs or combinations of known design features. Members may provide that such protection shall not extend to designs dictated essentially by technical or functional considerations. (2) Each Member shall ensure that requirements for securing protection for textile designs, in particular in regard to any cost, examination, or publication, do not unreasonably impair the opportunity to seek and obtain such protection. Members shall be free to meet this obligation through industrial design law or through copyright law."*

While Article 26 stipulates that, *" (1) The owner of a protected industrial design shall have the right to prevent third parties not having the owner's consent from making, selling or importing articles bearing or embodying a design which is a copy, or substantially a copy, of the protected design when such acts are undertaken for commercial purposes. (2) Members may provide limited exceptions to the protection of industrial designs, provided that such exceptions do not unreasonably conflict with the normal exploitation of protected industrial designs and do not unreasonably prejudice the legitimate interests of the owner of the protected design, taking account of the legitimate interests of third parties. (3) The duration of protection available shall amount to at least ten years."*

E. <u>Berne Convention (Berne Convention for the Protection of Literary and Artistic Works, 1886)</u>

Article 2 (1) of the Berne Convention stipulates that *"the expression 'literary and artistic works" shall include every protection in the literary, scientific and artistic domain, whatever may be the mode or form of its expressions, such as books, pamphlets, and other writings; lectures, addresses, sermons and other works of the same nature; dramatic or musical works; choreographic works and entertainments in dumb show; musical compositions with or without words; cinematographic works to which are assimilated works expressed by a process analogous to cinematography; works of drawing, painting, architecture, sculpture, engraving, and lithography; photographic works to which are assimilated works expressed by a process analogous to photography; works of applied art; illustrations, maps, plans, sketches and three-dimensional works relative to geography, topography, architecture or science".*

Article 2 (7) of the Berne Convention states that *"subject to the provisions of Article 7 (4) of this Convention, it shall be a matter for legislation in the countries of the Union to determine the extent of the application of their laws to works of applied art and industrial designs and models, as well as the conditions under which such works, designs, and models shall be protected. Works protected in the country of origin solely as designs and models shall be entitled in another country of the Union only to such special protection as is granted in that country to designs and models; however, if no such special protection is granted in that country, such works shall be protected as artistic works".*

In accordance with the provisions of Article 2(7), it is considered a renowned principle to protect the applied works and industrial designs at an equal footing. While leaving discretionary powers with each member country to regulate conditions for the protection of a design, *"this term shall last at least until the end of a period of twenty-five years from the making of such work"* (Article 7 (4)). The term of protection granted by this Convention shall be the very life of the author and fifty years after the author's death (Article 7 (1)).

VI.   Remedies

Infringement of an industrial design pertains to fraudulent copying of an existing design or the illegal act to use a registered design without authorization from the owner, therefore if a person without the consent of the actual owner tends to publish, use or import an already registered design for fraudulent imitation then any such owner who is a victim in this case of infringement can file for a suit against the infringer to recover damages. Remedies vary from country to country but in general are categories into civil and criminal remedies.

Generally, the remedies for infringement of a registered industrial design includes:

A.   CIVIL REMEDIES

* Injunction

IPRs are mainly negative in character i.e. they confer on their owners the very right to stop and prevent others from doing certain acts, without the owner's consent. The practical manifestation of the ability to stop infringers' is the prohibitory remedy of injunction. An injunction is therefore an order, made by the court, requiring an individual or group of individuals to refrain from doing certain acts, which are the exclusive preserve of the intellectual property right owner. In most infringement cases, injunction by far and away is one of the most important remedies in practice.

TRIPS Article 44.1 states, *"The judicial authorities shall have the authority to order a party to desist from an infringement, inter alia to prevent the entry into the channels of commerce in their jurisdiction of imported goods that involve the infringement of an intellectual property right, immediately after customs clearance of such goods. Members are not obliged to accord such authority in respect of protected subject-matter acquired or ordered by a person prior to knowing or having reasonable grounds to know that dealing in such subject matter would entail the infringement of an intellectual property right."*

An injunction is not used as a remedy for past invasion of rights, but it is used for protecting an existing right. The basis of the applicability of the remedy is the level of threat, either actual or implied, on part of the defendant who tries to do an act in violation of the plaintiff's right. Grant of an injunction involves a matter requiring the exercise of discretion by the relevant Court while on the other hand ensuring whether a *prima facie* case has been made i.e. only if it can be established that there are bona fide contentions between the parties or a serious matter to be tried. Furthermore, an additional condition that generally needs to be satisfied to grant a remedy of injunction is that the *balance of convenience* must be in favour of the owner. The balance of convenience refers to the comparative mischief/inconvenience likely to be caused to the owner in case the injunction is not granted versus the inconvenience that might be caused to the other party if an injunction is granted. Finally, the owner should prove that he has or could suffer an *irreparable injury* if such injunction is not granted i.e. a material injury, incapable of being adequately remedied by damages.

Temporary Injunction

Temporary Injunction pending full ventilation of the dispute has been one of the most common civil remedies for breach of IP rights. An IP owner in any case of infringement does not have to wait until it wins on the liability at the trial to secure an injunction i.e. it can obtain an injunction on an interim emergency basis, pending a full trial. It aims at restoring the status quo, halting the infringing act, and providing parties with a clear preview of the opponent's case leading to various cases subsequently settled without entering the trial. Solving the purpose to regulate and preserve the rights of parties pending the final determination of the case, it is decided on an urgent basis and settled without a full hearing, making it one of the most cost-effective remedies at hand. However, the civil remedy of interim injunction cannot be enforced as a right and is ultimately the discretion of the court.

Damages

Damages mainly constitute the difference between the pecuniary condition of the plaintiff after the infringement and subsequently considering what the condition would have been if the infringement had not taken place. Damages are generally calculated separately after the validity of a design and an instance of infringement has been decided upon.

Intellectual Property Rights are generally income-earning wherein a person whose right has been infringed has the option of seeking a remedy of damages on account of profits. The measure of damages accounts for the loss of profits in respect of those infringing articles that the artist could have made and subsequently sold. Such loss of profit is usually because the owner

      a. sells fewer products than he could have,

      b. charges lower prices in order to compete with the infringer, or

      c. has increased his production costs.

Article 45 of the TRIPS Agreement states that *"Courts must be able to order the infringer to pay the right holder damages adequate to compensate for the injury and to pay the right holder expenses, which may include appropriate attorney's fees."* The problem of quantification of damages makes it a less preferred mode of civil remedy. Courts face great difficulty in determining the compensation in case of infringement of a design.

Indemnification of Defendant

Article 48 of the TRIPS agreement provides for a civil remedy of indemnification of the defendant. In an instance wherein there has been an abuse of procedure by the plaintiff and none of the measures are justified, the defendant can claim a remedy of Indemnification of Defendant.

Indemnification includes compensating the defendant for the occurrence of his expenses including appropriate attorney's fees.

Delivery up/destruction of items

Delivery of goods is a remedy that is ancillary to an injunction. Its purpose is to act as an aid to the injunction by protecting the right holders from any further use however it is done at the discretion of the court. The TRIPS contain 2 provisions pertaining to the disposal/delivery or destruction of infringing goods i.e. Article 46 which is of general application applies to the disposal or destruction of infringing goods, irrespective of whether they are counterfeit, while Article 59 deals with the imported counterfeit goods in hands of the customs authorities. There is no automatic entitlement to delivery up / destruction of items, however, once the infringement is proved, orders requiring either or both of these are usually made.

Criminal Remedies & Sanctions

Criminal Sanctions under the TRIPS Agreement are provided under Article 61, which includes the following remedies:

- Imprisonment and/or monetary fines:
    - (a) sufficient to provide a deterrent;
    - (b) consistently with the level of penalties for crimes of a corresponding gravity.

- Seizure, forfeiture, and destruction of the infringing articles or any materials and implements used for the commission of the offense.

4.4 DOMAIN NAME

The unique name which helps in identifying any particular website is called a domain name. Like taking an example of Facebook, it is https://www.facebook.com

Each and every website has its own domain name that serves as an address, which is used to access the particular website.

For the growth of ones' brand in this technologically advanced world, it is crucial to maintain an exclusive symbol for each access considering how nowadays a domain name is easily accessible to all internet users worldwide.

Domain name describes the address of a website forming part of the URL (Uniform Resource Locator). It has definitely made the procedure of searching a website quite simple.

The suffix of the website, which represent the top level domain are either:

- gTLD (Generic Top Level Domain Names)- most commonly and often used by commercials, non-profit organisations, etc.; this suffix helps in identifying the type of website the domain name represents. Eg: .com, .org, etc.
- ccTLD (Country Code Top Level Domain Names)- this helps in the identification of the location and target audience of that particular website. Eg: .in, .dk, etc.

It is a well-known fact that deceptively similar domain names lead to confusion of the source and results in misleading the public of some sort of association between the similar domain names; hence invoking the reputation of a well-known brand. Such deception not only leads to a confusion of the source but the receipt of unsought for services as well.

The IP Address is translated as per the domain name appears in the address bar of the web browser; and this defines the server where the website is located.

This translation is performed dynamically by a service called DNS. Domain names are formed by the rules and procedures of the Domain Name System (DNS).

One of the major roles/ functions of domain name is to identify and distinguish goods and services of one entity to that of others.

Similarly, domain names are also relevant to the customers by performing the same function and role that a trademark forms on the online platforms and entire online space.

Hence, the deceptive similarity of a domain name has similar consequences as that of conventional trademark infringement.

ICANN & UDRP

The non-profit organisation board, Internet Corporation for Assigned Names and Numbers (ICANN) has the role of managing the top-level development. It has the responsibility to set up protocol of internet addresses, allocation of relevant and necessary space, identification of suitable assignment and generic country code and further system management.

On October 24, 1999, the ICANN Board adopted a set of rules for Uniform Domain Name Dispute Resolution Policy, known as the UDRP Rules, with an objective of setting out the procedures and other requirements for each stage of the dispute resolution administrative procedure. And this dispute resolution procedure is administered by Dispute Resolution Service Providers that are accredited by ICANN. The WIPO Arbitration and Mediation Centre is one such Dispute Resolution Service Provider.

The legal framework is set up under these UDRP Rules for resolution of disputes that arise between the domain name registrant and the third party invoking the rights of the said domain name registrant.

It has been reported that this Policy has till now helped the Board to solve over 5000 cases w.r.t. domain names. Hence, UDRP is designed to be effective, not only in terms of its resolution but also in matters of cost.

With the adoption of the said rules, the value of the domain name is becoming more valuable now due to the ongoing phase of internet revolution in companies and henceforth, these have become more valuable to corporate assets.

With the gradual increase of digitization, the potential of such disputes are also getting high.

Disputes Relating to Domain Name

1. Use of a domain name resulting in the likelihood of an association with the marks having reputation and goodwill- Wherein a domain name is similar to a distinctive or a well-known mark, it might cause trademark infringement, which might result in tarnishment whereby the domain name owners harm the reputation and distinctive character of the well-established mark.

2. Cybersquatting- Generally known as bad faith registration of another's trademark in a domain name. It exploits the first come first serve nature of domain name registration systems by selling it beyond the price of registration. The cybersquatted makes an attempt to make money from trademark holders through domain name selling at much higher prices.

   Case: *Yahoo! Inc. v. Akash Arora (1999)*

   The Yahoo! Inc. is considered as a landmark case on cybersquatting in India as it was for the primary time that the High Court of Delhi held that a registered website name similar to the trademark giving it the entitled, equal protection. It presents an important issue of law pertaining to the passing off under Trademark law in India. The case discusses Sections 27 and 29 of the Trade and Merchandise Marks Act (now repealed by Trademark Act) and its applicability to the case.

3. Reverse-cybersquatting- Another type where an innocent holder is exploited through malafide intention. Trademark holder initiates proceedings to harass the innocent owner of a domain name to transfer the domain name to them. Most basically known as a false cybersquatting proceeding, it is generally employed by large dominant companies that tend to use this practice against small companies or individuals for creating and staying in a dominant position in the corporate world.

4. Typo-squatting- It targets internet users who incorrectly type the URL into the web browser. Here, the cyber squatter registers the domain name that is slightly in variation to the target brand to get traffic on their slightly varied domain.

5. Confusion and deception by the use of phonetically similar domain names by third parties in order to lead confusion in mind of the consumer with a sole motive of creating a

connection between the domain names and trading upon the reputation of the similar domain name.

The domain name acts as a business idea on the internet and the same is entitled to equal protection as the act of infringement of trademark.

Domain Name Transfer Agreement

The agreement related to the realm of domain name is Transfer Agreement. The transfer of Domain name usually arises where rights transfer to the assignee, and in the case of a license, the transfer is for a certain period and lays certain conditions limiting the use of domain name by the licensee. It is an agreement between the assignor and assignee to transfer the domain name from the assignor to the assignee.

The situations where there is a need of Domain Name Transfer Agreement are:

- when a website is being sold to another person or business;
- when a domain name is related to organization being purchased or merged by another person or business;
- when a domain name is being acquired by another organization or business, and the agreement did not include the transfer of the domain name.

Cyber-Squatting

(Refer to Chapter 2)

4.5 Patent Protection

"The patent system adds the fuel of interest to the fire of genius"- Abraham Lincoln

MEANING

A patent is a monopoly right granted by the Patent Office to an inventor to use his invention for a limited period of time, subject to the provisions of the Patents Act. The inventor has the right to prevent anyone from commercializing his invention. The term patent refers to an invention.

It is a right to prevent anyone from creating, using, importing, or selling the patented invention during its term. It is a property right that the state grants to inventors in return for a promise to share the details of their invention with the general public. The inventor's exclusive rights under the Patents Act may be exercised by anyone other than the inventor with the latter's prior permission.

The aim of patent law is to promote scientific innovation, new technology, and technological advancement. The grant of an exclusive right to own, use, or sell a patented method or product for a limited time encourages new commercially useful inventions. The price of the monopoly is the disclosure of the invention at the Patent Office, which then passes into the public domain after the monopoly term has expired.

In India, the Patent Act, 1970 governs the concept of patent.

DEFINITIONS

- According to **Section 2(1)(m)** of the Patent Act, defines *patent* as *a patent for any invention granted under the Act.*
- **Section 2 (1)(j)** of the Act defines an *invention* as *a new product or process involving an inventive step and capable of industrial application.*
- The definition makes it clear that for a process to be termed as an invention it is not necessary that the product or process should be totally a new one. Even a process involving an inventive step will come under the said definition of an invention.
- **Section 2 (1) (ja)** of the Act defines an *inventive step* as *a feature of an invention that involves technical advance as compared to the existing knowledge or having economic significance or both and that makes the invention not obvious to a person skilled in the art.*

To meet the requirement of an inventive step, the patentee has to prove that the invention includes any technical advancement or has economic significance or both. If the invention was obvious, it would not constitute an inventive step. It refers to a feature of an innovation that involves a technological improvement as compared to already existing knowledge, or that has economic significance, or both, and that makes the invention not obvious to a person skilled in the art.

- **Section 2 (1) (ac)** of the Act defines *capable of industrial application* in relation to *an invention to mean that it is capable of being made and used in any industry.*

In the context of an invention, industrial applicability means that the invention's subject matter must be capable of being produced or used in any industry.

- **Section 2 (1) (l)** defines a *new invention* as *any invention or technology which has not been anticipated by publication in any document or used in the country or elsewhere in the world before the date of filing of a patent application with complete specification, i.e., the subject matter has not fallen in the public domain or that it does not form part of the state of the art.*

In order to be patentable, an innovation should be new or novel and should be capable of industrial application. A new invention is one that has not been anticipated by prior art. All information that existed prior to the relevant filing or priority date of a patent application, whether it was disclosed in written or oral form, is referred to as "prior art". It is a characteristic of an invention that has not been anticipated by prior publication of any paper or used anywhere in the world prior to the filing of a patent application, indicating that the invention's subject matter may not be in the public domain or part of the state of the art.

Patent Infringement

When a person uses an invention of a patentee for which he was granted the patent without his permission, this is said to be patent infringement.

A patent may sometimes be infringed by taking only a part of the invention, but that depends on whether the part for which protection is asked is a new and material part. If it is not new and material, the court must consider what is the substance of the invention, and to do so it has to consider the relative importance of all parts of the invention. The essential part or the substance of the plaintiff's invention is the use of pressure and therefore there could be no infringement unless the use of pressure by the defendants in their process was proved.

Types of Infringement

There are two forms of infringements:

- **Direct infringement**- It happens when a product is significantly similar to a patented product, or when the marketing or commercial use of the invention is carried out without the owner's permission.
- **Indirect infringement**- It occurs when there is a deception or accidental infringement that occurs without the intent to infringe.

Remedies

In certain cases, patent protection is sought to maintain and preserve the competitive and commercial advantage that an invention may provide, as well as to cover the expense associated with developing an invention. If patent rights are of minimal value unless implemented to prevent potential infringers and provide a redress for those whose rights have been infringed.

Under section 108 of the Act, the following reliefs are available-

a.   Injunctive relief

b.   Damages or an account of profits

Penalties are discussed in Chapter XX, Sections 118-124 of the Patents Act of 1970. The Patent Office has established various parameters to impose penalties on any act that is prohibited by Patent law.

Section 118- Contravention of secrecy provisions relating to certain inventions: *In this case, if any person fails to comply with the directions given under section 35 or makes an application for grant of Patent in contravention of section 39 of the Patents Act, 1970, then he shall be liable for punishment with imprisonment for a term of which may extend to 2 years or fine or with both.*

Section 119- Falsification of entries in register, etc: *If any person makes false entry in the register of Patent, or writing falsely purporting to be a copy of an entry in such a register, knowingly or unknowingly, he shall be punishable with imprisonment for a term which may extend to 2 years or fine or with both.*

Section 120- Unauthorized claim of Patents rights: *If any person falsely claims or represent any article sold by him is patented in India or if the article is stamped, engraved or impressed on or otherwise applied to, the article the word "patent" or "patented" or some other word expressing or implying that the patent of the article has been obtained in India or; that an article is the subject of an application for a patent in India, or if the article is stamped, engraved or impressed on or otherwise applied to, the article the word "patent" or "patented" or some other word expressing or implying that the patent of the article has been made in India, he shall be punishable with fine which may extend to 1-lakh rupees.*

Section 121- Wrongful use of words patent office: *If any person uses on his place of business or on any of the document issued by him the word patent office or in any other way which would lead to belief that his place of business or document issued by him are related to or connected with the patent office, then such offence shall be punishable with imprisonment for a term which may extend to 6 months or with fine, or with both.*

Section 122- Refusal or failure to supply information: *In any case, if the person fails to furnish or refuses any information which is false, and which he either knows or it does not believe to be true, as required by the central government under section 100(5) of the Patents act, 1970 or any information related to working of patents which is require to be furnished under section 146 of the Patents Act, 1970.*

He shall be punishable with a fine which may extend to 10-lakh rupees or in case of providing false information as required under section 146, the offence shall be punishable with imprisonment which may extend to 6 months or with fine, or with both.

Section 123- Practice by non-registered patent agents: *If any person contravenes the provisions of section 129, he shall be punishable with a fine which may extend to 1-lakh rupees in the first offence and 5-lakh rupees in the second offence.*

Section 124- Offence by companies: *If any company as well as every person in charge of, and in response to that company found responsible for the conduct of his/ their business at the time of the commission of the offence shall be deemed to be guilty of that offence and shall be liable to be proceeded against and punished accordingly.*

4.6 TRADE SECRET

Intellectual property is a wide term that refers to a business's collection of assets in both physical and in form of data storage that are covered under the law against unauthorised use or application of such property. Intellectual property refers to the idea that some creations of human intelligence must be protected in the very same way as a physical property is protected.

Any Brand's or Enterprises method or technique that is mostly unknown beyond the company's knowledge is considered a trade secret. Trade secrets are frequently the result of inside research and innovation and provide the enterprise with a competitive edge. An enterprise must make a rational attempt to keep the knowledge shrouded in secrecy in order for it to be declared a trade secret and that secret must have fundamental commercial importance; and must be inclusive of data. Trade secrets are a type of intellectual property that an enterprise owns. A trade secret, is not primarily known to world at large.

Trade secrets can include anything from an unique process, technology, method, form, ingredient, recipe, approach, or practice that is not widely known which can be used to develop a business that has an edge over rivals or gives value based satisfaction to its customers.

Nature & Characteristics

Trade secrets are characterized variable in different state jurisdictions, yet they all share the same characteristics:

- They aren't available to the general public.
- Their owner holds some form of financial advantage primarily from the notion that it is not widely known.
- Their privacy is strictly guarded.

Trade secrets are the "classified information" of an enterprise or an industry , just as concealed documents are tightly protected by government organizations, as sensitive data. Organizations have an impetus to discover what makes their opponents profitable because the cost of producing some products is substantially higher than the cost of advanced analytics. A company's trade secrets may be protected by requiring staff with access to the knowledge to undertake non-compete or non- disclosure agreements (NDA) when they are hired.

The goal of trade secret law is

- To keep and encourage the highest possible levels of confidentiality.
- Fairness and equal competition are two concepts that come to mind while thinking about business ethics.

- One of the main goals of trade secret legislation is not to encourage people to share their secrets.

Enterprise's or Industries should develop their economic power and outgrow their business by reserving a significant amount of time and resources into developing commercially efficient inventions, but particularly those that aren't patentable or not worth the cost of filing a patent application The rivals could utilize these if they aren't protected under trade secret law and that too without having to bear the financial risk or burdens of creativity

When you start a new business or want to outshine in the market the new ideas are the one basic thing which makes you stand out in a market flooded with similar businesses. There are a number of challenges that must be overcome. First of all the the two things to be cleared about are:-

- The information which is detrimental to my business and what will happen if it were to be traded loosely by employees or is exposed?
- And to have personnel dedicated to data input and regulatory compliances

The secrets could include anything within a list of essential suppliers and/or purchasers to the use of product design software applications to the inventory control of the full production process

Almost any piece of knowledge essential for a business to maintain its name or brand and keep up its customer base can be classified as a trade secret.

- A trade secret can be expertise about a formula, pattern, or procedure. a gadget or other collection of data which is in use for a long period of time in an enterprise.
- A trade secret is frequently technical information employed in the production process. A method for producing items
- A trade secret could be about promotion, sales, or sales methods, or it could be about a business or the procedures for accounting or other associated material with business management methods, as well as programming that is utilized for a variety of commercial applications.
- Other types of trade secrets encompass technological, intellectual, and financial information, financial data such as accounting records, registers of customer databases and other confidential information.

Core trade secrets are used to secure software-based revenue streams that enable an integrated sales strategy predicated on subtlety and rapidity to deliver a fashion products (For instance, ZARA, a Spanish fashion retail chain, employs an unique information systems (IT) system to cut their manufacturing cycle — that is, the time it takes from spotting a new fad to shipping the final piece – to just 30 days. The majority of their counterparts take between 4 and 12 months. Regular emails from sales associates alert the market to new fads, material, and trims, allowing its developers to instantly develop new designs. The cloth is cut in a computerized process being sent to manufacturing shops right away. With over 400 shafts and 200 kilometres of subterranean traces, a slightly elevated supply chain guarantees that complete goods are dispatched and reach in outlets within 48 hours.

(Other fashion businesses manufacture bespoke merchandise in relation to a customer's request using technology. For instance, Shirtsdotnet (www.shirtsdotnet.com) wants to change the traditional garment industry by reversing the decision-making process and adopting a made-to-order business model. Shirtsdotnet is a B2B apparel software platform that provides mail order enterprises with made-to-measure, mass customisation garments. The virtual shop allows customers to create and order clothes immediately. The company runs on proprietary software that is both a trade secret and protected by copyright laws.)

Safeguarding Trade Secret

Trade Secrets are generally the easiest means to help uplift a business because they usually have no filing expenses; neither do they need declaration or licensing. The security guaranteed under Trade Secret is not time-limited retroactively. But they generally have some drawbacks as the secret embedded in a product can be found and properly utilized by using the technology of "reverse engineering." Trade secret only safeguards privileged data or sensitive information against unauthorized access, usage, or exposure. It is harder to regulate than a patent since the amount of safety is much lower. If an individual has produced the identical idea through lawful means, then that individual may patent that trade secret.

Misappropriation of trade secrets is one of the biggest concerns in the Fashion Industry. A trade secret cannot be shielded from being acquired by rational and honest means. Authentic methods, such as self-invention or self-thought are considered as honest means. If a person who does not have rightful claim to trade confidential information and that person does so decodes the secret without resorting to any illegal methods, no such action can be taken against him.

If a trade secret is revealed it is impossible to prevent an individual from using the knowledge that has been revealed. In these certain situations, the proprietor of a trade secret has no recourse. It is really necessary to understand what leads to the leak of secret information of an industry or enterprise.

Internal trade secrets are increasing due to intense rivalry in both domestic and global markets has resulted in an increase in the price of goods. Beyond the industrial outlets, stealing of secret information by employees, also known as industrial espionage, is on the rise. Because of increased worldwide rivalry and lesser duration frames, activities are on the upswing. Product cycles are shortening, business ratios are shrinking, and staff loyalty is eroding. Corporate espionage with criminal syndicates targeting specific advancements, cyberterrorism (hacks), and data breaches : External dangers include getting software and raw data. Targeting staffers to provide company knowledge, innovations, business strategies, and customer databases)

Theft from within the company is usually done by unhappy employees or ex-employees.

Sometimes they deliberately hire personnel to steal the information. Some of these individuals allow themselves to be manipulated by rival spy agencies, either for financial gain or for personal gain. The sake of profit or simply the sake of being spiteful derives them to steal data and provide it to rival industries. A sacked or retrenched employee may approach a competitor and offer to reveal the trade secrets, marketing strategy, or new product plans in exchange for retribution or a fee, despite signed nondisclosure or confidentiality agreements. Competitive intelligence rival officers may tap phone lines or listen in on conversations and dig through a company's data on a daily basis or break into computers systems, to steal a trade secret.

In a lawsuit between Nike and its ex-employees who began working for Adidas exemplifies the menace that employees pose to businesses. The individuals allegedly plotted to obtain Nike's trade secrets and apply this while working for Adidas, . If this is factual, then this type of action poses a genuine threat to Nike's business, as it allowed an adversary to reap the benefit from Nike's efforts . The employees described their purported strategy on companies laptops and phones, and Nike discovered the scheme despite the attempts to wipe the evidence before handing in their systems. Despite the fact that the matter was agreed to settle after months of investigation, it exemplifies how easily trade secrets and classified info can be seized and abused, even when an organization takes precautions to secure its resources.

To protect their trade secrets, businesses should take measures and implement strict processes and practices . In case if one organization is in a legal spat over stolen secret information, the court will take the corporation's efforts to safeguard the secret information into consideration If the court determines that the corporation's measures are insufficient, the trade secret won't be considered as stolen information.

Remedies

To seek remedy in court against the infringement of trade secrecy , the company has to be aware about certain points ,that the individual alleged to have stolen the data must have gained a strategic edge . It is necessary for the owner to take all the feasible precautions to keep the information hidden. And there has to be a misappropriation because the data collected has to be used or shared in contravention of fair business practices. The court can order prohibiting the offender from profiting or exploiting the trade secret in the future. An order for compensatory damages based on the original loss suffered as a result of the misappropriation of a trade secret. An order for detention may be issued based , that might include an investigation of the offender's property in order to attain data to justify trade secret theft. Preventative retention of materials containing misappropriated trade secrets, as well as the products arising from their use or misuse. A court may order that the action which helped in securing the secret to make the products be termed as unlawful and the same product/item be destroyed. Legal penalty may be imposed in some states for wilful promotion of trade secret theft.

The Principles of Intellectual Property can be defined as a proprietary interest that arises or is formed from humans intellectual ability.Intellectual property rights can be classified as a right to profit, with intellectual property taking the form of knowledge, art, literature, and technology, and requiring the investment of energy, time, money, and mind in order to actualize. The occurrence of such investments adds value to intellectual endeavour. The protection of people is more prevalent in the principles of intellectual property rights, but to balance the interests of individuals with the interests of society, the principles of intellectual property are based on the notion of natural justice.

In the realm of capital and commerce, trade secret safety is extremely valuable because it allows key strategic knowledge that is not covered by patent, copyright, or trademark to be safeguarded As an example, in order to gain a patent protection, it must be true to discover something new, meet the inventive step requirements, and meet the Patent Office's very complex conditions, whereas trade secrets can be managed conveniently due to the legal obligations, which are not as stringent as in the patent legal system.

4.7 Counterfeiting

The clothing industry is currently experiencing a number of challenges, including developing new trends and satisfying the expectations of an ever-changing consumer market. Counterfeiting is the most serious problem that has been degrading high-end fashion brands for years. According to the World Customs Organization (WCO), 7-9% of global trade consists of counterfeit products. In India, counterfeit products cause over Rs 1 lakh crore loss annually India as claimed by ASPA which is a body working on anti-counterfeiting solutions

Counterfeit means to imitate something. Product counterfeiting is a consumer fraud in which a product is sold as something it is not. Counterfeit goods are imitated copies of original products.

Counterfeit goods are often created to benefit from the superior value of the imitated product. They have illegally manufactured items that look and perform like real goods but are of poorer quality in terms of performance, efficiency, and durability. Counterfeit consumer goods are known for being of poor quality (and even not working at all) and can even contain toxic substances.

Counterfeiting on e-commerce platforms

E-commerce platforms have made the lives of consumers very convenient; they have enabled us to purchase products from the comfort of our homes. They have allowed us to experience the joy of shopping without the hassles of long queues and waiting for seasonal sales. However, as there has been a stark rise in the number of counterfeit products being sold online, the consumer has no way to know if the products sold to them through the websites are authentic. After all, counterfeiters have started producing products that are so identical to the original one except in terms of quality which is often determined by its long-term use of the product and by then it is too late.

All major e-commerce platforms whether it is Amazon, Flipkart or Snapdeal have borne the brunt of having a history of counterfeit products being sold on their platform. In November 2019, Nike ended its partnership with Amazon and stopped selling its products on the platform due to the number of counterfeit copies of Nike being sold on the platform. "According to a November 2018 survey, 37 % of purchasers reported that they had received a counterfeit product from Snapdeal. In July 2019, Snapdeal's founders were accused of criminal conduct in India for selling counterfeit products there. The various right holders have also sued Snapdeal for selling counterfeit goods." The Khadi and Village Industries Commission (KVIC) in September 2020 forced e-commerce portals Amazon, Flipkart, Snapdeal, and others to remove over 160 web links selling products under the brand name of 'Khadi'

Online Counterfeiting

In the wake of the covid 19 pandemic, as online shopping became the new normal, there was a pressing need to hold e-commerce platforms accountable for the products they sell on their website. Most online sellers and e-commerce platforms did not disclose their identity and hence in the event of a fake product being received, there was not much a consumer could do. To tackle this issue, the Consumer Protection Act 2019 was introduced.

Counterfeiting has been around for decades, but the scope has grown tremendously as a result of the new means that technology has made accessible to reach consumers. Counterfeiters take advantage of the world's largest and most popular distribution network, which is low-cost and accessible to billions of people- the INTERNET.

A large number of counterfeits are acquired online since the consumer depends only on the seller's information, which can be easily manipulated. Counterfeiters can now offer fake items as there is no chance of consumer examination thanks to the Internet. They mostly operate online, offering customers professional-looking websites, low prices, faster delivery, and a larger choice of delivery options, posing a serious threat to luxury brands.

Two kinds of markets for counterfeiters

- **Deceptive Market-** Customers who are ill-informed or unfamiliar with the product are unable to differentiate between genuine and counterfeit items, resulting in the purchase of counterfeit goods by accident.
- **Non-deceptive Market-** This type of market applies more to the luxury goods industry because consumers are fully aware they are purchasing a counterfeit as customers can easily distinguish fake from authentic. Here, buyers are accomplices rather than victims in this case.

Why Do People Choose Counterfeit Goods?

There are three primary motivations for people to purchase counterfeits.

- The counterfeit is significantly less expensive than the original i.e. the utility and value for money;
- The quality of the counterfeit is similar to the original;
- Buyers see no need to support the firm that makes the legitimate item, which pertains to the company's social responsibility.
- Social motivation or the peer effect.
- The ever-changing needs and transient nature of fashion trends.

Impact of Counterfeiting

A. The ultimate victims of unfair competition are the consumers
B. The consumer receives poor-quality goods at an excessive price
C. Consumers are sometimes exposed to health and safety dangers.
D. Governments lose out on unpaid tax (direct and indirect) and incur large costs in enforcing intellectual property rights.
E. Industry worldwide loses large amounts to counterfeiters.
F. Counterfeiting and piracy are unlawful in and of themselves, but they also promote larger criminality by supplying cash for other illegal acts like terrorism, smuggling, etc. More money invariably strengthens criminal organizations and makes it more difficult to mitigate

the negative social repercussions of their actions, which might include lost lives, increased security expenses, and physical and emotional effects.

G. Consumers are sometimes exposed to health and safety dangers. Since they are not subject to the same regulatory requirements and production standards as real items.

H. As counterfeits are manufactured in an unregulated circumstance, counterfeiters frequently employ pollution-producing and harmful technology and materials. Not only that but once law enforcement seizes large numbers of counterfeits, the items are frequently incinerated. As a result, there is pollution released into the air. This is especially troublesome for products that were designed to decrease users' environmental footprints and for brands whose primary business models are based on sustainable practices.

I. If you sell a product and a counterfeiter competes with you by providing customers with a lower-cost counterfeit of your original product, you will lose some sales to these lower-cost goods.

J. The harm caused by counterfeiters extends beyond customer relationships. Because of the acts of counterfeiters, distributors, retailers, and other business partners sometimes lose faith in legitimate firms.

<u>Consumer Protection Act, 2019</u>

The act received the assent of the President on 9th August 2019, it came into effect on 20th July 2020. The Act replaces the previous act from 1986. It aims to protect the interest of the consumers and provide them with timely redressal through effective administration.

The main features of the Consumer Protection Act are

• Inclusion of E-commerce, Direct selling, and Establishment of Central Consumer Protection Authority (CCPA)

• Strict Norms for Misleading Advertisement

• Strict Norms for product liability

• Changes in the Pecuniary Jurisdiction

• Greater ease to dispute resolution Addition in the clause of "Unfair Trade Practice":

• Unfair Contract

• Alternate Dispute Resolution through mediation

Consumer Dispute Redressal Agencies

Three Consumer Disputes Redressal Agencies have been established to ensure speedy and inexpensive redressal to make sure the grievances of the consumers have been heard.

• District Consumer Disputes Redressal Commission or District Commission

• State Consumer Protection Council known as the State Council

• National Consumer Disputes Redressal Commission or National Commission.

The Pecuniary Jurisdiction Of Commissions

District commission- Up to 1 crore

State Commission- 1crore to 10 crores

National Commission- Above 10 crores

In case of a dispute, a complaint can be filed in a District Commission within the local limits of whose jurisdiction the:

• Place of business or residence of opposite parties, or

• Place of business or residence of the complainant, or

• where the cause of action, wholly or in part, arises

Salient Features

- The draft rules make it mandatory for every e-commerce platform to provide details regarding the seller, their legal name, address, website, contact details, the identity of the business, and the kinds of products they sell.
- If an e-commerce platform is selling imported goods, they are required to mention where did they procure the goods from, the name and contact details of the importer from whom they purchased the goods or if the person is a seller on the platform, then they are required to mention their business details. This is to ensure accountability on behalf of the sellers.
- E-commerce entities to appoint a nodal person of contact or an alternate senior designated functionary who is resident in India, to ensure compliance with the provisions of the Act or the Rules

- A grievance officer must acknowledge receipt of any consumer complaint within forty-eight hours and redress the complaint within one month from the date of the complaint to ensure a speedy trial.

- Every marketplace e-commerce entity shall make reasonable efforts to maintain a record of relevant information allowing for the identification of all sellers who have repeatedly offered goods or services that have previously been removed or access to which has previously been disabled under the Copyright Act, 1957, the Trade Marks Act, 1999 or the Information Technology Act, 2000

- No seller offering goods or services through a marketplace e-commerce entity shall refuse to take back goods, or withdraw or discontinue services purchased or agreed to be purchased, or refuse to refund consideration if paid if such goods or services are defective, deficient, or spurious.

Remedies

Although there is no legislation specifically dealing with counterfeiting and piracy in India, legislators have given statutory, civil, criminal, and administrative remedies through various statutes. It results in patent infringement or trademark infringement in the case of goods.

TRADEMARK ACT 1999

The law of trademarks in India is governed by this act, it provides civil as well as criminal statutory remedies against cases of infringement for unregistered as well as registered trademarks. The trademark law provides administrative remedies, where the aggrieved person can redress their grievance by seeking intervention from the Trademark Registry, which acts through the Registrar of Trademarks. In the case of an unregistered trademark, a remedy can be sought under common law by a suit of passing off. Trademarks can further be divided into service marks, wordmark, certificate marks, etc. according to the classification of goods. The term of protection offered is 10 years from the date of application, it can be renewed from time to time. Sec 103 provides a penalty for applying for false trademark and/or trade description etc with imprisonment for a term which shall not be less than six months but which may extend to three years and with a fine which shall not be less than fifty thousand rupees but which may extend to two lakh rupees.

COPYRIGHT ACT, 1957

Copyright protects original artistic, literary work, and cinematographic films. It subsists in music, films, computer works, etc. In order to obtain copyright protection, registration is not a mandate. The copyright comes into existence as soon as the work exists in tangible form.

Sec 55 of the act talks about the civil remedies available to a person, these are remedies by way of injunction, damages, accounts, and otherwise as are or may be conferred by law for the infringement of a right. The statute gives the right to the police officers to proceed with the investigation by seizing all the infringing copies. Further, the registrar of copyright has the power to investigate any alleged ship, dock, or premise and order to confiscate them. Section 63 of the Act provides for imprisonment up to three years and a fine for indulging in activities of infringement.

The term of protection offered for literary, dramatic, musical, and artistic works is the life of the author plus 60 years from the beginning of the calendar year following the author's death. The term of protection for films, photographs, and sound recordings is 60 years from the beginning of the calendar year following the work's publication.

PATENTS ACT, 1970

Under the statute, a patentee is granted a monopoly right in respect of an invention for a term of 20 years. Any violation necessitates the judiciary to intrude and secure such right. However, the patentee is required to institute a suit for seeking remedies, such as interlocutory/interim injunction, damages or account of profits, and permanent injunction, these are recognized as civil remedies. The Patents Act does not provide criminal remedies.

DESIGN ACT, 2000

The act is applicable to subject matters of a design like a shape, pattern, configuration of colours, etc. Protection is only offered to those features in the finished article that appeal to or are judged solely by the eye. Section 22 provides that anyone committing an act of piracy shall be liable to pay to the rights holder up to ₹ 50, 000 (approximately $1,000) per registered design. The rights holder may also seek interim relief and an injunction, provided that the right holder must prove that the alleged infringing act involves their design resulting in an economic loss. The remedies offered are of a civil nature. The term of protection is 15 years in total: an initial 10 years, extendable by a single five-year period.

INDIAN PENAL CODE, 1860

The Penal Code sets out punishments for cheating, counterfeiting, and possession of instruments for making counterfeits, etc. The provisions of the code can be invoked in criminal actions, in addition to the provisions of specific statutes.

Innovative Ways to Fight Off Counterfeits

Blockchain is a data recording system that makes it difficult or impossible to change, hack, or cheat the system. Blockchain technology is a collection of records and data called blocks that are encrypted and related to each other for security and safety. Manufacturers and designers can protect their products from counterfeiting through the use of blockchain. Its origin and ownership can be traced up to the origins of each fashion item. Counterfeit products or replicas will not have a genuine record chain, and will thus be quickly rooted out. As the technology spreads throughout the supply chain, customers will obtain even more information from an embedded chip. Consumers would have the information they need to reject products that are counterfeit or that the buyer does not ethically support using materials and production facilities.

The *Group Project* aspires to create a blockchain-based solution that will save the fashion clothing sector $500 billion in annual losses due to counterfeit products. Small and big businesses will benefit from the system's usage of Crypto-TagTM and mobile applications to secure their products from being copied and sold.

Supply chain- Monitoring- Effective controls are critical because there is so much leakage in the manufacturing, supply, and distribution chains. Brands need to know where counterfeit items are coming from, whether it's through third-party factories or approved production facilities that turn out unlicensed originals at the end of the day. They must also comprehend how counterfeit products reach the market. Once the product source or potential leakage in the distribution network has been discovered, the brand owner should undertake factory raids, potentially with the help of local law enforcement officers, to target locations where counterfeit goods are made and distributed.

Monitoring- An effective online monitoring program that assists in identifying popular places, including legitimate sites, where counterfeits may be offered and establishing effective takedown systems.

Technology- Many companies use technology to improve product security like radio frequency identification tags, security tags, holograms, watermarks, and customized fibres. These technologies make it impossible to copy items and allow customs authorities, wholesalers, merchants, and customers to check for authenticity.

A Pune-based start-up hopes to eliminate the usage of radio-frequency identification (RFID) tags and holograms, which are commonly used to identify counterfeits, by utilizing Artificial Intelligence (AI). *NeuroTags* creates mathematically linked tags - both open and secured - using algorithms and artificial intelligence. The open tag is placed on the front of the cover or box and can be scanned by anybody with a smartphone to obtain product information. It also serves as a guarantee of authenticity (with a certain probability).

QR code- A unique code or a unique number registered with the site can help to tackle counterfeit, this QR code should be registered under the official website of the Company. So the consumer can scan the code and see the genuinity of the product. This method will make sure the authenticity of the product and it will also prevent counterfeiting of the same.

Amazon- Product serialization is facilitated by a unique code that brands attach during the manufacturing or packaging process, and it allows us to scan and validate the originality of each and every purchase of enrolled items from Amazon's shops. Amazon's automatic safeguards monitor more than 5 billion attempted daily product listing changes throughout the world for fraudulent listings.

Under government directions- All industries relating to fashion should come under Government or if not totally under the control of Government, the Respective government should appoint a person as his watchdog to prevent counterfeiting in industry.

Media Trial

There is no doubt that social media has a big impact on our daily lives, it has the power to amplify a message once a related post or video goes viral. Fashion watchdogs like Diet Prada which goes by the name of @diet_prada on Instagram often highlight cases where big fashion brands have taken "inspiration" from smaller labels and independent designers to an extent where the products are almost identical.

On May 21, 2021, designer Cecilia Monge (@ceciliamariamakes) turned to the social media platform TikTok and made a clip titled "Ouch @converse." In her video, which has amassed over 12 million views as of this writing, Cecilia called out the shoe company for shamelessly copying two styles she designed specifically for Converse when she applied for a 2019 internship. The designer explained to Diet Prada, she saw that Converse had dropped a National Parks line incredibly similar to her own designs, she "was initially sceptical that such a large corporation could've actually noticed her work however it was not just one design that was similar and hence it became harder for her to dismiss it as a coincidence, Cecilia showed followers a second example of the national park's designs she shared with Converse. The color palette of the design that was introduced by converse and the one made by Cecilia were quite similar down to the order of the colors and the actual hues of the color.

The issue soon became viral and eventually reached Converse, they clarified the matter and denied having used the designer's designs that she had submitted as part of her internship application. Social media played a crucial role here in pushing Converse to release an official statement which may not have happened otherwise.

Palika Bazaar's Intriguing Case

Palika Bazaar, one of the country's first air-conditioned underground markets, has evolved over the last two three decades into one of the capital's largest counterfeit markets, attracting a diverse group of young and old customers who prefer to buy a variety of counterfeits, ranging from clothing, bags, and footwear to electronics and home décor. Thousands of tourists, including foreigners, come to the market to buy counterfeit goods and other low-cost items.

4.8 Landmark Cases

Cartier International Ag & Ors. vs Gaurav Bhatia & Ors. (226 (2016) DLT 662)

The Delhi High Court was presented with a case in which the defendants were selling counterfeit products online at a significant discount. CARTIER (recognized as a well-known mark under S. 2 (zg) of the Act). PANERAI, VACHERON CONSTANTIN, and JAEGER LECOULTRE were the brands in question. The court granted a permanent injunction based on the evidence presented, which included screenshots from websites and complaints made to authorities by several duped customers. The court ordered the plaintiff to be given details of all transactions and punitive damages of Rs 1 crore.

Christian Louboutin Sas vs Nakul Bajaj & Ors. (CS (COMM) 344/2018)

In this case, it was determined that the defendants had been selling shoes on their website, claiming that they were the plaintiff Christian Louboutin's original products and suggesting that they were affiliated with the plaintiffs by prominently displaying the mark CHRISTIAN LOUBOUTIN. Louboutin argued that goods would be considered counterfeit if they were sold without proper permission, authorization, or quality control and that the normal grey market rule would not apply to products sold on the internet because the risk of harm was much higher, making it impossible for the mark's owner to exercise any quality control. Christian Louboutin was granted relief by the Delhi High Court.

4.9 Complaint Mechanism

What Is Counterfeiting/ Intellectual Property Theft?

Counterfeiting is known to be a federal and state crime, involving the manufacturing or distribution of goods under someone else's name, and without their permission. Counterfeit goods are generally made from lower quality components, in an attempt to sell a cheap imitation of similar goods produced by brands consumers know and trust. Goods that can be counterfeited are the goods that span across multiple industries including everything from apparel, accessories, music, software, medications and cigarettes, to automobile and airplane parts, consumer goods, toys and electronics.

Anti Piracy (Acting Against The Piracy Of Copyrighted Material)

Anti-piracy steps are efforts to fight against copyright infringement, counterfeiting, and other violations of intellectual property laws. It includes, but is by no means limited to, the combined efforts of corporate associations, law enforcement agencies, and various international governments to combat copyright infringement relating to various types of creative works, such as software, music and films.

How To Combat Counterfeiting?

Counterfeiting is one of the biggest threats facing brand owners, threatening profits, corporate reputation and, potentially, customer safety and loyalty. However, creating a resilient anti-counterfeiting or anti-piracy strategy can be challenging given the global nature of the crime, as well as local nuances which come into play in different jurisdictions. It is one of the growing threats; especially with the rise of digital technologies and Internet file sharing networks. And much of the theft takes place overseas, where laws are often lax and enforcement is more difficult. All told, intellectual property theft costs U.S. businesses billions of dollars a year and robs the nation of jobs and tax revenues.

In India, the Copyright Act provides for both civil and criminal remedies for infringement. Section 55 provides for civil remedies and declares that, upon infringement, *"the owner of the copyright shall be entitled to all such remedies by way of injunction, damages, and accounts and otherwise as are or may be conferred by law for the infringement of a right."* Civil suits are instituted at the appropriate district court having jurisdiction (where the plaintiff resides).

When it comes to Criminal remedy, Chapter 12 (Section 63-70) of the Act gives criminal penalties for infringing copyrights which are typically punishable with terms of imprisonment which *'may extend up to 3 years along with a fine'*. These offences would be taken cognizance of and tried at the court of the Metropolitan Magistrate or Judicial Magistrate of the First class under Section 70, in the same manner as all cognizable offences in India (under the Code of Criminal Procedure, 1973).

Section 64 of the Copyright Act dealing with police powers was amended in 1984 to give plenary powers to police officers, of the rank of a sub-inspector and above, to seize without warrant all infringing copies of works *"if he is satisfied"* that an offence of infringement under Section 63, *"has been, is being, or is likely to be, committed"*. Earlier, this power could only be exercised by a police officer when the matter had already been taken cognizance of by a Magistrate. Moreover under the Income Tax Act, dealing with the far more sensitive issue of tax evasion, a search and seizure can only be conducted based on information already in the possession of the investigating authority. The procedure that is followed in suits is contained in Section 26 to 35A of the civil procedure Code and the rules of procedure in the First Schedule.

In a suit for infringement of copyright the plaintiff has to establish the following:

1. He is the owner of the copyright within the meaning of Section 54, i.e. he is the actual owner of the copyright, or he is one who is entitled to the remedies provided for infringement in Section 55.
2. Copyright subsists in the work infringed at the time the defendant committed the infringement.
3. Particulars of the infringement complained of,
4. The nature of the damage if any suffered by him or likely to suffer (if any),
5. What the defendant has done or is proposing to do.

What Should The Plaint Contain?

1. The name of the court in which suit is brought;
2. The name, description and place of residence of the plaintiff.
3. The name, description and place of residence of the defendant, so far as they may be ascertained.
4. The facts constituting the cause of action and when it arose.
5. The facts showing that the court has jurisdiction; and
6. The relief which the plaintiff claims.
7. Every pleading should contain a statement in a concise form of the material facts on which the party pleading relies for his claim {Evidence in support of the claim (such documents in a list to be added or annexed to the plaint)}

PROCEDURE AFTER FILING OF FIR

1. The investigation of a cognizable offence (as in the case of copyright infringement) begins when a police officer in charge of a Police Station has reason to suspect the commission of the offence.

2. When a reasonable suspicion of the commission of infringement of Copyright exists, the SHO (Station House Officer) must immediately send a report of the circumstances creating the suspicion to a Magistrate having power.

3. The SHO shall then proceed in person, or shall depute his subordinate officer to proceed to the spot, to investigate the facts and circumstances of the case, and to take measures for the discovery and seizure.

NASSCOM & BSA are working in conjunction to stop the menus of piracy from the society. They have established a special Anti-Piracy (Hotline) in Delhi. This alliance, with the help of the Police and Judiciary appointed Commissioners are carrying out the operations against anti-piracy. They are facilitating police raids against such menus, providing information of infringement.

Piracy Of Registered Designs

The designs are also prone to infringement and they can also be copied by the competitors or some other person. If a design has been copied then the owner of that design can claim damages and can also apply for an injunction. Section 22 of the Design Act, 2000 deals with the piracy of designs (registered). Any obvious or fraudulent imitation of a design which is already registered without the consent of its proprietor is unlawful and also prohibits the import of any material which closely resembles a registered design. This section also states that if any civil suit is brought then compensation should not exceed than Rs. 50000 for the infringement.

If there arises any question regarding the ascertainment of infringement then the Court will directly look for the design from the point of view of an average customer. In other words, the Court will consider whether there is any confusion which is obvious or some material facts in the minds of the customers regarding the two articles.

In the case of *Chanel and Adidas vs. Amazon Sellers,* In separate lawsuits Chanel, arbiter of luxury, and Adidas, patron saint of ath leisure, are going after dozens of web sites and Amazon store operators for selling merchandise with fake logos and trademarks and seeking combined damages of $249 million. While the damages being sought will likely be trimmed heavily by the court, it's clear that big, popular companies are getting better and better about finding counterfeiters and shutting them down through the courts.

Product Liability And Consumer Protection

Product liability and consumer protection laws both differ from country to country. But the basic reasoning behind this is to deal with the protection and safety of consumers, even if the damage is caused by the consumer's own negligence. The area of law in which manufacturers, distributors, suppliers and retailers are held responsible for any injuries products cause is called Product Liability. The Consumer Protection Act therefore introduced statutory liability for defective products.

Rights Available To Protect The Consumer From Defective Products

Civil law and criminal law both may be used to some extent to regulate unsafe/defective products. Under the consumer protection laws available in different countries for example UK, USA, Turkey, EU and India they provide some common rights to the consumers, like if any defect is found out in the product then the consumer can demand for the free repairing of the product or can exchange the defective product, and can also reduce the price for the defective part of the product, and also he can bring a legal action against the manufacturer or supplier or both for the breach of contract between   them.

In India, the consumer has *"right to choose"* which states that a consumer can demand the traders. A consumer also has *"right to be informed"* which describes that a consumer has a right to be informed about the quality and quantity standard, price and the health safety of the product. If he gets any wrong information about it or misleads about the expiry date of the product, a consumer can then file a suit against the traders.

Consumer protection Act, 1987 deals with the Strict liability (Strict liability is the legal process in which the claim filed by the plaintiff is focused not on the manufacturer's conduct, but rather the quality of the manufactured product) imposed on the manufacturer of the goods for any defect in the product. It means that if a consumer suffers any injury, then a claim can be brought against the manufacturer.

Coming to the defences, if any:

1. The product is compliant with the requisite statutory standards.
2. The product is not defective or unsafe.
3. Contractually agreeing to the disclaimer or limitations on warranties in terms of scope, period, recourse and amount.

4. The user of the product not being a consumer as defined in CPA 2019.

5. No harm caused to the consumer defined under CPA 2019.

6. The consumer is under the influence of alcohol or any kind of drugs

Within the **U.S.,** the ***National Intellectual Property Rights Coordination Center*** is working diligently to stop IP theft on a global basis. This center partners with more than 20 additional agencies located across the world to identify and curb IP theft as much as possible. Some of these agencies include the governments of Mexico and Canada, Europol, Interpol, and the FBI. These federal agencies are responsible for investigating any instances of IP theft and bringing perpetrators to justice. If an agency locates a potential target of IP theft, the investigation could take months or years before it is complete. Federal defense attorneys must have extensive evidence of IP theft, along with expert witnesses that can verify what is being present in court.

The Intellectual Property Unit, composed of special agents and analysts, recognizes the threat posed by intellectual property theft and provides the coordination of both IPR Center and field personnel needed to facilitate successful investigations into the criminal organizations involved in such activity. This unit also oversees enforcement operations relative to threats identified in the intellectual property environment, including the increasing health and safety risks posed by counterfeit products. The FBI also houses their IP headquarters program at the IPR Center. FBI program managers have oversight over the FBI's dedicated IPR field agents, whose priorities include counterfeit goods that pose a health and safety threat and the theft of trade secrets.

Chapter 5. Fashion and Employment

The fashion industry, taken as a whole, is a major provider of work to adults. One in eight of the world's adult population works in the fashion industry, from growing cotton crops to sewing garments for retail. This work enables individuals to earn money, build up skills and for some, to have a profession. However it is estimated that 181 million people are in vulnerable, or insecure, work40. That's equivalent to the combined populations of the UK, France and South Korea. Or just over 2.2% of the world's population.

In the garment and textile industry, work-related insecurity manifests itself in several ways. Workers are affected right across the global supply chain. Insecure, vulnerable or precarious work can have any of these characteristics:

- low pay
- lack of social benefits such as sickness pay or pensions
- lack of contracts or inadequate contracts – including 'zero hours' working
- employment on a casual or piece-rate basis, including from home
- greater risk of illness or injury
- lack of workers' rights or representation.

The industry employs major workforce as contractual workers for special period of time, purpose etc. Thus, understanding about the employment and rights relating to the workforce become important.

5.1 EMPLOYMENT NATURE AND AGREEMENTS

In the legal landscape, there are numerous contractual obligations that need to be complied with, before an employment agreement is entered into. Since both the employer and the employee are bound by such obligations, it becomes crucial to understand the extent of contracts because contractual violations often lead to adverse legal consequences.

The following chronological order is to be followed while formulating the contracts:

1. OFFER AND ACCEPTANCE

Offer and acceptance are the primary ingredients of a successful contract under the Indian Contract Act, 1872. In the fashion industry, the offer will be in terms of a job or a vacant position, the acceptance must be granted by the employee/worker, the consideration will be remuneration for the work done along with an intention to enter into a legal contract.

---

40 World Employment and Social Outlook - Trends 2018, International Labour Organization

In situations where an employee approaches the fashion brand, the individual approach shall be considered as an invitation to offer instead of an actual offer. Moreover, it must be considered that a written contract is preferable since it demarcates the rights and duties of the parties involved thereby avoiding controversies. The contract must contain the terms and conditions that are to be agreed upon.

2.   CLAUSE OF EXCLUSIVITY

In the fashion industry, it is possible that a person provides his/her labour to several employers. Therefore, clauses of exclusivity play an important role. The clause of exclusivity binds an employee to the employer and thus, prevents him from extending his services to multiple employers.

3.   RESTRAINT OF TRADE CLAUSE

The Fashion industry thrives on the concept of creativity and innovation. Therefore, the following restraint covenants can be applied on the employee, for a particular period of time after he quits the job, to prevent him from:

a.   working for a competitor of the employer

b.   setting up in business in competition with the employer

c.   canvassing, enticing or soliciting the customers of the employer

d.   interfering with the suppliers of, or supplies to, the employer

e.   canvassing, enticing, inducing, soliciting or poaching the employees of the employer

f.   dealing with the customers of the employer

g.   disclosing or exploiting the confidential information or trade secrets of the employer

This secures the employers by aiding them to prevent a future violation of their fashion trends.

4.   CONTENTS OF THE EMPLOYER-EMPLOYEE CONTRACT

The contract must be exhaustive in nature and shall contain all the relevant details with regards to the nature of the employment. These details include the duration of the job, working hours, salary, place of work, probation period, deductions, holidays and other benefits, restrictive covenants, pension (if any), grievance and disciplinary provisions, severability, jurisdiction and particulars of the employment among others. The contract must also clarify whether the employee will be a salaried employee or a contracted professional.

It is also crucial to establish that the employment is voluntary (at-will) in nature and is not forced upon the employee. However, the employees shall not possess the power to alter the terms of the contract verbally. The Fashion Industry heavily relies on its employees and shall therefore ensure that a proper procedure is followed to determine the nature of their employment.

Besides, the fashion industry functions under an umbrella of multiple agreements at different stages of production and distribution. These agreements include:

i. Licensing Agreements

ii. Manufacturer Agreements

iii. Vendor Agreement

iv. Supplier Agreement

v. Distribution Agreements

vi. Modelling Agreements

vii. Celebrity/Influencers Agreements

viii. Marketing and Advertising Agreements

ix. Non-Disclosure Agreements

x. Franchise Agreements

These agreements govern the complete product life-cycle to prevent any form of legal lacunae or conflicts during the process. They also provide a safety lock to the rights of the manufacturing company as well as its employees to avert the violation of the prevailing laws.

5.2 Informal Workers

The existence of flexible contracts and hiring through the informal sector is the beginning of exploitation. Fast fashion brands depend on developing countries to provide cheap labour. To deal with growing competition in the industry and offer cheaper products, workers, mostly women are hired under unregulated conditions. Legal restrictions restricted the use of short-term contracts for a long period. Reducing legal criteria for short-term contracting and employment termination has been a major part of many governments' labour law reform agendas (not just in Asia). Short-term contracting, as a form of flexible employment, is typically accompanied by flexibility in wage payment, work organization, working hours, and workforce makeup. These workers are subjected to insecure working conditions, including excessive hours and little pay.

A textile worker's wage in developing countries nowadays is only 0.5% to 4% of the final retail cost of a garment product. Not only have workers at the bottom of the supply chain been pushed to face the costs connected with customer expectations for low pricing but they have also been made to bear the risks associated with the industry's fluctuating supply and demand.

Such places use a Piece rate system to pay employees. Workers' livelihoods are jeopardized by the piecework pay system, which bases compensation on the number of garments assembled.

5.3 Working Conditions

Exploitation Of Garment Workers – An International Human Rights Crisis

The story of the unjust treatment of garment workers in Third World countries is becoming exceedingly common. It's unfortunately common in advanced countries also. Big Fashion houses like H&M and Zara employ garment workers in countries like Bangladesh, India, Vietnam, China, etc. Different problems arise in different countries in terms of garment workers. The overview of general problems is excessive overtime, flexible or no contracts, lack of collective bargaining in some countries, lack or absence thereof of social security, ignorance of international law principles. It is nearly an everyday occurrence that there is news of workers being exploited in India and Bangladesh by the garment industry. Top fast fashion and supermarket chains like Marks and Spencer are more in news for their mistreatment of labourers and employers rather than impeccable fashion pieces. COVID 19 has further aggravated the living conditions of workers. They already depended on low wages which weren't great in comparison to the living wage required.

Understanding Statistics Of Garment Workers

- China is World's leading garment exporter.
- According to studies conducted by these brands, only about 2% of global fashion workers are given a decent wage.
- In the nine countries, among the top 10 apparel exporters to The United States,15 wages for garment workers in five countries—Bangladesh, Mexico, Honduras, Cambodia, and El Salvador—declined in real terms during the period from 2001 to 2011 by an average of 14.6 percent on a per-country basis.
- As of September 2020, about one-half of all garment workers in the region lived in nations where all but essential workplaces, including garment factories, were compelled to close. Nearly half of all garment supply chain jobs in the region were reliant on domestic or international consumer demand from nations with strict trade restrictions, which saw severe drops in retail sales.

Sweatshops, Home-Based- Workers, And Laws & Legislation to Protect Garment Workers

One might suppose that countries like the United States of America might be more advanced in treatment towards garment workers, and once upon a time, American garment workers were treated equitably. Today, though, the scenario is quite different.

The word sweatshops or as these arduous unethical places of work are colloquially called, are the diamond mines where garment workers toil away for hours without decent pay and safety conditions.

The manner of exploitation is that these workers are paid per item rather than being paid per hour. It can be noticed that this technique has been used in several other countries to exploit garment workers. The piece rate can fluctuate to as low as $0.3 per task, totalling around $4-6 an hour.

This has caused California to introduce a bill, known as the Garment worker protection act. While the bill failed in the state assembly, it still has started a conversation around the struggles of garment workers. Among the many aims of this historic bill, one of them was to fix a basic minimum hourly wage for garment workers. It also planned to hold fashion retailers accountable for their actions especially when they tried to save on costs by denying basic wages to employees.

Another factor was that many fashion businesses also supported the bill as they believed this would bring equality in the market, as certain companies only earned a larger margin of profits by saving on the costs of workers. According to the department of labour, the definition of a sweatshop is any factory that violates two or more labour laws.

The two types of common workers in India - Contract workers & Home labour. Homeworkers do paid work normally on a piece-rate basis. Similarly in India, home-based garment workers suffer at the hands of major western brands. This leads to a different technique, the end result being the same, that of wage theft and exploitation Conditions have worsened during COVID -19 as women have lost their jobs at factories and are condoned to the homework manner. Nationally, 60 to 80% of the workers are women in the garment sector with millions of them employed in informal, unorganized, or home-based units.

As husbands have lost jobs, it leaves women as the major breadwinners of the family which leads to them being forced to continue in their jobs.

Not just is the wage problematic, to make the wage decent they are forced to work arduously long hours. Children and young teens under the age of 17 are also employed.

Home-based workers are common in India. Child labour and extremely low wages strain this community. Child labour is extremely common as since it happens in a home-based format it goes unnoticed.

Research by the University of California found that women and girls from the most marginalized communities toiled for as little as 15 cents (11p) an hour in homes across India. Roughly one in five home-based garment workers in India are aged 17 and under, according to the study, which draws on interviews with 1,452 workers. Roughly one in five home-based garment workers in India are aged 17 and under, according to the study, which draws on interviews with 1,452 workers. When a survey was done in New Delhi, there were roughly 342 garment workers working from Home, and they all received less than the government ordained minimum wage.

Even though there is a clear violation of law, home-based workers would be unable to speak against it, as they lack unity and are isolated. The financial background of the workers is weak and hence they wouldn't risk losing the employment they have. Such women could really use a government scheme that particularly recognized them as labourers and gives them social security.

Garment workers have suffered for a long at the hands of employers, be it in a factory/ sweatshop type set up with flexible contracts and short-term contracts or as home-based workers on a piece-rate system, it is high time that countries begin to protect garment workers. They should receive social security benefits immediately as COVID 19 increases losses for such workers drastically, it is all the more important to realize the damage done.

Modern Slavery in Fast-Fashion Brands

Off-late ethical fashion has been quite the buzzword, even more so after the advent of the pandemic. Advocates like Lucy Siegle have made their voice been heard, loud and clear that "fast fashion is not free and someone, somewhere is paying" (Stanton, 2021). However, lines of morality tend to get blurred when we have to listen to our conscience on one hand and control the urge to lay our hands on the latest spring/summer collection, on the other.

Most of the world's most famous brands, from Shein and H&M to Levi's and Zara, all have faced accusations of profiting from the forced labor. It is in-fact hard to pin down a brand that has not had charges levelled against it. In today's day and age of globalisation, international apparel brands have grown increasingly used to benefiting from oppressive worker conditions that exist in countries like China, India, Myanmar and Bangladesh among various others. What all these places share in common is cheap cost of production, which in turn reflects incredibly alarming working conditions.

The supply chains that exist in such businesses are 'long and opaque', with violations happening at different stages of the clothing item's journey from field to shelf-starting from cotton mills to the weaving, dyeing and finishing stage.

A major reason why the fashion industry is not able to tackle the issue of labour abuses and exploitation in a proper manner, is because it is very hard to pin-point breaches in the first place. The field of fashion is an industry of industries.

It is "very closely connected to agriculture for the production of raw materials such as cotton, to the chemical industry for dyes and to the garment-manufacturing industry in a vast array of developed and developing nations. A garment could have been through five different countries, all with different legislation and definitions of modern slavery, before it ends up on the shop floor"[41]

With this level of complexity, it should not come as a surprise that there end up existing a slew of issues.

Another reason is the fact that it is an incredibly difficult task to streamline and form a unified approach across different organisations and regulating bodies that exist across the planet. Each country tends to have its own specific code of conduct and legislation(the same being non-existent in many) and ensuring compliance with all of them(especially countries whose GDP thrives on the profits accrued from sweatshop-like working conditions) is a herculean undertaking, which these Multi-National Brands are not happy to take up in the first place. All it does, is increase their load and their share of responsibility while cutting down their profit margins at the same time.

Strict enforcement of laws around modern slavery is, without an iota of doubt, the prime reason why these violations happen in the first place; why modern slavery is able to exist even in the 21st century.

From lack of policing to a lackadaisical approach adopted by regulatory bodies in general (assuming, there exist these organisations), there are a number of factors why laws, even if they happen to exist in specific regions, fail to have the desired effect of curbing modern slavery.

An NGO called Anti-Slavery International, provides the following definition- It is "the severe exploitation of other people for personal or commercial gain". Furthermore, the International Labour Organization and the Walk Free Foundation (WFF) claim that approximately "40 million modern slaves" exist globally today out of which, 71% are girls and women while one-fourth are children[42].

A host of reasons like sharp increase in poverty, access to beneficiary schemes being limited coupled with the pressure on companies and other organisations to win contracts from global MNCs at the lowest price possible, has created such circumstances wherein those belonging to the financially weaker sections of society, mostly female and migrants, end up experiencing violation of the most basic of rights.

41 Wang, V. and Paton, E., 2021. Global Brands Find It Hard to Untangle Themselves From Xinjiang Cotton. [online] Nytimes.com. Available at: <https://www.nytimes.com/2021/04/06/business/xinjiang-china-cotton-brands.html> [Accessed 30 August 2021].
42 CLEANING UP FAST FASHION. RSA Journal, [online] 166(2), p.34. Available at: <https://www.jstor.org/stable/10.2307/27008580> [Accessed 30 August 2021].

Talking about India, pretty most of our go-to brands in a typical market space or arcade have had allegations levelled against them. Modern slavery has been found to exist in the Indian garment sector with female migrants being exploited in garment factories that supply to some of the world's biggest international fashion brands from Benetton and Gap Inc to Levi Strauss.

The International Labour Organization (ILO) lists out eleven indicators for forced labour, out of which five were found to exist in the Bangalore city's garment industry. The factors being as follows:

"Abuse of vulnerability; deception as a result of false promises (wages etc); restriction of movement in the hostel; intimidation and threats; and abusive working and living conditions"[43].

It is important to note herein, that the effects of these aspects are felt much more strongly by migrant workers as compared to local employees. They find themselves to be doubly disadvantaged due to the interplay of other socio-economic factors as well, but all ultimately stemming from their position of vulnerability.

The only way that such blatant violations can be dealt with, is if the companies who are effecting the same, take cognisance of the infringement of their workers' rights, followed by concrete commitments to remedy the situation.

One can hope that apart from simply making public statements and issuing apologies claiming to 'look into the matter', brands start owning up to their predatory behaviour and doing the needful. It is high time! The glamour and prestige in the trendiest of clothing amounts to nothing, if what it ultimately feeds is hunger and unhappiness.

5.4 Case Studies

Boohoo

Dingy sweatshops with garment workers toiling in hazardous conditions should be limited to a page out of history textbooks. Sadly, the same situation continues to persist even in today's times in the fashion industry. As glamorous as it may appear on the face of it, the world of fast fashion in reality

---

43 Modern slavery uncovered in India's garment sector – Just Style. [online] Just Style. Available at: <https://www.just-style.com/news/modern-slavery-uncovered-in-indias-garment-sector> [Accessed 30 August 2021].

is nothing but brutal when we look at the horrific conditions the workers employed in these factories have to endure. Coupled with the problem of unfair wages, it is nothing but modern day exploitation that workers across textile factories are subjected to. The Boohoo Group, owner of some of the hottest brands in the world, such as, Karen Millen, Oasis and PrettyLittleThing among others, has in particular been slammed with a slew of charges. The Sunday Times undertook an undercover investigation as per which, the production factories coming under its aegis did not abide by the Covid-19 social distancing protocol. They apparently also forced workers to come to work even if they showed symptoms and paid them salaries as meagre as 3.5GBP/per hour. This revelation ultimately led to temporary delisting of all brands owned by Boohoo, by partners like Next and Asos. As a consequence, the Boohoo group has launched "an immediate and independent" review of its supply chains across the UK as well as taken the pledge to spend 10 Million GBP in order to wipe out malpractice.[44]

Shein

The brand Shein, tops charts across the world as one of the most downloaded shopping apps. It even beat Amazon's record in May this year. Loved across the world, Shein, finding most of its consumer base in young girls and millennial women, has been facing flak off late for not making "full public disclosures about working conditions in its supply chains", which is a legal requirement in the United Kingdom.[45]

What is worse is the fact that the company falsely states on its website that the conditions its factories house, "have been certified by international labor standards bodies", as per Reuters' findings. In fact, "Shein has a "social responsibility" page which claims that it never, ever engages in child or forced labor", but at the same time does not give out information about its supply chains, that is required as per the country's Modern Slavery Act of 2015. In the context of blatant violations on the part of Shein, the proverb that comes to mind is,-actions speak louder than words![46]

---

44 Analysis: Why can't fashion wash out the dark stain of modern slavery?. [online] Drapers. Available at: <https://www.drapersonline.com/insight/analysis/analysis-why-cant-fashion-wash-out-the-dark-stain-of-modern-slavery> [Accessed 30 August 2021].
45 Shein is Falling Short of Modern Slavery Reporting Rules, According to New Report | The Fashion Law. [online] Available at: <https://www.thefashionlaw.com/shein-is-falling-short-of-modern-slavery-reporting-rules-according-to-new-report/> [Accessed 7 September 2021].
46 Chinese retailer Shein lacks disclosures, made false statements about factories. [online] Reuters. Available at: <https://www.reuters.com/business/retail-consumer/exclusive-chinese-retailer-shein-lacks-disclosures-made-false-statements-about-2021-08-06/> [Accessed 7 September 2021].

5.5 Prevention of Sexual Harassment

Sexual harassment can be extremely damaging, causing severe distress as well as economic losses to victims. Many people within the fashion industry have been reluctant to speak out against sexual harassment, due to a fear of retaliation or blackballing and the inability to secure work with the most prestigious and powerful tastemakers. Quid pro quo harassment occurs when a person with authority tries to trade sexual favors for employment benefits. For example, if your agent promised to book you a plum modeling gig if you would sleep with him, this would be considered quid pro quo harassment. By contrast, a hostile work environment occurs if the harassment is so severe or pervasive that it renders the workplace hostile or offensive to a reasonable person. For example, if you are working with a fashion magazine in which the photographers and editors routinely denigrate women, make lewd remarks about your body parts, and touch you inappropriately, you may have been subject to a hostile work environment.

Prevention of Sexual Harassment (POSH) of women at the workplace

Definitions

1. **Sexual Harassment**

Sexual Harassment is not restricted to the use of sexual behavior to control, influence, or affect the career, salary, or job of another person, but is also extended between co-workers in cases where harassment occurs between an ABC employee and someone that employee deals with in the course of his/her work who is not employed by the Company.

'Sexual Harassment' includes one or more of the following unwelcome acts (whether directly or by implication):

    a. Any unwelcome sexually determined behavior, or pattern of conduct, that would cause discomfort and/or humiliate the person at whom any of the following behavior or conduct is directed:

      i. Physical contact and advances

     ii. Demand or request for sexual favors

   iii. Remarks of a sexual nature about a person's clothing or body or sexually colored remarks

   iv. Showing pornography, making or posting sexual pranks, sexual teasing, sexual jokes, sexually demeaning or offensive pictures, cartoons or other materials through email, SMS, etc.

    v. Repeatedly asking to socialize during off-duty hours or continued expressions of sexual interest against a person's wish

   vi. Giving sexually suggestive gifts

vii. Eve teasing, innuendos, and taunts, physical confinement against one's will or any such act likely to intrude upon one's privacy;

viii. Persistent watching, following, contacting of a person; and

ix. Any other unwelcome physical, verbal or non-verbal conduct of sexual nature

b. The following circumstances if it occurs or is present in relation to any sexually determined act or behavior will amount to sexual harassment:

- Implied or explicit promise of preferential treatment in employment
- The implied or explicit threat of detrimental treatment in employment
- The implied or explicit threat about the present or future employment status
- Interference with the person's work or creating an intimidating or offensive or hostile work environment, or
- Humiliating treatment is likely to affect her health or safety.

The determination of whether the conduct was offensive or not will be done by applying the reasonable person standard. Further, it is important to note that the occurrence of sexual harassment does not depend on the intention of the people but on the experience of the aggrieved woman.

2. Employer

i. A person responsible for management, supervision, and control of the workplace with the capacity to 'hire and fire' the employee.

ii. Any officer specified by the order of appropriate government or local authority.

3. Employee

A person employed at the workplace, for any work on a regular, temporary, ad-hoc or daily wage basis, either directly or through an agent, including a contractor, with or without the knowledge of the principal employer, whether for remuneration or not, or working on a voluntary basis or otherwise, whether the terms of employment are express or implied and includes a coworker, a contract worker, probationer, trainee, apprentice or by any other such name.

4. Workplace

A workplace, in addition to the place of work (Head office/Branch offices, Factories) shall also include any place where the aggrieved woman or the respondent visits in connection with the work, during the course of and/or arising out of employment/contract/engagement with ABC, including transportation provided for undertaking such a journey.

5. Aggrieved Woman

In relation to a workplace, a woman, of any age, whether employed or not, alleges to have been subjected to any act of sexual harassment by the respondent and includes contractual, temporary visitors.

6. Internal Complaints Committee

It refers to an internal complaints committee which would be explained further in the next section. Hereinafter, it should be referred to as IC.

7. Presiding Officer

The Presiding Officer is a member of the IC who shall be a woman employed at a senior level in the workplace amongst her colleagues.

8. Respondent

A person against whom a complaint of sexual harassment has been made.

Principles of the Policy

The following procedures and redressal mechanisms shall be followed while lodging a sexual harassment complaint at the workplace:

1. The Internal Complaints Committee

The IC shall consist of:

a.   A presiding officer as mentioned above. However, in the absence of a presiding officer based on seniority, a senior-level woman employee can either be employed from the administrative departments of the same workplace or, from a different work of the same employer (in case of absence of a woman employee in the same workplace).

b.   At least two members from the employees preferably committed to the cause of women or with experience in social work or with legal knowledge.

c.   One member from a non-governmental organization or association committed to the cause of women or a person familiar with the issues relating to sexual harassment.

Every member of the IC shall hold their offices for at most 3 years from their due date of appointment.

The functions of the IC include:

- Implementing policies related to sexual harassment.
- Receiving complaints pertaining to sexual and other forms of physical harassment.
- Brainstorming strategies to redress the grievances of the client.
- Initiating and investigating the complaints given by the complainant by conducting inquiries.
- Coordinating with the employer in executing appropriate actions.
- Maintaining strict confidentiality and respect for the privacy of the complainant.
- Submitting annual reports.

2. Lodging a Complaint

The complainant needs to submit a detailed complaint, along with any documentary evidence available or names of witnesses, to any of the committee members at the workplace.

The complaint must be lodged within 3 months from the date of the incident/ last incident. The Committee can extend the timeline by another 3 months for reasons recorded in writing if satisfied that these reasons prevented the lodging of the complaint.

Provided that where such a complaint cannot be made in writing, the Presiding Officer or any Member of the Internal Complaint Committee shall render all reasonable assistance to the women for making the complaint in writing.

If the aggrieved woman is unable to lodge the complaint in account of her incapacity, the following may do so on her behalf, with her written consent.

- Legal heir, relative, or friend
- Co-worker
- Any person having knowledge of the incident

If the initial complaint is made to a person other than a committee member, upon receiving such a complaint, it will be the responsibility of the complaint receiver to report the same to the committee immediately.

Wherever possible ABC ensures that all the complaints of harassment are dealt with speedily, discreetly, and as close as possible to the point of origin.

The head of the legal department of ABC will be responsible for tracking the real-time status of the complaint. A web-based system shall be devised for the same in order to create transparency and ensure maximum satisfaction of the employees.

3. Modes of Redressal

The modes of redressal are as follows:

i.Conciliation

The IC may, before initiating an inquiry, and/or at the request of the aggrieved woman, try to settle this complaint between the complainant and the respondent privately at first. However, it must be ensured that money would not be placed as the basis for this conciliation. If a settlement was able to be reached, then:

The IC shall record the settlement so arrived and forward the same to the employer to act as specified in the settlement. The IC shall provide copies of the settlement to the aggrieved woman and the respondent. Where such settlement has arrived, no further inquiry shall be conducted by the Internal Committee.

ii.   Inquiry into the complaint

Where the respondent is an employee, proceed to make an inquiry into the complaint in accordance with the provisions of the service rules applicable to the respondent and where no such rules exist, in such manner as may be prescribed.

- The committee, within seven working days of receiving the complaint, shall forward one copy thereof to the respondent for obtaining a response.
- The respondent shall file the reply within ten working days of receiving the complaint along with a list of supporting documents, names, and addresses of witnesses.
- The IC shall consider the reply from the respondent and initiate an inquiry. The complainant or the respondent to the complaint shall not be allowed to bring any legal practitioner to represent them at any stage of the proceedings before the IC. IC shall hear both the complainant and the respondent on the date(s) intimated to them in advance and the whole procedure would be conducted according to the principles of natural justice.
- If the respondent or the complainant failed to attend the personal hearing before IC on three consecutive dates (intimated in advance) without sufficient cause, the IC shall have the right to terminate the inquiry proceedings or give an ex-parte decision. However, before such termination, the IC shall serve a notice in writing to the parties, fifteen days in advance. The inquiry process shall be completed maximum within ninety days from the date of receipt of the complaint.

Where the conduct of Sexual Harassment amounts to a specific offence under the Indian Penal Code (45 of 1860) or under any other law, the IC has to immediately inform the complainant of their right to initiate action in accordance with the law with the appropriate authority and to give advice and guidance regarding the same.

- Where the committee concludes that the allegation against the respondent has not been proved, it recommends to the employer that no action is required to be taken in this matter. Further, the committee ensures that both parties understand that the matter has been fully investigated, that the matter is now concluded, and neither will be disadvantaged within the company.

- Where the committee concludes that the allegation against the respondent has been proved, it recommends to the employer to take necessary action for sexual harassment as misconduct, in accordance with the applicable service rules and policies, and this may include:

a. Counselling

b. Censure or reprimand

c. Apology to be tendered by respondent

d. Written warning

e. Withholding offers for new opportunities

f. Suspension

g. or any other action that the Management may deem fit.

iii. Interim Relief

During the time in which the inquiry is going on, the complainant, on a written request, ask the committee to recommend to the employer to –

- Transfer the aggrieved individual or the respondent to any other workplace, or
- Grant such other relief to the aggrieved individual as may be found to be appropriate, or
- Restraint the respondent from reporting to work.

iv. Termination of Inquiry

The committee at ABC may terminate the inquiry or give an ex-parte decision, if the complainant or respondent respectively is absent for 3 consecutive hearings, without reason. 15 day written notice to be given to the party, before termination or ex-parte order.

v. Confidentiality

Notwithstanding anything contained in the Right to Information Act, 2005, contents of the complaint, the identity and addresses of the Aggrieved Woman, Respondent, and witnesses, and any other kind of information relating to conciliation and inquiry proceedings, recommendations of the Internal Complaints Committee, and the action was taken by ABC shall not be published, communicated or made known to the public, press and proceedings media in any manner.

vi. Malicious Allegations

If the IC concludes that the allegation against the respondent is malicious or the complainant or anyone else making the complaint has made the complaint knowing it to be false or either of the above two people has produced any forged or misleading document, it may recommend to the employer to take action against the woman or the person making the complaint. The action recommended should be like the ones proposed for the respondent in case of substantiated complaints. While deciding malicious intent, the committee should consider that mere inability to substantiate a complaint need not mean malicious intent. Malicious intent must be established through a separate inquiry.

vii.   Harassment by Outsiders

If a woman brings to the IC, any instances of sexual harassment where the respondent is not from the fashion industry, the Management or any person delegated by the Management shall assist the aggrieved individual, if such aggrieved individual so chooses, to file a complaint with the IC of the respondent's employer or under the IPC or any other law for the time being in force, as may be appropriate.

viii.   Appeal

Finally, if, in case, any of the parties is not satisfied or further aggrieved by the implementation or non-implementation of recommendations made, they may appeal to the appellate authority in accordance with the Act and rules, within 90 days of the recommendations being.

ABC is extremely devoted to ensuring that no employee, who brings forward a sexual harassment concern, is subjected to any form of reprisal and any such reprisal shall invite disciplinary action. It is the duty of ABC as an entertainment, and therefore a public enterprise, to make sure that everyone working under the union is in safe conditions with people who do not have any malicious intentions. Through this policy, ABC shall try to ensure that the victim or witnesses are not victimized or discriminated against while dealing with complaints of sexual harassment.

5.6 Case Laws

The Vishaka Judgement

In 1992, Bhanwari Devi, a dalit woman employed in the rural development programme of the Government of Rajasthan, was brutally gang raped by five Gujjar men on account of her efforts to curb the then prevalent practice of child marriage.

As a *"saathin"* in the programme, her work was to spread awareness about hygiene, family planning and the necessity of educating girls, along with campaigning against female foeticide, dowry.

Harassed in the course of work, she was brutally raped as a "punishment" for stopping the wedding of a nine month old Gujjar girl.

This incident revealed the hazards that working women were exposed to on a day to day basis and highlighted the urgency for safeguards to be implemented in this regard.

Fighting against the cause of working women in the country, women rights activists and lawyers filed public interest litigation in the Supreme Court under the banner of Vishaka. It was the first time that the Supreme Court acknowledged the workplace sexual harassment as a human rights violation and acknowledged legislative inadequacy related to the issue.

In framing the Vishaka Guidelines, the Supreme Court placed reliance on the India ratified Convention on Elimination of All Forms of Discrimination against Women, adopted by the General Assembly of the United Nations, in 1979.

As per the judgment, 'Sexual Harassment' includes such unwelcome sexually determined behaviour (whether directly or by implication) as:

A.   Physical contact and advances

B.   A demand or request for sexual favours;

C.   Sexually coloured remarks;

D.   Showing pornography;

E.   Any other unwelcome physical, verbal or nonverbal conduct of sexual nature.

Adverse consequences might result if the victim does not consent to the conduct in question or raises any objection thereto.

Post Vishaka – Some Other Judgments and finally enactment of law

Apparel Export Promotion Council v. A.K Chopra

The Vishaka judgment initiated a nationwide discourse on workplace sexual harassment and threw out wide open an issue that was swept under the carpet for the longest time. The first case before the Supreme Court after Vishaka in this respect was the case of Apparel Export Promotion Council v. A.K Chopra.

In this case, the Supreme Court reiterated the law laid down in the Vishaka Judgment and upheld the dismissal of a superior officer of the Delhi based Apparel Export Promotion Council who was found guilty of sexually harassing a subordinate female employee at the workplace and also widened the definition of sexual harassment by ruling that physical contact is not a necessary condition in order to amount an act of sexual harassment.

The Supreme Court explained that "sexual harassment is a form of sex discrimination projected through unwelcome sexual advances, request for sexual favours and other verbal or physical conduct with sexual overtones, whether directly or by implication, particularly when submission to or rejection of such conduct by the female employee was capable of being used for affecting the employment of the female employee and unreasonably interfering with her work performance and had the effect of creating an intimidating or hostile work environment for her."

Medha Kotwal Lele & Ors. V. Union of India & Ors.

A letter written by Dr. Medha Kotwal of NGO Aalochana highlighted a number of individual cases of sexual harassment stating that the Vishaka Guidelines were not being effectively implemented at the grass root level.

The letter was presumed as a writ petition and the Supreme Court took cognizance and undertook monitoring of implementation of the Vishaka Guidelines across the country by directing State Governments to file affidavits emphasizing on the steps taken by them to implement the Vishaka Guidelines and directed states to put a sufficient mechanisms in order to ensure effective implementation of the Vishaka Guidelines.

Sixteen years later, sexual harassment at the work place was finally as an offence under the Sexual Harassment of Women at the Workplace (Prevention, Prohibition and Redressal) Act, 2013. The POSH Act mandates that an employer create a safe workplace environment for every female employee and has a number of clauses that every employer has to mandatorily comply with, including training and sensitization of employees, formation of ICC and strict penalties for violations.

Though people are aware of the consequences they are using different direct or indirect ways to sexually harass women in the workplace so that it becomes difficult for any woman to prove it, so one has to really read between the lines to find and prove the issue. POSH has defined sexual harassment under "section 2 (n) that states any of the following: (1) physical contact and advances; (2) a demand or request for sexual favours; (3) making sexually coloured remarks; (4) showing pornography; (5) any other unwelcome physical, verbal or non-verbal conduct of sexual nature."

Sexual harassment has a wide scope because it's just not limited to physical contact harassment but also psychological harassment. The laws have been crafted in such a way that it can deal with every kind of harassment to women in their workplace and leaving no space for the offender to escape. It is the responsibility of employers to maintain a disciplinary environment amongst their employees but still if any such complaint comes, then he must initiate a disciplinary action against act/acts that outrage the modesty and dignity of women in the workplace.

Any kind of inappropriate physical touch or makes any filthy jokes to a woman or shows any erotica content or any implied sexual gesture or making any deal of sexual pleasure that makes a woman uncomfortable or uneasy to work within that environment of the workplace. Further, the uncomforted or uneasiness for every woman could differ means the act doesn't strain any women to feel all the gestures mentioned in the section 2 (n) of the POSH act as sexual harassment. It gives a women immense liberty to choose her way of comfort with her colleagues in the workplace but if a woman faces any sexual harassment, then she can approach to her employer and file a complaint in the Internal Complaint Committee.

POSH has not confined sexual harassment to verbal or nonverbal gestures but it also includes circumstances defined under "section 3 of the act by providing that any of the following circumstances, related to sexual harassment, may also amount to Sexual Harassment: (1) implied or explicit promise of preferential treatment in the victim's employment; (2) implied or explicit threat of detrimental treatment in the victim's employment; (3) implied or explicit threat about the victim's present or future employment status; (4) interferes with the victim's work or creating an intimidating or offensive or hostile work environment for her and (4) humiliating treatment likely to affect the victim's health or safety."

Sexual harassment can be on the basis of circumstances wherein if there is any promise done for unfair preference or any detrimental treatment or any sort of threat to hamper her current or future working position or deliberately disturbing her to work or creating an uneasy environment for her or embarrass her that can affect the victim's health or safety. If any employee faces any of the aforesaid circumstances in her workplace, that puts her in a compromising situation wherein she is forced to act or accept or let go anything that hampers her modesty. Rights of women to work in any place with dignity and peace is her constitutional right enshrined under Article 14, 15 and 21 of the Constitution.

There is a need for establishment of a proper mechanism which can have proper process by which there can be protection of women, prevention and redressal of complaints of sexual harassment in workplace. Every workplace that has employed 10 or more employees is required to constitute an Internal Complaint Committee by order in writing under section 4(1) of the POSH Act. This committee will exclusively work on complaints relating to sexual harassment of women at workplace and will not just take disciplinary action against the offender but can also provide aid to the victim in ways possible. Infact government has also interfered to form the Local Complaint Committee at each District, which have similar tasks to perform as the Internal Complaint Committee.

The Internal Complaint Committee has to be constituted in compliance with the POSH Act namely the Sexual Harassment of Women at Workplace (Prevention, Prohibition and Redressal) Rules, 2013 ("POSH Rules"). ICC is a form of redressal mechanism setted up for immediate and effective solution to the victim. According to the rules of POSH one half members of the committee should be women. The committee is constituted with 4 minimum members, presided by a senior chairperson of a senior women employee. Further, it will not include less than two members from amongst the employees.

The framework of the committee requires that , the employer should involve members who are committed to the causes related to women or has experience in social work or legal knowledge in order to maintain the checks and balances against misuse and also includes a third party members being a social worker from NGO committed to the cause of women or familiar with the issues relating to sexual harassment. Every committee member is supposed to hold the membership for a tenure of three years from the date of nomination as per the rules. Moreover, every company that has Subsidy Company will form a separate ICC.

To implement the rules mentioned in the POSH act there is a proper procedure established:

- The POSH act has limited the time period of three months from the date of incident or if there are series of incidents then from the last date of the last incident, for the filing of the complaint.

- The POSH act has allowed extension of 3 months for filing of the complaint under some grave circumstances that prevented her to make the complaint:

1. Physical incapacity - her relative/friends/co-worker/officer of the State Women's Commission can file a complaint.

2. Mental incapacity - her relative Friend /qualified psychiatrist or psychologist/special educator can file complaint

3. Any other reason (Death of aggrieved - complaint may be filed by any person who has knowledge of the incident with the written consent of her legal heir

After a complaint is filed there is proper inquiry that takes place to collect information. The committee is required to complete the inquiry within a period of 90 days. Thereafter, a complete report of inquiry will be sent to the employer and within 60 days action to the report will take place. If a prima facie case exists then ICC should forward the complaint to the Police within the period of seven days under Section 509 of Indian Penal Code (Outrage of modesty) or any other relevant provision of IPC applicable under this.

- The Internal Committee has the same powers are vested in a civil court:

I. Summoning and enforcing attendance of any person and examining him/her on oath

II. Requiring the discovery and production of documents e.g. .call record

- ICC decision is binding on the company management
- Members can be asked to deposit before the High Court if required.
- Conciliation

I. The ICC can take steps to settle matters between the aggrieved women and the respondent however this option must be used only at the request of women with extreme caution

II. The act also provides that monetary settlement shall not be made a basis of conciliation.

A COMPARATIVE VIEW

In Australia, the Sex Discrimination Act 1984 states that the Employers can be held vicariously liable for acts of discrimination or harassment that occur in the workplace or in connection with a person's employment, provided the Employers prove that 'all reasonable steps' were taken to prevent or avoid the discrimination or harassment.

Stepping out of the traditional gender identities, in the United Kingdom, the Equality Act, 2010 prohibits harassment on the basis of sexual orientation.

Brazil enacted a criminal law in 2001 criminalising sexual harassment at workplace as against most countries where harassment is dealt under civil or quasi-criminal laws.

Denmark, Australia and Switzerland have sexual harassment laws which are applicable to men and women alike.

In view of the position of the sexual harassment laws in other countries it is pertinent to note that Sexual harassment faced by men often receives ridicule in India. Whatsoever, the increasing incidents of sexual harassment experienced by men require immediate attention. Additionally, sexual harassment faced by the LGBTQ at workplace remains unaddressed. The Act is gender biased in this sense; ignoring to address the sexual harassment faced by men and the LGBTQ, thereby not providing any remedy to these victims. Legislative intervention is henceforth necessary to enact a gender-neutral law prohibiting sexual harassment at workplace.

Furthermore, the law is not sensitive towards the different nature of 'workplace' in express terms. The definition of workplace is restrictive as it includes only the traditional concept, leaving a gap as regards the idea of 'work from home' and the possibility of cybercrimes. However, the judiciary has evolved the theory of notional extension of the workplace to fill in this gap.

Whether there can be 'Sexual Harassment' while working from home?

CASE- NOTIONAL EXTENSION OF WORKPLACE

The theory of notional extension is applied to cases under Workmen Compensation to ensure the applicability of the beneficial legislation to situations wherein the course of employment cannot be limited to the time or place of the specific work. *Saurashtra Salt Manufacturing Co. v. Bai Valu Raja & Ors.* was a case concerning Workmen Compensation, wherein the Hon'ble Supreme Court thus observed-

"As a rule, the employment of a workman does not commence until he has reached the place of employment and does not continue when he has left the place of employment, the journey to and from the place of employment being excluded. It is now well-settled, however, that this is subject to the theory of notional extension of the employer's premises so as to include an area which the workman passes and repasses in going to and in leaving the actual place of work. There may be some reasonable extension in both time and place and a workman may be regarded as in the course of his employment even though he had not reached or had left his employer's premises. The facts and circumstances of each case will have to be examined very carefully in order to determine whether the accident arose out of and in the course of the employment of a workman, keeping in view at all times this theory of notional extension."

This concept of notional extension of workplace was applied by the Hon'ble High Court of Delhi with respect to the definition of 'Workplace' under the Prevention of Sexual Harassment Act, 2013 in *Saurabh Kumar Mallick v. the Comptroller and Auditor General of India & Anr.* **Delhi High Court.**

FACTS- In this case a senior female officer filed a complaint of sexual harassment against her colleague for assaulting her in the mess where all the officers resided temporarily. The issue was whether the mess where the employees temporarily resided would fall within the definition of 'workplace', thereby calling upon the application of The Prevention of Sexual Harassment of Women at Workplace Act, 2013.

OBSERVATION- The Hon'ble High Court of Delhi observed that the word 'workplace' could not be given a restrictive meaning. Finding no merit in the contentions advanced on behalf of the petitioner the petition was dismissed. While coming at the said conclusion the Court observed-

"21. It is imperative to take into consideration the recent trend which has emerged with the advent of computer and internet technology and advancement of information technology. A person can interact or do business conferences with other people while sitting in some other country by means of video-conferencing. It is also becoming a trend that offices are run by certain CEOs from their residence. Obviously, members of the public would not have access to that place, though personal staff of such an officer would be present there. In a case like, this if such an officer indulges into an act of sexual harassment with an employee, say, his private secretary, it would not be open for him to say that he had not committed the act at 'workplace', but at his 'residence' and get away with the same. It is also a matter of common knowledge that in educational institutions, hostel accommodation is provided to students and teachers are also provided the residential flats. These may be within the vicinity of the college complex. An officer or teacher may work from the accommodation allotted to him. He would not be allowed to say that it is not a workplace. These are some of the illustrations which are given to bring home the point that we cannot accept the narrow definition of the expression 'workplace' as sought to be projected by the learned Counsel for the petitioner.

22. Once it is accepted that for achieving justice adapting to such changes is imperative, the question that arises is as to how these changes may be affected. No doubt, one method is to incorporate such changes through legislation. However, in the absence of legislation, as in the present case where the term 'workplace' is not defined, that would not mean that such changes are not to be judicially recognized and taken note of while defining such an expression. In the process one of the conceptual tinkering and use of equity are the accepted judicial methods. Sir Henry Maine propounded the classic thesis that what he called 'progressive societies' develop beyond the point at which 'static societies' stop through the use of fiction, equity and finally legislation. The judgment in the case of Vishaka (supra) itself is recognition of change through judicial method."

The Convention on the Elimination of All Forms of Discrimination against Women, 1979 (CEDAW) and sexual harassment at workplace

Sexual harassment can be translated as any unwelcomed behavior in the form of physical contact, forcefully showing pornography, sexually colored remarks or any other sexual demands extended by words or actions. Such behavioural conduct is considered to be humiliating and might affect the health and safety of the victim.

If objecting to such behavior poses the challenge of discrimination or disadvantage at workplace, it leads to the creation of a hostile working environment. Under CEDAW or 'Convention on the Elimination of All Forms of Discrimination Against Women' such gender-based violence is structured by inequality. CEDAW is an international treaty that was established with the aim of empowering women and establishing their rights. India is a party to CEDAW.

The sexual harassment at workplace has gained momentum in the global scenario and is contemplated as a form of gender-based violence against women. Any such act is considered to be in violation of the rights of a woman.

Lack of official data of work participation of women, loosens the idea of establishing safety norms for women at the workplace. However, upon analysing the ground reality, the need solid legislations to protect women from gendered discrimination and assaults becomes clearly eminent.

The employment of women in the informal sector widens the challenge to secure a workplace for women. The informal sector is not protected by laws and hence the women employed there are left vulnerable to abuse. Since the informal sector is out of the reach of legal jurisprudence, proactive measures should be established to ensure security of women in the informal sector.

CEDAW and the judgment of the Apex court protecting rights of women in the light of Sexual Harassment of Women at Workplace (Prevention, Prohibition and Redressal) Act, 2013 have laid the foundation of protection of women at workplace.

The Fashion industry is not limited to an office set-up where the incidents of sexual harassment can be reported with ease. The long chain of manufacturing and distributing the product makes it an arduous task to manage complaints related to sexual harassment.

Illustration

If company A procures cotton from a farmer B during the months of October-December, then it becomes extremely complex to determine whether B can be protected under POSH guidelines for the whole year, only from October-December, or whether he is completely out of the purview of POSH guidelines.

However, the Act provides that every district must also set up a legal complaints committee to receive complaints from workers of the informal sector, street vendors, construction workers, domestic workers, and people involved in weaving and other crafts among others. The victim has a three to six-month time period to file a complaint.

Although, in the words of a garment factory worker, there is often no one to listen to their plight whilst they are constantly abused and harassed at their workplace. The Union Federation leaders who received these anonymous letters from the garment factory workers expressed their concern over the fact that the women fear retaliation at the factory as well as their homes and therefore restraint themselves from filing a formal complaint.

In a utopian world, the structure of the POSH Act would fit with the grassroots level situation and grant justice to working women belonging to all sectors of the country. However, the reality is quite different from the outcomes that were expected while formulating the said Act.

Another major issue with the implementation of the Act is the severe lack of awareness among women belonging to the unorganized and informal sector. The managers and seniors can easily track down the complainant forcing them to endure a double-torture; one caused by the process of establishing the complaint of sexual harassment and the other caused by the behavior of seniors upon discovering that a complaint has been filed.

The employees are left with no choice but to remain silent in such situations. Furthermore, the horrors of the process of establishing the claims of sexual harassment compel the victim to normalize their torment. It is a common observation that sexual harassment victims have to go through a dual trauma of the harassment as well as the societal judgments and secondary victimization.

The Fashion industry needs to witness a revolution with regards to laws that prevent sexual harassment at the workplace. Employers must strive to create a positive workspace for the employees by ensuring that a brand-level grievance committee is set up. Such committees shall be accessible to the independent contractors and informal sectors workers that are remotely connected with the brand.

Regular awareness campaigns for women as well as men shall be conducted to ensure that women are aware of their rights in this regard and the men are enlightened to prevent the occurrence of such atrocities. It has become extremely essential to spread awareness about right and wrong behavior, the line between which has diminished over the period of time.

Lastly, the concept of bystander intervention shall be promoted in order to make sure that the employees stand for each other and eliminate sexual harassment from the workplace.

Importance of Bystander Intervention in offences related to Sexual Harassment

Bystander intervention is a strategy used as a precautionary measure to prevent rape, sexual assault, racist or homophobic nature among others. A bystander is defined as any person present in the setting where an offence is likely to happen. When such a person notices a troublesome situation, he shall immediately make attempts to settle down the situation and allow the matter to cool down. The bystander, in his personal capacity, takes the responsibility and intervenes, with the bona fide aim of preventing the escalation of such a situation.

The intervention of a bystander can prove to be life-threatening in nature. It might also become the cause of fights or confrontations. The term bystander intervention is synonymous with bystander education for the reason that it is structured upon the training of a group of people who then lead the training of others and the chain continues. It is basically the process of starting a forest fire in the right direction with the aim of spreading awareness among the people of society. It is meant to spread from one individual to another.

The bystander intervention doesn't permit an individual to infringe upon the privacy of others. Therefore, a bystander must be careful while analysing the situation and deciding whether or not to intervene. A small interaction between two individuals has the capacity to escalate into a heinous crime and therefore, evaluation of a situation is critically important in such matters.

A bystander shall intervene when:

- The behavior of a person seems inappropriate or coercive
- Offensive and degrading jokes or comments are being passed
- A person displays over-possessiveness, aggression, or extreme jealousy
- Acting inappropriately
- Intervention is also necessary when a situation gives the impression of danger or doesn't appear to stop itself

Illustration

A and B are college friends and go to a party together to celebrate A's birthday. A gets completely drunk and is out of her senses when B tries to take her to a private room or hotel. A bystander shall take necessary steps to intervene and prevent B from doing so.

5.7 Rights of Fashion Models

Since Elizabethen times, fashion was considered to be viewed from the definitive visions and archaic notions. Fashion has always tried to portray the sentiments of the public and sometimes brings afresh the new idea of the new generation(s). Earlier fashion houses were only limited to the female models to match the set norm of present standards of beauty. Plus-size models, male and LGBTQ+ models are only now considered to be the fashion icons in this industry.

As an initiative to be more inclusive and diverse in the fashion industry, British Fashion Council set up its *Diverse & Inclusion Steering Committee*. One of its primary aim was to:

1. Hear the diverse and often unrepresented voices,
2. and focus on the impact of black culture and other ethnic or minority communities' industries on the British fashion industry.

    Since then, there have been collaborations with Black, Asian and Minority Ethnic fashion communities to fight against the apparent discrimination in the industry.

Major Concerns Regarding Rights Of Models

Following are the major concerns that beg for rights of models in the fashion industry:

- The network of human trafficking disguised within some modelling agencies and scouts;
- Fake casting calls;
- Invasive backstage photography;
- Clicking pictures of models while they change behind the runway shows which end up on pornographic websites;
- Photoshop of their photos without their consent;
- Racial discrimination;
- Underage models who travel to a foreign country and work illegally without a proper wage or knowing exactly what kind of work they are going to do.

The above-mentioned concerns are reflective of violation of both human and fundamental rights of the models. The rights as mentioned and guaranteed in the Universal Declaration of Human Rights, the Declaration of the Rights of the Child, the Convention on the Rights of the Child, the European Convention on Human Rights, the European Social Charter or in several Constitutions are blatantly overlooked in case of models in the fashion industry.

Right to physical and psychological integrity, the prohibition of discrimination, the right to health, the right to education, the prohibition of a human being's exploitation or the right for each person to control the use of his or her image are some of such rights. Affirmation of such rights is crucial for the personal development of a model and is inherent to his/her human dignity.

Every workspace as per the government regulations must have a committee or a cell to address sexual harassment cases and this basic step is not incorporated in the fashion industry. The reason could be that this is not an organized sector with a definite office and the crew keeps changing from project to project. However, this doesn't stop the fashion houses to have their in-house sexual harassment redressal cells which overlook the models' concerns while they undertake a project of their fashion house. Rarely are the models given proper work conditions unless they are big faces in the industry. There is a need for definite rules which give basic amenities to models.

While sexual harassment is one major concern, the other is employing underage models. We often see creative advertisements with minors performing not just simple acts but sometimes the ads go extreme. It does not come as a surprise to see minors drop out of their schools and colleges to get into modelling for easy money. At such an age and with desperation to go ahead as they have left behind their education, they are at a vulnerable position both in terms of sexual exploitation and in terms of making them do almost everything and anything a designer and a photographer wishes.

As per several national legislations, the work of an underage model is subjected to authorization. For instance, The **New York** labour law states that a minor begins work, they should have a *Child Performer Permit*, issued by the *Department of Labour*, which would be valid only for a year, and, in addition to this, the modelling agency or fashion house must have a *Certificate of Eligibility*, valid for a minimum of 3 years, to be able to hire an underage model.

In **Portugal**, the modelling agency or the fashion house which organizes the runway show or the photoshoot must require an authorization from the *'Commission for the Protection of Children and Young People'* to be able to hire underage models. In case it is single participation on a runway show or photoshoot, that happens within 24 hours with a child who is at least 13 years old and has never worked as a model 180 days before the event, the casting agency or fashion house must communicate the participation of the child to the committee

In most of the countries with a huge fashion industry like India, there is no such legislation to protect the rights of minors and it is high time for that to happen.

In short, the fashion industry must have a strict *Code of Ethics* which regulates every workspace in the fashion industry.

While on the outside, the life of a model and the whole fashion industry as a whole looks glamorous and glittery, it is no guarantee that it is the same on the Inside. What attracts outsiders towards the industry is the portrayal of it, which is often filled with the latest fashion, impeccable makeup, and an elite lifestyle. However, there is a lot that goes on the inside that we're not aware of. From struggles to capture that one perfect photo, to unreasonable and unhealthy body standards, there is a lot a fashion model has to endure. There is no executive law in India that protects the models, however, there is a list of statutes that come together to give some relief.

EQUAL REMUNERATION ACT 1976

The objective behind The Equal Remuneration Act, 1976 was to provide for equal pay for the same amount of work done by men and women. It is no secret that there is a huge disparity between the pay given to men and women for the same amount of work. The act makes an attempt at eliminating this disparity by incorporating the concept of equity in pay, ensuring treatment of equal with equals and unequal with unequal. The act provides for equal pay for equal work. While it makes way for equal remuneration for both the genders in equal work, it does not override any special treatment provided to women in the country. Section 4 of the Equal Remuneration Act, 1976 provides that it is the duty of the employer to pay equal salaries to both men and women for the same work or work of similar nature. The issue of disparity in remuneration based on gender first came to light and gained prominence when it was recognized in the International Labour Organisation's constitution of 1919. It also subsequently made its way into the International Labour Organisation's Convention on Equal Remuneration 1951. Similar principles are found in Articles 14 and 15 of the Constitution of India.

When it comes to the gender pay gap, which plagues each and every industry in the nation, the fashion industry is one such industry where the situation seems to be reversed. In an industry heavily dominated by women, men in the industry lag behind women, in payment as well as representation. It has been reported that the ratio averages at around 1:3.

MATERNITY BENEFIT ACT 1961

The Act was enacted as a means to advance the welfare of women in the workforce while giving them space to embrace motherhood. The act provides for a 'maternity benefit' to be given to women, which includes payment of full wage during her absence from work owing to pregnancy, childbirth, and subsequent care of the child. It also protects women from being terminated from employment during the period of their absence because of pregnancy.

The Act mandates a maternity leave of a period of 26 weeks, for the first two children. Apart from that, a woman adopting a child under the age of 3 or the one who chooses surrogacy will qualify for a maternity leave of 12 weeks. Further, the Act also provides for availing a work-from-home facility to the mother whenever possible. Further, the 2017 amendment to the act had also introduced Creche facilities for working mothers. It states that along with other common facilities, creche facilities must be given permission for at least four visits a day to the creche. The facilities are to be set up either at the workplace site or nearby, within 500 meters of the neighbourhood of the workplace.

SEXUAL HARASSMENT AT WORKPLACE (PREVENTION, PROHIBITION, AND REDRESSAL) ACT, 2013

The purpose of the act was to provide for the creation of a safe working environment for females. Sexual harassment of working women in their workplace is a wrong happening in every industry. The fashion industry is one of the most susceptible to it. Instances of sexual harassment against fashion models have time and again cropped up in news. From lack of private changing rooms to models undergoing strict scrutiny of their bodies, and to comments and objectifying innuendos, models endure a plethora of hardships in terms of sexual harassment. What makes things worse is the fact that if they choose to raise their voices, they are conveniently side-lined and replaced by the ones who are ready to keep quiet and take it. Not only females, but male models have also complained of the rampant plague of sexual harassment in the fashion industry.

After 16 years of the Vishakha judgment and a constant back and forth, the Sexual Harassment of Women at Workplace (Prevention, Prohibition and Redressal) Act 2013 ("the Act") was enacted with the objective to provide protection against sexual harassment of women at workplace and provide a redressal mechanism for complaints of sexual harassment. As per the Act, sexual harassment is defined as *"unwelcome acts or behaviour (whether directly or by implication) namely, physical contact and advances, a demand or request for sexual favours, making sexually coloured remarks, showing pornography, any other unwelcome physical, verbal or non-verbal conduct of sexual nature"*. Further, in terms of redressal mechanism, the act provides for the setting of an Internal Complaints Committee at every office of the organization or institution, having more than 10 employees. In offices where the number of employees is less than 10, the Act provides for the setting up of Local Committee in every district by the District Officer.

INDECENT REPRESENTATION OF WOMEN (PROHIBITION) ACT, 1986

Fashion models are known to represent brands, designers, agencies, and even photographers. However, they have little or no autonomy over their representation. They are often objectified and showcased in an obscene, indecent manner through various platforms via media - leading to severe human rights violations. This Act ensures a regulatory framework that is inclusive of all forms of media and also imposes penalties in case of violation of the law - thus serving as a deterrent.

Section 2 (c) defines "indecent representation" of women as "the depiction in any manner of the figure of a woman, her form or body or any part thereof in such a way as to have the effect of being indecent, or derogatory to, or denigrating, women, or is likely to deprave, corrupt or injure the public morality or morals. It states that no person shall publish or cause to publish or cause to be published or arrange to take part in the publication or exhibition of any advertisement which contains indecent representation of women in any form." Section 4 prohibits the production, sale, hire, distribution, circulation, sending by post any books, pamphlets, slides, films, writing, drawing, painting, etc., which contain an indecent representation of women in any form.

However, the degree of indecency is subject to and intricately linked to the current values and standards of morality prevailing in a concerned society. Meaning, just like fashion trends, the terms of defining what's indecent and what's not are also ephemeral, owing to the continual evolution of societal values. Despite that, this Act deters media platforms from portraying fashion models indecently and curbs the circulation of obscene advertisements.

IMMORAL TRAFFIC (PREVENTION) ACT, 1956

Based on International Labour Organisation's estimate, at any given time in 2016, an estimated 40.3 million people were in modern slavery, including 24.9 million in forced labour. The fashion industry worldwide is infamous for commoditizing models and capitalizing on trafficking and prostitution.

The act aims to put an end to immoral trafficking and prostitution in India. It focuses on the prevention of trafficking, prosecution of traffickers, and Protection of victims. It contains provisions to punish those who engage in commercial sexual exploitation - which is rampant in the fashion industry. The punishments imposed under the act are varied and can be found in sections 3-9, 11, 18, 20, and 21. Offenses such as keeping and using premises as a brothel, pimping for prostitution, soliciting for prostitution are punished with fines and even rigorous punishments, depending upon the nature of the offence. It permits states to appoint Special Police Officers (SPOs) to deal with offences, set up protective homes, and establish courts for providing speedy trials (Ministry of Home Affairs, 2009).

Fashion Model's Rights In Other Countries

Other nations have started taking measures to protect the rights of models in the industry. There is a need to promote a healthy set of standards for models. From unrealistic body standards to sexual and physical harassment, models often go through a lot. Further, oftentimes, girls from a really young age are pushed into the field, unaware of their rights and not knowing what is good for them.

ISRAEL

Israel was the first country to enact legislation that aimed to prevent fashion models from losing weight to the detriment of their health, back in 2013. It prohibits the hiring of women and men for modelling jobs with a BMI of less than 18.5 . This law is also called the "photoshop law" because it has an additional regulation placed on advertisers requiring clear labelling on ads featuring digitally altered images of models.

However, the Knesset Research and Information Center of Israel found that the law, without any stringent punishments and deterrents, doesn't guarantee effective change. A lot more than harmless legislation is required to improve the conditions of models and protect their rights.

FRANCE

Popularly known as the 'fashion capital' of the World, France has never been off the news when it comes to Fashion. It is barely a surprise that the word "modelling" originates from the Middle French word "modelle". Fashion models across the globe chase the idea of working in Paris - a city that's perched on the pinnacle in the world of fashion since the 17th century.

Undoubtedly, models need to be exceptionally talented and hard-working to set foot in this city, but they are also expected to adhere to certain mortifying standards of the 'ideal' model body.

The former editor of Australian Vogue Kirstie Clements talked about aspiring models gaining aesthetic eligibility by becoming 'Paris thin' in order to thrive in their International careers. In the fashion industry, this is looked at as an achievement of some sort, to starve oneself and live off cigarettes and diet coke.

Kirstie mentioned that the top designer ateliers or workrooms in Paris choose 'fit' models and design their clothes around them. These fit models, in reality, deprive themselves of food to an extent where they become anorexic. Isabelle Caro, an anorexic French model, died at the tender age of 28. She weighed only 60 pounds at the time of her death.

Many, like Isabelle, are required to be deceptively fit in order to make it big in the fashion capital. They are appreciated for losing the extra kilos and then easily fit into the unrealistically small sample sizes created by designers. This incentivizes the models and pushes them to further lose more weight, thinking it would make them more desirable. Model agencies, designers, brands, magazine editors, and other powerful members of the fashion community are complicit in glorifying these toxic and unattainable body images for models.

In 2017, the French government published a law aimed specifically at the fashion industry. The law aims to "avoid the promotion of beauty ideals that are inaccessible and to prevent anorexia in young people," according to France's Minister of Social Affairs and Health Marisol Touraine.

Models are now required to have a medical certificate, valid for up to two years, confirming their general physical well-being and the fact they are not excessively underweight. According to the law, models need a doctor's note stating that their BMI (Body Mass Index) is well above 18.5 to prove their well-being, based on the World Health Organisation's classification that a person is underweight if their BMI is below 18.5. If a model's BMI falls below 18.5, they'll be classified as underweight and considered at risk for health problems. This aspect of the law faced severe backlash as the BMI cannot be considered an absolute indicator of an individual's overall health. It was also criticized for its complete disregard for naturally thin but healthy models.

Moreover, digitally altered photos will have to be marked *"photographie retouchée"*(English: retouched photograph). Employers violating the law could face fines up to 75,000 euros and up to 6 months in jail.

When it comes to its effectiveness, Paris-based attorney Céline Bondard says that it does not guarantee that such a law will, in fact, be enforced. Bondard says that she has not encountered any cases involving the law since it was enacted.

However, this law has been supplemented by voluntary charters adopted by Kering and LVMH (Moët Hennessy Louis Vuitton) . LVMH and Kering feel that they have a specific responsibility, as leaders in the industry, to go one step further with their brands. These two giants, in September 2017, came up with a charter that promises good working conditions to fashion models. It entails seven commitments, ranging from child models and their rights to protect the physical and mental health of models.

USA

Initiatives have been taken by the New York legislators to protect underage child models. Via the Child Performers Protection Act, 2015, child models working in the state of New York are covered under the New York Department of Labor (NYDOL). This protects the "print and runway models" under strict labour regulations to protect individuals under the age of 18.

In addition to the NYDOL, a non-union collective known by the name Model Alliance works constantly towards the protection and promotion of working rights of the models and was one of the major figures in the aforementioned law.

As per the law, the houses that are casting models below the age of 18 are mandated to obtain a certificate prior to engagement of the young age model. Apart from that, the fashion house is also required to maintain a carefully curated list of all the underage models that they have worked with, for the perusal of the Department of Labour in the event of an inquiry. In case of a violation, a penalty of $1000 is imposed in the first instance of offence, and for subsequent repetition of the offence, the penalty may extend up to $2000-3000.

Following is the checklist of compliances to be fulfilled by a fashion house in case of casing a model under the age of 18-

1. obtain a certificate of eligibility that permits the employment of a "child performer", duly issued by the NYDOL.

2. A notice about the employment of the child performer must be furnished at the NYDOL at least two days prior to each event, this includes, fittings, runways, photoshoots, etc.

3. ensure that the child model has a proper work permit and maintenance of the same throughout.

4. ensure strict compliance to the rules regarding working hours and breaks after every four hours of work

5. maintenance of a document evidencing model's trust account that holds 15 percent of their earnings.

When it comes to ensuring a healthy standard of body image, laws in the USA are still falling behind. While in countries such as Italy, France, Spain, models are required to meet a certain BMI, the law in the USA is still blind to this side of the industry. As per a new study by the *International Journal of Eating Disorders,* it was highlighted that out of all the models that were interviewed, 65 percent were asked to lose weight, either by someone in the industry or their agency itself. Further, a striking 81 percent of the women interviewed were under the category of "underweight" as per their BMI. The harsh reality of unhealthy body image and ugly eating disorders is not secret, it is high time that lawmakers in the USA pulled up their socks and took initiative regarding the same.

ITALY

When it comes to health and body standards, there is already a lot of backlash in the industry with regards to unrealistic body standards. While the industry has come a long way from enforcing size zero and skinny figures, there is still a long road ahead. Models have opened up about struggling with issues such as eating disorders and body image disorders. From following a "cotton ball diet" to eating nothing at all for days, models have gone to dangerous extents to conform themselves to these standards. Law can be a hugely helpful tool to protect these models.

Italy has followed countries like France, Spain, and Israel, in order to enforce a healthy body standard and ensure that a realistic and healthy image is being pushed forward. Models are required by law to meet a certain body image to ensure that they aren't dangerously thin. The modelling agencies that cast models under a BMI of 18 could face penal consequences. Further, models themselves are required to maintain a certain healthy BMI.

Way forward

Government of India have took a major step to define and identify gig workers under 'The Code on Social Security, 2020', where fashion models, photographers or artisans under contract can be identified. The Act provides:

- **Social security funds for unorganised workers, gig workers and platform workers**: The 2020 Code empowered the central government to set up social security funds for unorganised workers, gig workers and platform workers. The 2020 Code states that the central government *will* set up such a fund. Further, state governments will also set up and administer separate social security funds for unorganised workers. The 2020 Code also makes provisions for registration of all three categories of workers - unorganised workers, gig workers and platform workers.

- **National Social Security for gig workers and platform workers**: The Code provided for the establishment of a national and various state-level boards for administering schemes for unorganised sector workers. The Act states that in addition to unorganised workers, the National Social Security Board may also act as the Board for the purposes of welfare of gig workers and platform workers and can recommend and monitor schemes for gig workers and platform workers. In such cases, the Board will comprise of a different set of members including: (i) five representatives of aggregators, nominated by the central government, (ii) five representatives of gig workers and platform workers, nominated by the central government, (iii) Director General of the ESIC, and (iv) five representatives of state governments.

Chapter 6. Sustainable & Ethical Fashion

Sustainable and Ethical fashion is an approach towards sourcing, manufacturing and designing clothes which maximizes the benefits to the fashion industry and society at large, while at the same time minimizing its impact on the environment. The two concepts overlap in ideology, but they each have slightly different concerns, both equally critical to the future of fashion.

We love fashion as much as the next person: fun outfits, glamorous accessories, individuality… what's not to love?!

Well, devastating environmental damage and severe human rights abuses, to name a couple.

Fashion, as it turns out, is a whole lot more complex than pencil skirts and shoulder pads, and with all the greenwashing it certainly doesn't make it easy to find ethical and sustainable clothing.

While the road towards sustainability in general isn't easy, it's now critical that we all learn what qualifies as truly sustainable and ethical fashion. Let us understand in this chapter about these two terms 'Sustainable' and 'Ethical' fashion.

6.1 Sustainable Fashion

In recent times we hear the words sustainability and sustainable fashion quite a lot, but are we aware of what it means? With the increase in knowledge about climate change and global warming, consumers have become more aware of what impacts the ecosystem as a whole. The fashion industry is a huge contributor to this impact and therefore, with changing times there is a need for fashion enthusiasts to make an effort towards making fashion more sustainable. But is this what sustainable fashion is? This is just the tip of the iceberg.

The knowledge of sustainable fashion has developed in a few recent decades as a part of modern environmental issues. Right from production to consumption of the product, there are aspects for which we as people are responsible, to help the uplifting of sustainable fashion. To make fashion more sustainable we need to re-think and revamp the entire system and we need to take action towards it.

Somethings that we as consumers need to ask ourselves before we buy any product

1. Would I want it even after 24 hrs from now?
2. How long will the product last?
3. What is it majorly made of?
4. Will I wear and re-wear it, till it is no longer wearable?

By asking these questions to ourselves we can make a rational decision and create an impact. It is not about a few people thinking about all four questions and making a decision but millions of people at least thinking about two of these questions and making a decision. If people start thinking in terms of these questions there can be a tremendous change in the mindset of the consumers and this will promote the companies to work towards sustainable fashion.

One of the biggest threats to our planet is 'fast fashion ', clothes that are cheap, accessible, and trendy causing unsustainable fashion. Due to the high and fast demand for such clothes they are produced on a large scale which causes a massive impact on the environment. Due to new trends and constant change in fashion, fast-fashion chains like Zara, H&M, etc, release a continuous series of collections and products. It reduces the utility of clothes merely to a particular period or a season resulting in fast fashion brands making 10-12 collections a year. These products are made of harmful fibres and not natural fibres. People buy such products frequently and constantly due to which the landfills are filling up. Laborers in such factories face bad working conditions and work on extremely poor wages as these fast fashion brands set up their factories in poor and underdeveloped countries causing a backlash to the country and on a larger picture it puts a brake on the growth of the world as a whole. The cycle of fast fashion is distant from the concept of sustainability as it reduces natural resources at a rapid rate, exploits laborers around the world, and causes a huge amount of waste.

"Regardless of what your background is, we can all agree on some really basic things—no one should die to make a T-shirt, and we shouldn't be pouring toxins into our planet."

Sustainable fashion is a term created for the type of products that quite literally can be consumed and sustained in a way that will protect the environment and the people making these products. Cutting emission of harmful gases, producing enough products, reducing pollution and minimizing waste, ensuring that the laborers are paid fair wages in safe working conditions are critical aspects to the notion of Sustainable Fashion.

Just because a product is labelled as 'sustainable' isn't enough; is the product sustainable? Many brands believe sustainable fashion is clothes made from recycled fabrics and term such products as sustainable, but such recycling of products cause almost equal amounts of emission of harmful chemicals and harm the environment.

The thought of moving towards sustainable fashion and leaving behind the old habits of shopping seems to be a scary thought for many. Moving to sustainable fashion means having limited options and might seem to be a tad bit heavy on the pocket at first but in the long run, it will be worth it. Livia Firth, the co-founder and creative director of Eco-Age, along with her team came up with a 10 step solution named "Make every step count" to help and navigate fashion followers to challenge misconceptions, re-engage and make a difference. It seems overwhelming but our simple act of getting dressed daily causes global issues such as climate crisis and low wage labor.

'To see the change, be the change'

When every person makes a conscious effort to make their wardrobe sustainable we make a difference. By following a few notions given by the experts in the field on rethinking our shopping habits and consumption of the product we can take a step forward.

1. Re wear Forever

   We need to stay away from pieces that are statement one-time wear dresses and instead invest in garments with a long life that can be worn again and again. Pick more versatile pieces which can be styled in different ways and not something that has limited usage. When you buy a garment, think about how many times are you going to wear it, do you see yourself wearing that particular garment 10 years down the line? You will be astonished to know the number of times you don't buy any garments.

2. Have adequate information

   It is important to know what we buy and from where we buy. Understand the brand and their process before actually purchasing. Many brands come forward to tell their story, make sure the story you know is authentic and flaunt your look.

3. Opt for multi-seasonal clothes

   Try to have a wardrobe in which the clothes can be worn around the year such as denim, tops, timeless jackets, and coats. Do not invest in season particular clothes as their usage is low and cannot be re-worn for a long time.

4. Donate your extras

   Keep only the ones which you know you can wear or you would wear. The garments which no longer fit you or for any reason wouldn't be worn by you can be donated. Always make sure to have a one-in-one out system. When you buy one you donate one.

5. Treasure your vintage and second hands

   The most interesting thing about vintage clothing is that it would last forever no matter how much they have been used. The best ones are the ones which are of our parents or grandparents, some garments which have been handed down.

6. Take proper care

   This is a very crucial aspect to make sure your clothes are sustainable and live longer. Keep the clothes in a proper wardrobe, keep them clean. Go the extra mile to ensure you can use them till the end.

7. Always choose quality over quantity

   Make sure to read the labels before purchasing. Know what you are buying and what the quality of the garments is. Quality garments will last longer and cause less effect on the environment. Buy a few pieces, but buy quality pieces.

8. Customize every garment

Instead of buying fast fashion fast, readymade garments find good tailors in your locality and make customized and unique clothes for yourself. This will help prevent overproduction and give the local workers a chance to earn a better living.

9.   Borrowing, sharing and Renting

Many of us get bored and tired of wearing the same clothes over and over again so instead of throwing them away you can exchange them or borrow garments from your siblings or friends in this way you can expand your wardrobe and you get to experiment with new styles and trends. Sometimes when you want to try something out of the box or when you need garments for particular occasions renting is always the best solution, as it serves the purpose and also saves money and unnecessary buying.

10.   Change your attitude

When we speak of change we must make sure we are the first ones to act upon it. When we talk about sustainability we need to question our thoughts, our habits, and our perspective towards it. We need to make the small changes that we have always spoken about. Making sustainable fashion sustainable is in our hands and we need to make sure to do our bit and help save the planet.

"I don't think that 'eco' should be a word that immediately conjures up images of oatmeal-colored garments or garments that are oversized or lacking in any sort of luxury or beauty or detailing or desirability," says Stella McCartney. "I don't think that things have to look ugly because they're organic; why can't they be beautiful as well? You can't ask a consumer to compromise. I don't think you can say, 'Here is this jacket that looks terrible but it's organic, and here is a really beautiful jacket that's cheaper but don't buy it because it's not organic.'

As the industry is still growing and evolving around the concept of sustainable fashion and how to elevate the environmental and social standards, we must stand by them and do our part in making the fashion industry more sustainable and making sustainable fashion the new thing which will be followed in the coming time.

Laws Applicable

I.Sustainable laws in Fashion Industry

The legal and regulatory landscape of the fashion and textiles sector is evolving as a result of a greater focus on sustainability and environmental stewardship posing new problems for textile and garment makers, distributors, and retailers. The various participants in a fashion industry need to understand the issues to navigate sustainability throughout their supply chain. To successfully identify applicable environmental standards, regulations, and requirements as well as follow changes as they occur, it is essential to know the materials utilized in your merchandise and the intricacies of your production process. With its large ecological impact, the fashion and textiles industry, in particular, requires a thorough grasp of manufacturing operations and accompanying policies and procedures to assure compliance and reduce environmental enforcement risk.

A.   Products used in the manufacturing & construction of merchandise

Textile makers must have a solid understanding of the materials utilized in their merchandise' design and production. Textile makers, importers, and consumers who use or sell articles containing particular elements or chemicals are subject to chemical composition rules and regulations, responsible sourcing standards, and recycled content mandates. The European Union (EU), for example, has put restrictions on the chemicals that can be used in textiles. The EU's primary chemical regulation, the Registration, Evaluation, Authorization and Restriction of Chemicals (REACH) law, curtails the use of phosphates, phosphinoxides, biphenyls, and other chemicals in the expansion of textile articles, with legal restrictions for toxins that come into contact with the skin. With some exceptions, EU REACH also prohibits the use of the commercially used perfluorooctanoic acid (PFOA) chemical and its salts in goods.

In addition, conflict mineral disclosure standards exist in the United States (US) and the European Union (EU) for some minerals used by the fashion market in finishing details, decorations, and jewellery, such as gold, diamonds, and mica. In addition to these limitations, recycled content rules and labelling requirements are becoming more frequent in the United States and around the world.

B.   Eliminate supply chain risks by conducting active monitoring

Regulators in the United States and around the world are increasingly focused on responsible sourcing. For example, alleged human rights violations in China's Xinjiang Uyghur Autonomous Region (XUAR) sparked regulatory action against products imported into the United States lately. On humanitarian principles, the US Customs and Border Protection agency issued Withhold Release

Orders for a variety of items coming from the XUAR, including cotton and cotton products, preventing their clearance from US ports.

To address human rights violations inside supply chains, some countries have implemented or are seriously considering due diligence and modern slavery regulations. As a result, firms with complicated supply chains must do proper research to eliminate possible risks related to human rights and modern slavery. Companies can also use this due diligence to offer information to authorities in the event that they take disciplinary action.

C. Follow the advancement of environmental standards in all jurisdictions where the company does business

Ecological laws and regulations differ significantly between countries and even within nations. Understanding the environmental legal systems in the nations and regions where you operate is crucial for reducing risk exposure. Furthermore, as the world's attention turns to climate change and sustainability, many national governments are enacting or considering new domestic environmental laws and regulations, as well as international treaty obligations.

Emerging fields such as per- and polyfluoroalkyl substances (PFAS), advanced recycling, microplastics, and microfibers are all expected to see new environmental rules and regulations in the immediate future. To lessen the possibility of being prosecuted, it's critical to study the environmental laws and regulations that affect your operations in major countries on a regular basis and to be proactive in adapting to any changes.

D. Meet the Additional Producer Responsibility criteria if applicable

A number of states have proposed new Extended Producer Responsibility (EPR) legislation for plastic packaging, which has ramifications for the fashion and textile industries. California, Hawaii, New York, Oregon, and Washington have all considered packaging-related EPR legislation. The Oregon Senate, for example, introduced a bill to reform the state's recycling system by, among several other things, boosting product liability and compelling companies to pay a fee for any covered product they sell in Oregon.

As several states explore EPR legislation, it's critical to know the scope of the law and policies in each jurisdiction where your organization does business. Textile disposal rules, such as France's Anti-Waste law, which prohibits enterprises from discarding existing stock such as garments, shoes, and other products, could also affect companies with worldwide operations.

E. <u>Assess Green Marketing Rule Compliance in Eco-Friendly Marketing Campaigns</u>

Corporations that want to make green claims about their commodities need to assure that the claims are legitimate and backed up by evidence. The Federal Trade Commission (FTC), in the USA has filed a lawsuit against textile producers and distributors for making deceitful statements about their products' environmental impact, which are in violation of the FTC Green Guides, which explain how the FTC interprets green marketing rules. The FTC and the US Department of Agriculture, for example, scrutinize claims regarding a textile's biodegradability, recyclability, and organic nature, with significant penalties for inaccurate or misleading statements.

To make an unequivocal sustainable claim in the United States, for example, companies must be able to demonstrate that the product portfolio or packaging will totally degrade and return to nature within a reasonable amount of time after normal disposal. One year is the FTC's definition of a reasonable amount of time. Manufacturers must have credible empirical proof that all materials in the product or packaging will break down into or become a component of usable manure safely and in about the same time as the materials with which it is composted in order to make biodegradable claims.

II. **Rules and Resolutions to Change the Future of Fashion – Enhancing Sustainability**

A. **UNITED KINGDOM**

According to experts, the fashion business accounts for 4% of yearly worldwide carbon emissions, while textile production produces carbon pollution equal to those of France, Germany, and the United Kingdom combined. The government of the United Kingdom has announced initiatives to minimize waste in a variety of areas. Proposals for measures to increase action on fast fashion production and hold manufacturers accountable for textile waste are among these suggestions. The initiatives are part of a new wide-ranging Waste Prevention Programme for England (2021), which outlines how the industry and government can work together to eliminate pollution and work towards a more resource-efficient economy in seven key sectors: construction, textile industries, furniture, electrical products, commercial vehicles, manufacturing process, plastic containers, and single-use items; and food.

The government will consult participants on textile possibilities by the end of 2022, based on the Resources and Waste Strategy. For example, its Extended Producer Responsibility plan, which is backed up by steps to stimulate effective version and labelling, would ensure that the sector contributes to the costs of recycling. This will aid in the remanufacturing of textiles, as well as lowering the industry's ecological consequences.

Further, Environment Audit Committee in its February 2021 Report, stated that it will continue its investigation into Fixing Fashion: Clothing Consumption and Sustainability, which began in 2018. Given the ongoing worries about the fashion industry's environmental effect and labour conditions in UK garment manufacturers, the Committee has decided to revisit the subject to track progress. Most of the Committee's proposals were rejected by the government in 2019, ranging from a producer's responsibility to enhance textile collection by giving due diligence on recycling across fashion supply chains to ferret out forced or child labour. Textile waste, on the other hand, has been highlighted as a priority area for the government's Resources and Waste Strategy.

Fast fashion also contributes to waste in the United Kingdom and other developing nations. Every year, British consumers buy more new garments than consumers of any other Eu nation and discard over a million tons of apparel. Although two-thirds of clothing is given or collected for resale or low-quality recycling, around 336,000 tons of textile is discarded in home trash for landfills. The Covid-19 outbreak has shone a spotlight on Leicester's garment industry. Inadequate working conditions have been reported, implying that little has changed since the Committee's report, which suggested frequent audits and firms engaging with unions for their employees.

FRANCE

President Emmanuel Macron in 2019 gave François-Henri Pinault, Chairman and Chief Executive Officer of Kering, a mission to pull together the leading players in fashion and textile and minimize the sector's effect on the environment. Global warming, ecology, and oceans are all addressed in this agreement. The 32 clothing and textile companies that signed the accord each participate in their own way to create the sector more sustainable, but their aggregate impact will be considerably greater. Stopping climate change (zero greenhouse gas emissions by 2050), restoring natural habitats and protecting species, and eradicating single-use plastics from our oceans while lowering the industry's harmful impact are the three goals. ADIDAS, Armani, H&M, Selfridges, and Stella McCartney are among the 32 brands.

From 2021, unsold apparel in France is now prohibited from being destroyed or thrown away according to a new French law. The *Project de loi relatif à la lutte contre le gaspillage et à l'économie circulaire* or Bill on the battle against waste and the circular economy means that French businesses can now expect to follow the government's guidelines for more than 100 sustainable inputs. The law requires manufacturers, importers, and sellers, including e-commerce platforms like Amazon, to donate unsold non-food commodities and save those that pose a health or safety risk. Under the polluter pays clause, businesses will be required to pay for the elimination of garbage they generate, affecting everything from tobacco industries to the fashion sector and more.

C. USA

In the United States, there are already rules designed to safeguard consumers and decrease waste in the textile sector. There are now rules in place to reduce factory environmental consequences, as well as water treatment plants that keep pollutants out of drinking water supplies. For example, tax deductions are available for clothing donations to charitable organizations in the United States. This incentivizes the general population to donate unwanted clothing in exchange for rewards. To recycle fabrics and limit the amount of clothes that end up in landfills, donated items are resold to low-income populations in other nations. The Trans-America Trading Company is the largest organization in the United States that promotes sustainability. Textiles are manually divided into 300 different categories based on item, size, and fibre composition.

D. SWEDEN

Sweden has long been the world leader in terms of sustainability, making it a smart and sustainable country. They imposed a chemical tax on devices in 2017, and towards the end of 2019, they indicated that they would impose a chemical tax on clothing. This tax will not only safeguard workers and consumers from health dangers, but it will also preserve the environment. Other countries have begun to follow Sweden's lead, although there is still dispute about whether it is the consumer perspective that needs to evolve in order for change to occur. According to the Swedish Fashion Council, consumer attitudes have shifted, but if sustainable items are difficult to get, consumers will be unable to actively modify their habits.

III.   Application and Practice of Laws and Standards Relating to Sustainability

A garment was once produced and sold within a 20-mile radius of where the materials used to make it were produced, but as transport infrastructure and economies globalized, the industry became increasingly diverse, with endless supply chains and manufacturing methods, all with completely unstandardized practices. Several fast-fashion businesses manufacture their products with a single purpose in mind - maximum revenue, which almost invariably requires manufacturing in developing nations with neither the means nor the motivation to govern environmental effect. Vietnam and Bangladesh for instance lack the organizational mechanisms to hold fashion brands accountable for emissions, and even if they did, it's unlikely that they'd be successful; these sectors survive because they can lower manufacturing costs in wealthy countries. Increasing regulation would need costly reorganization, which would entirely undermine that one purpose i.e., maximum profit.

The Resource Conservation and Recovery Act (RCRA) was passed in 1976 in the United States, imposing penalties and fines for dumping excessive chemicals and garbage into nearby rivers and lakes. These regulations lead to the decline of harmful chemicals and pollutants in water bodies in the US. However, the solution to these US imposed restrictions is to shift production to developing countries, causing havoc on their environment and people, which has only lately attracted recognition in the last few years as a result of the humongous Bangladesh factory collapse, which killed 1,100 people and injured 2,000 others.

In 2017, the Organization for Economic Cooperation and Development (OECD), which was founded in 1961, developed a common instruction on companies' due diligence requirements for their supply chain in terms of child slavery, slave labor, workers' salaries, and union contracts. While the recommendation is not legally obligatory, it has been ratified by OECD member states, and businesses in this field are expected to follow it. Similarly, the Sustainable Garment Coalition (SAC) was founded in 2009 with the goal of creating a framework for an environmentally sustainable apparel industry. It has over 200 global members and created the HIGG index, which allows businesses to self-assess and monitor sustainable development across their supply chains.

In 2019, the UN Environment Assembly launched the United Nations Alliance for Sustainable Fashion, to halt the environmentally destructive practices involved in the fashion industry and make efforts to harness the industry to improve the world's ecosystems. The United Nations Alliance for Sustainable Fashion is a collaboration of UN agencies and other partners aimed at helping to attain the objective of Sustainable Development through concerted action in the fashion industry. The Alliance strives to promote programs and policies that ensure that the fashion value chain contributes to the fulfilment of the Sustainable Development Goals' targets, as well as to assist collaboration across UN entities working in fashion. Sustainability involves both social responsibilities, such as improving working conditions and remuneration for workers, as well as ecological issues, such as reducing the industry's waste stream, reducing water contamination, and mitigating climate change. The UN pledges to change the direction of fashion, decreasing its adverse environmental and health implications, and transforming fashion into a driver of the Sustainable Development Goals' implementation through the Alliance.

Way Forward

The fashion world has definitely reached a point where change is absolutely necessary and something that has become inevitable. Pushing towards a greener future to help the planet flourish shall be a mantra that should be followed. Sustainability in fashion is very important as it gives people a way to express and enjoy fashion without causing any harm.

Due to the awareness among consumers, fashion houses have now started maintaining a lot more transparency around their materials and supply chains so that consumers know exactly what they are buying and not causing harm to the environment in any way.

Demand for Sustainable fashion has increased in the past few years because of aware and thoughtful consumers. The percentage of sustainable consumers has increased quite a lot in the past few years especially with the young generation understanding the harmful way fast fashion companies affect the environment.

The consumer demand for sustainable fashion is so powerful that fashion brands have now started researching and making sustainable clothes.

Sustainable Fashion has become a priority in the fashion industry due to climate crisis and also because of sustainably aware consumers but Sustainable fashion requires advanced technology and hence it is expensive and cannot be produced in bulk which acts as a hurdle in the process and needs to be attended to at the earliest. The number of aspects involved in the problem of fashion sustainability makes it difficult to get a grip on. The rational model of consumption considers a consumer to consume according to his needs and ability to spend by making calculative judgments taking into consideration the best result in the aspects of cost, benefits, and the effect on the environment. The psychology of a human being is considered to be self-oriented, decisions especially related to fashion are made majorly by excitement and pleasure which is hard to resist. For many consumers, shopping is just a matter of pleasure and excitement and they shop just because they wish to do so. The need of consumers to possess more and more is hard to change. The desire for new clothes is something that will never change and hence fashion brands try to use modern technology while designing their products that can be easily recycled, upscaled, and don't cause any harm.

Wearing sustainable fashion does not mean you have to wear out of style or boring-looking clothes. The whole point of sustainable fashion is to use the same innovation and creativity but change the fabrics that they use to make clothes that are sustainable yet super fashionable and in style. Currently, the fashion industry is making constant but moderate efforts to make fashion more sustainable and have a lasting impact on society. Many ways have been undertaken by brands and consumers to be more sustainable. Brands have started in-house recycling of old products, sustainability has become an eye-catching marketing technique for fashion brands in times when consumers have become more educated about sustainable fashion.

Brands should aim at setting up new systems and technology to design products that can be made of less harmful chemicals by using creativity and innovations. With the new upcoming technologies and innovations, there has been the introduction of new fabrics such as eco-friendly rubber from algae, mushroom leather, pineapple leaves the leather, wool from coconut husk, bacteria-based dyes, etc. Such innovations help to make more usable fabrics by creating less damage to the environment. By cleaning the fashion supply chain we can reduce a significant amount of pollution around various communities around the globe.

Humans have always used fashion as a way to express themselves so the biggest challenge fashion brands have to face is still providing enough designs for people to be able to express themselves without compromising on the environment. Today due to the consciousness and awareness around sustainable fashion consumers demand fashionable and eco-friendly garments and few brands have worked their way up towards creating something on such lines. It is a great start but there is a long way to go. To a few big and small brands have taken up some great initiatives such as-

Levi's – being a brand majorly in the production of denim they have managed to use 96% less water in their new collection. They have committed themselves towards creating sustainable fashion and would adopt the usage of 100% sustainably sourced cotton and recycle old denim.

H&M Conscious- H&M being a fast-fashion brand is trying to move away from that by their conscious collection which has products made from organic cotton and recycled polyester. By taking this step towards sustainability H&M is trying to reduce the environmental footprint they create. They aim to be sustainable by the year 2030.

Swarovski- is a well-renowned jewellery brand that has aimed at creating sustainable fashion. In a letter of address from the historic brand's CEO Robert Buchbauer, the company revealed its: 'six key commitment focuses: greenhouse gas emissions, conscious materials, empowerment and education, waste and circular economy, equality, diversity and inclusion, and of course respect for our people.'

There are other brands such as TenTree, Everlance, Patagonia, Eileen Fisher, etc. who have been making efforts to move away from fast fashion to more eco-friendly options and creating an impact on the industry. This is just a small drop in the ocean but slowly and steadily with the need of time, more brands have been moving forward towards sustainability.

Instead of making people feel bad for wearing fast fashion or ethically correcting them, it is important to make them aware of the harmful effects that fast fashion has on the environment. Most people still wear fast fashion brands because they are not aware of the available options. After all, these options often don't get the recognition or attention. As many consumers are becoming aware of sustainable fashion and demand for it there is a segment of people who have no clue or very little clue about this. It is important for brands and influencing people like fashion bloggers and actors who influence people into buying new and trendy clothes to educate and spread awareness towards sustainable fashion. The percentage of sustainable consumers has increased quite a lot in the past few years especially with the young generation understanding the harmful way fast fashion companies affect the world.

Creating a path and moving forward to achieving the goal with the help of the right channels.
The consumer has great power and if educated properly they along with the brands can create a huge impact. Consumers shall be more thoughtful and rational while buying and think of every purchase as an investment, rather than impulsive buying and wasting of money and resources. By asking the right questions regarding the fabrics used to make clothes, who made the clothes, where were the materials obtained from, and asking for transparency from brands, the brands will be compelled to give answers and if they do not have answers they can work towards that Consumers can shift from fast fashion and opt for slow fashion, which means they can go to independent designers or tailors who will make limited and necessary products which eventually will reduce the carbon footprint.

One part of sustainable fashion is called thrifting.
Thrifting means you thrift/ buy pre-loved clothes in perfectly good condition from other people and wear it. The other part of sustainable fashion is making clothes from products that do not affect the climate and do not underpay the laborers. Thrifting has become a rage among the young generation as it is cheap and affordable along with no adverse effect on the environment.
The most sustainable clothes are the ones that are hanging in your wardrobe. Using your wardrobe most effectively is an excellent step towards sustainability, try to create new trends and mix-matching your pre-existing clothes. Make sure to keep the clothes in good condition which will increase the life of the garment.
Laws such as 'The Bribery Act 2010 (UK)', Grenelle II regulation (France), REACH regulation(EU), Transparency in supply chain act(California, US), Government of India launched a soil health and management scheme to promote sustainable agriculture which in turn promotes organic fibres, keep a track on the supply chain, payments to workers, carbon footprints, risks posed by chemicals, etc. These are just a few of the laws and regulations which people and brands are bound to comply with, but most of all it is important to have an intent to work ethically. Moving forward towards making the Fashion industry sustainable along with a few laws scattered here and there which are just local solutions, there need to be few laws that need to be set in motion globally

to guarantee the working towards saving the planet. The global nature of the fashion industry needs the co-operation of the world to come together to face the problems.

Consumers and brands together must be motivated to move towards sustainability, in the aspects of the attitude of the consumers and the supply and manufacturing chain of the brands. Along with this, a few laws shall be enforced on a global level, all these efforts taken together will help the world achieve Sustainable fashion effectively.

6.2 ETHICAL FASHION

The Fast Fashion industry has taken the world by storm with its promise of endless trends, accessibility, low prices, and convenience that come with it. In the last few years, we have been accustomed to seeing new designs of clothing being pumped out every week, all with the click of a mouse. More and more, we are building homes with bedroom-sized wardrobes and consuming "disposable" clothing at a rate never seen before. "**Ethical Fashion**" is the only remedy to this Fast Fashion world which has become a social as well as an environmental crisis.

The idea of Ethical Fashion is on the ascent, but why bother and what is the significance here? As a result, various people define Ethical Fashion in different ways. We all have various ethics and beliefs that we resonate with.

*"**Ethical Fashion is defined as** fashion that strives to have minimal negative impact on the environment, animals and people. Clothing production includes design, manpower and inputs. Every step of the journey, from seeds to clothes, Ethical Fashion is respectful to the world and people."*

There is a slight difference between Ethical Fashion and Sustainable Fashion. Unlike Sustainable Fashion, Ethical Fashion focuses on the social impact of the fashion business: ethical actually means "**morally right**". 'Ethical' and 'Sustainable' are progressively becoming as essential to shoppers as are the style and price of the outfits.

TRADITIONAL PRACTICES

Ecological and social welfare are protected by Ethical Fashion, which requires a reasonable use of natural resources. The established traditional practices of tying, dyeing and weaving exquisite textiles and drapes give a solid framework for the production and acquisition of sustainable raw materials of all kinds. These geographically-designated processes and goods, such as Lucknow chikankari or Kotpad handloom or Mysore silk or Orissa ikat, can be purchased from authorised sources.

In addition, a large number of highly skilled young adults and a robust infrastructure make the area ideal for supporting the production and supply of raw materials and the final product. Khadi and ittar/attar (essential oils) are well-known ethical products to Indian consumers, who utilise them on a regular basis. A global awareness of Ethical Fashion has led to the introduction of high-end and creative sustainable items into the Indian market by established and emerging brands.

MATERIALS:

It's not difficult to take a gander at a dress in your closet and not consider how it got there. Our clothes don't start life looking anything like the ones we wear on our bodies.

Each fabric like Cotton, Denim, Linen, Polyester has a varied influence on the earth and its people, and Ethical Fashion is all about choosing the fabrics that have the least impact on the environment. Workers who generate the material, such as those who harvest cotton crops, are compensated fairly in the Ethical Fashion process. When the statistics like the suicide of 2,50,000 cotton farmers in the last 15 years are brought to our attention, Ethical Fashion becomes a necessity and not just a priority. This is when we start to think about the scope of the problem and the implications of consumer decisions.

DYES:

The colour of the rivers in China is said to reveal the popular colour of the season. Strange, right? In the Fast Fashion industry, clothing is dyed with chemicals to give it that ideal shade the influencers tell us is "on trend."

The drinking and bathing water of adjacent villages is contaminated when factories fail to properly contain and manage their waste. The consequences of reckless dye use include stillbirths, mutations, and other life-altering diseases, as well as the loss of plant life and ecosystems. Ethical Fashion, on the other hand, focuses on using closed loop systems, natural or recycling dyes, or not changing the colour at all.

The cost of conventional colours and methods to humans and the environment is simply not worth it, and brands that follow Ethical Fashion principles fully acknowledge this.

LABOUR:

1 in 6 individuals worldwide are employed in the fashion sector, and the majority of them make less than $3 a day on average. In addition, to being mistreated and underpaid, the working conditions of growers, producers, makers, manufacturers, packers, and sellers are horrendous. Workers in apparel industries do not have access to clean drinking water, frequent breaks, comfortable workplaces, or fundamental human rights because they labour in facilities without these amenities. However, the Rana Plaza disaster in 2013 pushed the world to acknowledge the fashion industry's cruelty, but the issues persist years later.

DIRTY SECRETS OF TEXTILE INDUSTRY:

Do you really know about the origins of the fabric? Cotton, for an instance, is heavily reliant on chemical pesticides and requires a large quantity of water to cultivate and harvest. It is also worth noting that, at a time when shoppers are more aware of the zeitgeist's watchwords, such as "**ethical**" and "**sustainable**," sales of organic cotton have actually declined.

The following are the top most significant ethical concerns in the fashion industry, notably in the apparel manufacturing sector:

#1: HUMAN RIGHTS VIOLATION

Let's start with a problem that most of us are aware of in one way or another. Specifically, millions of people's working conditions. According to the Fair Fashion Center, the global apparel business affects 150 million people every day. The majority of these individuals do not get a decent wage and work in deplorable conditions. To cite a few of the ethical transgressions:

- Unlivable pay
- child labour
- physical and verbal abuse
- modern slavery
- hazardous working conditions
- migrant exploitation
- gender discrimination (the bulk of these workers are young females)
- extra working hours

#2: LACK OF TRANSPARENCY AND COMPLEX SUPPLY CHAINS

Because it's so difficult to have complete visibility over all components of the supply chain, every business that creates anything has contributed to modern slavery in some way. The process of making a single garment is extremely long and complicated, with numerous manual modifications along the way. A seed-to-shelf supply chain essentially entails the following steps:

- Obtaining raw ingredients for all of the fabrics involved

- Raw materials are spun into fibre

- Fabric is made by transforming fibre

- Preparing and dyeing fabrics

- Design

- Garment production (extras like thread, buttons, and zippers)

- Adding the finishing touches like adding tags, etc.

- Ship to consumers and sellers all over the world

All of this is subject to change with each season, so each brand isn't always dealing with the same set of suppliers.

#3: WATER WASTE & WATER POLLUTION:

Fashion is also the world's second greatest water consumer, consuming between 7 to 9 trillion litres every year. Cotton is an extremely thirsty crop; one pair of jeans requires about 2000 gallons of water.

But, after all, isn't there enough water in the world? Not so much, to be honest. Cotton farming is already doing havoc on the environment.

#4: CHEMICAL USE IN FASHION PRODUCTION

When we think about pollution, we see carbon-emitting factories, gas-pumping oil refineries, and other noxious images. The fashion industry is not something that comes to mind. Nonetheless, the fashion sector has been identified as one of the most environmentally destructive sectors.

Cotton is used in about half of all textiles. Being the dirtiest crop, cotton needs the highest amount of chemicals: 25% of the world's insecticides and 18% of the world's pesticides when cultivated conventionally. Even a typical T-shirt is cultivated with an average of 17 teaspoons of chemical pesticides and fertilisers. Toxic chemicals are not only employed in the production of fibres, but they are also found in the dyeing and processing of textiles. Heavy metals (such as nickel, lead, and chromium), phthalates (known carcinogens), and formaldehyde are among these substances.

These chemicals are hazardous not just to growers and producers, but also to us, the consumers. Certainly, fashion cannot merit the cost of wearing formaldehyde.

BEWARE OF GREENWASHING IN "ETHICAL" FASHION:

Brands can claim to be doing something exceptional when in reality they are just conforming to fundamental human rights rules and regulations across the fashion industry, which raises concerns about "**greenwashing**". Companies should adhere to a few essential human rights norms, and doing so is neither special nor extra ethical.

WHY IS ETHICAL FASHION IMPORTANT?

It is important to dress ethically because the consumption patterns to which we are accustomed are totally unsustainable. As we have seen, the long-term effects can wreak havoc on the health of the planet and the people who live on it:

Environment:

The world population consumes 400 percent more clothing than at the beginning of the millennium, cotton production accounts for 25% of insecticide and 18% of pesticide use, and the resources used to raise livestock for leather production has a huge impact on the health of our planet. Because Fast Fashion is produced overseas, it pollutes all types of water bodies and produces 20 percent of the world's wastewater. And 97 percent of Fast Fashion items are made in poor nations.

Garment workers:

A garment factory in Dhaka, Bangladesh collapsed on April 24th, 2013 commonly known as "**Rana Plaza Disaster**"[47], killed 1,134 persons. Most of these persons were women, including children who were being cared for while their moms worked. Cracks were detected the day before the collapse, but its owner ignored instructions to stop utilising the building, pushing garment workers to resume business as usual despite the danger.

Our clothes are made by people who have been exploited by Fast Fashion. 80 percent of textile workers who are women face all kinds of abuse and works in unsafe and unfair conditions; the Rana Plaza incident is just one of many reminders of the significance of Ethical Fashion.

Us:

We all know that our largest organ is our skin. The creams we use on our skin are carefully chosen, and we spend hundreds of dollars on them, but there is something that does not make sense. We appear to be failing to remember that the clothing we purchased from our number one Fast Fashion stores were splashed with chemical substances at each phase of production and eventually on our bodies.

HOW THE FASHION INDUSTRY CAN BE MORE ETHICAL?

In 2020, the Global Organic Textile Standard (**GOTS**) certified facilities was increased by 35% globally, in order to inspire change and strive for the future of Ethical Fashion. One of the most important requirements for a textile product to bear the GOTS "organic" label is that it contains at least 95% certified organic fibres.

Some clothing producers fight Fast Fashion by utilising natural dyes thereby avoiding polyester and other man-made materials made from plastic that have been proven to harm oceans and other waterways.

INDIAN LAWS SUPPORT ETHICAL FASHION:

In both text and spirit, Indian laws favour Ethical Fashion. A Soil Health and Management Programme were started by the Indian government in 2017 in order to encourage sustainable agriculture, which in turn stimulates the production of organic fibres. Environmental laws also impose criminal penalties and damages for infractions. We have laws safeguarding

---

47 Rana Plaza Disaster- https://www.ilo.org/global/topics/geip/WCMS_614394/lang--en/index.htm

geographical indications and traditional knowledge, including handloom items and procedures, that are unique to us.

Minimum salaries and humane working conditions are guaranteed by employment and labour laws, which are also a topic of Ethical Fashion. Indian laws provide protection against sexual harassment and maternity allowances in the workplace to encourage gender equality. Exotic skins and furs for clothes and accessories are also prohibited under wildlife conservation legislation.

'A lot' is being done in this area in terms of law, but it is done in a scatter-gun manner. The problem is that the phrases "ethical" and "sustainable" do not have a legal definition that is universally recognised. According to lingerie buyer on South Molton Street, the terms ethical and sustainable mean something quite separate from what a factory manager in Bangalore means by those terms. Because the law doesn't really help with this ambiguity, the consequence is a jumble of regulations and "best practise standards" that individuals in the sector are supposed to follow.

Proactive Approach:

India's abundance of resources and supportive policies make it possible to build global sustainable fashion businesses. Proactive marketing and promotion, as well as compliance with current laws should help overcome the hurdles.

CONCLUSION

Ethical Fashion is not black and white like law. Supply chains in manufacturing and distribution are convoluted and clogged up. This makes it feasible for us to encourage those who are making conscious changes to do better by shopping for the best in the worst and supporting the ones who are doing better. Buying the most gorgeous handmade, organic linen dress is not the only approach to transform the fashion industry.

We should be concerned because we would never want the emotional and mental hardship of a cotton farmer or the working circumstances of garment factory workers on our worst enemy, so why do we continue to turn a blind eye on them? We should be concerned about Ethical Fashion if we want to continue to survive on this globe. Our current rate of resource consumption is not sustainable for our planet. We should be concerned about Ethical Fashion, because **"there is no beauty in the finest cloth if it makes hunger and unhappiness."- Mahatma Gandhi**[48].

---

48 https://www.euronews.com/green/2019/04/17/there-is-no-beauty-in-the-finest-cloth-if-it-makes-hunger-and-unhappiness

6.3 Concept of Greenwashing

In a recent interview with Vogue Scandinavia Greta Thunberg the Swedish climate activist strongly condemned the fashion industry for being one of the biggest contributors to climate-and ecological emergency.[49] Thunberg did not hesitate to call out the industry for its greenwashed campaigns stating that one "cannot mass produce fashion or consume sustainably as the world is shaped today. That is one of the many reasons why we will need a system change."[50] The greenwashing referred by Thunberg in her interview is also known as 'green sheen'. The term first coined by the environmentalist Jay Westervelt in 1986 refers to the act of a company using "misleading or false claims to suggest it's doing more for the environment than it actually is."[51] With scientific reports as recent as that 2021 from the Intergovernmental Panel on Climate Change (IPCC) and others suggesting the irreparable damage caused by climate change, 'sustainable' and 'eco-friendly' fashion is the newest trend in the fashion industry. "Green is the new black, sustainable is the it look, and veganism is in while animal products are out."[52] Thus, with an aim to sell their product to the climate conscious Gen Z popular fast fashion brands such as H&M, Zara, Mango, Asos[53] and several others have resorted to greenwashing, advertising their products as eco-friendly and sustainable even when it is not. The article aims to analyse the reason for the emergence of greenwashed advertising campaigns carried out by fast fashion brands and their impact on the targeted consumer base, while exploring existing the laws and regulations against greenwashing prevalent in the developing nations of the world.

WHY ARE FAST FASHION BRANDS GREENWASHING THEIR CAMPAIGNS ?

The demographic born between the year 1996 and 2010 is popularly known as Gen Z, while the oldest member of the generation is only 24 years old, in 2020 Gen Z became the largest generation surpassing Baby Boomers and Millennials.[54] This generation constitutes a whopping 32 percent of the global population, which approximately estimates to 2.47 billion out of the 7.7 billion human population on earth.[55] Having being born in the age of climate crisis the youngest and the largest generation is

---

49Pattinson T, "Read Greta Thunberg's Vogue SCANDINAVIA Cover INTERVIEW: Greta on Activism, Trump and Becoming the Voice of a Generation" (*Vogue Scandinavia*August 8, 2021)
<https://www.voguescandinavia.com/articles/greta-the-great> accessed August 29, 2021.
50BBC, "Thunberg Calls out Climate Impact of Fashion Brands in Vogue Interview" (*BBC News*August 9, 2021)
<https://www.bbc.com/news/world-europe-58145465> accessed August 29, 2021.
51 Chan E, "6 Ways to Be Greenwashing Vigilant" (*British Vogue*February 12, 2020)
<https://www.vogue.co.uk/news/article/greenwashing-in-fashion> accessed August 29, 2021.
52 Mlaba K, "Greenwashing: What Is It and How to Avoid It" (*Global Citizen*August 20, 2021)
<https://www.globalcitizen.org/en/content/greenwashing-what-is-it-and-how-to-avoid-it/> accessed August 29, 2021.
53 Langa, "5 Earth Day Fashion Campaigns Which Are Actually Just Greenwashing" (*Popdust*April 22, 2021)
<https://www.popdust.com/earth-day-greenwashing-2652663175.html> accessed August 29, 2021.
54 Spitznagel E, "Generation z Is Bigger than Millennials - and They're out to Change the World" (*New York Post*January 25, 2020) <https://nypost.com/2020/01/25/generation-z-is-bigger-than-millennials-and-theyre-out-to-change-the-world/> accessed August 29, 2021.
55 Spitznagel E, "Generation z Is Bigger than Millennials - and They're out to Change the World" (*New York Post*January 25, 2020) <https://nypost.com/2020/01/25/generation-z-is-bigger-than-millennials-and-theyre-out-to-change-the-world/> accessed August 29, 2021.

environment conscious and they want to purchase from brands that resonate with their values of being eco- friendly and sustainable. "But as some companies attempt to meet Gen Z's demands for sustainability, others might merely be presenting a façade."[56] Greenwashing is a deceptive practice of branding adopted by companies that allows them to project themselves as environment-friendly even without them practicing any such legitimate sustainable operations.[57]

While the motives of fast fashion brands remain the same - to sell more and to sell fast, the needs of their target consumer demographic is changing. However, even with the change in needs one factor remains constant, the consumer's limited budget. The real problem lies in the fact that Gen Z wants sustainable fashion, but they also want trendy clothes within their budget whereas in reality ethically sourced garments that are sustainable are naturally above the price point generally offered by fast fashion brands. Therefore, being conscious of Gen Z's growing desire for affordable sustainable products the brands have adopted sustainability-targeted marketing in an attempt to appeal to their consumers. Many prominent fast fashion brands have been quick and creative in generating greenwashed campaigns to trick their consumer base into buying their products while projecting their brand to be environmentally conscious and sustainable. Such campaigns projected to be backed by verified data and evidence gives the consumer the required peace of mind while purchasing. "This year, more than a quarter of millennials and Gen Zs worldwide said that their buying decisions have been influenced by the impact of certain businesses on the environment."[58] Thus, fast fashion brands are using the façade of sustainability to only further their own motives, while consumers limited by budget are left with little option.

6.4 Laws And Regulations Against Greenwashing

The consumer protection authorities from over 65 countries (such as US, UK, Canada, prominent EU nations, Australia, China, Japan and others) have formed a global network called the International Consumer Protection and Enforcement Network (ICPEN) that is responsible for cross border coordination to ensure enforcement and compliance of greenwashing guidelines by companies.[59] While at times soft enforcement such as warning letters are sufficient other times

---

56 Jahns K, "The Environment Is Gen Z's No. 1 Concern – and Some Companies Are Taking Advantage of That" (*CNBC*August 11, 2021) <https://www.cnbc.com/2021/08/10/the-environment-is-gen-zs-no-1-concern-but-beware-of-greenwashing.html> accessed August 29, 2021.
57 Jahns K, "The Environment Is Gen Z's No. 1 Concern – and Some Companies Are Taking Advantage of That" (*CNBC*August 11, 2021) <https://www.cnbc.com/2021/08/10/the-environment-is-gen-zs-no-1-concern-but-beware-of-greenwashing.html> accessed August 29, 2021.
58 Jahns K, "The Environment Is Gen Z's No. 1 Concern – and Some Companies Are Taking Advantage of That" (*CNBC*August 11, 2021) <https://www.cnbc.com/2021/08/10/the-environment-is-gen-zs-no-1-concern-but-beware-of-greenwashing.html> accessed August 29, 2021.
59 Webb B, "The Big Global Greenwashing Crackdown" (*Vogue Business*May 27, 2021) <https://www.voguebusiness.com/sustainability/the-big-global-greenwashing-crackdown> accessed August 29, 2021.

formal investigations are directed where the offence committed is criminal in nature.[60] In a recent survey of global websites conducted by the enforcement network ICPEN claims to have recorded approximately forty percent misleading environmental claims by companies who are trying to target the environment conscious customer says Josephine Palumbo, president of ICPEN and deputy commissioner of deceptive marketing practices directorate at Competition Bureau Canada.[61]

In the European Union widespread greenwashing campaigns led to rise in consumer distrust in the market which subsequently resulted in the establishment of a standard of minimum requirements in 2020 for brands who wished to avail the tag of an 'EU Ecolabel' 62 or other sustainability marks/logos.63 Further this also mandated companies to substantiate their brand's environmental claims by showing reliable data such as environmental footprint of products and organisations. While UK derived most of its environmental laws and regulations from the EU, post Brexit it is required to establish its own regulations which match up to the standards previously established by EU.[64]

Taking a conscious step to avoid greenwashing the UK government launched an investigation on all 'green' deals in August 2021, aiming to prevent consumer misinformation. [65] The government assigned the Green Technical Advisory Group (GTAG) for conducting the investigation.66 GTAG comprises of 28 stakeholders such as the Cambridge Institute, FTSE Russel, and others, headed by Ingrid Holmes of the Green Finance Institute.[67] Furthermore, the Competition and Markets Authority (CAM) will be launching its own guideline in September 2021 after running an investigation on the existing 'eco-friendly' claims in the market.[68] The collaboration between international regulatory bodies such as ICPEN, EU, Dutch Authorities for Consumer Markets, CMA

---

60 Webb B, "The Big Global Greenwashing Crackdown" (*Vogue Business*May 27, 2021)
<https://www.voguebusiness.com/sustainability/the-big-global-greenwashing-crackdown> accessed August 29, 2021.
61 Webb B, "The Big Global Greenwashing Crackdown" (*Vogue Business* May 27, 2021)
<https://www.voguebusiness.com/sustainability/the-big-global-greenwashing-crackdown> accessed August 29, 2021.
62 https://ec.europa.eu/environment/ecolabel/eu-ecolabel-for-businesses.html.
63 Abbie, "Op-Ed: Greenwashing regulations in 2021 – the year of the level playing field" (*Compare ethics* Jan 28,2021) <https://compareethics.com/greenwashing-regulations-level-playing-field/> accessed August 29, 2021.
64 Abbie, "Op-Ed: Greenwashing regulations in 2021 – the year of the level playing field" (*Compare ethics* Jan 28,2021) <https://compareethics.com/greenwashing-regulations-level-playing-field/> accessed August 29, 2021.
65 Thomas H, "UK Business Is on Notice for 'Greenwashing' Claims" (*Become an FT subscriber to read | Financial Times* August 19, 2021) <https://www.ft.com/content/b907d46f-1ca3-4cc8-9a59-da921da656e7> accessed September 5, 2021.
66 Mellor S, "A Raft of New Financial Products Claim to Be 'Green'. The U.K. Government Isn't so Sure" (*Fortune*June 9, 2021) <https://fortune.com/2021/06/09/a-raft-of-new-financial-products-claim-to-be-green-the-u-k-government-isnt-so-sure/> accessed September 8, 2021.
67 Mellor S, "A Raft of New Financial Products Claim to Be 'Green'. The U.K. Government Isn't so Sure" (*Fortune*June 9, 2021) <https://fortune.com/2021/06/09/a-raft-of-new-financial-products-claim-to-be-green-the-u-k-government-isnt-so-sure/> accessed September 8, 2021.
68 Thomas H, "UK Business Is on Notice for 'Greenwashing' Claims" (*Become an FT subscriber to read | Financial Times* August 19, 2021) <https://www.ft.com/content/b907d46f-1ca3-4cc8-9a59-da921da656e7> accessed September 5, 2021.

along with the UK government post Brexit is an important collaboration that could possibly reform the existing regulations against greenwashing for a better future. 69

In Netherlands in the beginning of May 2021, the Authority for Consumers and Markets (ACM) began investigating the environmental claims of its largest local businesses including seventy fashion brands.70 The investigation was subsequent to the announcement of five "rules of thumb" for environmental claims made by the regulatory body in January in the same year.71 The Green Guides of the Federal Trade Commission (FTC) in the US outlines the rules prohibiting greenwashing by companies however the said guide has not been updated for almost a decade.72 However, both policy collective called Politically in Fashion and Amendi, the contemporary denim fashion in the US are calling out the FTC to review and update its guidelines.73 The Commission responded by a press release of a 'statement of basis and purpose' where it clarified its objective is to continue battling against deceptive and unfair practices rather than creating rigid definitions or standards that would be counterproductive in its purpose.74 Now the American Association of Advertising Agencies has come up with a comprehensive guideline for brands promoting eco-friendly campaigns.75

On the other hand, France has become one the world's first countries to direct its legal sanctions in combatting greenwashing. 76 The legal sanctions introduced by the government can levy up to 80% fine on organisations found to be guilty of greenwashing their campaigns and brand image. 77 The government's action will discourage brands from committing greenwashing campaign frauds and subsequently save the consumer as well as the environment.78

---

69 Abbie, "Op-Ed: Greenwashing regulations in 2021 – the year of the level playing field" (*Compare ethics* Jan 28,2021) <https://compareethics.com/greenwashing-regulations-level-playing-field/> accessed August 29, 2021.
70 Webb B, "The Big Global Greenwashing Crackdown" (*Vogue Business* May 27, 2021)
<https://www.voguebusiness.com/sustainability/the-big-global-greenwashing-crackdown> accessed August 29, 2021.
71 Webb B, "The Big Global Greenwashing Crackdown" (*Vogue Business* May 27, 2021)
<https://www.voguebusiness.com/sustainability/the-big-global-greenwashing-crackdown> accessed August 29, 2021.
72 Webb B, "The Big Global Greenwashing Crackdown" (*Vogue Business* May 27, 2021)
<https://www.voguebusiness.com/sustainability/the-big-global-greenwashing-crackdown> accessed August 29, 2021.
73 Webb B, "The Big Global Greenwashing Crackdown" (*Vogue Business*May 27, 2021)
<https://www.voguebusiness.com/sustainability/the-big-global-greenwashing-crackdown> accessed August 29, 2021.
74 FCT, "FCT Green Guides Statement of Purpose "(*FCT*) <https://www.ftc.gov/sites/default/files/attachments/press-releases/ftc-issues-revised-green-guides/greenguidesstatement.pdf> accessed August 29, 2021.
75 4A's, "What Marketers Need to Know about Greenwashing in Advertising" (*4A's*August 11, 2021)
<https://www.aaaa.org/what-marketers-need-to-know-about-greenwashing-in-advertising/?cn-reloaded=1> accessed September 8, 2021.
76 James M, "France Introduces One of the World's FIRST GREENWASHING Laws" (*Communicate magazine*April 16, 2021) <https://www.communicatemagazine.com/news/2021/france-introduces-one-of-the-world-s-first-greenwashing-laws/>, accessed August 29, 2021.
77 James M, "France Introduces One of the World's FIRST GREENWASHING Laws" (*Communicate magazine*April 16, 2021) <https://www.communicatemagazine.com/news/2021/france-introduces-one-of-the-world-s-first-greenwashing-laws> accessed August 29, 2021.
78 James M, "France Introduces One of the World's FIRST GREENWASHING Laws" (*Communicate magazine*April 16, 2021) <https://www.communicatemagazine.com/news/2021/france-introduces-one-of-the-world-s-first-greenwashing-laws> accessed August 29, 2021.

Studies indicate that lapses in the advertisement regulations in India has given scope for rise in greenwashed advertisements which constituted 51.7% of the advertisements in the state in 2014.79 Unfortunately, the environmental laws or trademarks laws presently in India do not comprise of any specific regulations that address greenwashing in the country.80 Instead there exists a self-regulatory organization by the name of ASCI (The Advertising Standards Council of India) that was founded in 1985 for the purposes of monitoring advertising content within the state.81 The ASCI is an independent body that functions to preserve the sanctity of advertising within the Republic of India and to ensure the maintenance of public confidence in advertising and communications published by compliance of its Code for Self-Regulation.82 Even though the regulations mandate the advertisements to be truthful, legal, decent, non-hazardous or harmful there are existing loopholes which could be rectified by guidelines addressing the issues concerning environmental claims and green advertising.83 It is important to note that that the lack of appropriate regulations is not just harming the customers but also the state's reputation as "it is committed to fulfilling sustainable Development Goals set up by United Nations by 2030."84

CONCLUSION

Today's consumer wants to invest their money in green and ethical fashion, however they are limited by their budget. Fast fashion brands are aware of their consumers needs as well as their limitations thus greenwashed advertisements and campaigns are successfully generated to mislead such consumers. Therefore, with the willingness to invest in sustainable fashion the customers are also required to be aware of the brands and their practices beyond the over-advertised greenwashed campaigns in the absence of appropriate regulations. As developed nations continue to focus on economic developments of the state turning a blind eye the environmental deterioration, consumer research becomes crucial. Chief brand officer at sustainability consultancy Eco-Age Mr. Harriet

---

79 Fernando AG, Sivakumaran B and Suganthi L, "Nature of Green Advertisements in India: Are They Greenwashed?" (2014) 24 Asian Journal of Communication 222   DOI: 10.1080/01292986.2014.885537.
80 Narula R, "Deception of Greenwashing" (*Legal Developments*May 18, 2021) <https://www.legal500.com/developments/thought-leadership/deception-of-greenwashing/> accessed August 29, 2021.
81 The CSR Journal, "Opinion: Are Our Ads 'Greenwashing' You?" (*The CSR Journal*April 18, 2017) <https://thecsrjournal.in/opinion-are-our-ads-greenwashing-you/> accessed August 29, 2021.
82 The CSR Journal, "Opinion: Are Our Ads 'Greenwashing' You?" (*The CSR Journal*April 18, 2017) <https://thecsrjournal.in/opinion-are-our-ads-greenwashing-you/> accessed August 29, 2021.
83 Narula R, "Deception of Greenwashing" (*Legal Developments*May 18, 2021) <https://www.legal500.com/developments/thought-leadership/deception-of-greenwashing/> accessed August 29, 2021.
84 Narula R, "Deception of Greenwashing" (*Legal Developments*May 18, 2021) <https://www.legal500.com/developments/thought-leadership/deception-of-greenwashing/> accessed August 29, 2021.

Vocking suggests, "Don't just listen to the marketing, look at the company's website and read what they are doing."[85]

However, aware customers alone cannot fix a broken system. There is a dire need for government initiatives and regulatory bodies that monitor the market to ensure companies are complying to the environmental regulations and not simply pretending to be eco-friendly and sustainable to their customers. Suggesting such a mechanism is easier than establishing one as industry lobbying coupled with corruption creates a roadblock in the formulation of a robust environmental legislation in most developing countries including India.[86] While countries around the world are taking their first steps towards regulations against greenwashing, there is lot left to be done. A strict standard of compliance to regulations upon the violation of which corporations will be subjected to serious penalties can bring about a change in the attitude of such corporations. The fight against greenwashing must be a united one, the government, self -regulating bodies, corporations, and consumers themselves have to collectively take the onus to put an end to greenwashed campaigns . Meanwhile in the absence of a robust regulatory system that holds fast fashion brands accountable Gen Z has started to shop from small businesses and thrift stores leading to their rising popularity in today's day and age.

---

85 Chan E, "6 Ways to Be Greenwashing Vigilant" (*British Vogue*February 12, 2020) <https://www.vogue.co.uk/news/article/greenwashing-in-fashion> accessed August 29, 2021.
86 Fernando AG, Sivakumaran B and Suganthi L, "Nature of Green Advertisements in India: Are They Greenwashed?" (2014) 24 Asian Journal of Communication 222.
DOI: 10.1080/01292986.2014.885537.

Chapter 7. Marketing, Promotion in Fashion & Law

Starting a fashion company has never been easier. There are an estimated 20,000 D2C fashion brands globally, with new brands launching every week.[87] Being an enterprise fashion company, however, has never been harder.

Every fashion brand needs a good marketing strategy in place to help it stay ahead of its competition. A good strategy will not only help them stay afloat in the treacherous sea that is eCommerce, but also grow as others flounder in confusion. As for you, it doesn't matter if you're brand new to the fashion world or a seasoned veteran — no matter where you lie, you need an effective marketing strategy. Digital marketing for fashion brands specifically has changed dramatically over the past few years and it's vital that your business is constantly looking to adapt and evolve to stay ahead of the competition.

In the past, traditional wholesalers served as gatekeepers. They provided scaled distribution to fashion companies with sufficient brand recognition and sales, limiting competition to the biggest and best-known players. Today, e-commerce has removed the barriers to distribution, resulting in an explosion of competitors.

Media. Previously, mass-market advertising—primarily television and print—was expensive and required money upfront, which gave an edge to large brands that were able to use those media channels to reach large audiences and reinforce their branding. Digital advertising requires no upfront commitments; brands pay as they grow.

Each of the traditional growth pillars was effective in a world that rewarded size. Today, the benefits of being big—lower prices, greater access to consumers, and scaled communication—can be realized by the small. So the area of competition shifts naturally to delivering compelling consumer experiences and interactions. In other words, it shifts to marketing. Notable D2C brands such as Warby Parker, Allbirds, and ThirdLove all compete by creating innovative, tailored experiences for consumers.

Enterprise fashion companies find themselves at a decided disadvantage because they have honed their strategies and processes for the old world of marketing. These processes—centered on mass-

---

87 https://www.bcg.com/publications/2021/modern-marketing-for-sustained-advantage-and-growth-in-the-fashion-industry accessed on 8th Sept, 2021

market advertising—are linear, siloed, and static. The new marketing world calls for a whole new set of processes—ones that are iterative, cross-functional, and dynamic.

Acknowledging this change, most enterprise fashion companies have tried to modify the old marketing ways. The chasm between the old and new, though, is too large for such hybrid approaches to be effective. Instead, it's imperative that brands revisit the fundamentals of how marketing works.

The right kind of fashion marketing plays a key role in the growth and developments of the fashion industry. With the help of fashion marketing, the creations of the fashion designers from different parts of the world is brought into the vicinity of the consumers and the buyers.

While the fashion industry adopted new ways of marketing, then there is need to understand the legal side to address the disputes that can arise. This chapter talks about rights and obligations of celebrity, influencers, photographers etc.

7.1 Celebrity and Personality Rights in Fashion Industry

This section is authored by Chitra Sahay[88]

The public's recognition of a person's unique qualities determines his celebrity status. Voice, mannerisms, and clothes that aid in the formation of a well-known personality are commercially valuable indicia. Controlling the commercial use of one's identify is an inherent right of every human being. Famous people like actors and fashion influencers are well aware that, rather than being hurt by public exposure of their likenesses, they would be severely disadvantaged if they were no longer paid for authorising advertisements popularising their likenesses, unless they could make this right of publicity the subject of an exclusive grant that prohibited any other advertiser from using their likenesses without their consent. Where an individual's commercial worth is utilised without prior agreement, responsibility is assigned, such as his or her name, likeness or any other identity indication for commercial purposes.

Celebrity is the idea of being widely known. Somebody who is a big-name, famous and visible amongst the public will be considered as a celebrity. Celebrities have economic associative value, or in other words brand value of their own, because they are well known to the public. Since, these people have their image reflected on the minds of the public, protection of celebrity rights is getting

---

88 Editorial Board Member, Fashion Law Journal, IP professional with an LLM in Intellectual Property Laws.

significantly developed with the development of technology. Celebrity rights are being granted in countries like the United States of America without the status of being a celebrity, anybody can claim for publicity rights without even being a celebrity, whereas in India the components of celebrity rights are still ambiguous. Certain celebrities have an interest that may be protected from the unauthorized commercial exploitation of that identity, the famous ones have an exclusive legal right during life to control and profit from the commercial use of their name and personality.[89] It is largely common for the celebrities to lend their names, voices, faces etc. to various entertainment portals, sometimes for free as well as for some monetary gains, but there have been many instances where the image of the celebrities have been used without any prior permission from that respective celebrity.

CELEBRITIES AND RIGHT TO PUBLICITY

Unwanted publicity can harm the individual, physically and mentally. Key interests such as human dignity and personality should be protected under law. Right to publicity was conferred to the people with the purpose the law also should protect at least a minimal threshold of emotional equilibrium for the celebrities to be protected from unwanted exposure and publicity in the press.[90] Earlier, appropriation cases were concerned with mental anguish of individuals caused due to portrayal of their likeness without any prior consent. With the evolution of concept of privacy, people started asserting privacy claims that sought remuneration for the use of likeness or persona of the private individuals rather than mental discomfort arising from the unauthorised commercial appropriation. Later, the concept of publicity was distinguished from the right of privacy, and right of publicity started controlling and preventing exploiting of name and likeness of private individuals.

The objective of the right to publicity is protection of the commercial value of the identity whose false likeness was being used. A man has a right to the publicity value of his photograph in addition to and independent of his right to privacy, which is referred to as a "right of publicity." Many famous people (especially actors and athletes) are well aware that, rather than having their feelings hurt by public exposure of their likenesses, they would be severely deprived if they were no longer paid for authorising advertisements popularising their likenesses in newspapers, magazines, buses, trains, and subways, unless they could make this right of publicity the subject of an exclusive grant that prohibited any other advertiser from utilising their name, likeness or any other indicia. When the commercial value of an individual is used without any prior consent, such as the name, likeness or any other indicia of identity for commercial benefit is subject to liability.

89 Alvin Antony,Celebrity Rights, Is it important in India? MONDAQ (January 31, 2019) https://www.mondaq.com/india/trademark/777368/celebrity-rights-is-it-important-in-india
90 Warren and Brandeis, "The Right to Privacy" (mit.edu)

The right of publicity is not defined under any specific statue, but it is recognised in India. The right of publicity was categorized as an enforceable right by the Delhi High Court as "The right of publicity has evolved from the right of privacy and can inhere only in an individual or in any indicia of an individual's personality like his name, personality trait, signature, voice. etc."[91] A suit for permanent injunction was filed by the famous journalist Rajat Sharma against the zee media for insulting his name in their advertisement as 'India Mein Rajat Ki Adalat Ab Band'.[92] The court reiterated well-known principles of personality rights or right of publicity of celebrities. The plaintiff has an unassailable right attached to his famous television host persona and insulting such name will amount to false advertising. The above advertisement was declared illegal and an injunction was issued against Zee media from using Rajat Sharma's name in all its print and electronic advertisements and remove all hoardings across the country which mention the name of the plaintiff. The right of privacy has twin objective, first is the general law of privacy which affords a tort action for damages resulting from an unlawful invasion of privacy, where the name or likeness of a person is violated without any authorised consent.[93] The right of publicity is a part of the right to privacy which generates from the likeness in his name, personality trait, signature, voice, etc. from an individual, and such right is vested in that particular individual and he alone is entitled to gain profit from it.[94]

WIPO held that using unauthorized name of a famous individual will not be categorised as a bona bide use and if the application intended to lure people, any legitimate rights cannot be conferred by the infringer. Also, the right to commercially use or exploit one's own name, vests with the person who has worked to create the fame and can lawfully restrict any other third parties from exploiting that fame for commercial purposes. Interfering with someone's privacy, publicly divulging private facts, disseminating material that casts a person in a wrong light, and the right of publicity are the four sorts of right to privacy. Whether or not a celebrity's name or identification is used, the right of publicity protects the appropriation of that identity of the celebrity. It was held that "the right to grant the exclusive privilege of publishing one's picture is protected under the right to publicity". When the commercial value of an individual is used without any prior consent, such as the name, likeness or any other indicia of identity for commercial benefit is subject to liability.[95] "The inherent right of every human being to control the commercial use of his or her identity".[96]

91 ICC Development (International) Ltd v Arvee Enterprises, 2003 VIIAD Delhi 405.
92 Rajat Sharma v Zee Telefilms, Delhi HC, 2019
93 R. Rajagopal v State of Tamil Nadu, (AutoShankar's Case) (1994) 6 SCC 632
94 ICC Development (International) v Arvee Enterprises and Anr 2003 (26) PTC 245 (Del)
95 Restatement (Third) on Unfair Competition § 46
96 McCarthy, The Rights of Publicity and Privacy § 1:3 (2d ed. 2000)

7.2 Papparazi, Social Media And Celebrity Rights

Is it possible to sue celebrities for posting paparazzi photos of themselves on social media? The answer is, Yes. The photograph is capable of being an original, as the product developed is a mixture of the skill, labour, and the intellectual asset of the individual, and how the skills come into play by following their own aesthetic sense to create the visual effect. Not only the ownership of content was disputed, the subject matter of content was also under the ambit of infringement. However, the poses or manners which are present in the public domain, cannot amount to infringement.

Celebrities like Gigi Hadid, Victoria Beckham, Khloe Kardashian and Jennifer Lopez have engaged in lawsuits relating to copyright infringement on sharing of pictures of their own on social media platforms, which were posted without permission on social media platforms. While most of the cases were mutually settled, others have chosen to fight back. One of the first cases that addressed the issue of the use of images uploaded by individuals on social media was that between a photographer and the Agence France-Presse and Getty Images. The photographer took photos of the 2010 earthquake and shared them on TwitPic, a website that allowed photographers to post pictures on Twitter. These pictures were then reposted by another twitter user and the pictures were then distributed by The Agence France-Presse and Getty Images. The jury held that Agence France-Presse and Getty Images unmannerly infringed the copyrightability of the images and awarded the photographer $1.22 million. The court made a significant observation that a photographer does not wilfully forfeit his rights by posting a picture on social media.

Similarly, Versace was sued for sharing a photograph without the permission of the photographer. As a result of the lawsuit, the celebrities are hiring their photographers, which clearly is not an efficient solution. In Indian context, Delhi High Court recognized that the photographs uploaded on Facebook are protected under copyright, where some damages were awarded to the aggrieved party along with the permanent injunction. The poses or manners which are present in the public domain, such as the pose of a nude and pregnant women cannot amount to infringement. In the case of the iconic jump of Michael Jordan, only the photographer's emotion, as well as the selection and layout of the shot, was protected, not the pose itself. Copyright also subsists in derivative works under the ambit of the Act provided it resulted after application of little bit of skill, labour and capital of an author. Any work can be qualified as a fair use when the work does not replace the original work as a whole, but instead incorporates something new, with a different purpose or character.

The expansion of scope of copyright laws is protecting the traditional media, and with the shrinking of public domain, fair use comes into play which allows the creators to incorporate the work of other creators and safeguard the interest of their own as well as other creators. There have been many cases of copyright infringement, but each case has different facts and should be dealt accordingly.

THE "IMAGE" ATTACHED WITH CELEBRITIES

Celebrity status has evolved throughout time, especially when people earn popularity from their first, and often nearly exclusive exposure on the internet. According to research, endorsements done by celebrities can have a significant impact on the purchase decisions of potential customers. When it comes to connecting with customers, using well-known celebrities and their well-known attributes is considered an effective strategy. Whether we like or dislike celebrities and their impact on society, they will certainly continue to be a significant part of the social behaviour, and as such, will likely continue to affect how people act and dress. Celebrities and their stylists, as well as fashion manufacturers, negotiate behind-the-scenes arrangements that allow some apparels to make it onto the year's most visible red carpets in place of others. Celebrities are regularly paid to promote fashion labels and sell items through social media. As some celebrities can have millions of social media followers, corporations are extremely aware that dedicated fans can be directly responsible for buying goods marketed on social media sites of such celebrities.

McCracken's Meaning Transfer Model explains associative appropriation as when a celebrity is perceived to embody particular positive attributes or ideals, such attributes or ideals are passed on to products the celebrity is associated with, where an additional commercial advantage comes into the picture which is directly and substantially connected to the associative value of the celebrity's identity, further making the products become more 'desirable'.

The determination of misappropriation requires showing that a third party has used the identity of the plaintiff, and such use was for commercial gain.[97] In some cases, where the facts persist, it is not necessary to prove that the defendant had an economic advantage by using someone's name or likeness.[98] Personality rights can be claimed when there is certain application of name, picture, voice, or any other characteristic directly linked as a part of the image or likeness of a famous personality. For Example, Ariana Grande sued the fashion brand Forever 21 for using a model whose persona resembled with the singer, further trying to convince their customers that the celebrity is endorsing their products.[99] On establishing the violation to right to publicity, general damages and special damages can be awarded to the aggrieved party.[100] The right of publicity entails that the reaction of public to a person's name and likeness, which can be accidental or directed and planned, endows the person's name and likeness with financially exploitable prospects, as the heart

---

97 Moore v. Big Picture Co., 828 F.2d 270, 275 (5th Cir. 1995)
98 Henley v. Dillard Dept. Stores, 46 F.Supp.2d. 587, 597 (N.D.Tex.,1999).
99 Julia Jacobs, Ariana Grande Sues Forever 21 Over 'Look-Alike Model' in Ads, New York Times (3rd September, 2019) https://www.nytimes.com/2019/09/03/arts/music/ariana-grande-forever-21.html
100 National Bank of Commerce v. Shaklee Corp., 503 F. Supp. 533, 540 (W.D.Tex.1980)

of the law of privacy is the protection of one's name and likeness against unwelcome intrusion or exploitation.[101]

Interfering with someone's privacy, publicly divulging private facts, disseminating material that casts a person in a wrong light, and the right of publicity are the four sorts of right to privacy. Whether or not a celebrity's name or identification is used, such right protects the appropriation of that identity of the celebrity. A well-known phrase introducing a show host was protected as the phrase is associated with a show which is viewed by substantial segment of television viewing audience, so the commercial value of the phrase cannot be neglected.[102] All uses of identification in a commercial setting, such as advertising or merchandising, are planned to capitalise on the affective bond between the celebrity and the customer, these uses succeed in doing so when they evoke the celebrity in the mind of audience. There is no need to separate distinct actionable indicators of identity because all kinds of identification are by their very nature "evocative," albeit to varying degrees, because audiences react to the celebrity in all of its manifestations. If any restrictions are to be placed on an ever-expanding right of publicity, a restrictive view of identity is not the way to go. Liability is not the same as evocation, other aspects of the right of publicity claim must be met. Attracting customers is the first stage in marketing a product or service, people respond almost immediately to appeal having the name or image of a celebrity.

"An unauthorized commercial appropriation of identity of an individual converts the potential economic value in that identity to another's advantage."[103]If the essence of commercial appropriation is defined by an associative use, the judicial examination should focus on the connection between the defendant's commercial advantage and the associative value of the plaintiff's identity. The plaintiff should be required to show, by appropriate evidence, that the defendant's real or intended pecuniary advantage was directly and substantially related to the exploitation of the plaintiff's identity's associative value.

In the Karate Kid case, it was debated that whether a stage name is protected under right to publicity if it is closely identified with the user. A claim was bought by William J. DeClemente claiming that he is the original karate kid under New York Civil Rights Law § 51, for violation of his right of publicity. The court held that the public personality as 'The Karate kid' is not so notorious because of which it "had come closely and widely identified with the person who bears it". It was mentioned that the celebrity is not being identified as karate kid by public at large, in exclusion of his real

---

101 Lugosi v. Universal Pictures, 25 Cal.3d 813, 160 Cal.Rptr. 323 (1979).
102 Carson v Here's Johnny Portable Toilets (6th Cir, 1983)
103 Lugosi v Universal Pictures

name. The public personality of the celebrity as the Karate Kid simply has not reached the magnitude of public notoriety necessary to be actionable under the statute as a matter of law.[104]

In a claim of infringing the right of publicity and violation of Section 43(a) of the Lanham Act, 15 U.S.C. § 1125(a), Illinois Consumer Fraud and Deceptive Business Practices Act and Illinois Uniform Deceptive Trade Practices Act, the court said that since the plaintiff is not a well-known public figure, and only one person knew that she was modelled in the disputed matter, the plaintiff have to show that her identity is "inextricably intertwined" in the public mind with the main model, and since the plaintiff is unable to do so, not being a widely known martial artist, there is no infringement of publicity rights.[105] It is important to establish that before there is unauthorized use of the name, likeness or persona of an individual, there was certain commercial value attached to the image of the plaintiff prior to such use.[106] A similar judgment was given by the court saying that the plaintiff alleging unauthorized use of his likeness must determine that the likeness was recognizable.[107] When a false article was published about a love triangle involving petitioner and telecasted advertisements featuring petitioner's name, photograph, and mentioning the petitioner prominently the subject of the article by a newspaper, the court held that newspaper had commercially exploited his name, photograph, and likeness under both the common law and Cal. Civ. Code § 3344(a), and such conduct would constitute as infringement of right of publicity of the petitioner.[108]

The statute's reference to "name or likeness" is not limited to present or current use, and there was a violation of publicity rights when the former name of the applicant was used without any consent.[109] "Picture of a well-known personality, used in an ad and instantly recognizable, will still serve as a badge of approval"[110]. The court in this case held that the use of a "lookalike" of a widely popular personality for commercial purposes violates the right of privacy, stating that "there is no free ride, the commercial hitchhiker seeking to travel on the fame of another will have to learn to pay the fare or stand on his own two feet"[111]. When an agency is using soundalikes of a famous personality, and the celebrity is distinctively popular for his voice, there has been a violation regarding the appropriation of the attributes of the celebrity, leading to infringement to right to publicity.[112]

---

104 DeClemente v. Columbia Pictures, 860 F. Supp. 30, 53 (E.D.N.Y. 1994)
105 Pesina v. Midway Mfg. Co., 948 F. Supp. 40 (N.D. Ill. 1996)
106 Bi-Rite Enter.'s, Inc. v. Button Master, Inc., 555 F. Supp. 1188, 1198-99 (S.D.N.Y.1983)
107 Leval v. Prudential Health Care Plan, Inc., 610 F. Supp. 279, 281 (N.D.Ill.1985)
108 Eastwood v. Superior Court (National Enquirer, Inc.) (1983)
109 Abdul-Jabbar v General Motors (9th Cir, 1996)
110 Onassis v Christian Dior (NY Sup Ct, 1984)
111 Id.
112 Midler v Ford Motor (9th Cir, 1988)

A common law right of publicity that predates the passage of the statutory right and it remains valid and additive to the statutory right has been established in California.[113] Any unauthorized use of name, voice, signature, photograph, or likeness of an individual on products or merchandise, or for the purposes of advertising or promotion will result in civil claim, but use of unauthorized signature in a political campaign will also emerge in criminal action.[114] Also, right to privacy is a classified under tort on the basis of whether the claimed injury is an economic or dignitary one.[115]

When a suit was filed against The Velvet Elvis Nightclub, where the nightclub intended to be a parody of an era of popularity of the celebrity, but the painting and other Elvis memorabilia were treated as infringement of right of privacy but the night club alone was not an infringement. The nightclub was not unauthorised commercial exploitation of the identity of the celebrity as nothing was taken, the value of "The Velvet Elvis" was from evoking an era of Elvis Presly, not Elvis alone.[116] An injunction was granted to prohibit advertisements that use image or likeness of Elvis and phrases inextricably linked to the identity of Elvis.

INFLUENCER ADVERTISING ON DIGITAL MEDIA IN INDIA

With the development of technology, there has been a rise in the sector of social media influencers. Social media influencers as the name suggests are people who leave a certain impact on an individual's mind through their content posted on social media platforms. Social media has been a catapult for several entrepreneurial individuals, Forbes recognizing the popularity of social media influencers, announced for the first time its inaugural Top Influencers list.[117]Social media influencers include celebrities, artists, bloggers, critics, musician, vloggers, academicians, students and so on.

"Influencer advertising on digital media" rules were published by the Advertising Standards Council of India (ASCI) with the major goal to guarantee that customers can tell when something is being pushed with the purpose of influencing their behaviour for immediate or future commercial advantage, according to the document. The influencer or publishing account on which the advertising is published, or the advertiser for whose brand the advertisement is, must make a disclosure in the form of clarification that a piece of communication is an advertisement.

---

113 Comedy III Productions, Inc. v. Gary Saderup, Inc. (2001) 25 Cal.4th 387
114 Cal. Civ. Code § 3344
115 Dora v. Frontline Video, Inc., 15 Cal. App.4th 536 (1993)
116 Elvis Presley Enterprises v Capece (5th Cir, 1998)
117 Clare O'Connor, Forbes Top Influencers: Meet The 30 Social Media Stars Of Fashion, Parenting And Pets (Yes, Pets), Forbes (Sep 26,2017) https://www.forbes.com/sites/clareoconnor/2017/09/26/forbes-top-influencers-fashion-pets-parenting/?sh=4a1a21ba7683

Consumers will be able to see when influencers are being compensated for endorsing a product or influencing views and behaviours. Influencers must comply with strict disclosure rules, and both marketers and influencers are held accountable. According to the guidelines, influencers are those who have access to an audience and the capacity to influence the purchase decisions or views about a product, service, brand or experience of their audience due to their authority, knowledge, position, or relationship with their audience. Influencers do not have to have a minimum number of followers or be 'verified' on a social media platform in order to be considered influential. This definition of an influencer includes anyone who has the potential to influence the decisions of consumers in some way.

To comply with the Guidelines, an influencer cannot rely solely on a social media platform's disclosure feature. A simple "Sponsored" Instagram tag may not be enough for an influencer to fulfil their responsibilities under the Guidelines. In the event that there is a "material relationship" between the advertiser and the influencer, advertisements produced by social media influencers are obliged to be explicitly labelled as advertisements. Because social media platforms provide influencers a number of ways to promote such as posts, stories, reels, livestreams, podcasts, etc., the Guidelines specify disclosure standards for each sort of marketing based on its format. The Guidelines also stipulate that disclosures must be made in English or in the language of the advertising like Advertisement, Ad, Sponsored, Collaboration, Partnership, Employee, or a Free gift. In order to ensure compliance with the Guidelines, advertisers must take extra caution when negotiating with influencers. Influencer agreements might include termination clauses that allow sponsors to terminate influencers if they receive unfavourable press. In addition, influencers may be required to remove all content related to the business from their social media channels.

POSSIBLE ACTIONS FOR UNJUSTIFIABLY ENFORCING CELEBRITY RIGHTS IN INDIA

1. Right to publicity

Celebrities are well-known persons whose identities should not be commercialized without their consent, and they should have the freedom to determine when, when, and how their identities are used. The court determined breach of the right to publicity in the Daler Mehndi case because the singer is well-known, his persona has added economic value, and the court cannot allow commercial exploitation of his personality features. The contested use of a person's picture must show that it is significant, adequate, or substantial to show that the defendant has taken the persona or some of its basic characteristics. In the Titan Case, the defendant was found guilty of copyright infringement and misuse of personality rights for using images that were previously part of a promotion without permission. It was held that when a prominent celebrity's name appears in the title of a film, it is easy to deduce that the audience's opinion of the film is solely focused on the celebrity and not on anyone else. If a celebrity's name is used without permission, the aggrieved celebrity is entitled to an injunction if the celebrity can be easily identified through the disputed act.[118] The Court relied on the famous Titan Industries and the Shivaji Rao Gaikwad cases to reiterate well-known principles of personality rights or right of publicity of celebrities and came to the conclusion that the above advertisement was prima facie illegal and that the balance of convenience was in the favour of plaintiff.[119] The validity of the identify or persona of the human being who owns an enforceable right to his identity, as well as the individual's identifiability from illegal use, are the main criteria defining the liability for a violation of the right of publicity.[120]

2. Defamation

The freedom of speech and expression under article 19(1)(a) of the Constitution of India safeguards the freedom of speech and expression, but defamation is categorised as one of the reasonable restrictions on the fundamental right conferred to the citizen. Any false statement which harms the reputation, character, status of persona of the individual in the society is defamation. Such false communication may cause hatred or injury to the person himself, or his business or profession. Defamation is bifurcated into two parts, libel and slander, where the former deals with the communication being passed in a written form, latter focuses on the speech or gesture by which harm is inflicted on the image of the person.

3. Trademarks

Any mark that is eligible for is capable of being a trademark. According to the Trade Marks Act 1999, if the subject matter in question is a mark, and is eligible for graphical representation and supplies distinction in relation to other goods or services qualifies as a trademark unless it falls under any grounds of refusal of registration under section 9 and 10 of the Act. Section 9 deals with the absolute grounds of refusal, devoid of any distinctive character being the first ground. The mark should possess intrinsic characteristics within itself that will help in differentiating the goods or services of one person from those of other. For the test of inherent distinctiveness of a trademark, the mark must be analyzed in isolation without the involvement of external evidences gathered in the surroundings and examine that whether the mark is capable of distinguishing between two or more products or not. While analyzing the mark, the representation of the mark towards the public

---

118 Shivaji Rao Gaekwad v Varsha Production, Madras HC, 2015
119 Rajat Sharma v Zee Telefilms, Delhi HC, 2019
120 Titan Industries Ltd.v M/s Ramkumar Jewellers, CS(OS) No.2662/2011, Delhi HC

shall be taken into consideration. The mark in question shall not have the potential to deceive the public or likely to cause any instance of confusion. Section 2(zb) of the Act has certain requirements for the mark to be categorised as a trademark, and the mark consisting of names of celebrities is capable of being represented graphically and is also capable of distinguishing the goods and services it offers from others and by aforementioned justifications regarding grounds of refusal, it can be concluded that such names can be registered as a trademark. The purpose of registering the trademark in case of celebrities is to protect the brand value of the individual. Registration of a celebrity's name as a trademark prevents any form of misuse in the trade practices associated with the trademark. It is also necessary to register the trademark with respect to a particular class belonging to a set of goods and services. The wordmark 'Alia Bhatt' has been registered under class 35[121], class 25[122], class 18[123], class 14[124], class 9[125] and class 3[126] by the celebrity Ms Alia Bhatt herself. Celebrities are registering their names as trademarks across the globe to protect their image. If we particularly talk about India, Shahrukh Khan has registered the wordmark 'SHAH RUKH KHAN' in class 41.[127] Sachin Tendulkar has also registered the wordmark 'SACHIN TENDULKAR' in class 41.[128] Actress Kajol has registered the wordmark 'KAJOL' and 'KAJOL LABEL' in class 41.[129] Salman Khan has registered 'SALMAN KHAN VENTURES' and 'SALMAN KHAN FILMS' in the same class.[130] Deepika Padukone has also her own name in class 41.[131] Ajay Devgan has also registered his name as well as his signature in class 41.[132]

Section 14 of the Trademarks Act prohibits any individual to register a trademark similar to any celebrity, whether the person is alive or has died twenty years before the application of trademark was filed, without the consent of the celebrity himself or his legal representatives respectively. Indian law of succession allows the rights of the deceased to be devolved on the successor of the deceased after his death, and they can legally represent the individual if required. However, the right of publicity extends to the people who are dead in the United States, but are subject to certain duration and other requirements.

121 https://ipindiaonline.gov.in/tmrpublicsearch/tmsearch.aspx?tn=203980123&st=Wordmark
122 https://ipindiaonline.gov.in/tmrpublicsearch/tmsearch.aspx?tn=203980175&st=Wordmark
123 https://ipindiaonline.gov.in/tmrpublicsearch/tmsearch.aspx?tn=203980189&st=Wordmark
124 https://ipindiaonline.gov.in/tmrpublicsearch/tmsearch.aspx?tn=203980213&st=Wordmark
125 https://ipindiaonline.gov.in/tmrpublicsearch/tmsearch.aspx?tn=203980204&st=Wordmark
126 https://ipindiaonline.gov.in/tmrpublicsearch/tmsearch.aspx?tn=203980232&st=Wordmark
127 https://ipindiaonline.gov.in/tmrpublicsearch/tmsearch.aspx?tn=204034082&st=Wordmark
128 https://ipindiaonline.gov.in/tmrpublicsearch/tmsearch.aspx?tn=204034536&st=Wordmark
129 https://ipindiaonline.gov.in/tmrpublicsearch/tmsearch.aspx?tn=204034704&st=Wordmark
130 https://ipindiaonline.gov.in/tmrpublicsearch/tmsearch.aspx?tn=204037913&st=Wordmark
131 https://ipindiaonline.gov.in/tmrpublicsearch/tmsearch.aspx?tn=204038242&st=Wordmark
132 https://ipindiaonline.gov.in/tmrpublicsearch/tmsearch.aspx?tn=204041832&st=Wordmark

4. Passing Off

The claims related to passing off made by the celebrities are generally for the usage of name, likeness of image, vocal similarity or any other personality traits that could mislead the consumers into believing that the particular celebrity is involved with the brand by giving their consent. Passing off is a phenomenon which occurs when there is a confusion created on the part of any business entity to mislead or deceive their consumers into believing that the goods that were being delivered by the particular company belongs to another supplier where the reputation of that supplier is also attached with the goods delivered. The essence of passing off is that any individual cannot represent his goods as the goods of another individual. Passing off has three requirements to be fulfilled, a goodwill or reputation must be associated with the individual, misrepresentation should have occurred which caused confusion and lead the public into believing that the goods belonged to someone else and establishment of certain damage that has caused or is likely to be caused in the future.

CONCLUSION

A celebrity status is determined by the well-known status of a person, who is identified by the public for his specific attributes. A distinctive indicia like voice, mannerism, or clothing that help in emergence of a famous personality are commercially valuable. When a celebrity is perceived to embody particular positive attributes or ideals, such attributes or ideals are passed on to products the celebrity is associated with, where an additional commercial advantage comes into the picture which is directly and substantially connected to the associative value of the celebrity's identity, further making the products become more 'desirable'. When an individual is using the image of any celebrity without prior consent, it will always lead to violation of the personality rights of the celebrity.

7.3 Fashion Influencers and Law

Fashion influencers and Fashion enthusiasts love Instagram when it comes to getting inspiration for outfits. With Instagram reels have turned into an endless virtual runway, the fashion hauls and #OOTD stories and posts have not only fulfilled our love for aesthetics but have even upped our wardrobe game by exposing us to the latest trends.

As the famous quote goes, with great power comes great responsibility. The same applies in the context of social media influencers; the greater the influencer bigger the responsibility. Influencers have a responsibility towards the audience that follows them and to keep a check on this, certain legal frameworks have been implemented.

Brands adore social media influencers because they can start trends and persuade their fans to purchase the goods they support. Celebrity endorsement spawned influencer marketing. It has always been in the knowledge of the businesses that when a celebrity supports or endorses their product, sales increase. Many businesses, especially high-end brands, continue to use celebrities as influencers.

Common people were able to gain fame via social media platforms such as YouTube, Instagram, and Twitter, resulting in the emergence of social media influencers.

Many people, especially teenagers, are influenced by social media influencers. Influencers are also working with celebrities to promote their films.

People trust social media influencers more than conventional celebrities because they have the picture of a girl/boy next door, making them more relatable. Since influencers communicate with their followers on a regular basis, followers, especially young people, feel closer to them.

Brands also tend to work with social media influencers over traditional celebrities because of the impact they have on young people and because supported content can easily be incorporated into the influencers' regular content. It is clearly seen that influencer marketing is on the rise, and it's influencing young people's buying decisions. Furthermore, young people are more likely to study a product before purchasing it. They'll even look at the ratings left by the influencers they follow.

The influence of advertising is undeniable. It holds the audience's attention and encourages them to imitate a lifestyle that they believe is led by their heroes. In the early twenty-first century, no means of communication had a greater effect on the lives of ordinary people than television, and the same impact can now be seen across social media. Using goods or services recommended by celebrities or influencers allows ordinary people to feel closer to their heroes.

Influencer marketing, the newest type of marketing, entails businesses or organisations contacting Social Media Influencers to promote their brands. Companies nowadays use this technique by sending free goods to social media influencers in exchange for feedback or photos, inviting them to attend events where all is taken care of by the company, or sharing a specific message with their audience.

However, the problem with this type of marketing is that influencers may spread false or misleading information on these social media sites. This has been seen often with celebrities promoting goods with false statements in television ads and print media. To combat misleading ads, the government enacted new provisions in the Indian Consumer Protection Act, 2019, imposing penalties and liability on manufacturers and endorsers who promote or publish wrongful and misleading advertisements, as well as prohibiting the endorser from endorsing any products/services for a year.

The Consumer Protection Act, 2019

This bill aimed to move further towards *caveat venditor* from the prior existing notion of *caveat emptor*. The bill proposed the establishment of a regulatory authority called the Central Consumer Protection Authority (CCPA) powers of enforcement, unlike the existing Consumer Protection Councils which are only advisory bodies. It was the very first legislation that emphasized targeted advertising, market campaigns through influencers and celebrities. The changes brought celebrities and influencers under the purview of services and hence they could be held liable for advertisements that could harm the consumers.

The CCPA aimed to promote, protect, and enforce the rights of consumers qua misleading advertisements and unfair trade practices. They will have the power to initiate class-action suits including recall, refund and return of the product. It is a well-known fact that the courts in India are overburdened with existing cases and hence Mediation as an alternative method for dispute resolution can be implemented if agreed by both parties. The bill placed importance on Celebrities and promoters to check the validity of the claims made by the advertisement before promoting them. In the past we have seen many celebrities face backlash due to the lack of diligence for example; Amitabh Bachchan in the Maggi case, MS Dhoni in the Amrapali case and so on. The bill did not just affect Bollywood A-listers but also influencers across various platforms who now needed to be careful of what they are endorsing. In case of failure to comply a penalty from 10-50 Lakhs can be imposed in case of failure to comply with the rules. A ban from future endorsements can also be imposed for a period of 1-3 years.

Judicial Precedents

In the recent case of *Marico Limited v Abhijeet Bhansali,* a YouTube video by an influencer was taken down for undervaluing Marico's Parachute Coconut Oil which led to damage to the reputation of the company. The influencer used certain questionable techniques and claimed that the oil was not pure. The court observed that the influencer was promoting competitors of Parachute while portraying Parachute coconut oil in a bad light. In the case of *Reckitt & Colman v Kiwi T.T.K. Ltd.* the court held that:

"A manufacturer is not entitled to say that his competitor's goods are bad so as to puff and promote his goods. It, therefore, appears that if an action lies for defamation, an injunction may be granted."

Even though the influencer tried to take the defence under article 19(2) of the constitution and said that he had a right to freedom of speech, however, the Bombay High Court ruled that as he was comparing it oil with other competitors it is commercial speech and relied on the Supreme Court judgement in *Tata Press Limited v Mahanagar Telephone Nigam Limited* that commercial speech that is misleading is not protected under Article 19(2) of the constitution. The court ordered the removal of the video from YouTube to protect the plaintiff- company from irreparable harm and injury

Guidelines by Advertising Standards Council of India (ASCI)

On 27 May 2021, final guidelines for Influencers were released by the Advertising Standards Council of India which was to be applicable from 14th June 2021. The term influencer was defined by the ASCI in a broad sense as "someone who has access to an audience and the power to affect their audiences' purchasing decisions or opinions about a product, service, brand or experience, because of the influencer's authority, knowledge, position, or relationship with their audience" This definition also included Virtual influencers that are computer-generated 'people' or avatars like Miquela Sousa, a 19-year-old intelligent robot in LA who has 3 million followers on Instagram.

The main purpose of these guidelines was to ensure a customer's interests are protected by distinguishing between promotional content and other content of the influencer. This was done to prevent the manufactures and brands from using influencers as a source of marketing their products without giving a heads up to the consumer that the said promotion or review is a paid one. After the implementation of the guidelines, social media influencers are required to put disclosure labels as per the specifications of the guidelines to identify paid posts as advertisements. This includes "Material Connections" which is any connection between an advertiser and influencer that may affect the weight or credibility of the representation made by the influencer. This includes but is not limited to benefits and incentives like monetary compensation, free products, hotel stays, awards, family or employment connection between the influencer and advertiser etc.

The placement of the disclosure should be such that it should be easily visible and in a prominent, hard to miss manner and not hidden in hashtags. The disclosure labels that can be used are "Advertisement", "Ad", "Sponsored", "Collaboration", "Employee", "Free Gift." A virtual influencer would be required to disclose to the customers that the interaction is not with a real human being.

It is also advisable that influencers carry out Due diligence themselves to review that the advertiser is in the position to substantiate the claims that are being made in the advertisement.

The Code for Self-Regulation of Advertising by ASCI

The code aims to control the contents of advertisements so that they are not offensive and to ensure that the representations made are true and honest. The code applies to advertisers, advertising agencies and media. lays down various guidelines to ensure there is no discrimination based on these advertisements like` the Guidelines of Advertising for Skin Lightening or Fairness

Improvement Products, Guidelines for Advertising of Educational Institutions and Programs etc. A detailed Complaint Procedure is also aid out to cater for redressal.

Endorsement Agreement

An agreement that permits a company to use a celebrity's or an influencer's name and social status to promote a product or a service by his or her consent is called an **Endorsement Agreement**. Such an endorser must be a renowned personality within the field of the aforementioned product or service. The endorser gets an endorsement fee for allowing the company to use his or her name and promoting the product or service on their behalf. Such endorsement agreement elucidates the terms and conditions of the endorsement, which may include advertising guidelines for the endorser, usage of the product or service, how to use such product or avail such service, etc. The agreement may also include additional responsibilities of the endorser, such as what clothes to wear while endorsing, how to act in the advertisement, how to promote the product or service in a specified way, etc.

Usually, there are only two parties indulged in an endorsement agreement, the company that produces the product or facilitates the service and the celebrity or influencer who endorses said product or service. To avoid any dispute arising between the parties at any point in time in future, the validity period of the agreement between the company and the endorser is cited in the agreement itself. Throughout the period till the agreement is valid, the company approves the providence of the product or service to the endorser as per the demand made by him or her, which shall be provided free of cost and will also form a part of the endorsement compensation.

Advertisements are made for the purpose of influencing consumers and creating an urge to use these products or services. But the company would not want to create a negative impulse. Thus, the endorsement agreement includes a moral clause that serves as the guideline on how to regulate detrimental activities of the endorser, which may reflect immoral effects on the brand image or the product or service. The purpose of such moral provisions is to strictly forbid some of the adverse behaviours in the personal life of the endorsers, which can be seen as sexual acts, drug abuse, scandals, etc., which might influence the consumers in a negative way.

Endorsement agreement contracts majorly are of two types, Sports Endorsement Agreement or Celebrity Endorsement Agreement. When the company manufactures sports products or facilitates sports activities or services, the agreement made is Sports Endorsement Agreement. The company associates with one of the celebrated sportspersons to endorse their product or service. Every now and then, the company may also select a particular sports team, who has a higher probability of success in the tournament they are associated with and provide them with sponsorships, for which the company signs the sports sponsorship agreement. For example, the MPL advertisement on the Indian Cricket Team jersey reflects that MPL holds one of the main sponsorships for the Indian

Cricket Team and has signed the sports sponsorship agreement with BCCI. Since MPL is an e-sports platform, getting the services endorsed by a sports team will help the company target the right set of audience.

When the company manufactures a product or provides a service that is not related to sports, the agreement made is Celebrity Endorsement Agreement. One of the efficacious ways to endorse a good or service is getting a celebrity or an influencer to endorse their product or service. This method is highly effective as these celebrities and influencers are highly decorated and thus have a massive fan base to back their promotion. For example, supermodel Gigi Hadid is the brand ambassador of Maybelline. Since Maybelline is a cosmetics and makeup brand, getting the products endorsed by a supermodel will provide the right market segmentation.

Since these endorsement agreements are a form of contracts, there can be a breach in them. In a contract breach situation, both the parties involved have the right to terminate the contract, making it null and void. When a company forfeits the guidelines given in the agreement, the endorser can terminate the contract or file a suit against the company. Likewise, if the endorser forfeits the guidelines crafted by the company under the agreement, then the company can terminate the contract. The endorser should comprehend the guidelines stated by the company beforehand and then sign the agreement. Similarly, a company should analyse all the requirements crafted by the endorser beforehand and then sign the contract. Thus, both parties must make sure that they get assisted by an attorney to determine whether to sign the contract or not.

We could see many a time in the past where endorsers failed to do their homework on the brands they are endorsing, resulting in legal action, such as the widely publicised Pierce Brosnan-Pan Parag controversy, in which Brosnan denied ever agreeing to endorse a pan masala product with cancerous side effects, and Pan Bahar was held responsible for abusing Brosnan's celebrity for personal gain. In situations like this, the endorser must perform Due Diligence on their own or with the assistance of a legal advisor to ensure they are not putting themselves in jeopardy by endorsing the statements made by the brands.

How can Influencers avoid liabilities?

1. Social media influencers ought to ensure the product they are promoting does not violate or hurt any sentiments of a particular section of society.
2. A background check and research about the company can go a long way in building trust and confidence
3. It has become extremely crucial for Influencers to disclose any paid promotions, advertisements to their customers and followers on social media.

4. Along with the disclosure message, relevant hashtags like #collaboration #sponsored #paidpromotion #ad can help the customers to know when a product is based on personal opinion and when it is a part of an advertisement. However, the disclosure for an advertisement should not merely be just these hashtags as they are easy to miss.

5. Having a contract in place is always advisable, this is to ensure that there are no ambiguities in the agreements and there is proof of too.

6. Transparency is the best policy; a deprecating statement about a product they have not tried or used and giving a fabricated review of the experience is not allowed by law.

7. Due diligence, background checks, and personal research are non-negotiables for influencers now.

7.4 Fashion Photographers And Their Rights

Without photographs, fashion would be nothing. Photographers play a key role in the fashion industry and that is why we need to make them aware of their rights so that nobody takes advantage of their work. In the fashion industry, every single course of action is bound by agreements and contracts, be it hiring a model, photographer, designer, etc. With the pandemic around the corner, everything is digitalized. Social media being the perfect platform for reach for photographers can be a boon and bane at the same time. A lot of upcoming fashion photographers struggle with publishing their photos because of their work being stolen and shared by others without giving them any credits. With the help of various editing tools, watermarks can be removed thereby stealing their credit.

A photographer may register a copyright in a photograph, however, this is a recommendation rather than a requirement. Copyright protection begins the moment the work is created. The expression of a concept is copyrightable, but not the idea, according to copyright law. Normally, social media platforms have their own copyright rules. For example, Instagram states its Copyright rules which tells its users how to protect their own copyrighted works and avoid infringing the copyrights of other people when posting on Instagram, as well as how Instagram addresses reports of copyright infringements. But we must note that laws in different countries may vary. If the issue is still not resolved using its Help Centre, then it is better to move legally.

Countries pass laws to safeguard intellectual property for two primary reasons: first, to give statutory voice to the creator's moral and economic rights, and second, to foster creativity in order to encourage fair trade and accelerate the creator's and country's economic and social growth. The laws controlling Copyright protect intellectual property rights on photos. Legislators have taken strenuous attempts to protect photographers' rights by categorizing images in the "Artistic Category," which includes photographers under the idea of "Authors." The law grants the author-specific rights that can only be exercised by the author. The Indian Copyright Act of 1957 is comprehensive. It protects not only traditional paper images but also online photographs, despite the fact that they are not specifically addressed. The "first owners" of a literary work, according to Section 17(a) of the Indian Copyright Act, are the authors of that work, and first ownership will always remain with the author, even if the rights to the literary work have been transferred. In short, this section states that the photographer is the original proprietor of the photograph and that he has all rights to it. The existing copyright legislation is capable of meeting the difficulties brought by modern technology and provides a solid legal foundation for copyright protection. Section 51 of the Indian Copyright Act of 1957 safeguards photographers' expression from infringement. Copyright infringement is defined as any violation or infringement of the author's rights. In addition, Indian courts have ruled that publishing a photograph without the author's or owner's consent from another published material constitutes an infringement of the photograph. However, infringement does not occur when the identical photograph is utilised by another person without the goal of obtaining illicit profits. Also, if the photograph is used for legislative or academic purposes, it will not be considered a copyright infringement and will be considered authorised use of photographs without the photographer's prior authorization.

The Copyright Act of 1957 grants creators (photographers) of artistic works certain exclusive rights. The photographer's rights are as follows:

(1) Right to reproduce, which means that no one may make one or more copies of a work, or a major portion of it, without the copyright owner's permission. He can use the right to reproduce as a legal basis for various sorts of exploitation of copyrighted work.

(2) Right to make any adaptation of the work, which means it entails the creation of a new work or the alteration of existing work in a similar or different form.

According to Section 57 which deals with authors special rights, the author of a work shall have the right to claim authorship of his work, to restrain or claim damages in respect of any distortion, mutilation, modification, or other act in relation to the said work, whether or not the author's copyright has been assigned entirely or partially if such acts would be prejudicial to his honour or reputation.

WATERMARKS

Watermarks serve a similar purpose as trademarks. Its purpose is to indicate that the shot was taken by a specific photographer. Anyone who wants to use the photo will see the watermark and be able to find out who took it. It is up to him whether or not he contacts the photographer and asks for permission. Watermarks don't play a legal role in the court of law. The evidence that can be adduced are agreements, circumstantial evidence, other photos in the series, etc.

REMEDIES

Injunction, damages and accounts, delivery of illegal copies, and damages for conversion are covered by civil remedies (Sections 55 to 62).

Criminal remedies (Sections 63–66) deal with the accused's imprisonment or fine, or both, as well as the seizure and transfer of infringing copies to the copyright owner. In other words, it aims to penalize individuals who engage in piracy on a commercial basis.

Administrative remedies (Section 53) – involve petitioning the Registrar of Copyrights to prohibit the importation of infringing copies into India, as well as the delivery of confiscated infringing copies to the copyright owner.

Other than this there are various non-legal ways in which we can address this issue. The trending ways of going 'live' or posting their concerns on the social media platform have been proved very effective. But we should always bear in mind that these too have their consequences like defamation, wrong allegations, etc.

7.5 Fashion Blog, Bloggers And The Law

Blogging is the art of expressing one's opinion and is a revelation of character to the outer world. The culture of blogging to a fast pace with the advent of social media and the need to constantly feed consumers with information. Blogging is therefore identified by its potential to assess and forecast trends in the industry and roll out new pieces of information with eye-catching graphics which also help create a large reader base. With the advent of vlogging, which is the video-graphic representation of information, blogging has received a competitor of concern. As a result of which many bloggers have shifted to vlogging as it is a more popular and mass-friendly form of info-communication. Blogging is to date a lucrative form of business for many who had spent countless hours perfecting their craft. Many bloggers have had the opportunity to represent brands and vouch for them through their platform. This commercial aspect of blogging is considered the root of many lawsuits. Violation of contracts, pay discrepancy, IP infringement, defamation and copying within the blogger community, are some of the most noticeable forms of conflicts in the blogging space. With major fashion houses across the globe tapping into the blogger reservoir, many issues emerge as to the viability and standardization of these collaborations. It has been found that many bloggers eventually turn into mere puppets at the disposal of these fashion houses and are left with no creative freedom, being bound by stringent contracts. There have been incidents of conscious awakening in the blogging community in terms of walking hand-in-hand with fast fashion and constantly helping gain traction to the latest trends. A shift from trends to styles is what dominates the blogging scene today. With the advent of Instagram influencers, the art of blogging is receiving a setback like never seen before. In yesteryears, fashion frenzies used to read and scroll through the artistic explanations of latest trends and collections launched by brands, but today, "insta-celebs" do the work for you by just posting a picture which is then virtually hunted by the followers. The blogging landscape is meeting with changes assisted by technology therefore it is pertinent to understand the emerging issues in this field and forecast some legal trends for fashion bloggers.

Blogging & the Laws

In terms of IPR, both, the presenter/blogger and the represented/the concerned fashion brand or celebrity are at high risk of being infringed, copied, and misinterpreted. The fashion industry has always been susceptible to these risks.

The photographs used by both fashion brands and bloggers in their campaigns are subject to illegal use outside the dimensions of fair use doctrine. In one of the instances, back in 2011, ZARA was accused of stealing photographs and design work of bloggers and imprinting the same on their clothes, and making money out of it. This serves as a perfect example of a case where a fashion brand had infringed on the IP of a fashion blogger. After massive criticism and outcry from the blogging community, the t-shirts and other items of clothing were taken down by Inditex.

Fashion bloggers often endorse certain brands to raise their own profile and also to help the brand gain customers. This is a fair and universally acknowledged practice but the only concern is that bloggers have to reveal any form of paid promotion or brand deals that underwent in their publication. The FTC Regulation of Native Advertising mandate that all the paid promotions be revealed to the consumers so that they can make informed choices and decided for a brands' worth on their own.

Blogs offer a platform for interaction between readers and consumers who like to put forth their opinions on literally everything. So it is the responsibility of the fashion blog to lay out certain rules of privacy and terms and conditions to ensure that the community engaging over their platform is not being disrespectful to anyone or a group of individuals. In doing so, the accountability of the blog owner is enhanced and guarantees protection from legal sharks in case of any possible disputes.

Conclusion

The ambiguity with regard to what is eligible to be put by fashion bloggers is bound to stay. But bloggers can take certain precautions to protect their own IP and safeguard themselves from possible lawsuits from celebrities and brands that they tend to cover in their blog pieces. Blogs are the brands of trendy journaling and thus need mechanisms to protect and foster brand quality and image.

Starting off by registering a domain name guarantees website protection and no other blogger or fashion brand can then use it. Bloggers can then get copyright over their exclusive photographs and imagery and also for their content. They could also rope in Blockchain technology to detect infringers of their copyrighted work.

On the contrary, fashion should also be very cautious about the way in which they use the copyrighted work of photographers, brands and also should respect celebrity/model rights. Procuring licenses from modeling or photograph agencies should be the ideal way to use pictures on blogs. If not then due credit should be given to these agencies and photographers. Giving credit does not eliminate the risk of being sued but assures the copyright owner of fair use. Blog owners should also respect the limits of criticism and must ensure that it does not turn into defamation. Defamation is bad-mouthing about someone or something without solid evidence to back it up. Therefore, bloggers should refrain from engaging in defamatory activities as it is also not considered good practice for their own brand value as well.

Following these basic steps could help bloggers stay away from the parameters of court and legal authorities. But at the same time, it is often the responsibility of the judiciary to check the balance between freedom of expression and curtailment of free speech. It, therefore, becomes quintessential for bloggers to understand the balance and harmonize their content to build a platform of trust.

7.6 Social Media, Fashion and Law

Within the pristine comforts of our homes we, with the utmost causality perform the action of 'select and post', what we think is entrapped within the space of our feed and is only visible to the select of our 'social media audience' is in-fact visible data to the far and near, if as students we consider SCC online as an open access server, our social media is an open access version of our lives encapsulated with data, tauntingly laid out for absolutely anybody to go through and use. However, sticking to the parallel, if any sort of research material is used from the said SCC online the user is made aware and given due credit, a resultant of the complex citations, but such cannot be said regarding data on social media.

Social media is the "most distinctive medium for communication" for sales of counterfeit goods, thereby undermining brand protection and resulting in both loss of revenue and damage to brand reputation, as well as causing issues for both government and consumers. - The UK Intellectual Property Office (2015).

The sudden growth of counterfeit products on social media sites is astounding, fake-goods vendors have progressed in droves to social media platforms like Facebook and Instagram to ply their trade taking superiority of the fact as to how anything on social media is open to everyone. Social media has quickly evolved into an under-reported yet crucial hub for counterfeiters. It's past time for businesses to adapt, just as counterfeiters have, and reclaim control of their brand on social media. Counterfeiters have swiftly figured out where to sell each type of product and how to advertise them adequately. For example, it appears that counterfeiters' preferred channel for selling imitation beauty items is Instagram. A survey indicated that a fifth to a third of the comments on some trademarked hashtags on the network were from counterfeit product dealers.[133]
Using social media to promote counterfeit goods is not a novel tactic. In reality, some social media personalities have been chastised in recent years for actively promoting counterfeit goods.

Because of the rise of e-commerce and the financial incentives presented by counterfeiters, many social media influencers are inclined to endorse counterfeit items. Social media sites are perfect forums for illicit activities because of their capacity to swiftly connect and share information with people all over the world. Counterfeiters and other entities can use social media platforms to target specific consumers based on their online activity. It appears that no prominent social media platform is immune to these problems, and many companies are grappling with how to prevent bad actors from abusing the platform in ways that harm consumers. It can be understood that social media is particularly favoured because:

1. Low entrance hurdles- anyone may create an account and duplicate photographs from reputable sites that are nearly identical.

2. Use of hashtags, spam bots, advertisements, and other techniques to increase reach and visibility.

3. Social platforms' increased "Buy now" features make it simple to collect payment outside of the platforms.

4. Closed groups and direct communications for social selling and perceived trust.

---

133 The growth of fake products on social media, Red Points (2021), https://www.redpoints.com/blog/the-growth-of-fake-products-on-social-media/ (last visited Jan 24, 2022).

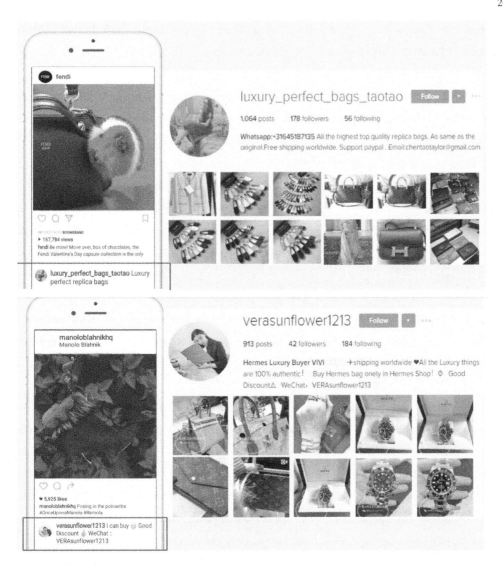

Which ultimately results in-

1. Loss of industry revenue as a direct result.

2. Indirect impact: Impairment to the industry's and individual companies' credibility

3. Indirect effects: tax revenue losses and rising unemployment

4. Concerns about standards of quality

To further aggravate the problem, Swindlers utilise social media networks to market a variety of scams to a big audience; posts could range from investment possibilities to commodities or services for sale. They will also send direct messages to anyone attempting to extract money or personal

information that can be used to get access to bank accounts and credit cards. The following are some examples of frauds that have surfaced on social media sites:

Scams using cryptocurrency - Fraudsters cold call and pitch 'get rich overnight' mining and cryptocurrency investments on social media. To register a trading account, victims sign up for bitcoin investment platforms and provide personal information. Victims may not realise they have been cheated until the website has been disabled and suspects can no longer be reached.

Scams involving free tickets or coupons - be wary of posts or messages offering to offer 'freebies.' Messages circulating on the internet say that supermarkets and other businesses are giving out coupons and tickets. Those who click on links are frequently sent to a fake website or put in contact with a con artist.

Personal information - Fraudsters can get your personal information from your social media profiles and use it to impersonate you. Make sure your privacy settings are set to private so that strangers can't read your postings or access your data.[134]

There is a prospect that personal data will be exposed if users use a service that values personal information. This could happen by accident or through security flaws. Because ones account is filled with personal information that online crooks can exploit for a variety of purposes, they target social media platforms. The data acquired can be used against individuals in the form of blackmail or impersonation. A cybercriminal can open a credit card or bank account in your name if he or she obtains enough of one's personal information. If hackers gain access to a user's account, they can fool people into believing they are legitimate firms. They can then use naïve parties to supply credit card information for things they will never receive to syphon money right into their pockets. The majority of people's smartphones currently track and record location data . Location data can be targeted by burglars or stalkers because of geo-location information shared by them. Social media apps are particularly interested in their data because it provides insight into your habits and whereabouts, which advertisers can use to target ads to you at specific times of the day.[135]

Many social networking apps' privacy agreements specify that the platform owns the content users post, such as photos, videos, and messages, even if you opt to remove your account. For example, Instagram states that it does not claim ownership of the content created by its users. However, the

134Social Media Fraud, https://www.herts.police.uk/Information-and-services/Advice/Crime-prevention/Protect-your-money/Social-media-fraud (last visited Jan 24, 2022).
135 8 reasons why social media is bad for your data security, 8 Reasons Why Social Media is Bad for Your Data Security, https://www.hp.com/us-en/shop/tech-takes/8-reasons-why-social-media-is-bad (last visited Jan 24, 2022).

user offers Instagram a "non-exclusive, fully paid and royalty-free, transferable, sub-licensable, global right to use their content," according to the rules. This means that, other from the fact that it is not an exclusive licence, Instagram has all of the rights of the original content owner. Photographers should be aware of this because if they sell a picture under an exclusive licence, uploading the image on Instagram would be a violation of that licence. Instagram has the ability to sublicense private material. This implies it might freely licence a user's photograph or video to any third party without asking permission, notifying the user, or offering compensation. It may potentially take a user's content and licence it to another company in exchange for a fee, which Instagram retains. Similarly, Instagram can utilise any user's content for its own purposes or marketing without asking permission, notifying the user, or paying the user. The ability to edit, alter, share, copy, and convey the content is also included. Instagram can not only sublicense, use, distribute, alter, run, copy, publicly perform, show, translate, and create derivative works of a user's content, but it can also pass the rights to do so to a third party — all without the user's permission. It is able to do so since the terms of the licence say that it is transferrable. This means Instagram can freely assign or licence the rights to utilise its users' content to other businesses or individuals. The accord has no geographical restrictions, so it might perform any of the aforementioned things anywhere on the planet. The same laws do not apply to Instagram's material, which is protected by Intellectual Property and cannot be copied, modified, edited, published, used, or licenced, according to the terms.

Telecom service providers, network service providers, internet service providers, web-hosting service providers, search engines like Google, online payment sites, online auction sites, e-commerce platforms like Amazon and Flipkart, and platforms like Facebook, Twitter, Blogspot, and WordPress are all considered social media intermediaries under the new IT Rules 2021. Currently, Section 79 of the Information Technology Act (IT Act) protects intermediaries, including social media intermediaries, from responsibility for content uploaded by third parties, including users, on their websites. It codifies the 'safe harbour' framework, which protects intermediaries from legal accountability for anything illegal that their users do as long as they follow specific due diligence guidelines, such as complying with the government's content takedown requests. In the meantime, legitimate publishers, such as newspapers, are in charge of the content they host. Publishers are said to have complete control over the information they host, yet there can be further implementations to protect an users data, Individual rights should be at the centre of privacy and data protection, according to the first principle of the Indian Privacy Code. As a result, the Bill's user rights must be evaluated to ensure that users' right to privacy takes precedence and data fiduciaries' interests are met through restricted exceptions. Users in India who are identified as "major data fiduciaries" are required to set up infrastructure that allows them to verify their accounts willingly. This regulation restricts internet anonymity and, as a result, the right to privacy. It will also provide social media companies access to people's government-issued identification documents. This may result in the collection of demographic data from various companies and databases. This opens up a lot of opportunities for businesses to establish granular user profiles and commercialise personal and sensitive personal data. Allowing the Data Protection Authority to control non-personal and anonymised data, as a result, the focus would shift to the protection of citizens' digital rights, as well as the establishment of solid regulatory procedures for non-personal data. Data fiduciaries should only acquire as much information as they require. There needs to be a more in-depth conversation about the types of data that businesses demand, and their objectives cannot jeopardise people's basic privacy.

Chapter 8. Fashion and Technology

The fashion industry is one of the largest economic contributors to any economy due to this, fashion has always been forward-looking. It continuously incorporates new technologies and embraces innovations to keep up with the transient trends of the 21st century. In this chapter, we'll understand about the application of technology in fashion, new trends and law.

8.1 Artificial Intelligence and Blockchain

Artificial Intelligence much like fashion is evolving at an exponential rate. The challenges confronting the global fashion industry ranging from raw material acquisition, labor conditions, factory information, as well as environmental and sustainability concerns- are often complex and hard to tackle.

This is where AI, Blockchain, and emerging technologies present an opportunity to leverage sustainability, social impact, and ethical sourcing in one of the world's biggest industries.

Blockchain and Artificial Intelligence (AI) are often referred to as the yin and the yang of predicting and recording reality through the use of algorithms and cryptography.

Blockchain, as the name suggests, are chunks of blocks used to store and contain transactions sequentially in an open-source ledger that is accessible to all the stakeholders of that transaction. It is distributed and verified across a peer-to-peer network, designed to efficiently manage enormous amounts of data in real-time on a decentralized platform. Simultaneously, its encryption model effectively keeps unwanted eyes off the network, with no possibility of tampering with the same by a central authority or intermediary.

The concern regarding the duplicity of goods runs deep in the fashion industry, particularly in the luxury brands section, where consumers constantly are fearful of acquiring unoriginal and counterfeit products. The application of Blockchain technology enables brands to narrate a story and give credit to all the people involved in the process by spreading throughout the supply chain. Consumers may now avail information ranging from the procurement of raw materials and factory details to how finished products were packed and transported. The complete disclosure of facts and transparency also offers customers with the knowledge they may need to select/reject counterfeit items, products, or materials that violate environmental, ethical or moral codes of conduct, thereby confirming authenticity across the supply chain.

By leveraging this technology, manufacturers and designers can also protect their brands against replicas and counterfeiting by providing traceability and eliminating all duplicate materials at the source. The mandatory registration of merchandise helps fashion brands to preserve and secure their digital identity in a convenient manner. Moreover, the immutability and decentralisation of records simplify royalty tracking, allowing designers to generate an unalterable proof of production and track both licenced designs and trademarks, encouraging corporate social responsibility and adding confidence and security to the fashion sector.

E.g., For example,The Shanghai Fashion Week witnessed Babyghost collaborating with technology providers to enable everyone in the supply chain, including customers, to validate the legitimacy of its apparel. The firm embedded little chips inside its clothes and accessories, which anybody could scan to establish if the authenticity of the outfit.

In contrast, cloud-based Artificial Intelligence (AI) is emerging from a position of continually learning, analysing and documenting an individual's attributes based on their search. It creates high predictability of fashion websites, where machine algorithms frequently produce advertisements, posts, articles, and searches that cater best to our tastes and preferences.

With over big % of population using social media, the fashion and style industry is deeply entwined to act as an expert tool by connecting brands directly with the consumers. AI algorithms are responsible for providing well-informed and relevant product recommendations to online retail clients. Fashion brands develop advertisements for target audiences using internet cookies that marketers can track. Scrutinising customer's trends and purchase habits, these cookies are subsequently delivered as adverts to chosen persons who then function as possible clients. This not only assists marketers in meticulous Market Segmentation and Geo location-based sales but also helps in improving business operations, demand forecasts and inventory optimization. Manufacturers obtain a good understanding of inventory checks and restocking depending on seasons and establish locations based on ongoing trend forecasting.

The intended result is to elevate customer experiences via personalization that helps foster long-term growth and success.

Apart from that, AI is bridging the gap between brand owners and customers by introducing product development strategies that aid in the interfaces with employees, partners, and consumers, enabling the large-scale creation and development of a new company.

Their influence is felt primarily through the optimization and improvement of Visual Searching in the fashion industry by utilising its investigative history and predictability to accurately forecast trends and product demand, allowing retailers to better manage inventory and cater to customers' needs and demands. This is accomplished by helping consumers visualise their ideas by capitalising on their personal dilemmas and limited understanding and exposing them to AI chatbot, Virtual stylists, organising prizes, reacting to posts comments, and getting consumer feedback.

Artificial Intelligence is the ability given to computers to perform tasks that generally require human intelligence. The machines are incorporated with artificial human-like intelligence which allows them to perform tasks similar to humans. AI is the talk of the decade as it considerably reduces the amount of human intervention and helps in saving time and costs which are crucial for any industry. AI can be designed to do a particular task with the ability to teach itself with each outcome allowing it to become better and faster with each action.

We interact with Artificial Intelligence daily without dwelling much into it, right from when you ask Alexa about the weather to when you upload a picture on Facebook where the face recognition feature suggests friends to tag.

IS THE FASHION INDUSTRY READY FOR AN AI REVOLUTION?

Gone are the days where people wore whatever was created by designers, people have now started becoming very conscious of how they dress, what kinds of clothes suits them and the way a person dresses up has become accepted as a medium to express creativity and individuality,

To understand the preferences of the consumer, fashion retailers need insights into the behaviour of the customer, for this reason, the fashion industry is gradually becoming data-driven. By collecting data on consumer behaviour, the brands can understand the needs and demands of their customer, this in turn would increase the likelihood that their product would be purchased. Online shopping is becoming the new normal hence online fashion retail stores are becoming extremely popular among brands. These online stores are on their way to replace the traditional brick and mortar stores, due to this reason fashion retailers must make their brands digitally mature. AI is the future and one after another it has paved its way into each industry. To keep up with the competitors an AI revolution is essential, especially for smaller brands.

Many reports suggest that by the year 2020, over 80% of retailers would be using chatbots in some or the other capacity. And rightly predicted, gradually all online stores have introduced provisions to interact with their consumers through chatbots, the customers can select from filters, style preferences and seek help from these chatbots by clarifying their queries and resolving grievances. As these chatbots can learn from previous data they prove to be extremely helpful in gauging consumer mentality and dealing with similar issues more accurately in the future.

It is safe to say that artificial intelligence is no longer a distant future, the fashion industry has started to meet technology. The industry utilizes artificial intelligence in a variety of ways including providing a forecast of the trends in the future or merchandising.

8.2 Application of AI in Fashion

- *Artificial intelligence as a designer*

Amazon

Artificial Intelligence has successfully donned several roles, it might not come as a surprise to see AI excelling as a fashion stylist and designer. If you were asked to name the top high fashion brands, it is highly unlikely that you would mention Amazon, this is because Amazon is not synonymous with fashion, YET. However, they plan to change that notion. Since its very inception, Amazon has used AI to suggest recommendations based on what the user has previously purchased. The company now wants to further expand its horizon and create the next generation of brands rather than just a platform on which brands sell their products. Amazon has created an AI fashion designer that utilizes machine learning to notice and track fashion trends. It's research team at San Francisco has developed an AI designer; it is an algorithm that allows them to take inspiration from images of a particular style in fashion and by taking this inspiration, it creates new pieces which are similar in style. In 2017 the company had also announced an Echo Look camera that was intended to be a fashion-focused stylist. The Alexa- enabled camera was designed to act as a personal stylist that would give you feedback on your outfits while working in sync with the Look's companion application. It allowed the user to take pictures, videos and share them on social media However after three years from its launch the product was discontinued by Amazon.

Tommy Hilfiger

We live in a world that is moving at a very fast pace, everybody wants things done at the earliest, right from instant coffee in the morning to anticipating a "next day delivery" after ordering something online. Technology is impacting the supply chain to move at a faster pace; incorporation of computer vision, natural language understanding and deep learning are being used to produce key insights on trends to both expedite the initial design process and better predict demand for products.

International Business Machines Corporation (IBM) had teamed up with Tommy Hilfiger and The Fashion Institute of Technology (FIT) on a project called the Reimagine Retail project. The project aimed to prove how by utilizing AI retailers can gain an edge in terms of speed and make the design process more efficient. Students of FIT were given access to IBM research's AI capabilities including computer vision, natural language understanding, and deep learning techniques specifically trained with fashion data. Those tools were applied to an extensive library of Tommy Hilfiger products, runway images and thousands of patterns from fabric sites. They then brought about key silhouettes, colours, and novel prints and patterns that could be used as informed inspiration to the students' designs. The machine analysis provided insights into the colours, patterns and silhouettes in an extensive manner, the design students were able to take inspiration from popular trends in fashion and combine that with the essence of Tommy Hilfiger and create completely new design concepts

Myntra

It is one of the biggest fashion retailers in India, its Rapid project works with an AI-based software that tells them what designs are most likely to be sold. The software has helped the design team cut down the time taken to design clothes from 6 months to merely 1 month. The team at Rapid affectionately calls the algorithm as 'Ratatouille.' After the key requirements are entered for the product, 'Ratatouille' produces designs that have the potential to become a bestseller. Myntra's brand Moda Rapido and Here & Now are the brainchild of the Rapid project and they are some of the largest apparel brands on Myntra. Human input is also encouraged to keep up with the cultural nuances and the ability to connect with the clothes to give them a personality. Data-backed designs also improve the confidence of designers, hence AI compliments the creative flow of designers while also making it data-driven.

- *Trend forecasting*

In 2018 the fast-fashion brand H&M revealed in their quarterly report that they have $4.3 billion worth of unsold clothes in their inventories. Due to this their profits took a massive hit. A fashion brand needs to understand the demand of the consumer so they can bring similar goods to the market. This is where trend forecasting plays an important role, fashion trends are important because it tells us about the popular styles of clothes and accessories which the consumer is likely to purchase. Trend forecasting in fashion essentially focuses on colours, technique, fabric, patterns that are likely to become popular.

Forecasting is extremely important for any business because it helps in understanding the future of the market; what kind of products need to be manufactured and in what quantity. Trend forecasting is essential for any e-business especially in the fashion industry as fashion is always evolving. Traditionally forecasting was done by analyzing data from sales, social and political trends and fashion shows. Now there is a wide range of innovative technologies available that can be used to draw insights.

WGSN

It is one of the largest fashion forecasters in the world, they predict and forecast upcoming trends. Artificial intelligence analyzes hundreds and thousands of images from Runway shows or even social media networking sites like Instagram and Pinterest and generates insights relating to the colour and patterns and the fabric which is most prevalent in the upcoming season. The most prominent colours are recorded and it analyses which colours are being repeated. A similar analysis is also done for patterns for fabrics and different Runway shows.

This analysis also plays a very important role in uplifting an important aspect prevalent in the fashion industry i.e. sustainability. By manufacturing new clothes according to predicted future trends, fashion brands can save a lot of time and effort as they would have an idea about what the customer demands. The amount that could be wasted would be a lot lesser and this would minimise unsold inventory and reduce the waste which would be a big step towards fashion sustainability

Manually the process of analysing fashion trends by going over data is time-consuming as there is a lot of data that is involved and there is always the risk of human error but with artificial intelligence in the equation, the process of predicting trends becomes extremely easy and efficient. These trends can be predicted 1-2 years in advance or for the next season this gives time to the company to produce similar goods in the meantime.

- *Virtual Style Assistant*

Do you love the idea of buying clothes but find it difficult to identify your style and understand what looks best on you? Young fashion shoppers today are demanding personalization more than ever. According to an IBM study, 52% of female Generation Z would like to see tools that allow them to customize products for themselves. Fashion companies like Stitch Fix, Wantable have tried to address this issue by hiring professional stylists who provide personalized recommendations based on custom parameters set by you. Customers can sign up and fill out a detailed questionnaire which helps these companies in understanding individual preferences.

It is no surprise that in today's time social media plays a very important role in shaping our ideas, inspirations and opinions. Fashion companies have identified this and they are already using social networking sites like Instagram and Pinterest to track the latest trends in fashion and understand what the customers want so that they can produce similar goods.

Stitch Fix

Every month, Stitch Fix sends a box of clothes or accessories based on the responses and information that the customer has provided about themselves. The customers can keep the clothes that they like and return the ones that they don't like. This works out well for the customers as they have an expert stylist who is shopping on their behalf after knowing their recommendations and preferences.

The algorithm learns about your preferences each month based on the information you provided along with the data of the clothes that you keep and the ones you return. They also gather information from your Pinterest and Instagram accounts to understand your aesthetic and help you in discovering your style. They provide you with the feedback form after each shipment so that if so that they can keep up with the customer service

The Yes

Another similar AI shopping app is "The Yes", it takes items from retailers and brand websites and shows them to the customer. If you like the dress or you would like to buy similar styles tap on "yes" if you are not interested then tap "no." With each recommendation given due to artificial intelligence and machine learning the results are improved and tailored according to the person's personal preference. Other platforms that offer similar services are Wishi, Trunk Club and Wantable, they aim to help you in building your version of a perfect wardrobe.

- ● *Virtual Fitting Rooms*

Do you remember in 2016 when Pokémon Go sent the world into a frenzy, this game changed the way augmented reality (AR) was perceived. Since then, AR has entered many industries; from Gaming to Fashion and Education. It has become a popular way for brands to advertise their products.

The fashion industry has used AR to interact with its customers through visual try-on. A variety of retailers in the fashion industry such as Nike, Burberry, Gucci, and Converse have adopted this technology. The technology that argument reality works on is that it generates graphics on top of actual reality, in simple words this means that it does not create a world of its own but rather adds something graphically to the already existing reality around us.

Style Me

Fashion companies like Style Me have developed a way to personalize the shopping journey of a person. The individual can create an avatar of themselves including the measurement, body shape, skin tone, hairstyle etc. in a three-dimensional version. This allows the customers to try on clothes without leaving the comfort of their own homes and also getting an idea of how the clothes or accessories would fit on them.

Virtual fitting rooms enable the shoppers to try out items virtually without physically touching the items. It is predicted that global virtual fitting rooms will grow from $3 million in 2019 to $6.5 million by 2025. The covid-19 pandemic has accelerated the growth of this technology and made it more prevalent, Virtual fitting rooms can work by using augmented reality as well as be powered by artificial intelligence, these technologies create a three-dimensional full-body replica of the person by using algorithms, machine learning, web cameras, etc.

Gucci

The fashion brand made a debut with AI by launching its augmented reality "try on" sneakers. The shoppers could virtually try the luxury brand's line of Ace sneakers. The customer just had to download the application on their mobile and enable the camera to point downwards, a range of sneakers were available for the user to select from. The user could see a virtual image of the selected Modi sneakers on his feet

Sephora

Sephora has introduced a virtual assistant, which allows you to get virtual makeovers, experiment with hundreds of eyeshadows, lip colour and even eyelashes till you find the one that is perfect for you. All the customer needs to do is download the Sephora mobile application and select the product which they want to try, the makeup app uses the facial recognition feature that enables the customer to try the products, the application scans your face and detects eyes, lips and cheeks to understand the application of the product on your face. After the scan is complete, you can virtually try on what eyeliner would suit you or what lipstick would look good on you. You can compare colour swatches from a variety of brands side by side on your virtual arm. It also allows you to get virtual step-by-step tutorials that are customised for your face and also in line with the outfit that you wear.

- ### Counterfeiting

The World Customs Organization estimates that 7-9 % of global trading relates to fake products. Today we live in a world where the internet has become an indispensable part of our life, the world has become a common marketplace that has enabled people to purchase products online. At the same time, it also accelerated the sale of counterfeit products. The problem with counterfeit products that are sold on e-commerce sites is that it is impossible to identify the product is not authentic until it arrives, by then the person has generally paid for the purchase and there is little that can be done for redressal.

Machine learning and deep learning can be used in anti-counterfeit applications, Artificial intelligence utilizes computer vision to recognize fake products. Machines and algorithms are used to detect the close details and through these details, authentic items are separated from counterfeit ones. Data science can identify counterfeit products, for instance, if the fabric in question is of lower quality; deep learning algorithms identify this deviation and hence report the item as a duplicate.

Entrupy

It is an artificial intelligence startup that identifies counterfeit products of various luxury brands. They have an extremely user-friendly process, they provide their user with a custom camera with a microscope lens and their application, the user has to scan the product to determine whether it is original. For instance, if a retailer wants to determine whether a Louis Vuitton bag is original he would scan the handbag and as he does so the machine learning algorithm would determine its authenticity. The startup claims to have an accuracy rate of 98% which makes them quite popular with luxury brands.

DataWeave

It is a Seattle-based company that utilizes deep learning to detect and remove fake products from E-Commerce websites. DataWeave has a built-in Fashion Tagger that assigns labels to the various attributes of fashion products, for instance, the colour, material, patterns and other specifications are automatically assigned to the clothes that are processed. Anshul Garg who worked as a former AI specialist at the company explained in his blog post how the technology functions. "The image is then converted to 0s and 1s, and fed into our home-brewed convolutional neural network trained on millions of images with several variations. These images were acquired from diverse sources on the Web, such as user-generated content (UGC), social media, fashion shows, and hundreds of eCommerce websites around the world. If present, text-based information associated with images, like product title, metadata, and product descriptions are used to enhance the accuracy of the output and leverage non-visual cues for the product, like the type of fabric. Natural-language processing, normalization and several other text processing techniques are applied here. In these scenarios, the text and image pipelines are merged based on assigned weightage and priorities to generate the final list of product attributes" Initiatives like Amazon's Anti-Counterfeiting Coalition, Big Data Anti-Counterfeiting Alliance launched by Alibaba have been to counter the issue of counterfeit goods, this alliance also included brands like Swarovski, and Huawei, Samsung, Louis Vuitton.

- *AI as Fashion Models*

Stakeholders in the fashion industry, especially models and influencers are put under a lot of scrutiny for promoting unrealistic standards of beauty. This case might become stronger with the coming of AI- Influencers.

Miquela (@lilmiquela)

She is a Brazilian American model, singer and a social media influencer with an Instagram following of 3 million. Much like any popular fashion influencer she wears clothes designed by luxury labels like Chanel and Prada, promotes fashion brands and designers on her social media handle, however what separates her from other influences is the fact she is completely artificial. Even though she is an AI model she is living the dream, in 2018 she made modelling debut at Milan Fashion Week, she promoted Prada's collection by three dimensional GIFs and modelled for Pat McGrath's make-up line.

Shudu

The French luxury fashion brand Balmain had enlisted 3 digitally created models for its pre-fall 2018 campaign. These models wore digitally created versions of the collection. These Computer-Generated imageries (CGI) Models are Margot, Zhi and Shudu. Shudu is the world's first digital supermodel, she is the computer-generated creation of British photographer Cameron-James Wilson. Despite being just a three-dimensional character, she has an Instagram following of 140,000 followers. She has been a part of various campaigns for Fenty Beauty. She has featured in Vogue, Hyperbeast, V Magazine and she was named as one of the most influential people on the internet by Time.

Lalaland

Similarly, Lalaland is a start-up in Amsterdam that aims to bring together both tangible aspects and imagination in the world of AI. They wish to make online shopping more inclusive and sustainable while also ensuring profitability. The startup develops hyper-realistic AI-driven virtual models for e-commerce platforms. They create fully AI-generated models that fashion retailers can use to promote their brands while showcasing their products online. The consumer can select a model that is closest to their skin colour, age and height to understand how the clothes would fit them.

8.3 IP AND ARTIFICIAL INTELLIGENCE

Artificial Intelligence has incorporated itself into our daily lives, whether when we go shopping or listen to music, we are interacting with AI in one way or another. AI has slowly found its way into the creative industry as well, musicians for a long time have relied on AI to help them in creating songs and melodies. The legendary singer David Bowie used an application called Verbasizer that helped him in creating new combinations of words that he could use as part of the lyrics in his songs. A Google-owned company called DeepMind is a software that is capable of creating music after listening to recordings.

With sophisticated techniques being combined with the flourishing technology it is only a matter of time before machines can start producing inventions, artistic work without any human intervention. In such scenarios which go beyond the conventional borders of humans acting as owners as the copyright and patent rights are challenged the question of ownership in Intellectual Property particularly Copyright and Patents arises for these robotic artists.

Copyright Protection

Copyright is an exclusive right that is granted to the creator of an original work allowing them to have exclusive control over the use and distribution of these rights. The rationale and justification behind this were the notions that the author is an originator merged with Locke's economic theory of possessive individualism. To obtain a copyright, it is essential that the work should be original and should be in tangible form. The subject matter that copyright deals with is artistic and literary work.

There have been many areas where AI can be applied creatively, whether it is to write novels, compose music or create paintings. The question that arises in this regard is whether works created by AI can be protected under copyright law and if so, who you be considered the creator. There can be two outcomes here, either the work can be created with some human interference, in these cases, there is human interaction; the creativity can be drawn from the human and the implementation of the same can be done by AI. In such cases, the human is considered to be the author. The laws regarding the creation of an artistic work by AI without any human intervention are ambiguous and uncertain. Most jurisdictions like Spain and Germany state that only works that are created by humans are entitled to copyright protection.

However, due to the technological boom, computers and machines are no longer just working from the sidelines, they can now actually make decisions and engage in creative processes without human intervention. In such a scenario, if the work created by the AI is deemed to be free of copyright protection as the author is not a human, then it would be very convenient for the competitors and to use the product for free and this would lead to huge losses for the company that originally invested in the technology since they do not have any legal right available to protect themselves. In such instances, the authorship may rest with the person who developed the AI.

In the case of Naruto v. Slater which is popularly known as the "monkey selfie case" in the United States of America determined that a copyright can not exist for a picture that is taken by a monkey, since this picture was taken without any human intervention. Along the same lines, the US Copyright Office does not consider works made by non-humans to be copyrightable, a work must be made by a human to be registrable. Australia has a similar stance about this issue, in the case of Acohs Pty Ltd v Ucorp Pty Ltd, it was declared by the court that any works that are created without the intervention of humans cannot be offered copyright protection.

In India, a standard of 'modicum of creativity' needs to be established to get protection under copyright law, this was laid down in Eastern Book Company and Ors. V. D.B. Modak and Anr, here the court held that for any work to be copyrightable there should be a degree of creativity involved in it. For any work created by AI, it needs to be shown that AI would fall under the definition of "author" as mentioned in the copyright act. Since AI is not recognized as a legal person in India it is difficult to establish the same.

However, some countries like the United Kingdom, Ireland, and New Zealand do grant copyright-like protection. The UK Copyright Designs and Patents Act 1988, for example, creates a legal fiction for computer-generated works where there is no human author. Section 9(3) of the act states that "the author shall be taken to be the person by whom the arrangements necessary for the creation of the work are undertaken." However, it is essential to point out the overtone that this provision is applicable for works created with some human assistance along with AI and not for an outcome generated solely by AI. Hence countries like the United Kingdom, New Zealand provide authorship to the programmer for the creation of the work. The granting of copyright to the person who invested and made the operation of AI possible also seems to be a viable option that would fulfil the objective of intellectual property rights as it will encourage the companies to invest and create new technologies and also keeping in mind the interest of the general public.

In the future, more artists are likely to incorporate elements of AI in their creative works and machines will become better at creating artistic work. This will further blur the lines between the distinction that can be made for an artwork created by a human and one made by a computer. Machines can be taught to process the entered data and learn to become better with each outcome, there might soon come a time when it will become tough to distinguish between human-generated and machine-generated content. The scale at which AI is independently involved in generating artistic work is much lower today than it would be in the near future, we must identify and address the concerns relating to the manner and mode of protection at the earliest.

Patents

WIPO's first Technology Trends report reveals the massive surge in AI-based innovations that have taken place in the past few decades. Since AI emerged in the 1960s, innovators and researchers have filed patent applications for nearly 340,000 AI-related inventions and published over 1.6 million scientific publications on AI. AI-related patenting has soared in the past few years, however, like all evolving fields, there is a lot of scientific ambiguity around AI which in turn impacts its ability to be patented. The legal stance around the patentability of inventions created by AI also remains uncertain. Like we had discussed previously, it is much easier to determine if protection would be granted for intellectual property if it has been created with human intervention. This is since several countries have rejected that the word "inventor" goes beyond natural persons to include machines. an inventor on a patent application must have "legal capacity," meaning the "ability, according to a source of law, to be the subject of rights and duties."

World's first Patent where AI is an inventor

The patent office in South Africa became the first country to grant a patent for an invention that was conceived by AI, the inventor DABUS is an AI system. Stephen Thaler is the creator of DABUS and the patent applicant. The patent was given for "a food container based on fractal geometry," and was accepted by South Africa's Companies and Intellectual Property Commission on June 24 2021.

They had attempted to procure patents in European Union, United Kingdom and the United States as well where they were not successful and in their application was rejected. The European Patent Office rejected the DABUS patents on appeals for the rejection, the Board of Appeal after agreeing to the earlier decision of EPO said that, under the European Patent Convention, an inventor for a patent application must have "legal capacity," that is the "ability, according to a source of law, to be the subject of rights and duties."

Most recently, on 30th July 2021 Australia became the second country to confirm that DABUS can be an inventor in a patent. The Australian federal court in Thaler v Commissioner of Patents confirmed that inventions by AI system DABUS are patentable.

These landmark decisions have challenged our traditional notion that an "inventor" of a patent has to be a human being, while most jurisdictions still do not recognize AI as an inventor, the DABUS team argues that this current situation hampers the ongoing fourth industrial revolution that represents the fusion of advances in AI, robotics, genetic engineering and more.

These historic cases have opened new horizons in the legal recognition that is given to AI, there is a need to recognize and bring about a change in how we attribute inventions as earlier

The issue with AI Patent Ownership

We have surpassed the traditional notion around Intellectual Property that only humans can be inventors, with exponential growth in technology and science there is a pertinent need to update our definition of an inventor.

However, as machines have no consciousness of their own, they can not comprehend the rights and obligations that are associated with patents in such a scenario, it becomes difficult to grant them the status of an inventor. AI patent applications generally rely on multiple applications that cover techniques and their application both special and functional. Patent applications on AI and machine learning-based virtual assistance, image processing, medical diagnosis, biological modelling, vehicle control, and several others have received grants despite objections based on all patentability requirements.

8.4 Smart Contracts in the Fashion industry

To use smart contracts in the textile industry, we can think of the fourth industrial revolution and what it brought with it, namely, artificial intelligence and blockchain.

A smart contract consists of a computer program that executes agreements already established between two or more contracting parties with the aim that the conditions agreed upon in the contract are fulfilled. "The great contribution of smart contracts is that there is no need for a third party to verify whether or not the events have taken place". Smart contracts began with the creation of Ethereum (a global open source platform for decentralized applications) and we could indicate that in its application to the fashion industry, it would be very beneficial to be integrated into the blockchain, thus allowing most likely to have greater confidence in the contractual agreements between the parties and be limited to extra payments for mediation or arbitration, if applicable, since its purpose is compliance and automated execution according to what has been agreed in alphanumeric language and established in an unmodifiable blockchain, so extreme diligence must be exercised in the terms and conditions to be agreed. This really is a very exciting, novel and extensive topic that deserves to be developed in a new section.

Smart contracts are self-executing contracts with the terms of the agreement between buyer and seller being directly written into lines of code. The code and the agreements contained therein exist across a distributed, decentralized blockchain network. Smart contracts permit trusted transactions and agreements to be carried out among disparate, anonymous parties without the need for a central authority, legal system, or external enforcement mechanism. They render transactions traceable, transparent, and irreversible.

Smart contracts are a way to transform your business by automating it. They make trading quicker, easier, and more secure, and they can be used in almost any industry. They're especially useful in areas like financial services, real estate, or legal services, but you can use them wherever a middle person might otherwise be needed. Smart contracts make the process of doing business more secure and more efficient. The current trends including Metaverse and NFTs also use Smart Contract technology.

8.5 NFTs, Metaverse in Fashion

NFTs (Non-Fungible Tokens) have been around for about 9 years but have recently become more noticeable and used in various industries, including the art industry, entertainment, real estate (virtual real estate) and quickly seduced the fashion industry to be tokenised and trending.

It is anticipated that over time NFTs, could become a vital issue for individuals and businesses in various sectors, a clear example of this is that during this quarter the highest sales were in the art segment, followed by collectibles and then metaverses according to the NFT Q2 2021 REPORT.

To understand the scope and purpose of NFTs in the fashion industry, we must first understand their definition: NFTs, are a special type of digital tradable certificate called a non-fungible token (special asset class on the blockchain) and are secured with blockchain technology (A ledger of records, with the ability to record the production chain of an industry, the traceability of a product, etc. And all this information will be shared with all nodes in real time, providing a high degree of transparency) whose properties are broadcast, notarization and serialization; and the types of blockchain networks are: Public (e.g. Bitcoin, Ethereum, Litecoin, etc.), private (e.g. Pound, Corda, etc.) and consortium.

Often NFTs are used to represent and restrict a unique claim on a digital asset that is copyable, sharable, and sticky, like a digital file; in that sense, it creates a type of authenticity and is defined by metadata. Therefore, NFTs can be said to be unique and not interchangeable with each other, and can take the form of trading cards, images of physical objects, tweets, GIFs, virtual real estate, etc.

Today, the NFTs market is valued at hundreds of millions of dollars in various sectors, which has encouraged more than one to follow this digital path; however, it also has a lot of criticism due to various factors such as the high consumption of computer power used to encrypt their tokens (producing an energy and environmental impact) and the fact of cases of piracy of certain digital works, but there is also discontent among creators because of the legal loopholes that still exist.

Despite the successes and failures, it is now possible to value and enhance the value of great digital works such as the case of:

"IRIDESCENCE"

It was the first digital haute couture dress in the world, a piece of digital art negotiable, traceable and collectible designed by the digital fashion house "The Fabricant". The digital garment was sold for $9500 in 2019. Amber Jae Slooten, who was the creative director at The Fabricant, wrote the following text:

"A new cult is rising. The digital world is coming and we are no longer bound to physical space.

Our bodies are becoming fluid, our money decentralized, new powers are being formed. Slowly we are moving into a non-dual operating system. Intrinsic new patterns are being formed by systems that are closer to our nature by evolving rather than being controlled by a central power. This outfit provides a look into the future.

What can a body be when it is freed from physical restraints? What does identity mean when there are endless bits and bytes to express it? Connection is what we yearn for, and connection is what will rise now.

Our frequency is our energy in motion. It provides fluidity of movement, which is what forms this new line. We look for connection in technology. It is our new religion."

For her part, the new owner Mary said "I had to imagine what it would look like to wear the dress. There was a huge element of surprise that you wouldn't get with physical garments. It is like a green screen, you have to imagine what it will look like since the dress will be added in post production.

Of course this was the first of its kind, but I would love to be able to use the dress more often, and wear it wherever I like, not just limited to the pictures I got, but it should be something I can endlessly use over the pictures being taken so I can wear it in different situations.

In the future, it would help if digital clothing could be cheaper than physical clothing, so the element of pricing would be more attractive for people to purchase a digital item instead of a physical one.

It would be amazing to wear the outfit on TikTok to express yourself in these apps and have an extra special layer to use.

500 years ago we jumped on a ship to sail to the edge of the map, but all of the physical world has been discovered already. It is really exciting to discover a space that hasn't been explored yet, like the blockchain space, especially in combination with apparel."

The first luxury brand to launch its NFT

Gucci, the first luxury brand to launch its NFT, recently sold its bee-embroidered Gucci Dionysus bag for approximately $4,115, more than doubling its physical value; the sale was made through the Roblox gaming platform and the payment was made with virtual money from Roblox, note that the bag sold was not an "NFT" and the reason is because the bag cannot be exchanged outside that platform; however, we can highlight that it was in that way that the Gucci brand entered to conquer a gaming platform for the Z generation.

So if the Gucci Dionysus bag was not an NFT, what are Gucci's NFT launches? The augmented reality trainers sold by the Italian fashion house was an NFT, the luxury brand sold it for $11.99 on its app and almost $9 on the app of fashion tech company Wanna, who was also its technological ally in achieving this feat and Gucci's foray into the virtual world. The buyer of these trainers will never be able to physically pick them up or wear them; however, this is not a limitation for digital fashion buyers, as they will be able to debut them on Instagram, Roblox, VR Chat and other social networks as well as trade or auction them among digital fashion consumers.

But as Gucci's desires are infinite, it already plans to work on a complete line of digital products after having launched a while ago in the world of video games, as well as some brands such as Balenciaga, Hermès, Louis Vuitton, Valentino, Marc Jacobs and Burberry.

Paris fashion capital and NFT

Paris Fashion week 2020 was celebrated differently because of the pandemic times we still live in and, this year 2021 Arianee and the Federation of Haute Couture and Fashion who coordinate Paris Fashion Week and Haute Couture Week, are working to deliver a great experience in the project that will allow brands to broadcast digital assets "NFT", a fully personalized experience for journalists, influencer users, photographers, and buyers.

"This collaboration is an opportunity for Arianee to break new ground by co-creating a new form of NFT for one of the world's leading fashion events. As a French start-up and open source consortium, we hope to contribute to strengthening Paris' position not only as a fashion capital, but also as a capital of NFTs" commented NFT platform CEO and co-founder Pierre Nicolas Hurstel.

How to buy an NFT?

NFTs are sold on digital platforms, so you must choose the Marketplace in which you intend to buy, for it will be necessary to have a digital wallet service and cryptocurrencies, it will also be necessary to consider whether the NFT to be acquired, is part of an auction or is for sale at a certain time. Major marketplaces includes opensea, rarible etc.

Intellectual property and NFTs

NFTs are treated as "works" and are therefore a great proposition for copyright protection.

When acquiring an NFT, the intellectual property rights are not acquired automatically, this will only be transferred if the author of the original work expressly provides it; that is, without the authorization of the author, only an implicit, non-exclusive license will be possessed for their personal use.

In that sense, the rights that a buyer acquires over an NFT will depend on its creator, whether they are commercial rights or not over the work, so it will be very important to review the terms and conditions before making the purchase.

Some people will only own the digital ownership over the NFT and not the copyright; In other words, they will have a certificate of ownership, but they will not be able to exploit them commercially; However, all is not lost since on certain occasions they will also be able to acquire the rights of transmission, exhibition, and distribution.

NFTs can also be protected as trademarks and create a large space for intellectual property itself, helping creators to protect and generate income from their creations, decrease the number of orphan works, counterfeits, and piracy.

It is also possible that when a creator sells an NFT, he may receive royalties if his work is sold by its initial purchaser; In other words, while the work is sold from person to person, the creator can automatically receive these royalties.

While we understand or relate luxury with a high price or a limited quantity of products, on the digital platform this reality is totally different, as many of the products that we would consider luxury are within the reach of several people, and it is for this reason that many consumers do not hesitate to buy digital fashion from various luxury brands and then show them off and post them on social networks.

Approximately 67% of monthly active users on these digital platforms are under 16 years old, young people who belong to the Z generation, it is for this and other reasons that the big luxury brands are enlisting a new consumer segment that in a few years will probably be very active for their purchasing power as they spend much of their time on the internet.

For its part, the use of "NFT" in the fashion industry demonstrates to consumers when a brand is ethical and sustainable, as well as the traceability of the garment from its creation to the consumer's wardrobe, bringing the industry closer to selling original products; However, we cannot yet fully win the war against copying and piracy because although NFTs can authenticate the work and its ownership, counterfeiting can still occur in the case that if an original ledger entry is false or in error from the start, the NFTs will confirm and perpetuate that falsehood.

Finally, today we can say that we are facing the future of fashion, with the introduction of digital fashion, the hiring of influencers, the creation of avatars as models and a greater emphasis on e-commerce, the great exposure of "NFTs" in the fashion industry, blockchain, digital wallets, smart contracts, etc. All this digital trend leads many fashion brands to be more innovative and creative, to develop new creations for a generation hungry for technology, practicality, information and above all greater social awareness for the great responsibility of continuing to care for our planet. In this sense, the rise of NFTs could save the fashion industry and free it from the great responsibility of being one of the most polluting industries on the planet; also, in these times of pandemic that we live in, it has allowed several fashion brands to position themselves on a virtual platform with opportunities for growth without limiting their activities.

Technology is a field with exponential growth, given that its progress more often than not facilitates a quickening, never-ending cycle of development. In accordance with this, it is relevant to point out that the pandemic has favored said industry; demanding this cycle happen faster and faster. In other terms, as society's demands changed, tech giants were the only ones able to fulfill such peculiar conditions, which made each of their innovations a worldly affair. Home and online shopping, the purchase of better equipment for school and work, those are only a couple of examples of what has been a global reality ever since the breakout of COVID-19. But that's not all, as tech giants also used the pandemic as an opportunity to improve and make more money; rethinking their investments and following customer's needs. Gone are the days when used to call 'Technology is future of Fashion', now 'Technology is Present and Future'.

Chapter 9. Cultural Appropriation

This chapter is authored by Cindy K. Sotomayor[136]

Over the years, many fashion brands have been involved in cases of cultural appropriation, such as the iconography of the Dior "Dior Book Tote" bag vs. the traditional Mexican Macramé community of Huichol and Chamula, the Oxaqueño designs in the blouses and dresses of the Spanish brand Intropia vs. the Oaxacan indigenous people who defended the huipil chinanteco originating from their Mexican village, the traditional embroidery and designs that the Zara brand included in its garments vs. the traditional embroidery of the indigenous women of Chiapas, Carolina Herrera and the use of Mexican elements (embroidery and designs), the patterns of Nike leggings and the Samoan male tattoo called pe'a, the Kim Kardashian case and her line of modeling garments that she pretended to call kimono solutionwear, Louis Vuitton and the pattern of upholstery similar to the embroidery of the Mexican community of Tenango de Doria, and so on an endless number of controversies in this great trillion-dollar fashion industry, in which technology allows us to quickly and easily access the traditional knowledge and cultural expressions of any non-Western (indigenous) culture without the need to cross borders or to previously contextualize the cultural elements, so that brands and designers end up resignifying these cultures without any knowledge or recognition whatsoever.

9.1 What is Cultural Appropriation

To speak of cultural appropriation is synonymous with dispossession of indigenous culture and identity, insensitivity, colonization, oppression, disrespect, offence, illicit appropriation of traditional knowledge and imbalance of power against indigenous peoples and culture, due to the transgression carried out by a natural or legal person towards the traditional knowledge and cultural expressions of local peoples and communities. This violation evades any kind of ethical and social responsibility to give them due credit and economic benefit under the approach of the broad concept of solidarity economy. However, many brands, companies and/or individuals omit dialogue with the people of indigenous communities, the holders of such traditional knowledge, and without their authorization appropriate their culture, under the pretext of inspiration and appreciation. This discrediting of fashion brands towards indigenous peoples and/or communities damages and impacts their culture and craftsmanship.

---

136 Degree in Public Management from the Continental University, with specialized studies in Fashion Law, Intellectual Property Law by the World Intellectual Property Organization - WIPO Intellectual Property Organization - WIPO, the National Institute for the Defense of Competition and Protection of Intellectual Property - INDECOPI (Peru) and the National Institute of Industrial Property - INAPI (Chile), the only Latin American scholar of the Summer School 2021 at the Huazhou University of Science and Technology of Science and Technology of Huazhong-Wuhan (China), specialist in Administrative Law, Public Management and Administrative Law, Public Management and State Contracting in the national and international markets. Editor of Fashion Law Journal & Legal Desire Media and Insights from India.

For its part, Article 31 of the United Nations Declaration on the Rights of Indigenous Peoples (2007) is an important reference regarding the protection of their traditional knowledge and traditional cultural expressions, stating that*: "1. Indigenous peoples have the right to maintain, control, protect and develop their cultural heritage, traditional knowledge, traditional cultural expressions and the manifestations of their sciences, technologies and cultures, including human and genetic resources, seeds, medicines, knowledge of the properties of fauna and flora, oral traditions, literatures, designs, sports and traditional games and visual and performing arts. They also have the right to maintain, control, protect and develop their intellectual property of such cultural heritage, traditional knowledge and traditional cultural expressions. States shall, in conjunction with indigenous peoples, take effective measures to recognize and protect the exercise of these rights".*

In this aspect, it is possible to appreciate that the due regulation by the states in terms of intellectual property, public policies and unfair competition, will be a great support to face the problems of cultural appropriation; likewise, this protection must be accompanied by teachings that allow indigenous people to learn and/or receive the appropriate advice, with the purpose of having a good strategy of negotiation, commercialization and promotion of their products, avoiding in this way the undue exploitation and deception.

Cultural appropriation is a very sensitive issue that has become visible over the years in various industries and in the fashion industry, the forerunner of fashion law, Professor Susan Scafidi, in her book Who owns culture: Appropriation and authenticity in American law, defines cultural appropriation as follows: *"Taking the intellectual property, traditional knowledge, cultural expressions or artefacts of another person's culture without permission. This may include the unauthorized use of another culture's dance, dress, music, language, folklore, cuisine, traditional medicine, religious symbols, etc.".*

Professor Susan Scafidi's definition also makes us reflect on the justice and balance that should exist in intellectual property for the benefit of indigenous peoples through respect for their knowledge and traditions; in this context, if there is any type of infringement or misuse of intellectual property, we would be faced with the interposition of precautionary measures in order to prevent the illicit use of intellectual property rights, as well as the payment of fines for the damages caused. Although traditional knowledge and traditional cultural expressions are not protected by intellectual property per se, what are protected are the products and services of their people, related to this traditional knowledge and expressions.

9.2 Intellectual Property Rights and Cultural Appropriation

It is important to address intellectual property as a pillar of protection of traditional knowledge and traditional cultural expressions against cultural appropriation.

The copyrights of traditional cultural expressions, by their nature, are collective and protected through copyrights made by unknown groups of authors. While these traditional cultural expressions may serve as inspiration for others, they are also susceptible to being copied, inspiration is normatively acceptable, but copying transgresses copyright (copying and selling without authorization), so the copyright legislation of the country where the alleged infringement was committed should always be consulted. A clear example is what happened in the country of[137]Ghana with its Kente cloth.

On the other hand, in relation to patents, it is recognized that traditional knowledge is part of the state of the art, as long as it meets certain conditions, such as: if it was published, orally disclosed or used in a public way; however, to date very few patents have been granted to indigenous communities.

Finally, regarding certification marks, we can see that indigenous peoples and local communities could use them to certify the quality and accredit that their products are manufactured under traditional methods, a clear example of this is the certification mark of the Cowichan tribe in the province of British Columbia. A mark could also be owned by more than one person, whether natural or legal, which is why a community can create a collective mark as the property of an association or a cooperative and follow traditional methods to produce its products. For its part, a certification mark will be granted to third parties, as long as they comply with and respect the rules that are determined (for example, compliance with the regulations for the use of the mark and compliance with product quality) and thus protect the distinctive qualities of indigenous peoples.

In the case of trademark registration, it is important to take into consideration that, in some countries, such as the Andean Community countries (Bolivia, Colombia, Ecuador and Peru), article 136 g) of Decision 486 provides that they cannot be registered as trademarks when they "consist of the name of indigenous, Afro-American or local communities, or the name of the indigenous peoples, Afro-American or local communities, or the names, words, letters, characters or signs used to distinguish their products, services or the way they are processed, or which constitute the expression of their culture or practice, unless the application is filed by the community itself or with its express consent".

---

137 Gertrude Torkornoo (2012): "Building Capital from Culture: Rethinking the Provisions on the Expression of Folklore in Ghana's Copyright Law", Annual Survey on International and Comparative Law 18 (1), pp. 1 and 2, available at: http://digitalcommons.law.ggu.edu/ annlsurvey / vol18 / iss1 / 4 and Torkornoo, op. cit., pages 1 and 2. 4. Boatema Boateng: "Walking the tightrope tradition-modernity: gender contradictions in textile production and intellectual property in Ghana", Journal of Gender, Social Policy and Law 15 (2) , P. 342, available at: digitalcommons.wcl.american.edu/jgspl/vol15/iss2/

Geographical indications will also play an important role in protecting against cultural appropriation, using appellations of origin to receive a type of indirect protection.

Now let's talk about industrial designs, which are often also inspired by traditional knowledge and traditional cultural expressions, where a lot of caution should be taken when registering them and respecting this fine line of inspiration in order not to infringe the rights of third parties and thus avoid cancellation of their registration.

Another very important point is the unfair competition when they try to deceive us or make us believe that a product is endorsed by a community, confusing us and commercially discrediting a community.

THE SUSTAINABLE DEVELOPMENT GOALS (SDGS) AND THE 2030 AGENDA

The appropriation of cultural heritage is a violation of the rights of indigenous peoples, which not only has negative repercussions from an economic, social, cultural and spiritual point of view. Likewise, this negative action has repercussions in the discrediting and undervaluing of their culture and traditions. In this sense, the SDGs have a 2030 Agenda, in which 17 goals related to the exercise of the rights of indigenous peoples are indicated, but it seems that many of the collective rights of indigenous peoples in relation to land, resources, health, education, culture and ways of life are also being left out, which would prevent the development goals from being effectively achieved. In this regard, in the fifth report about indigenous peoples "Rights to lands, territories and resources", they concluded that the world still does not recognize indigenous rights.

Finally, let us not forget that the Sustainable Development Goals (SDGs) or 2030 Agenda is the roadmap towards a new development model in which all people, the planet, prosperity, peace and partnerships take a central role, with the 17 goals of the SDGs as guidelines; therefore, it is expected that all rights are included in it and that each of the planned goals are met.

9.3 The Boundary between Cultural Appropriation and Inspiration in the Fashion World

The intense debate on the boundary between cultural appropriation and inspiration leads us to question the difference between one and the other, as well as the legal mechanisms for protection against this problem.

What is clear is that there is a strong cultural, social and economic grievance towards indigenous peoples, since the cultural components are not taken into account, and they are not compensated monetarily.

It is also important to highlight that the characteristic of fashion is its multiculturalism and therefore its creations, inspired by the diverse nuances of cultural expressions, must be found in the valuable and very careful representation of what they are intended to represent in fashion. We accept that there is permissible inspiration, but not appropriation that harms and damages indigenous peoples, because when this harmony between permissive inspiration and creativity is disrupted by cultural appropriation, we are faced with direct damage, which must be dealt with normatively from the point of view of intellectual property and customary law; in that sense, we can say that we will be faced with cultural appropriation in the following scenarios:

- When traditional cultural expressions are not respected, for example, through a reinterpretation or transformation that transgresses the essence of the indigenous culture.

- When there is no recognition of the holders of that indigenous culture and tradition, which may be the case when their authorization has not been duly sought and their cooperation has not been respectfully sought through initial dialogue and subsequent formal agreements.

We know that, in the fashion industry, copying and piracy are like the needle and thread of the sewing machine, which is why the mere fact that a garment is shown in the market is threatened by the culture of copying and plagiarism. Now imagine that a copy is made of a fabric or embroidery whose lineage is ancestral with a millenary cultural science, which has initially reached the market because a designer, under the excuse of "inspiration", made it his own and transgressed the thin limit, then we would be facing cultural appropriation, but also copying and piracy on the part of a large market. That is why it is terrible to think that this fact alone would lead indigenous peoples to face great economic losses and the impact of this fact that will have repercussions on their community and family economy; it is because of this great problem that cultural appropriation goes beyond a simple definition, because the damage caused penetrates the sensitive fibers of creativity and the dignified work of indigenous peoples.

Finally, globalization and interculturality should allow us to treat all ethnic groups with respect, in all scenarios, so it is best to appreciate, understand and study every culture in the world before seeking inspiration; to always focus on equality, respect and equity before generating economic income for our brand.

Today we are at the perfect technological moment to virilize indigenous culture as a valuable heritage of traditional knowledge, whose science and creative process should be valued by those who appreciate and access it in different ways.

Chapter 10. The Use of Animals in the Fashion, Textile and Fashion Retail Industry

This chapter is authored by Annalucia Fasson Llosa[138]

Since ancient times, man has used animals to cover and protect himself from the cold, in fact since the time of the caves we see how our ancestors as homo sapiens were covered with skins of bears or cows, and is that even though some people to date are against the use of animals, the textile industry and fashion, often resorts to it, for example is of our knowledge that wool is obtained from sheep shearing, the silk of the worm cocoons, the leather under the tanning process comes from cattle, the skins of rabbits, ermine, mink, fox have been highly appreciated and in some cases the high social classes used them as a distinction of wealth and social position, also in some countries are used the skins of crocodiles or snakes and how not the feathers of birds such as goose, ostrich or peacock that are used not only in clothing but even in the decoration or bedding as bedspreads or down.

Now, although animals are currently used, there are certain ethical considerations that have been implemented for some time now, such as the non-torture of animals. In this regard, it is important to point out that many companies that manufacture and sell clothing have among their policies not to buy from breeders who use the "mulesing" procedure. This is a technique that consists of shearing sheep to prevent parasites in the wool and increase its quality, however, at the moment of shearing, a type of mutilation is performed, since it consists of cutting off pieces of meat from the sheep's loins or anus with pruning shears, without administering painkillers, as a cheap method of preventing worm infections (despite the fact that there are technical methods to control parasitosis). That is why many fashion retailers, such as Adolfo Dominguez, have within their animal welfare policies not to buy from these suppliers who use these cruelty methods on animals.

On the other hand, it is known by all that many cosmetic brands test their products on animals such as mice or rabbits, which is considered as animal torture, which is why there have been several

---

138 Lawyer graduated from Universidad de Lima with Magnum Cum Laude. Master in Finance and Corporate Law from ESAN University. She has a specialization in Fashion Law from the Fashion Law Institute at Fordham Law University, New York. She is currently partner of the corporate area and head of the fashion and retail law area of Muñiz, Olaya, Meléndez, Castro, Ono & Herrera Abogados, as well as professor of the Fashion and Retail Law courses at ESAN University, Universidad de Ciencias Aplicadas (UPC) and Instituto Centro de Altos de la Moda (CEAM) and of the Corporations III course at Universidad de Lima. She is a mentor of retail and fashion projects in the start-up incubator Emprende UP of the Universidad del Pacífico. She has written several articles in blogs and national and international media, as well as lectured in Peru and abroad on topics related to fashion law and retail. In 2019, 2020 and 2021 she was recognized as a Leader in Fashion Law by the legal magazine Leaders League. She is a member of the fashion law committee of ASIPI, of the Asociación de Expertos de Derecho de la Moda de España and of the Asociación de Fashion Law Latam de Perú. Coordinator of the First Ebook of Fashion Law in Peru, published in 2018. afasson@munizlaw.com.

campaigns against their use in experiments, including in this year 2021 a campaign launched by Humane Society International called "Save Ralph" that raises awareness among the population by publicizing the story of Ralph the rabbit, a member of a family of rabbits in a laboratory, the consequences of using his body in his work. In this sense, for those who do not wish to use this type of cosmetics, they can identify with the "Cruelty Free" seal the cosmetics that do not test their products on animals.

On the other hand, the skins of python snakes are highly valued in some countries and are used as leather to make handbags or shoes. For some time now they have been considered an endangered species, so much so that there are now controlled farms, since it was a common practice to preserve the brightness of their skin by skinning them alive, which is no longer acceptable because it is considered animal torture.

As you know the use of animal fur is very debatable and luxury brands are not exempt from this controversy and while some of them continue to use them in their proposals and even some countries are major producers of fur as China, Denmark or Finland, more and more luxury brands are considered "Fur Free" as for example Stella McCartney, symbol of sustainable fashion in the world or the PETA association (People for the Ethical treatment of animals) that fights against animal abuse, being one of the big trends in the fashion industry, the use of fake fur as for example the English brand Shrimp (luxury synthetic fur). It should be noted that the use of fake fur, in addition to personal beliefs, also helps those who are allergic to natural fur, they are cheaper, and you can use creativity by using prints such as animal print, among others.

Faced with this issue, there is a trend called "vegan leather", i.e. not derived from animals, since now with the use of technology many fashion start ups are applying it, these are disruptive business models that innovate using new materials in their proposals thanks to the use of technology, such as the reuse of fruit waste such as pineapple peel (piñatex leather) or Peruvian brands such as Evea Eco Fashion, which uses the Amazonian tree "Shiringa", which inside has a liquid called latex, and that through a traditional process becomes rubber and with that material produces the soles of their sneakers or Insecta brand that uses the cactus and transforms them into leather.

On the other hand, we cannot fail to mention the "Blue Economy", a concept that was launched by the author Gunter Pauli, who wrote a book called "The Blue Economy. 10 years. 100 innovations. 100 million jobs", which proposes a production alternative based on the use of waste.

In this regard, the Food and Agriculture Organization of the United Nations (FAO) has an initiative called "Blue Growth", which promotes the protection of communities that depend on fishing and its related industries.

That is to say, the "Blue Fashion" consists of the fact that although the first use of the fish is to be food, as a second use its skin would be used, turning it into leather for the design of shoes, wallets and purses, as for example in Peru there is the Rochi Kahn brand that uses the skin of the Amazon fish "Paiche" to manufacture its purses.

It should be noted that the use of alpaca and vicuña camelid fiber is also very important in Peru, so much that the National Alpaca Day is celebrated on August 1 as provided by Ministerial Resolution No. 429-2012-AG and the National Vicuña Day is celebrated on November 15, according to Ministerial Resolution No. 0458-2017-MINAGRI. It should be noted that the vicuña has been declared a National Natural Heritage by Law No. 28477, published on March 22, 2005.

In that sense, Peru is the first power worldwide in producing alpaca fiber, which is why the Commission for the Promotion of Peru for Export and Tourism (Promperu) launched in 2014 the sectoral brand "Alpaca del Peru" to promote the alpaca fiber at the international level for which a license agreement must be entered into free of charge and register its use in Class 16, 18, 23, 24, 25, 26, 35 and 41, with Certificate No. 41 00016671.

Regarding the vicuña, we have to mention that it is a symbol of the Peruvian national coat of arms, and its fiber is considered one of the finest in the world. It has been used since the time of the Inca empire, maintaining the ancestral shearing procedure called Chaccu, which is carried out from May 15 to November 15.

In that sense, anyone wishing to market and/or export vicuña fiber must first purchase it from the farming communities and then enter into a licensing agreement with the Peruvian government through the National Forestry and Wildlife Service (SERFOR) that will allow them to hold the rights to the Vicuña Perú and Vicuña Perú - Artesanía trademarks for five years.

Once this license agreement has been signed with SERFOR, the Vicuña Perú trademark must be registered with the Office of Distinctive Signs of the National Institute for the Defense of Competition and the Protection of Intellectual Property (Indecopi) in class 24 (fabrics and textiles) and class 25 (manufacture of pants, coats, shawls, scarves, sweaters and others).

In addition, the aforementioned agreement entails the fulfillment of several obligations, such as:

1. Communicate to SERFOR the contracts entered into with third parties for the purpose of purchasing vicuña fiber.
2. Prepare an annual report accrediting its activities, which must be submitted to SERFOR thirty (30) calendar days prior to the expiration of each year of the contract.
3. Submit reports on the performance of vicuña fiber transformation processes to products, in order to exercise better control over its commercialization.
4. Promote, directly or through third parties, the Vicuña Perú or Vicuña Perú - Artesanía brand, both nationally and internationally, for which from the third year onwards a documented report must be sent to SERFOR containing videos, dissemination material or advertising that accredits it.

It should be noted that the procedure for shearing both alpacas and vicuñas in Peru is duly regulated by the Peruvian State, as well as by the Technical Standards issued by Indecopi, in order to avoid any torture to these camelids.

In conclusion, I have cited some examples of the use of animals in the fashion, textile and fashion retail sector, which, although it is currently a trend to replace them with fake fur or other innovative materials, it cannot be denied that they are still used in the industry so it is necessary to use them with due care, without mistreating the animal, avoiding any kind of torture and rather maintaining their conservation so that the animals continue in our ecosystem in a sustainable way in the coming years.

References
- https://www.lavanguardia.com/natural/tu-huella/20190402/461424922243/ovejas-lana-merino-sufrimiento-mulesing-australia-mutilacion.html
- https://smoda.elpais.com/moda/mutilaciones-y-modificaciones-geneticas-los-secretos-de-tus-jerseis-de-lana/
- https://www.elmundo.es/yodona/2010/06/24/moda/1277375455.html
- https://cosas.pe/de-fondo/205953/save-ralph-apoya-al-conejito-comprando-marcas-cruelty-free-peruanas/
- https://shrimps.com/
- https://evea-ecofashion.com/es/
- https://insecta.pe/
- https://www.bbvaopenmind.com/ciencia/medioambiente/economia-azul-clave-futuro-planeta-verde/
- http://www.parthenon.pe/columnas/derecho-de-la-moda-retail/la-economia-azul-y-su-vinculacion-con-la-moda-sostenible/
- https://rochikahn.com/es/
- http://alpacadelperu.com.pe/es/home
- https://www.mincetur.gob.pe/marca-alpaca-del-peru-logra-posicionarse-en-nuevos-mercados-del-mundo/

Chapter 11. Contracts/Agreement in Fashion

Contracts/Agreements (hereinafter mentioned as "**Agreements**") make it to the top of the list when it comes to the effective functioning of a business, no matter what the industry is. The fashion industry has evolved tremendously in such a short span of time. The industry is home to numerous employees and contributes significantly to a nation's economy. This article shall focus upon the various Agreements which ensure smooth functioning of the industry with minimum liability. Divided into three stages, we will look at the most important facets of contracts which play a vital role in administering the fashion business with sample contract/agreements alongwith checklist and policies.

11.1 Agreements in various stages of a Fashion Business

Stage I: Making of the Product

This is the initial stage. Here we will take a look at the Agreements that are necessary for the manufacturing of the products i.e Manufacturing Agreements and Private Label/ White Label Agreements.

1. **Manufacturing Agreements**

   A manufacturing agreement is contracted between two parties, the designer and the manufacturer. Here, the product designer demands the creation of the goods (clothing items, accessories, footwear, bags, etc.) on his/her behalf from the manufacturer. The Manufacturing Agreement must include the following clauses:
   a. Quantity of the Product.
   b. Shipment: How will the products be shipped to the designer by the manufacturer.
   c. Modes of Payment: What shall be the outstanding amount and how will the payment be made.
   d. Dates of Delivery: When will the product be delivered?
   e. Product Specifications: Maintaining the quality of the product.
   f. Details about the manufacturer.
   g. Intellectual Property (IP) Rights: Designers ownership of the intellectual property.
   h. Liability of both the Parties.

2. **Private Label/ White Label Agreements**

   Under Private Label/White Label (A.G. Paphitis & Co.) Agreements the designer sells products manufactured under their brand. The manufacturing companies provide the designers with their product, the company on the other hand markets the product as their own. This method minimizes the designing cost, manages time, and lifts off the burden from the designer's head. A very popular example of a Private Label (Lamb) is AmazonBasics. It is an in-house brand of Amazon which includes a variety of products ranging from electronics to house goods at a much cheaper cost than other competitive brands. The Private Label/White Label Agreements must include the following clauses:

    a. Price of the Product.

    b. Quantity of the Product.

    c. An assurance of the quality of the product.

    d. Right of selling the product under a specified trademark.

    e. Liability of both the parties.'

Stage II: Breaking the Product Out

Under the second stage, we will look at the Agreements necessary for the product to reach the market i.e Consignment Agreement, Showroom Agreement, and Independent Sales Representation Agreement.

1. **Consignment Agreement**

   A Consignment Agreement (Practical Law Commercial) is a contract between the designer and the retailer where the former consents to the latter to sell the design at his/her marketplace for a particular period of time. If the goods are not sold by the retailer they are returned to the designer company.\

   The Consignment Agreement must include the following clauses:

       a. Term and Termination of the Agreement.

       b. Terms of Sale for the Designer Goods.

       c. Percentage/Profit Percentage each party tends to receive.

       d. Effect of non-sale on the Designer Goods.

2. **Showroom/Dealership Agreement**

   A Showroom/Dealership Agreement is a contract between the owner of the showroom and the designer. The dealer grants the designer permission to showcase his/her products at their showroom. The dealer owes the designer the responsibility to not only showcase his/her items but also to introduce the products to its buyers and sell them. A Showroom/Dealership Agreement must include the following clauses:

a. Term and Termination of the Agreement.

b. Quantity and Quality Assurance of the Products.

c. Modes of Payment.

d. Shipping Policy.

e. Dates and Methods of Delivery.

f. Specifications of the Product(s).

g. Details of the Designer.

h. Intellectual Property Rights

i. Liability of both the Parties.

3. Independent Sales Representation Agreement

An Independent Sales Representative (also known as Sales Rep Agreement) Agreement (Guillermo and Kolson, 178) is a contract between the designer company and a sales representative where the company assigns the representative to display their collection to the list of his/her customers. The representative is obligated to take orders and pass the details to the designer company. Representatives are offered a commission on the sales by the designer company. This Agreement is quite similar to the Showroom Agreement. The Sales Rep Agreement must include the following clauses:

a. Term and Termination of the Agreement.

b. Representative's Obligations.

c. Exclusivity of the Products.

d. Products and Territories covered by the Representative.

e. Commission of the Representative.

f. Guaranteed Percentage of Orders by the Representative.

g. Showroom Tariff.

Stage III: Expanding the Brand

The third stage is where we expand our fashion brand with the following agreements i.e Licensing Agreement, Joint Venture (JV) Agreement and Distribution Agreements. These agreements will safeguard and widen the business of the designer company.

1. Licensing Agreement

A Licensing Agreement is a contract between the designer company and a second party where the company permits the use of the trademark within a specified territory for a limited period. This process is generally used to increase territorial reach and ensure a constant supply of products without investing a huge amount of funds. The designer companies can avoid the struggle of building new manufacturing units and gathering the sales segment.

A Licensing Agreement must include the following clauses:

    a. Term and Termination of the Agreement.

    b. Assignment of Products.

    c. Clause of Exclusivity.

    d. Channel of Sale.

    e. Royalty Payments.

    f. Use of Manufacturers

    g. Use of Retailers

    h. Use of Wholesalers

    i. Licensed Trademarks

    j. Intellectual Property Rights (IP) Rights

    k. Liability of both the Parties.

2. Joint Venture (JV) Agreements

A Joint Venture (JV) Agreement is a contract between two companies where both come together to create a fresh establishment with their competence. Bally-Reliance Brand Limited (RBL), Karl Lagerfeld-Cover Story, Raghvendra Rathore-Reliance Brand Limited (RBL), Shantanu & Nikhil-Aditya Birla Fashion & Retail Limited (ABFRL) are a few of numerous JV's (Vogue Business) running in India. In a JV, both the brands invest and share the revenue plus profits.

A Joint Venture (JV) Agreement must include the following clauses:

    a. Term and Termination of the Agreement

    b. Initial Investments by both the Parties.

    c. Classification of Products.

    d. Registered Trademarks and Licenses.

    e. Intellectual Property (IP) Rights.

    f. Renewal of the Agreements.

    g. Profit Division.

    h. Advertisement & Marketing.

    i. Rights of Audit

3. **Distribution Agreements**

   A Distribution Agreement is a contract that is used to build trading relations between the distributor and retail outlets. The distributor collects the products from the designer company and trades them with the retail houses. The Distribution Agreements can be Exclusive, Non-Exclusive, Selective and Sole.

   a. Exclusive Distribution Agreement

   Under the Exclusive Distribution Agreement, the manufacturer allows only one distributor to trade the products with the retail outlets.

   b. Non-Exclusive Distribution Agreement

   Under the Non-Exclusive Distribution Agreement, the designer company authorises multiple distributors to resell the products to the retail houses.

   c. Selective Distribution Agreement

   Under the Selective Distribution Agreement, the company permits the distributors to resell to selected retail houses. This agreement is often used by luxury brands.

   d. Sole Distribution Agreement

   Under the Sole Distribution Agreement, the supplier appoints one distributor as their sole distributor within a geographical area.

   A Distribution Agreement must include the following clauses:
   a. Territories.
   b. Channels.
   c. Reserved Channels.
   d. Classification of Products.
   e. Intellectual Property (IP) Rights.
   f. Renewal of the Agreements.
   g. Distributor's Obligations.
   h. Fashion Company's Right to Terminate.
   i. Terms of Delivery
   j. Royalty Payments

Stage IV: Marketing and Promotion

Advertising and marketing service provider contracts, including agreements with advertisement agencies, online agencies, and market researchers.

Stage V: Franchising Agreement

One of the most popular way to start/expand your own company is through a franchise; a business organization in which a well-known firm with a successful product or service – the franchisor – enters into a contractual relationship with another business – the franchisee – that operates under the franchisor's name in exchange for a fee. Franchise agreements vary from franchise to franchise so it would be impossible to identify every term and issue that should be considered in all situations. One of the most popular way to start your own company is through a franchise; a business organization in which a well-known firm with a successful product or service – the franchisor – enters into a contractual relationship with another business – the franchisee – that operates under the franchisor's name in exchange for a fee. Franchise agreements vary from franchise to franchise so it would be impossible to identify every term and issue that should be considered in all situations. The checklist should be used in conjunction with the franchise agreement (provided after this checklist) – the document that will set out all the terms and conditions that will govern your ownership of the franchise – which will be drafted by the franchisor. In any event, you shouldn't sign it until you've discussed your options with your attorney.

Issues relating to the franchise cost terms

❑ What is the initial franchise fee? Is any part or the entire initial fee refundable?

❑ Does it include an ''opening" inventory of products and supplies?

❑ What are the payment terms: amount, time of payment, lump sum or installment, financing arrangements, etc.?

❑ Does the franchisor offer any financing, or offer help in finding financing?

❑ Are there any deferred balances? If so, who finances and at what interest rate?

❑ Does the contract clearly distinguish between ''total cost" and ''initial fee," ''initial cash required," or ''initial costs," etc.?

❑ Are there periodic royalties? If so, how much are they and how are they determined?

❑ How and when are sales and royalties reported, and how are royalties paid?

❑ If royalty payments are in whole or part payment for services by the franchisor, what services will be provided?

❑ Are accounting/bookkeeping services included or available?

❑ How are advertising and promotion costs divided?

❑ Is a specified amount of working capital required of the franchisee to cover operating costs until profits can be made?

❑ Must premises be purchased or rented, and are there further conditions on either of these (from franchisor, selected site, etc.)?

❑ How and by whom will the building be financed, if purchased?

❑ Does the franchisee have to make a down payment for construction and/or equipment?

Issues relating to the franchise location terms

❑ Does the franchise apply to a specific geographical area? If so, are the boundaries clearly defined?

❑ Who has the right to select the site?

❑ Will other franchisees be permitted to compete in the same area, now or later?

❑ Is the territory an exclusive one, and is it permanent or subject to reduction or modification under certain conditions?

❑ Does the franchisee have a first refusal option as to any additional franchises in the original territory if it is not exclusive?

❑ Does the franchisee have a contractual right to the franchisor's latest products or innovations? If so, at what cost?

❑ Will the franchisee have the right to use his own property and/or buildings? If not, will the franchisor sell or lease his property to the franchisee?

❑ Who is responsible for obtaining zoning variances, if required?

Issues relating to the buildings, equipment and supplies terms

❑ Are plans and specifications of the building determined by the franchisor? If so, does this control extend to selection of contractor and supervision of construction?

❑ Are there any restrictions on remodeling or redecorating?

❑ Must equipment or supplies be purchased from the franchisor or approved supplier, or is the franchisee free to make his own purchases?

❑ When the franchisee must buy from the franchisor, are sales considered on consignment? Or will they be financed and, if so, under what terms?

❑ Does the agreement provide for continuing supply and payment of inventory (by whom, under what terms, etc.)?

❑ Does the franchise agreement bind the franchisee to a minimum purchase quota?

❑ What controls are spelled out concerning facility appearance, equipment, fixture and furnishings, and maintenance or replacement of the same? Is there any limitation on expenditures involved in any of these?

❑ Does the franchisor have a group insurance plan? If not, what coverage will be required, at what limits and costs? Does the franchisor require that it be named as an insured party in the franchisee liability coverage?

Issues relating to the operating practices terms

❑ Must the franchisee participate personally in conducting the business? If so, to what extent and under what specific conditions?

❑ What degree of control does the franchisor have over franchise operations, particularly in maintaining franchise identity and product quality?

❑ What continuing management aid, training and assistance will be provided by the franchisor, and are these covered by the service or royalty fee?

❑ Will advertising be local or national and what will be the cost-sharing arrangement, if any, in either case?

❑ If local advertising is left to the franchisee, does the franchisor exercise any control over such campaigns or share any costs?

❑ Does the franchisor provide various promotional materials point-of-purchase, mail programs, etc. and at what cost?

❑ What are bookkeeping, accounting and reporting requirements, and who pays for what?

❑ Are sales or service quotas established? If so, what are the penalties for not meeting them?

❑ Are operating hours and days set forth in the franchise contract?

❑ Are there any limits as to what is or can be sold?

❑ Does the franchisor arrange for mass purchasing and is it mandatory for the franchisee to be a participant buyer?

❑ Who establishes hiring procedures initially and through the franchise term?

Issues relating to termination and renewal terms

❑ Does the franchisor have absolute privilege of terminating the franchise agreement if certain conditions have not been met, either during the term or at the end?

❑ Does the franchise agreement spell out the terms under which the franchisor may repurchase the business?

❑ Does the franchisor have an option or duty to buy any or all of the franchisee's equipment, furnishings, inventory, or other assets in the event the franchise is terminated for good cause, by either party?

❑ If the preceding situation occurs, how are purchase terms determined?

❑ Is there provision for independent appraisal? Is any weight given to good will or franchisee equity in the business?

❑ Does the original agreement include a clause that the repurchase price paid by the franchisor should not exceed the original franchise fee? If so, this eliminates any compensation for good will or equity.

❑ Under what conditions (illness, etc.) can the franchisee terminate the franchise? In such cases, do termination obligations differ?

❑ Is the franchisee restricted from engaging in a similar business after termination? If so, for how many years?

❑ If there is a lease, does it coincide with the franchise term?

❑ Does the contract provide sufficient time for amortization of capital payments?

❑ Has the franchisor, as required, provided for return of trademarks, trade names, and other identification symbols and for the removal of all signs bearing the franchisor's name and trademarks?

Other points to consider

❑ Can the franchisee sell the franchised business and assign the franchise agreement to the buyer?

❑ Is the franchise assignable to heirs, or may it be sold by the franchisee's estate on death or disability?

❑ Does the lease permit assignment to any permitted assignee of the franchisee?

❑ How long has the franchisor conducted business in its industry, and how long has it granted franchises?

❑ How many franchises and company-owned outlets are claimed, and can they be verified?

❑ If there is a trade name of a well-known person involved in the franchise, is he active, does he have any financial interest; does he receive compensation for work or solely for use of his name, etc.?

❑ Are all trademarks, trade names, or other marks fully identifiable and distinct, and are they clear of any possible interference or cancellation owing to any pending litigation?

❑ What is the duration of any patent or copyright material to the franchise? If time is limited, does the franchisor intend to renew, and is this spelled out in the franchise agreement?

❑ Has the franchisor met all law requirements (registration, escrow or bonding requirements, etc.), if applicable?

❑ Are there laws governing franchisor/franchisee relationships, including contract provisions, financing arrangements and terminations? If so, does the contract meet all requirements?

11.2 AGREEMENT TEMPLATES

> **NOTE:**
> The agreement templates are for reference purposes only. Consult a lawyer for drafting agreements as per your customized requirement/business.

11.3 FRANCHISE AGREEMENT

This Franchise Agreement ("Agreement") is made and effective this [DATE],

BETWEEN: **[YOUR COMPANY NAME]** (the "Franchisor"), a company organized and existing under the laws of [STATE/PROVINCE], with its head office located at:

[YOUR COMPLETE ADDRESS]

AND: **[FRANCHISEE NAME]** (the "Franchisee"), an individual with his main address located at OR a company organized and existing under the laws of [STATE/PROVINCE], with its head office located at:

[COMPLETE ADDRESS]

WHEREAS, Franchisor and certain of its Affiliates own, operate and franchise [DESCRIPTION] throughout [COUNTRY] which, among other things, rent, sell and market [PRODUCT/SERVICE] to the [GENERAL PUBLIC OR COPORATIONS OR GOVERNMENT]; and

WHEREAS, Franchisor and certain of its Affiliates acquire, produce, license market and sell [PRODUCT/SERVICE]; and

WHEREAS, Franchisee is willing to purchase on a per Location (the terms initially capitalized in this Agreement and not otherwise defined herein shall have the respective meanings set forth in Paragraph 18 of this Agreement) basis a specified number of [PRODUCT/SERVICE]; and

WHEREAS, Franchisor is willing to provide various marketing, advertising and promotional services and activities in support of Franchisee;

NOW, THEREFORE, based on the above premises and in consideration of the covenants and agreements contained herein, and intending to be legally bound, the parties agree hereto as follows:

1. AGREEMENT TERM

The term of this Agreement shall be for the period (the "Term"), commencing as of the date of this Agreement. Each year of the Term, as measured from the date of this Agreement, is a "Contract Year."

2. TERRITORY

The territory for purposes of this Agreement with respect to [PRODUCT/SERVICE] shall be [COUNTRY], their territories and possessions (the "Territory"), except with respect to those [PRODUCT/SERVICE] for which Franchisee has only [COUNTRY] Distribution Rights, in which case, the Territory with respect to such [PRODUCT/SERVICE] shall be limited to [COUNTRY] and, if and to the extent Franchisor owns or controls such rights, to territories and possessions of [COUNTRY]).

3. REVENUE SHARING

Franchisee shall remit to Franchisor [%] of the net profits of its business in the form of [ROYALTIES,
ETC]. [DESCRIBE IN DETAILS REVENUE SHARING BETWEEN FRANCHISOR AND FRANCHISEE].
Distribution of profits shall be made on the [DAY] of [MONTHS].

4. FRANCHISOR COMMITMENTS

Beginning as of the date of this Agreement for [NUMBER OF LOCATIONS] located in [COUNTRY] within [NUMBER] calendar months hereafter, and for Participating Franchises within [NUMBER] calendar months hereafter, Franchisee agrees as follows:

4.1 Purchasing

The following purchasing requirements shall apply to all Locations and Participating Franchises

    A. [FRANCHISEE REQUIREMENT]
    B. [FRANCHISEE REQUIREMENT]
    C. [FRANCHISEE REQUIREMENT]

4.2 Missing Products

For each [PRODUCT TYPE] that is lost, stolen or otherwise not reasonably accounted for, for more than [SPECIFY] calendar days during the period commencing upon delivery to Franchisor's distribution center and ending on the last day of the relevant Revenue Sharing Period, Franchisee shall pay [AMOUNT] to Franchisor. For any such [PRODUCT TYPE] Franchisee will reimburse Franchisor the applicable distribution wholesale price less the applicable average Purchase Price received by Franchisee.

4.3 Payment

The parties acknowledge and agree that if Franchisee fails to order [NUMBER OF UNITS] required under Paragraph 3.1, Franchisee shall pay [AMOUNT] to Franchisor, as liquidated damages, an amount equal to [AMOUNT] for each unit which Franchisee failed to order. If Franchisor fails to deliver the number or units ordered by Franchisee under Paragraph 3.1, Franchisor shall pay to Franchisee, as liquidated damages, an amount equal to [AMOUNT] for each unit which Franchisor failed to deliver. The parties hereto expressly agree and acknowledge that actual damages for purposes of this Subparagraph would be difficult to ascertain and that the amount set forth above represents the parties' reasonable estimate of such damages.

4.4 Marketing

With respect to advertising of [PRODUCT/SERVICE], Franchisee agrees to consult with Franchisor and to keep Franchisor reasonably appraised of its marketing plans and activities and to comply with Franchisor's then-current customary marketing support policies and practices to the extent they are reasonable and practicable. Franchisor shall have the right to approve such plans, and Franchisee shall provide a timely opportunity for said approval by Franchisor. Franchisor shall exercise its approval rights in a timely and reasonable manner.

Should Franchisee fail to comply in good faith with its obligations under Paragraph 3.4, Franchisor shall be entitled to give written notice to Franchisee of such failure. In no event shall Franchisor be obligated to provide such advertising which it would otherwise have been obligated to provide during such time as Franchisor's obligations hereunder were suspended because of Franchisee's failure to fulfill its obligations under this Paragraph 3.4.

4.5 Participating Franchises

While Franchisee cannot guarantee that its Franchises will adopt the Agreement, Franchisee will use good faith commercially reasonable efforts to recommend adoption of the Agreement to its Franchises and anticipates a high level of adoption thereby. Franchisor hereby agrees that each Participating Franchise shall execute a letter agreement, which has been approved by Franchisee in form and substance, in favor of Franchisor, agreeing to be bound by the terms and conditions of this Agreement as if it were a party hereto (the "Participating Franchise"). Franchisee shall be liable for each Participating Franchise's performance of its financial obligations hereunder as if such Participating Franchise were a Location. Franchisor shall have the right to proceed against Franchisee for money only for any failure of a Participating Franchise to fully perform the financial terms and conditions of this Agreement. Participating Franchises shall be subject to the same terms and conditions under the Agreement as Locations, unless specifically designated otherwise. Implementation of the Agreement at the Franchise level and Franchise payments there under will be administered by Franchisor.

4.6 Placement

Franchisee shall exercise good faith commercially reasonable efforts to maximize revenue on the [SALE OR RENTAL] of [PRODUCT/SERVICE]. At all times during the entire Revenue Sharing Period, Franchisee shall make available for [SALE OR RENTAL] at each Location all of the [PRODUCT/SERVICE] purchased for such Location.

4.7 Packing and Shipping

Franchisor will be solely responsible for making [PRODUCT/SERVICE] ready for consumer [PURCHASE/RENTAL] and for shipping the [PRODUCT/SERVICE] from its distribution center to Franchisee's Locations.

4.8 Returns/Exchanges

The purchase requirements set forth in Paragraph 3.1 shall not be subject to any returns by Franchisee. Franchisor will exchange defective or damaged products. Defective products shall mean those that are mechanically defective, mispackaged, physically blemished or contain extraneous material. Franchisee shall report defective or damaged products to Franchisor promptly following discovery of such defect or damage.

4.9 Location Count

Franchisee will report to Franchisor on a calendar month basis the number of currently operating Locations, including Participating Franchises, non-participating Franchises, New Franchisor Locations and recently closed Locations.

4.10 Demographic Information

Franchisee will provide to Franchisor, on an ongoing basis, information regarding the demographic make-up generally of Franchisee customers.

5. COMMITMENTS

5.1 Marketing Support

In lieu of specific marketing support programs such as rebate, co-op and MDF programs, and as payment for services and in consideration for the various other services and activities which Franchisee has agreed to perform hereunder for the benefit of Franchisor, such as sales and rental reporting functions, Franchisor agrees to credit on a per [PRODUCT/SERVICE] basis (on the relevant invoice) Franchisee with marketing support funds ("Marketing Support Funds") in the amount of [SPECIFY] OR of in the amount of [SPECIFY PERCENTAGE] of the Purchase Price generated by [PRODUCT/SERVICE]. Marketing Support Funds shall not be used to advertise, promote or otherwise market product not distributed by Franchisor. In addition to Marketing Support Funds, Franchisor shall continue to provide Franchisee with standard [IN-STORE/ON-LOCATION] point of purchase marketing materials as customarily utilized by Franchisor.

a. Franchisee shall use all of the Marketing Support Funds to advertise in measured media [PRODUCT/SERVICE]. With respect to said advertising of [PRODUCT/SERVICE], Franchisee agrees to consult with Franchisor and to keep Franchisor reasonably appraised of its marketing plans and activities and to comply with Franchisor then-current customary marketing support policies and practices to the extent that they are reasonable and practicable. Franchisor shall have the right to approve such plans, and Franchise shall provide a timely opportunity for said approval by Franchisor. Franchisor shall exercise approval rights in a timely and reasonable manner.

b. With respect to [SPECIFY PERCENTAGE] of the Marketing Support Funds, Franchisor and Franchisee shall jointly determine how said monies will be used to advertise, promote or otherwise market [PRODUCT/SERVICE].

c. Franchisor shall use [SPECIFY PERCENTAGE] of the Marketing Support Funds for [IN-STORE/ON-LOCATION] [PRODUCT/SERVICE] specific marketing and promotion.

d. Should Franchisee fail to comply in good faith with its obligations under paragraphs 4.1 A, B and C, Franchisor shall be entitled to give written notice to Franchisee of such failure. If Franchisee fails to remedy such failure to Franchisor's satisfaction within [NUMBER] calendar days following receipt of such notice, Franchisor shall be relieved of its obligations to provide Marketing Support Funds, until such time as Franchisee complies in good faith with its obligations under this Paragraph 4.1 D. In no event shall Franchisee be entitled to receive Marketing Support Funds which would otherwise have accrued during such time as Franchisee's rights hereunder were suspended because of its failure to fulfill its obligations under this Paragraph 4.1 D.

6. ELECTRONIC REPORTING

At no cost or expense to Franchisor, Franchisee will provide to Franchisor, electronically, daily access to all Franchisee [PRODUCT/SERVICE] information along with weekly summaries, in such form as may be reasonably specified by Franchisor from time to time, of all performance information as to Franchisee's [SALE OR RENTAL] of [PRODUCT/SERVICE], including, but not limited to, daily [SALES OR RENTAL] data, daily inventory and daily Revenue from each Location on a Location by Location, [PRODUCT/SERVICE] by [LOCATION] basis.

7. REVIEW

Within [SPECIFY NUMBER OF DAYS] calendar days following the end of each Contract Year, the parties shall meet and in good faith review the terms of this Agreement. Should no agreement be reached between the parties with respect to adjusting or amending the terms of the Agreement, the then current terms of the Agreement shall remain in full force and effect. Within the [SPECIFY NUMBER OF DAYS] calendar days following the end of the [SPECIFY] month of the Term, either party may give [NUMBER] months notice to terminate the Agreement. If such notice is given by either party, from such notification forward, Franchisee shall have no right or obligation to purchase additional [PRODUCT/SERVICE] under this Agreement and Franchisor shall be relieved of any right or obligation to sell [PRODUCT/SERVICE] to Franchisee under this Agreement.

8. TERMINATION

The following transactions or occurrences shall constitute material events of default (each an "Event of Default") by the applicable party (the "defaulting party") hereunder such that, in addition to and without prejudice to or limiting any other rights and remedies available to the non-defaulting party at law or in equity the non-defaulting party may elect to immediately and prospectively terminate this Agreement at the sole discretion of the non-defaulting party by giving written notice thereof to the other party at any time after the occurrence of an Event of Default setting forth sufficient facts to establish the existence of such Event of Default.

8.1 Material Breach

A material breach by a party of any material covenant, material warranty, or material representation contained herein, where such defaulting party fails to cure such breach within [NUMBER] calendar days after receipt of written notice thereof, or within such specific cure period as is expressly provided for elsewhere in this Agreement; or

8.2 Insolvency and/or Bankruptcy

A party makes an attempt to make any arrangement for the benefit of creditors, or a voluntary or involuntary bankruptcy, insolvency or assignment for the benefit of creditors of a party or in the event any action or proceeding is instituted relating to any of the foregoing and the same is not dismissed within [NUMBER] calendar days after such institution; or

8.3 Failure to Make Payment

A failure by either party to make payment of any monies payable pursuant to this Agreement, as and when payment is due. Except as otherwise provided herein, no termination of this Agreement for any reason shall relieve or discharge any party hereto from any duty, obligation or liability hereunder which was accrued as of the date of such termination.

9. PUBLIC DISCLOSURE AND CONFIDENTIALITY

9.1 Public Disclosure

Each party agrees that no press release or public announcement relating to the existence or terms of this Agreement (including within the context of a trade press or other interview or advertisement in any media) shall be issued without the express prior written approval of the other party hereto.

9.2 Confidential Information

During the Term and for a period of [SPECIFY YEARS/MONTHS] thereafter, Franchisee and Franchisor shall hold, and shall cause each of their directors, officers, employees and agents to hold in confidence the terms of this Agreement (including the financial terms and provisions hereof and all information received pursuant to, or developed in accordance with, this Agreement) specifically including but not limited to the Franchisor. Franchisee and Franchisor hereby acknowledge and agree that all information contained in, relating to or furnished pursuant to this Agreement, not otherwise known to the public, is confidential and proprietary and is not to be disclosed to third parties without the prior written consent of both Franchisee and Franchisor. Neither Franchisee nor Franchisor shall disclose such information to any third party (other than to officers, directors, employees, attorneys, accountants and agents of Franchisee and Franchisor or the affiliates of either, who have a business reason to know or have access to such information, and only after each of whom agrees to being bound by this paragraph) except:

    a. To the extent necessary to comply with any Law or the valid order of a governmental agency or court of competent jurisdiction or as part of its normal reporting or review procedure to regulatory agencies or as required by the rules of any major stock exchange on which either party's stock may be listed; provided, however, that the party making such disclosure shall seek, and use reasonable efforts to obtain, confidential treatment of said information and shall promptly, to the greatest extent practicable, notify the other party in advance of such disclosure;

    b. As part of the normal reporting or review procedure by its parent Franchisee, its auditors and its attorneys;

    c. To the extent necessary to obtain appropriate insurance, to its insurance agent or carrier, that such agent or carrier agrees to the confidential treatment of such information; and

    d. To actual or potential successors in interest, provided, however, that such person or entity shall have first agreed in writing to the confidential treatment of such information.

10. NO RIGHT TO USE NAMES

    a. Neither Franchisee nor Locations nor Participating Franchises shall acquire any right to use, nor shall use any copyrights, trademarks, characters or designs owned or controlled by Franchisor or any of its Affiliates, including without limitation, the names [SPECIFY], alone or in conjunction with other words or names, in any advertising, publicity or promotion, either express or implied, without Franchisor's prior consent in each case, and in no case shall any Franchisee or Location advertising, publicity, or promotion, express or imply any endorsement of the same.

b. Franchisee shall not acquire any right to use, nor shall use the name [SPECIFY] alone or in conjunction with other words or names, or any copyrights, trademarks, characters or designs of the same in any advertising, publicity or promotion, either express or implied, without Franchisor's prior consent in each case, and in no case shall any Franchisee advertising, publicity, or promotion, express or imply any endorsement of the same.

11. ASSIGNMENT

This Agreement and the rights and licenses granted hereunder are personal and neither party shall have the right to sell, assign, transfer, mortgage, pledge nor hypothecate (each an "Assignment") any such rights or licenses in whole or in part without the prior written consent of the non-assigning party, nor will any of said rights or licenses be assigned or transferred to any third party by operation of law, including, without limitation, by merger or consolidation or otherwise; provided, however, that an Assignment pursuant to or resulting from a sale of all or substantially all of the assets or all or a majority of the equity of Franchisee to any Person or Persons or any other form of business combination, such that the Franchisee business as currently existing remains substantially intact, including, without limitation, a sale to the public, shall not require such consent so long as such Assignment is not to [SPECIFY]; and provided further that any Assignment by (i) Franchisee, to [SPECIFY] or (ii) Franchisor to any Affiliate of Franchisor. In the event that Franchisee or Franchisor assigns its rights or interest in or to this Agreement in whole or in part, the assigning party will nevertheless continue to remain fully and primarily responsible and liable to the other party for prompt, full, complete and faithful performance of all terms and conditions of this Agreement.

12. AUDIT RIGHTS

a. During the Term and continuing until [SPECIFY] months following the date of expiration or earlier termination of this Agreement Franchisor may, audit the financial books, information systems and records of Franchisee as reasonably necessary to verify Franchisee's compliance with its obligations under this Agreement; provided, however, that

    i. Such audit shall be at the sole cost and expense of Franchisor (unless such audit reveals that payments due to Franchisor for any [SPECIFY] month period were understated by more than [SPECIFY] percent, in which case, in addition to all other rights which Franchisor may have, Franchisee shall promptly reimburse Franchisor to the extent of its reasonable out-of-pocket costs of such audit);

    ii. Franchisor may not audit more than twice per year (and no such audit shall continue for more than [NUMBER] calendar days from the date the auditors are given access to the applicable records), and

    iii. Any such audit shall be conducted only during regular business hours and in such a manner as not unreasonably to interfere with the normal business activities of Franchisee.

b. Franchisee shall keep and maintain complete and accurate books of account and records in connection with its obligations under this Agreement at its principal place of business until the date [SPECIFY] months following the date of rendering of the initial statement reflecting such records unless a legal action with regard thereto is commenced during such period.

c. During the Term and continuing until [SPECIFY] months following the date of expiration or earlier termination of this Agreement, Franchisor may inspect and audit the books, records and store premises of Locations and Participating Franchises as reasonably necessary to verify compliance with this Agreement; provided, however, that

d. Such audit shall be at the sole cost and expense of Franchisor (unless such audit reveals that payments due to Franchisor for any [NUMBER] month period were understated by more than [%], in which case, in addition to all other rights which Franchisor may have, Franchisee shall promptly reimburse Franchisor to the extent of its reasonable out-of-pocket costs of such audit), and (b) any such audit shall be conducted only during regular business hours and in such a manner as not unreasonably to interfere with the normal business activities of Location or Participating Franchises.

13. FRANCHISOR'S REPRESENTATIONS AND WARRANTIES

Franchisor represents and warrants that:

a. It is a corporation organized and existing under the laws of [SPECIFY COUNTRY AND/OR STATE/PROVINCE] with its principal place of business in [SPECIFY COUNTRY];

b. The undersigned has the full right, power and authority to sign this Agreement on behalf of Franchisor;

c. The execution, delivery and performance of this Agreement does not and will not, violate any provisions of [COUNTRY] articles or certificates of incorporation and bylaws, or any contract or other Agreement to which Franchisor is a party;

d. There is no broker, finder or intermediary involved in connection with the negotiations and discussions incident to the execution of this Agreement, and no broker, finder, agent or intermediary who might be entitled to a fee, commission or any other payment upon the consummation of the transactions contemplated by this Agreement;

e. This Agreement has been duly executed and delivered and constitutes a legal, valid and binding obligation, enforceable in accordance with its terms, except as enforceability may be limited by bankruptcy, insolvency, reorganization, moratorium or other similar laws now or hereinafter in effect, affecting the enforcement of creditors' rights in general and by general principles of equity, regardless of whether such enforceability is considered in a proceeding in equity or at law.

14. FRANCHISEE'S REPRESENTATIONS AND WARRANTIES

Franchisee represents and warrants that:

a. It is a corporation organized and existing under the laws of the [SPECIFY COUNTRY AND/OR STATE/PROVINCE] with its principal place of business in the [SPECIFY COUNTRY];

b. The undersigned has the full right, power and authority to sign this Agreement on behalf of Franchisee;

c. There is no broker, finder or intermediary involved in connection with the negotiations and discussions incident to the execution of this Agreement, and no broker, finder, agent or intermediary who might be entitled to a fee, commission or any other payment upon the consummation of the transactions contemplated by this Agreement;

d. This Agreement has been duly executed and delivered and constitutes the legal, valid and binding obligation of Franchisee enforceable in accordance with its terms, except as enforceability may be limited by bankruptcy, insolvency, reorganization, moratorium or other similar laws now or hereinafter in effect, affecting the enforcement of creditors' rights in general and by general principles of equity, regardless of whether such enforceability is considered in a proceeding in equity or at law; and

e. The execution, delivery and performance of this Agreement does not, and will not, violate any provisions of Franchisee's articles or certificates of incorporation and bylaws, or any contract or other Agreement to which Franchisee is a party.

15. FORCE MAJEURE

The duties and obligations of the parties hereunder may be suspended upon the occurrence and continuation of any "Event of Force Majeure" which inhibits or prevents performance hereunder, and for a reasonable start-up period thereafter. An "Event of Force Majeure" shall mean any act, cause, contingency or circumstance beyond the reasonable control of such party (whether or not reasonably foreseeable), including, without limitation, to the extent beyond the reasonable control of such party, any governmental action, nationalization, expropriation, confiscation, seizure, allocation, embargo, prohibition of import or export of goods or products, regulation, order or restriction (whether foreign, federal or state), war (whether or not declared), civil commotion, disobedience or unrest, insurrection, public strike, riot or revolution, lack or shortage of, or inability to obtain, any labor, machinery, materials, fuel, supplies or equipment from normal sources of supply, strike, work stoppage or slowdown, lockout or other labor dispute, fire, flood, earthquake, drought or other natural calamity, weather or damage or destruction to plants and/or equipment, commandeering of vessels or other carriers resulting from acts of God, or any other accident, condition, cause, contingency or circumstances including (without limitation, acts of God) within or without [COUNTRY]. Neither party shall, in any manner whatsoever, be liable or otherwise responsible for any delay or default in, or failure of, performance resulting from or arising out of or in connection with any Event of Force Majeure and no such delay, default in, or failure of, performance shall constitute a breach by either party hereunder. As soon as reasonably possible following the occurrence of an Event of Force Majeure, the affected party shall notify the other party, in writing, as to the date and nature of such Event of Force Majeure and the effects of same. If any Event of Force Majeure shall prevent the performance of a material obligation of either party hereunder, and if the same shall have continued for a period of longer than [SPECIFY] days, then either party hereto shall have the right to terminate this Agreement by written notice to the other party hereto.

16. INDEMNIFICATION

Each party (the "Indemnifying Party") shall indemnify and hold the other party and its affiliates and their respective employees, officers, agents, attorneys, stockholders and directors, and their respective permitted successors, licensees and assigns (the "Indemnified Party(ies)") harmless from and against (and shall pay as incurred) any and all claims, proceedings, actions, damages, costs, expenses and other liabilities and losses (whether under a theory of strict liability, or otherwise) of whatsoever kind or nature

("Claim(s)") incurred by, or threatened, imposed or filed against, any Indemnified Party (including, without limitation, (a) actual and reasonable costs of defense, which shall include without limitation court costs and reasonable attorney and other reasonable expert and reasonable third party fees; and (b) to the extent permitted by Law, any fines, penalties and forfeitures) in connection with any proceedings against an Indemnified Party caused by any breach (or, with respect to third party claims only, alleged breach) by the Indemnifying Party of any representation, term, warranty or agreement hereunder. Neither party shall settle, compromise or consent to the entry of any judgment in or otherwise seek to terminate any pending or threatened Claim in respect of which the Indemnified Party is entitled to indemnification hereunder (whether or not the Indemnified Party is a party thereto), without the prior written consent of the other party hereto; provided, however, that the Indemnifying Party shall be entitled to settle any claim without the written consent of the Indemnified Party so long as such settlement only involves the payment of money by the Indemnifying Party and in no way affects any rights of the Indemnified Party.

17. REMEDIES

No remedy conferred by any of the specific provisions of this Agreement is intended to be exclusive of any other remedy which is otherwise available at law, in equity, by statute or otherwise, and except as otherwise expressly provided for herein, each and every other remedy shall be cumulative and shall be in addition to every other remedy given hereunder or now or hereafter existing at law, in equity, by statute or otherwise and no provision hereof shall be construed so as to limit any party's available remedies in the event of a breach by the other party hereto. The election of any one or more of such remedies by any of the parties hereto shall not constitute a waiver by such party of the right to pursue any other available remedies.

18. DEFINITIONS

a. "Affiliate" shall mean an entity in which either party has a controlling interest.

b. "Franchise" shall mean all Franchisee Locations which Franchisee informs Franchisor are Franchises.

c. "Laws" shall mean all international, federal, national, state, provincial, municipal or other laws, ordinances, orders, statutes, rules or regulations.

d. "Location" shall mean any Location in [COUNTRY] or [COUNTRY], which, at any time during the Term of this Agreement, is wholly owned and/or operated by Franchisee, whether or not such Location is operated under the "Franchisee" trademarks. Should Franchisee undertake to own or operate outlets different than the outlets it has traditionally operated, such as by way of example, kiosks, carts, "Locations within a Location", "rack jobbing" operations or vending machines, the parties shall negotiate in good faith to agree upon terms for the inclusion of such retail outlets in this Agreement.

e. "New Franchisee Location" shall mean a Location which Franchisee or any of its Franchisees or Affiliates first owns or operates after the commencement date of this Agreement, excluding Franchisee's acquisition of franchised Franchisee Locations.

f. "Revenue Sharing Period" shall mean the period commencing on [SPECIFY DATE] and running through until the end of [SPECIFY PERIOD].

19. MISCELLANEOUS

a. This Agreement shall not constitute any partnership, joint venture or agency relationship between the parties hereto. The parties shall be considered independent contractors.

b. This Agreement, together with the attached [EXHIBITS IF INCLUDED], embodies the entire understanding of the parties with respect to the subject matter hereof and may not be altered, amended or otherwise modified except by an instrument in writing executed by both parties.

c. The headings in this Agreement are for convenience of reference only and shall not have any substantive effect.

d. All rights and remedies granted to the parties hereunder are cumulative and are in addition to any other rights or remedies that the parties may have at law or in equity.

e. Should any non-material provision of this Agreement be held to be void, invalid or inoperative, as a matter of law the remaining provisions hereof shall not be affected and shall continue in effect as though such unenforceable provision(s) have been deleted herefrom.

f. Unless otherwise indicated, all dollar amounts referenced herein shall refer to and be paid in [COUNTRY] dollars.

g. No waiver of any right under or breach of this Agreement shall be effective unless it is in writing and signed by the party to be charged.

h. This Agreement shall be governed by and construed in accordance with the internal Laws of [SPECIFY], applicable to Agreements entered into and wholly performed therein. Franchisee hereby consents to and submits to the jurisdiction of the Franchisor and any action or suit under this Agreement may be brought in any Court with appropriate jurisdiction over the subject matter established.

i. None of the provisions of this Agreement is intended for the benefit of or shall be enforceable by any third parties.

j. This Agreement may be executed in separate counterparts each of which shall be an original and all of which taken together shall constitute one and the same Agreement.

k. All notices shall be in writing and either personally delivered, mailed first-class mail (postage prepaid), sent by reputable overnight courier service (charges prepaid), or sent by transmittal by any electronic means whether now known or hereafter developed, including, but not limited to, email, facsimile, telex, or laser transmissions, able to be received by the party intended to receive notice, to the parties at the following addresses:

Franchisor Address:
[YOUR COMPLETE ADDRESS]

Franchisee Address:
[SPECIFY]

20. GOVERNING LAW

This Agreement shall be governed by, and construed under, the laws of [STATE/PROVINCE].

IN WITNESS WHEREOF, the parties hereto have executed this Agreement as of the day and year first above written.

FRANCHISOR   FRANCHISEE

_____   _____
Authorized Signature   Authorized Signature

_____   _____
Print Name and Title   Print Name and Title

11.4 MANUFACTURING AGREEMENT

This Manufacturing (the "Agreement") is effective [DATE],

BETWEEN: **[YOUR COMPANY NAME]** (the "Publisher"), a company organized and existing under the laws of the [State/Province] of [STATE/PROVINCE], with its head office located at:

[YOUR COMPLETE ADDRESS]

AND: **[MANUFACTURER NAME]** (the "Manufacturer"), a company organized and existing under the laws of the [State/Province] of [STATE/PROVINCE], with its head office located at:

[COMPLETE ADDRESS]

Recitals:

Publisher has expended considerable time, effort, and resources in the development and/or publishing of certain unique, copyrighted and proprietary interactive multimedia products and software, and the documentation and packaging materials related thereto (the "Publisher Products" as defined below);

Manufacturer desires to act as a Manufacturer of the Publisher Products bundled together with the products of Manufacturer or of third parties, and represents to Publisher that Manufacturer has sufficient expertise, resources, and personnel to perform its obligations under this Agreement.

Manufacturer further desires to manufacture the Publisher Products for purposes of such distribution; and

Publisher desires to have Manufacturer act as a Manufacturer of the Publisher Products on the terms and conditions set forth herein.

Therefore, in consideration of the mutual covenants and promises contained herein, the parties hereto agree as follows:

1.   DEFINITIONS

"Publisher Products" shall mean the products identified in Exhibit A attached hereto, together with any accompanying documentation, packaging, or other materials identified on Exhibit A (if any). Publisher, in its sole discretion, reserves the right to add Publisher Products to or delete Publisher Products from Exhibit A on [NUMBER] days notice.

"Bundles" shall mean the combination of the Publisher Products with hardware and/or software distributed as a unit by Manufacturer, as described in Exhibit C.

"Proprietary Rights" shall mean all rights of Publisher and its licensors in the Publisher Products including, without limitation, copyright, patent, design patent, trademark, trade dress, trade secret, and publicity rights, arising under applicable law and international conventions.

"Territory" shall be defined as the world.

2. GRANT OF LICENSES

2.1 Distribution License

Publisher grants to Manufacturer a non-transferrable and non-exclusive license during the term of this Agreement to include the Publisher Products in Bundles and to distribute Bundles directly or through distributors and retailers to end-users located in the Territory. In addition to the other terms and conditions of this Agreement, these licenses to distribute are expressly subject to the following conditions:

2.1.1 Manufacturer distribution to end-users, whether directly or through distributors and retailers, shall be made only pursuant to the end-user license included with the Publisher Products, and each license of a Publisher Product by Manufacturer to an end-user will be allowed only in jurisdictions where an enforceable copyright covering the Publisher Products exists; and

2.1.2 Manufacturer distribution to any entity other than end-users, including without limitation distribution to retailers or other distributors or sub-distributors, shall be made pursuant to written agreement(s) with Manufacturer which (i) comply with all of the terms of this Agreement, (ii) are no less protective of Publisher's rights than the terms of this Agreement, and (iii) expressly make Publisher a third-party beneficiary.

2.1.3 Manufacturer shall be entitled to distribute only those Publisher Products manufactured by Manufacturer.

2.2 Manufacturing License

Subject to the terms of this Agreement, Publisher grants to Manufacturer and Manufacturer accepts, for the term of this Agreement, the nonexclusive right to manufacture the Publisher Products only in the [COUNTRY] and only for distribution as otherwise provided in this Agreement, subject to the following limitations:

2.2.1 Manufacturer may manufacture the Publisher Products, provided that such manufacturing is at Manufacturer 's own cost and in accordance with this Agreement and otherwise prudent in protecting Publisher's and its Licensors' Proprietary Rights. Any and all copies of the Publisher Products manufactured by Manufacturer shall contain security coding in a form acceptable to Publisher. Manufacturer shall indemnify and pay Publisher for any unauthorized copies of the Publisher Products manufactured by Manufacturer or at its authorized facilities at the full retail price of such Publisher Products.

2.2.2 Manufacturer shall manufacture the Publisher Products in accordance with strict security procedures and shall keep detailed manufacturing and distribution records for all units manufactured. Manufacturer's manufacturing facilities and manufacturing and distribution records shall be open to Publisher's inspection without notice.

2.2.3 Manufacturer shall include with all copies of the Publisher Products manufactured by Manufacturer an end-user license in the form provided by Publisher. Changes to the terms of the end-user license shall be subject to approval by Publisher, in its sole discretion.

2.2.4 Manufacturer shall manufacture the Publisher Products from production masters of the Publisher Products (including without limitation production masters of packaging and related materials) provided by Publisher in accordance with the schedule set forth on Exhibit B. Manufacturer agrees not to alter the Publisher Products (including without limitation their packaging) without Publisher's prior written consent.

2.3 Prohibited Acts

Neither Manufacturer nor anyone to whom Manufacturer distributes the Publisher Products has the right to distribute or sell the Publisher Products except as part of Bundles within the Territory, without the express prior written approval of Publisher. Anyone who unbundles any Publisher Products shipped to Manufacturer for inclusion in Bundles shall be liable for the full wholesale price of all such unbundled Publisher Products plus all applicable attorneys' fees and costs incurred in investigating and prosecuting an action against the unbundling party. Manufacturer shall notify those to whom it distributes the Publisher Products in Bundles that unbundling is specifically prohibited, and that anyone who unbundles any Bundled Publisher Products shipped to or through Manufacturer shall be liable for the full wholesale price of all such unbundled Publisher Products plus all applicable attorneys' fees and costs incurred in investigating and prosecuting an action against the unbundling party.

2.4 Limitations

Title to the Publisher Products and all associated patents, copyrights, trademarks, trade dress, trade secrets and other proprietary rights shall remain with Publisher and its licensors. Except as expressly authorized by Publisher in writing, Manufacturer will not, and will cause its employees, agents and Manufacturer not to: (i) modify, translate, reverse engineer, decompile, disassemble, create derivative works of or copy the Publisher Pr6ducts or related documentation; (ii) remove, alter, or cover any copyright or trademark notices or other proprietary rights notices placed or embedded by Publisher on or in the Publisher Products.

2.5 Non-Exclusivity

The licenses granted in this Agreement are non-exclusive. Accordingly, nothing in this Agreement shall be construed as limiting in any manner Publisher's marketing or distribution activities (including without limitation the distribution of Publisher Products upgrades and Publisher Products to end users of Bundles) or Publisher's appointment of other dealers, distributors, value-added resellers, original equipment manufacturers, licensees or agents in the Territory.

2.6 Packaging, Advertising and Promotion

2.6.1 Packaging. Manufacturer shall not alter the packaging in which the Publisher Products are provided, including without limitation production masters for manufacturing of packaging.

2.6.2 Promotion and Advertising. Publisher shall have the right to approve any advertising or promotional materials regarding or including the Publisher Products which incorporates any original artwork not provided by Publisher. Any such advertising or promotional materials shall be submitted to Publisher for approval, in its sole discretion, and Publisher shall have [NUMBER] business days in which to approve or disapprove the advertising or promotional materials. Publisher's failure to approve or disapprove the materials within [NUMBER] business days shall constitute approval of the materials. Manufacturer shall not provide any copies of the Publisher Products or other materials to magazines, newspapers or other publications for review purposes.

2.7 Reserved Rights

Except as expressly provided in this Agreement, Publisher does not grant any right to Manufacturer to

(a) use, print, copy, or display (except for promotional purposes) the Publisher Products; (b) assign, sublicense, or otherwise transfer its rights or delegate its obligations under this Agreement or any of the rights, licenses, software, Publisher Products, or materials to which it applies; or (c) modify, amend, rewrite, translate to another language or otherwise vary the Publisher Products. Publisher shall at all times retain all right, title and interest to the Publisher Products. Publisher reserves the right at any time to terminate Manufacturer 's rights to manufacture or distribute any particular Publisher Product on [NUMBER] days notice. Upon the receipt of such notice, Manufacturer shall cease its manufacturing, marketing, selling, distribution, import and export of such Publisher Product within the time period specified in such notice.

3. COMPENSATION and STATEMENTS

3.1 License Fees

For each copy of the Publisher Products which Manufacturer manufactures, Manufacturer shall pay Publisher the license fees set forth in Exhibit B. Payment shall be made by Manufacturer within [NUMBER] days of purchase order date.

3.2 Minimum License Fees

At a minimum, Manufacturer shall be obligated to pay Publisher the minimum license fees set forth in Exhibit B, in the amounts and on the schedule and terms set forth in Exhibit B.

3.3 Purchase Orders

Manufacturer shall use its standard form purchase orders to indicate to Publisher the number of copies of the Publisher Products that Manufacturer will manufacture. Manufacturer shall be entitled to manufacture no more than the number of units of the Publisher Products shown on the Manufacturer purchase orders received by Publisher. No other term or condition of the Manufacturer purchase orders shall have any force or effect. Manufacturer shall be obligated to pay license fees for all units indicated on the purchase orders. The first [NUMBER] purchase orders, totaling [NUMBER] units, are attached to this Agreement as Exhibit E. Manufacturer shall pay license fees for these units based on the dates of the purchase orders.

3.4 Content Royalties

The initial payment and additional license fees shall include all royalties to be paid to third parties ("content royalties"). It will be Publisher's responsibility to ensure that all content royalties are paid when due.

3.5 Audit

Publisher shall have the right, upon reasonable request, to review those records of Manufacturer necessary to verify the units manufactured and license fees paid. Any such audit will be conducted at Publisher's expense and at such times and in such a manner as to not unreasonably interfere with Manufacturer 's normal operations; provided, however, that if any such audit reveals an error of at least [%] in the payment of royalties, then Manufacturer shall pay the costs of the audit. If a deficiency is shown by such audit, Manufacturer shall immediately pay that deficiency. Non-payment of any deficiency within [NUMBER] days of the date on which Manufacturer receives notice of such deficiency shall constitute a material breach of this Agreement.

4. WARRANTY

4.1 Warranty

Publisher warrants to Manufacturer that, for a period of [NUMBER] year from the shipment to Manufacturer (or, if earlier, termination of this Agreement), the Publisher Product masters will conform substantially to Publisher's published specifications. If Manufacturer discovers a material defect in the master for the Publisher Products within the warranty period, Manufacturer will promptly notify Publisher. Publisher's entire obligation and Manufacturer 's sole remedy will be for Publisher to use its best efforts promptly to correct any discovered defect and provide Manufacturer with a corrected version of the master for the Publisher Products.

4.2 Limited Warranty on Media

Publisher warrants the diskettes and/or compact disc on which the masters of the Publisher Products are recorded to be free from defects in materials and workmanship under normal use for a period of [NUMBER] days from the date of delivery. Publisher's entire liability and Manufacturer 's exclusive remedy regarding master diskettes and/or compact discs not meeting Publisher's limited warranty and which are returned to Publisher shall be replacement of the master disk or diskette or credit against future orders of Publisher Products, at Publisher's option. Publisher will have no responsibility to replace or credit a diskette/disc damaged by accident, abuse or misapplication.

4.3 Disclaimer

EXCEPT FOR THE ABOVE EXPRESS LIMITED WARRANTIES, PUBLISHER MAKES AND MANUFACTURER RECEIVES NO WARRANTIES ON THE PUBLISHER PRODUCTS, EXPRESS, IMPLIED, STATUTORY, OR IN ANY OTHER PROVISION OF THIS AGREEMENT OR COMMUNICATION With MANUFACTURER, AND PUBLISHER SPECIFICALLY DISCLAIMS ANY IMPLIED WARRANTIES OF MERCHANTABILITY OR FITNESS FOR A PARTICULAR PURPOSE. Publisher DOES NOT WARRANT THAT THE OPERATION OF THE Publisher PRODUCTS WILL BE UNINTERRUPTED OR ERROR FREE.

5. TRADEMARKS

5.1 Use

During the term of this Agreement, Manufacturer shall have the right to indicate to the public that it is an authorized Manufacturer of the Publisher Products and to advertise (within the Territory and solely in connection with Bundles) the Publisher Products under the trademarks, marks, and trade names that Publisher and its licensors may adopt from time to time for the Publisher Products. ("Trademarks"). Manufacturer will not and will ensure that its distributors and dealers will not, alter or remove any Trademark, or affix, without the prior written permission of Publisher, any other trademarks, marks or other logos on the Publisher Products. Nothing herein shall grant to Manufacturer any right, title or interest in the Trademarks. At no time during or after the term of this Agreement shall Manufacturer challenge or assist others to challenge the Trademarks or the registration thereof or attempt to register any trademarks, marks or trade names confusingly similar to those of Publisher and its licensors for the Publisher Products.

5.2 Approval

All representations of the Publisher Trademarks that Manufacturer intends to use shall first be submitted to Publisher for approval (which shall not be unreasonably withheld) of design, colour, and other details relating to the Trademarks.

6. INTELLECTUAL PROPERTY INDEMNITY

Publisher will defend at its expense any action brought against Manufacturer to the extent that it is based on a claim that the Publisher Products or any part thereof, when used within the scope of this Agreement, infringes a [COUNTRY] copyright or a [COUNTRY] patent issued and known to Publisher as of the date of this Agreement, and Publisher will pay any settlements and any costs, damages and attorneys' fees finally awarded against Manufacturer in such action which are attributable to such claim; provided, the foregoing obligation shall be subject to Manufacturer notifying Publisher promptly in writing of the claim, giving Publisher the exclusive control of the defense and settlement thereof, and providing all reasonable assistance in connection therewith. Publisher shall have no liability for any claim of infringement arising out of

    i) the use of other than a current unaltered release of the Publisher Products or

    ii) the use or combination of the Publisher Products with non-Publisher programs, data or equipment if such infringement was caused by such use or combination, and

    iii) Publisher shall have the right, upon either the occurrence of or the likelihood (in the opinion of Publisher) of the occurrence of a finding of infringement to:

        a) procure for Manufacturer the right to continue distributing the Publisher Products or

        b) replace the relevant portions of the Publisher Products with other equivalent, non-infringing portions. If Publisher is unable to accomplish either (iii)(a) or (b) above, then at Publisher's option, Publisher shall remove the Publisher Product in issue and refund to Manufacturer the amount paid to Publisher under this Agreement relating to that Publisher Product. THE FOREGOING IS IN LIEU OF ANY WARRANTIES OF NONINFRINGEMENT, WHICH ARE HEREBY DISCLAIMED, AND SETS FORTH PUBLISHER'S ENTIRE

LIABILITY FOR ANY INFRINGEMENT BY THE Publisher PRODUCTS OR ANY PART THEREOF.

7. TERMINATION

7.1 Termination without notice

This Agreement shall terminate automatically without notice, [NUMBER] year from the effective date first set forth above, unless the parties have mutually agreed in writing to renew it for an additional term.

7.2 Termination with or without a reason

Publisher may terminate this Agreement for any reason or no reason on [NUMBER] days' written notice. Until Manufacturer has fulfilled its minimum purchase commitment for the term of this Agreement as set forth in Section [SPECIFY], Manufacturer shall be entitled to terminate this Agreement only upon Publisher's breach of a material provision of this Agreement, which breach has not been cured within [NUMBER] days of Manufacturer giving written notice of such breach. After Manufacturer has satisfied its minimum purchase commitment for the term of this Agreement, Manufacturer may terminate this Agreement for any reason or no reason on [NUMBER] days' notice.

7.3 Termination in case of insolvency, receivership, or bankruptcy

This Agreement may be terminated automatically, without notice, (i) upon the institution by or against Manufacturer of insolvency, receivership or bankruptcy proceedings or any other proceedings for the settlement of Manufacturer 's debts, (ii) upon Manufacturer's making an assignment for the benefit of creditors, or (iii) upon Manufacturer's dissolution.

7.4 Effect of Termination

Upon the termination of this Agreement, the rights and licenses granted to Manufacturer pursuant to this Agreement (including without limitation the right to manufacture and the right to distribute the Publisher Products through distributors) will automatically cease, provided that all existing sublicenses to end users will continue for the duration of such sublicense. All payments owing from Manufacturer to Publisher shall become immediately due and payable upon termination. All Publisher trademarks, marks, trade names, patents, copyrights, designs, drawings, formulae or other data, photographs, samples, literature, and sales aids of every kind shall remain the property of Publisher. Within [NUMBER] days after the termination of this Agreement, Manufacturer shall prepare all such items in its possession for shipment, as Publisher may direct, at Publisher's expense. Manufacturer shall not make or retain any copies of any confidential items or information which may have been entrusted to it. Effective upon the termination of this Agreement, Manufacturer shall cease to use the Trademarks.

7.5 Sell-Off Period

Notwithstanding the provisions of section [NUMBER], if termination occurs because the term set forth in section [NUMBER] has expired, and not because of any breach of material provisions of this Agreement by Manufacturer or any other reason, Manufacturer shall be entitled to sell-off remaining Publisher Products manufactured in the ordinary course of business and currently in Manufacturer 's inventory as of the date of termination as part of Bundles according to the terms of this Agreement for a period of [NUMBER] days, provided that Manufacturer has paid any additional license fees owed for the manufacture of such Publisher Products. At the end of this sell-off period, Manufacturer shall, at Publisher's sole option, destroy all remaining copies of the Publisher Products in its inventory or return such copies to Publisher for a refund of license fees paid or payment of manufacturing costs (as may be applicable) for the copies returned in saleable condition. If termination occurs because of a breach of any material provision of this Agreement, or for any other reason other than expiration of the term of the license set forth in section [NUMBER] (including termination by Publisher at its option under section [NUMBER]), then all of Manufacturer's rights under this Agreement shall immediately terminate as provided in section [NUMBER], and Manufacturer shall have no right to sell off remaining Publisher Products in its inventory, which shall, at Publisher's sole option, be destroyed or returned to Publisher for a refund of license fees paid or payment of manufacturing costs (as may be applicable) for the copies returned in saleable condition.

7.6 Survival Provisions

If this Agreement is terminated for any reason, those provisions which by their nature would survive such termination will survive termination. Termination shall not affect any other rights which either party may have at law or in equity.

8. CUSTOMER SUPPORT

Publisher will be responsible for providing reasonable and customary customer and technical support for the Publisher Products.

9. LIMITATION OF LIABILITY

IN NO EVENT WILL PUBLISHER BE LIABLE FOR COSTS OF PROCUREMENT OF SUBSTITUTE PRODUCTS OR SERVICES, LOST PROFITS, OR ANY SPECIAL, INDIRECT, CONSEQUENTIAL, OR INCIDENTAL DAMAGES, HOWEVER CAUSED AND ON ANY THEORY OF LIABILITY, ARISING IN ANY WAY OUT OF THIS AGREEMENT OR THE TERMINATION THEREOF, WHETHER OR NOT PUBLISHER HAS BEEN ADVISED OF THE POSSIBILITY OF SUCH DAMAGE, AND NOTWITHSTANDING ANY FAILURE OF ESSENTIAL PURPOSE OF ANY LIMITED REMEDY PROVIDED IN THIS AGREEMENT.

10. INDEMNIFICATION OF PUBLISHER

Except for the warranty and infringement claims based on the Publisher Products discussed above, Manufacturer agrees to indemnify and hold Publisher and its licensors harmless against any cost, loss, liability, or expense (including attorneys' fees) arising out of third party claims against Publisher as a result of Manufacturer's or its distributors' or retailers' promotion or distribution of the Publisher Products or Bundles, including, without limitation, providing unauthorized representations or warranties to its customers regarding the Publisher Products or breaching any term, representation or warranty of this Agreement.

11. GENERAL TERMS

11.1 Non-assignability and Binding Effect

Manufacturer agrees that its rights and obligations under this Agreement may not be transferred or assigned directly or indirectly without the prior written consent of Publisher. Publisher may assign its rights and obligations under this Agreement without Manufacturer's consent. Subject to the foregoing, this Agreement shall be binding upon and inure to the benefit of the parties hereto, their successors and assigns.

11.2 Notices

Notices under this Agreement shall be sufficient only if personally delivered, delivered by a major commercial rapid delivery courier service, delivered by facsimile transmission confirmed by first class mail, or mailed by certified or registered mail, return receipt requested, to a party at its address first set forth above or as amended by notice pursuant to this subsection. If not received sooner, notice by any of these methods shall be deemed to occur [NUMBER] days after deposit.

11.3 Import and Export Controls

Manufacturer will comply with all export laws and restrictions and regulations of the Department of Commerce or other [COUNTRY] or foreign agency or authority, and will not export, or allow the export or re-export of any Publisher Products in violation of any such restrictions, laws or regulations.

11.4 Governing Law and Legal Actions

This Agreement shall be governed by and construed under the laws of the State of [SPECIFY STATE] without regard to choose of laws principles. The parties consent to the jurisdiction of the state and federal courts located in [STATE], [STATE], and agree that process may be served in the manner provided herein for giving of notices or otherwise as allowed by law.

11.5 Partial Invalidity

If any provision of this Agreement is held to be invalid, then the remaining provisions shall nevertheless remain in full force and effect, and the invalid or unenforceable provision shall be replaced by a term or provision that is valid and enforceable and that comes closest to expressing the intention of such invalid or unenforceable term or provision.

11.6 No Agency

The parties hereto are independent contractors. Nothing contained herein or done in pursuance of this Agreement shall constitute either party the agent of the other party for any purpose or in any sense whatsoever or constitute the parties as partners or joint venturers.

11.7 No Waiver

No waiver of any term or condition of this Agreement shall be valid or binding on either party unless the same shall have been mutually assented to in writing by both parties. The failure of either party to enforce at any time any of the provisions of this Agreement, or the failure to require at any time performance by the other party of any of the provisions of this Agreement, shall in no way be construed to be a present or future waiver of such provisions, nor in any way effect the ability of either party to enforce each and every such provision thereafter.

11.8 Force Majeure

Non-performance by either party shall be excused to the extent that performance is rendered impossible by strike, fire, flood, earthquake, or governmental acts, orders or restrictions;

provided that any such non-performance shall be cause for termination of this Agreement by the other party if the non-performance continues for more than [NUMBER] days.

11.9 Attorneys' Fees

The prevailing party in any legal action brought by one party against the other and arising out of this Agreement shall be entitled, in addition to any other rights and remedies it may have, to reimbursement for its expenses, including costs and reasonable attorneys' fees.

11.10 Entire Agreement

This Agreement sets forth the entire agreement and understanding of the parties relating to the subject matter herein and merges all prior discussions between them. No modification of or amendment to this Agreement, nor any waiver of any rights under this Agreement, shall be effective unless in writing signed by the parties.

11.11 Counterparts

This Agreement may be executed in two or more counterparts and all counterparts so executed shall for all purposes constitute one agreement, binding on all parties hereto.

IN WITNESS WHEREOF, each party to this agreement has caused it to be executed at [PLACE OF EXECUTION] on the date indicated above.

PUBLISHER   MANUFACTURER

_____   _____
Authorized Signature   Authorized Signature

_____   _____
Print Name and Title   Print Name and Title

EXHIBIT A
PUBLISHER PRODUCTS

(with documentation, packaging, and other materials, if any, as identified herein)

Publisher reserves the right to add Publisher Products to or delete Publisher Products from this Exhibit on [NUMBER] days' notice.

EXHIBIT B
LICENSED MANUFACTURING QUANTITIES SCHEDULE

Publisher shall deliver the Production Masters of the Publisher Products as follows:

Publisher Product	Delivery Date for Production Masters on or Before

Subject to the terms and conditions of the Agreement and if Manufacturer attaches purchase orders to this Agreement in Exhibit E for the units set forth below, Manufacturer shall be entitled to manufacture the Publisher Products as follows:

Publisher Product	Quantity Authorized for Manufacture	License Fee Per Copy Manufactured

Minimum manufacturing commitments for subsequent months shall be as follows:

Month	Products available for Manufacturing	Quantity of Each Product	Total Minimum License Fees to be Paid

EXHIBIT C
APPROVED BUNDLES

EXHIBIT D
TERRITORY

EXHIBIT E
PURCHASE ORDERS

11.5 TRADEMARK LICENSE

This Trademark License (the "Agreement") is effective [DATE],

BETWEEN: **[YOUR COMPANY NAME]** (the "Licensor"), a company organized and existing under the laws of the [State/Province] of [STATE/PROVINCE], with its head office located at:

[YOUR COMPLETE ADDRESS]

AND: **[COMPANY NAME]** (the "Licensee"), a company organized and existing under the laws of the [State/Province] of [STATE/PROVINCE], with its head office located at:

[COMPLETE ADDRESS]

For good and valuable consideration, the receipt and legal sufficiency of which are hereby expressly acknowledged, the parties hereto agree as follows:

WHEREAS pursuant to an asset purchase agreement dated on [SPECIFY] between Licensor and Licensee (the "Asset Purchase Agreement"), Licensor sold to Licensee substantially all of the property and assets (subject to the exceptions stated therein) of its [SPECIFY] business (the "Purchased Business") excluding, among other things, the Trade Marks (as hereinafter defined);

AND WHEREAS as a condition to the completion of the purchase and sale contemplated by the Asset Purchase Agreement, the Licensor agreed to grant to the Licensee a license to use the trade marks set forth in Schedule [SPECIFY] attached hereto (the "Trade Marks") with respect to the wares and services set forth in such Schedule [SPECIFY].

NOW, THEREFORE, the parties hereto agree as follows:

1.   **PREAMBLE**

1.1. The preamble shall form part hereof as if herein recited at length.

2.   **GRANT OF LICENSE**

2.1. Subject to the terms and conditions set out herein, Licensor hereby grants to Licensee the exclusive royalty free, right and license, with the right to have others licensed in conformity with the provisions of this agreement (the "Trade Mark License"), to use the Trade Marks and works in which copyright subsists as set forth in Article [NUMBER] of this agreement, in [COUNTRY] (the "Territory"), only on and in connection with the sale and distribution of the wares and services set forth in Schedule [SPECIFY] hereto, and, if the Licensor obtains an amendment to the registration of the Trade Marks (which it will apply for at the request and expense of the Licensee), the additional wares and services set forth in Schedule [SPECIFY] hereto if such additional wares and services are offered for sale in the ordinary course of business in substantially all of the [SPECIFY] stores in [COUNTRY] operated by the Licensee in respect of the Purchased Business and such other wares and services which are offered for sale in the ordinary course of business in substantially all the [SPECIFY] stores in [COUNTRY] operated by the Licensee in respect of the Purchased Business as may be mutually agreed upon (acting reasonably) by Licensor and Licensee from time to time (herein collectively referred to as "Designated Products and Services"). Licensee agrees that it shall not use any Trade Mark in connection with a ware or service which is not one of the Designated Products and Services nor shall it use any Trade Mark outside of the Territory.

2.2. Furthermore, Licensee shall not have the right to use any of the Trade Marks (i) in its corporate name, or (ii) other than pursuant to the terms and conditions of this Agreement. However, the Licensee may use the Trade Marks in public signage for the Licensee's [SPECIFY] outlets from which a significant variety of Designated Products and Services are offered for sale and, with the prior written consent of the Licensor (which consent cannot be unreasonably withheld) and upon satisfaction of such conditions as to the protection of the distinctiveness and goodwill of the Trade Marks as the Licensor may reasonably impose, may use the Trade Marks in association with other words or expressions in association with Designated Products and Services.

2.3. It is understood and agreed that the Trade Mark License is limited strictly to the rights granted hereunder and that all other rights in the Trade Marks in connection with the present and future businesses of Licensor and its affiliates throughout the world are reserved to Licensor and its affiliates.

2.4. Licensee shall have the right to assign the Trade Mark License in connection with any sale by the Licensee of all or substantially all of the Purchased Business or have further licenses granted to purchasers of all or substantially all of the Purchased Business in [SPECIFY] or to franchisees of the Licensee with or without royalties or other consideration being payable to Licensee, without the consent of Licensor and without any right on the part of Licensor to receive the whole or any part of any such other royalties or other consideration; provided, however, that Licensee shall promptly inform Licensor in writing of the identity and business address of any additional licensee or assignee and provided further that as a condition of such assignment or sublicense such additional licensee or assignee will be required to enter into a trade mark license agreement with Licensor more particularly described below. No assignment shall operate to release Licensee from its obligations hereunder.

2.3.1. The assignment by Licensee of this Trade Mark License shall take place only upon the assignee and the Licensor entering into a trade mark license agreement substantially the same as this Trade Mark License, which agreement the Licensor shall not unreasonably refuse to negotiate and execute at the sole expense of the Licensee.

2.3.2. The grant from time to time by Licensee to additional licensees of the right to use the Trade Marks shall be by license agreement between Licensor, Licensee and the additional licensee, which license agreement shall incorporate no less stringent obligations on the part of the additional licensee with respect to the use by such licensee of the Trade Marks than are required of Licensee by this agreement and shall not provide for the granting to any such licensee of greater rights to use the Trade Marks than are enjoyed by Licensee. Without limiting the generality of the foregoing, the additional licensee shall agree to be bound in such license agreement by the quality control and trade mark provisions set out in Articles [NUMBER] and [NUMBER] below.

2.5. Licensor hereby appoints Licensee as its agent to, and Licensee hereby agrees to, enforce compliance by all additional licensees appointed by Licensee with the provisions of their respective license agreements (including, without limiting the generality of the foregoing, the quality control provisions contained therein). The appointment of Licensee as an agent is solely for the purposes of this agreement.

3. TERM

Subject to the provisions of Article [NUMBER], this agreement shall remain in full force and effect for a term of [NUMBER] years from the date of this Agreement, subject to automatic renewal for an indefinite number of further [NUMBER] year terms unless (i) at least [NUMBER] days prior to the end of the initial term or any renewal term Licensee delivers a written notice to Licensor stating that it does not wish this agreement to be renewed, or (ii) Licensee is at the time of the renewal in default under Article [NUMBER] of this agreement.

4. QUALITY CONTROL

4.1. So as not to bring discredit upon the Trade marks, Licensee agrees that the Designated Products and Services sold and distributed by Licensee will at all times be of good quality and that the Designated Products and Services will be merchandised, distributed and sold by Licensee with packaging and sales promotion materials appropriate for good quality products and services. Licensee further agrees that all Designated Products and Services will be sold, labeled, packaged, merchandised, distributed, promoted and advertised in accordance with all applicable [YOUR COUNTRY LAW] and regulations.

4.2. Licensee shall ensure that the packaging, contents, workmanship and quality of all Designated Products and Services sold and distributed by Licensee are consistent with the reputation and prestige of the Trade Marks as a designation for good quality products and services.

4.3. Licensor and its duly authorized representatives will have the right, upon reasonable prior notice and during normal business hours, to examine the Designated Products and Services, and their packaging and labeling, for the purpose of maintaining quality and to ensure that Licensee is performing its obligations under this agreement.

4.4. Licensor acknowledges that all Designated Products and Services in existence as at the date hereof comply with the provisions of this Article [NUMBER].

5. TRADE MARKS

5.1. Licensee acknowledges that Licensor is recorded as the owner of (a) all right, title and interest in and to the Trade Marks and (b) of the goodwill attached to or which will become attached to the Trade Marks in connection with the Designated Products and Services, in relation to which the same are or will be used. Licensee will not, at any time, do any act or thing which adversely affects any rights of Licensor in and to the Trade Marks or any registration thereof.

5.2. Licensee will at Licensor's request and at Licensee's expense, execute any documents reasonably required by Licensor to confirm (i) Licensor's ownership of all rights in and to the Trade Marks in association with the Designated Products and Services in all jurisdictions in the Territory and (ii) the respective rights of Licensor and Licensee pursuant to this agreement.

5.3. Licensee will use the Trade Marks in the Territory strictly in compliance with the legal requirements applicable therein and will use such markings and notices in connection therewith as may reasonably be required in writing by Licensor in compliance with each jurisdiction's applicable legal provisions.

5.4. Licensor shall have a reasonable delay in which to comply with Licensor requirements for marking. Licensee will cause to appear on all Designated Products and Services (other than stock on hand of goods constituting Designated Products and Services in existence as at the date hereof and on the public signage for the Licensee's retail outlets) and on all materials on or in connection with which the Trade Marks are used and in a visible location in each of its [SPECIFY] outlets in association with which any of the Trade Marks is used, such legends, markings and notices as may reasonably be requested of it by Licensor in order to give appropriate notice of any copyright, trade mark, trade name or other rights therein or pertaining thereto.

5.5. Licensee will comply with all governmental regulations in connection with the distribution and sale of the Designated Products and Services. Licensee shall clearly indicate, with each incident of use of the Trade Marks (including, without limitation, on each label and package in respect of products and on point of sale and contract documents in respect of services) that any of the Trade Marks used is being so used by Licensee under license from the Licensor. Until otherwise notified by Licensor, such indication shall state: "Registered Trade Mark of [SPECIFY] Inc. Used under License".

5.6. Licensee will never challenge the Licensor's ownership of or the validity of the Trade Marks or any application for registration thereof, or any trade mark registrations thereof, or any rights of Licensor therein whether during the term of this agreement or subsequent to its expiration or termination.

5.7. In the event that Licensee or the Licensor learns of any actual or anticipated infringement or limitation of any of the Trade Marks or of any use by any person of a trade mark or trade name similar to, derived from or containing any of the Trade Marks in association with any of the Designated Products and Services (collectively "Infringing Trade Marks"), it will promptly notify the other in writing. Licensor may (but shall not be obliged to) take such action as it deems advisable for the protection of its rights in and to the Trade Marks and Licensee will, if requested to do so by Licensor, cooperate with Licensor in a commercially reasonable manner. It is understood that in the event that Licensor institutes court action to terminate the use of the Infringing Trade Marks, Licensee has the right to participate in such action should it so decide, but such participation shall be at its own cost and expense and to the extent that it is protecting its interests as Licensee of the Trade Marks, which interests are defined by this agreement.

5.8. In no event, however, will Licensor be required to take any action if it deems it inadvisable to do so. Licensor shall not be obliged to take any measures or proceedings whatsoever to seek or obtain the cessation of use of any Infringing Trade Marks by any third party. Licensor shall not be obliged to contest or oppose any application for registration of any Infringing Trade Marks by any third party. In the event that Licensor decides not to take any such action it shall so advise Licensee in writing within [NUMBER] days of receipt of notification from Licensee of such Infringing Trade Marks. In such event Licensee shall be free to take such action on its own in connection with any Infringing Trade Marks, keeping Licensor advised as developments occur. All expenses (including legal fees and disbursements) incurred by Licensor or Licensee in connection with investigating and prosecuting any claim with respect to any Infringing Trade Marks shall be borne by the party taking such action. Any damages recovered or sums obtained in settlement of or with respect to any such claim will belong to the party taking such action.

5.9. Should a third party at arm's length with Licensee ("Third Party") claim in writing that Licensee by acting in accordance with this agreement in its use of the Trade Marks is violating any intellectual property right of such Third Party, Licensee shall promptly notify Licensor accordingly in writing. Licensor may (but shall not be obliged to) take such action as it deems advisable for the protection of its rights in and to the Trade Marks and for the protection of Licensee, and Licensee will, if requested to do so by Licensor, cooperate with Licensor in a commercially reasonable manner. In no event, however, will Licensor be required to take any action if it deems it inadvisable to do so.

5.10. In the event that Licensor decides not to take any such action it shall so advise Licensee in writing within [NUMBER] days of receipt of notification from Licensee of the Third Party claim. In such event, Licensee shall be free to take such action on its own in connection with such Third Party claim, keeping Licensor advised as developments occur. All expenses (including legal fees and disbursements) incurred by Licensor or Licensee in connection with investigating and defending against any such Third Party claim shall be borne by the party taking such action. Any damages paid or recovered or sums paid or obtained in settlement of or with respect to any such Third Party claim shall be for the account of the party taking such action.

5.11. Subject to the foregoing provisions of this Article [NUMBER], the Licensor at Licensee's cost and expense shall take all such steps and execute all such documents as are necessary to maintain the validity of the Trade Marks and the registrations thereof in relationship to the Designated Products and Services and shall provide Licensee with copies of all correspondence with and notices from any third party, including governmental authorities, with respect to the Trade Marks insofar as the Designated Products and Services are concerned.

6. COPYRIGHT

6.1. Any copyright which may be created in any sketch, design, print, packaging, label, tag or advertising or promotional material or the like bearing any of the Trade Marks will be the property of Licensor, whether designed by or for Licensor or Licensee.

6.2. Licensee will ensure that proper copyright assignments in favor of Licensor are signed by the creator of the work in which such copyright subsists and, as the case may be, by the employer of the said creator.

6.3. Licensee will cooperate fully with Licensor in order to confirm Licensor's ownership of all rights in and to such copyright and the respective rights of Licensor and Licensee pursuant to this agreement, including executing all documents reasonably required by Licensor.

7. INDEMNIFICATION

7.1. Each of the Licensor and the Licensee (the "Indemnifying Party") does hereby indemnify and agrees to save and hold the other party (the "Indemnified Party") harmless of and from any and all liabilities, claims, causes of action, suits, damages and expenses (including reasonable attorney's fees and expenses) for which the Indemnified Party may become liable or may incur or be compelled to pay in any action or claim against the Indemnified Party or any of its affiliates, for or by reason of any acts, whether of omission or commission, that may be committed or suffered by the Indemnifying Party or any of its respective servants, agents or employees or in the case of the Licensee, its sublicensees in connection with the Indemnifying Party's or, as the case may be, any sublicensee's performance of this agreement and transactions arising therefrom provided that neither party shall be obliged to indemnify the other in respect of claims of trade mark infringement asserted by a third party as to and arising from either party's use of the Trade Marks in the Territory in accordance with this Agreement. The Indemnified Party will give prompt written notice to the Indemnifying Party of any such claim.

7.2. Licensee will procure and maintain at its own expense in full force and effect at all times during which Designated Products and Services are being sold or offered for sale, with a responsible insurance carrier, a public liability insurance policy including product liability coverage and contractual coverage relating to this agreement with respect to the Designated Products and Services with a limit of liability of not less than [AMOUNT]. Such insurance policy will be written for the benefit of Licensor and Licensee, as their respective interests may appear, and will provide for at least [NUMBER] days prior written notice to Licensor and Licensee of the cancellation or substantial modification thereof. Such insurance may be obtained by Licensee in conjunction with a policy of public liability insurance that covers products and services other than the Designated Products and Services. Licensee shall provide certificates of such insurance to Licensor from time to time at Licensor's request. Nothing contained in this paragraph 7.2 will be deemed to limit, in any way, the indemnification provisions of paragraph 7.1 above.

8. DEFAULT

8.1. Licensor will have the right to terminate this agreement forthwith by written notice to Licensee, if Licensee fails in a material respect to perform any covenant or obligation in this agreement on its part to be performed and Licensee fails to remedy such default within the [NUMBER] days after notice thereof has been given in writing by the Licensor to the Licensee, or in the case of any default which is not reasonably capable of being remedied within such [NUMBER]-day period, the Licensee commences to remedy such default within such [NUMBER]-day period and proceeds diligently to complete the remedy of such default as soon as possible thereafter.

8.2. If Licensee shall not generally pay its debts as such debts become due, or shall make a general assignment for the benefit of its creditors, or shall file a notice of intention to make a proposal under the Bankruptcy and Insolvency [ACT/LAW/RULE] ([COUNTRY]) or shall make a proposal under such Act, or any proceeding shall be instituted (or renewed after a stay) by or against the Licensee seeking to adjudicate it a bankrupt or insolvent, or seeking liquidation, winding up, reorganization, arrangement, sequestration, adjustment, protection, relief, or composition of the Licensee or its debts under any law relating to bankruptcy, insolvency or reorganization or relief of debtors, or seeking the entry of an order for relief or the appointment of a receiver, trustee or other similar official for the Licensee or for any substantial part of its property and assets and, in the case of any such proceeding against the Licensee, it shall not be dismissed or stayed within [NUMBER] days; or if an encumbrancer takes possession of all or a substantial part of the property and assets of the Licensee, or execution or other similar process is enforced against such property and assets and remains unsatisfied for a period in excess of [NUMBER] days, this agreement will terminate automatically without written notice to Licensee.

8.3. No assignee for the benefit of creditors, custodian, liquidator, sequestrator, receiver, administrator, trustee, trustee in bankruptcy, sheriff or any or any other officer of the court or official charged with taking over custody of Licensee's assets or business, will have any rights to continue this agreement or to exploit or in any way use the Trade Marks (or any of them) if termination occurs pursuant to paragraph 8.2 above.

9. TERMINATION

On the termination of this agreement, all the rights of Licensee hereunder will forthwith terminate and automatically revert to Licensor and Licensee shall forthwith discontinue any and all uses of the Trade Marks.

Notwithstanding the provisions of the foregoing sentence, in the event of termination of this agreement, Licensee will be entitled, for an additional period of [NUMBER] days only, on a non-exclusive basis, to continue to sell under the Trade Marks and in accordance with all of the terms and provisions of this agreement its inventory of goods constituting Designated Products and Services on hand on the date of such termination. Except as provided in the immediately preceding sentence, on the termination of this agreement, Licensee with forthwith discontinue all use of the Trade Marks, will no longer have the right to use the Trade Marks or any variation or simulation thereof, and will transfer to Licensor all registrations, filings and rights with regard to the Trade Marks which it may have possessed at any time.

Licensor may, in its sole discretion, at any time, enter into such arrangements as it desires pursuant to which Designated Products and Services may be sold, distributed and advertised in the Territory or any part thereof in association with the Trade Marks by it or by any duly authorized third party other than Licensee at any time subsequent to the date of termination of this agreement. Upon termination of this agreement for whatever reason, Licensor shall be entitled to demand that all officials and regulatory authorities having jurisdiction in the Territory immediately cancel any registration in favor of the Licensee of the Trade Marks, and the Licensee undertakes not to object in any manner to such cancellation. The Licensee covenants and undertakes to consent in writing to the above-mentioned cancellation, if Licensor or any such official or regulatory authority requires same, and the Licensee undertakes to execute and deliver to Licensor all necessary or useful documents required to effect the above-mentioned cancellation.

10. REPRESENTATIONS AND WARRANTIES

10.1. The Trade Mark License granted herein is on an "as is" basis, save and except for the Licensor's representation and warranty that the Trade Marks, in association with the wares and services described in Schedule [SPECIFY], are owned by the Licensor and are in good standing and for the representations and warranties as to the Trade Marks set forth in Section 3.1.27 of the Asset Purchase Agreement, which representations and warranties are limited to the use of the Trade Marks in association with the wares and services described in Schedule "A".

10.2. Licensee acknowledges that Licensor has enforceable legal rights in and to the Trade Marks in the Territory.

10.3. The representations and warranties set forth in Section [NUMBER] of the Asset Purchase Agreement are given and made by the Licensor for the exclusive benefit of the Licensee and shall not enure to the benefit of any sublicensee or assignee of the Licensee.

11. NOTICES

All notices or other communications provided for in this agreement shall be given in writing and shall be sent by prepaid registered or certified mail, or by telecopy or delivered in person at the following address for each party until such time as written notice, as provided hereby, of a change of address to be used thereafter, is given by one party to the other party:

Licensor:

Attention: President
Telecopier: I

Licensee:
Attention: The President
Telecopier: I

The receipt of any such notice or other communication shall be conclusively presumed to have occurred at the address to which it is delivered, transmitted by telecopy or mailed, at the time of delivery or on the business day next following such transmission or on the third business day next following such mailing (as the case may be).

12. BINDING EFFECT

Subject to the provisions of paragraph 10.3 hereof, this agreement will enure to the benefit of and will be binding upon the parties and their respective successors and permitted assigns, provided that any assignment by Licensee may only be made in connection with a sale by Licensee of all or substantially all of the Purchased Business or with the prior written consent of the Licensor (and, in either case, upon satisfaction of such conditions for the protection of the interest of the Licensor in and to the Trade Marks, as the Licensor may reasonably require). Licensor may assign this agreement without the prior written consent of (but on prior notice to) of Licensee. An assignment shall not release the assignor from its obligations hereunder.

13. FORCE MAJEURE

Neither the Licensor nor the Licensee shall be liable in damages or otherwise, nor shall they be subject to termination of this agreement by the other, for any delay or default in performing any obligation hereunder if that delay or default is caused by government orders or requirements, wars, fires, strikes, radioactive fallout, interruption of transportation facilities, labor troubles, riots, shortages of raw fuel or raw materials, or any other cause beyond the reasonable control of the Licensor or the Licensee, as the case may be, and is without fault or negligence of the Licensor or the Licensee, as the case may be.

14. MISCELLANEOUS

14.1. This agreement contains the entire understanding and agreement between the parties hereto with respect to the subject matter hereof, supersedes all prior oral and written understandings and agreements relating thereto. And may not be modified, discharged or terminated orally.

14.2. Nothing herein contained will be construed to constitute the parties hereto as partners or as joint ventures, or except as expressly set forth in paragraph 2.4 hereof, either party as agent of the other, and Licensee will not have the power to obligate or bind Licensor in any manner whatsoever. Licensor will have no responsibility for the operation or production of Licensee's distribution or sales facilities or for any decisions that may be made in connection therewith.

14.3. This agreement shall be governed by and construed in accordance with the [YOUR COUNTRY LAW] of the Province of [STATE/PROVINCE] and the federal [YOUR COUNTRY LAW] of [COUNTRY] applicable therein.

14.4. No waiver by either party, whether express or implied, of any provision of this agreement, or of any breach or default, will constitute a continuing waiver of such provision, breach or default, or any other provision, other breach or other default of this agreement.

14.5. If any provision or any portion of any provision of this agreement will be held to be void or unenforceable, the remaining provisions of this agreement and the remaining portion of any provision held void or unenforceable in part will continue in full force and effect.

14.6. Article headings appearing herein have been inserted for convenience only and shall not be used in the interpretation of this agreement.

14.7. Time is of the essence of this agreement and the mere lapse of time shall have the effects contemplated herein and by [YOUR COUNTRY LAW].

IN WITNESS WHEREOF, each party to this agreement has caused it to be executed at [PLACE OF EXECUTION] on the date indicated above.

LICENSOR   LICENSEE

_____   _____
Authorized Signature   Authorized Signature

_____   _____
Print Name and Title   Print Name and Title

11.6 FASHION MODEL RELEASE AND PERMISSION TO USE PHOTOPGRAPHS

This Model Release and Permission to Use Photographs (the "Agreement") is made and effective [DATE],

BETWEEN: **[YOUR COMPANY NAME]** (the "Website Owner"), a corporation organized and existing under the laws of the [State/Province] of [STATE/PROVINCE], with its head office located at:

[YOUR COMPLETE ADDRESS]

AND: **[MODEL NAME]** (the "Model"), an individual with his/her main address located at:

[COMPLETE ADDRESS]

RECITALS

For good and valuable consideration, the receipt and sufficiency of which are hereby acknowledged, the Model hereby irrevocably and perpetually grants to Website Owner the unrestricted right, power and authority to reproduce, publish, print, distribute, transmit, copy, or otherwise exploit, in whole or in part, in any medium known or later discovered, including but not limited to by means of digital transmission through the Internet, all photographs which are described in Exhibit "A" attached hereto, including but not limited to all photographs and images taken of the Model by [PHOTOGRAPH] at a photo shoot held at [LOCATION] on [DATE], and further including the photographs which are attached hereto and consecutively numbered [NUMBER] through [NUMBER] (all of the above are collectively defines herein as the "Photographs").

1. COPYRIGHTS AND USE OF PHOTOGRAPHS

The Model acknowledges and agrees that the Website Owner may use and exploit the Photographs in any manner, without restriction of any kind, and without the necessity of acknowledging the Model's identity, or by identifying him/her other than with his/her real name.

The Model hereby releases and holds the Website Owner harmless from and against all claims, suits, threats, demands, liabilities, actions and causes of action, in any way related to the Photographs or the Website Owner's use and exploitation of the Photographs, including but not limited to actions based upon invasion of privacy, violation of moral rights, defamation, false light, and all other potential legal theories of any nature or type, under and state, federal or local common law, statutory law, rule, regulation or court order, whether now known and available or whether later developed, discovered or created.

2. REPRESENTATIONS AND WARRANTIES

The Model represents and warrants that he/she is over the age of majority in the state in which this Release is executed and that the Model has full power and authority to execute this Release. The Model has produced a valid driver's license' birth certificate, or other proof of his/her age to the Website Owner. No other party has any interest or right in and to the Photographs or the exploitation thereof by the Website Owner.

3. ENTIRE AGREEMENT

This Agreement contains the entire agreement and understanding of the parties with respect to the subject matter hereof and supercedes and replaces all prior discussions, agreements, proposals, understandings, whether orally or in writing, between the parties related to the subject matter of this Agreement. This Agreement may be changed, modified or amended only in a written agreement that is duly executed by authorized representatives of the parties. If any provisions hereof is deemed to be illegal or unenforceable by a court of competent jurisdiction, the enforceability of effectiveness of the remainder of the Agreement shall not be effected and this Agreement shall be enforceable without reference to the unenforceable provision. No party's waiver of any breach or accommodation to the other party shall be deemed to be a waiver of any subsequent breach.

4. GOVERNING LAW

In interpreting the terms of this Agreement, the parties agree that the laws of the [State/Province] of [STATE/PROVINCE] shall be applicable. All suits permitted to be brought in any court shall be in [STATE/PROVINCE].

IN WITNESS WHEREOF, the parties have executed this Agreement on the dates set forth first above, with full knowledge of its content and significance and intending to be legally bound by the terms hereof.

WEBSITE OWNER   MODEL

_____   _____
Authorized Signature   Authorized Signature

_____   _____
Print Name and Title   Print Name and Title

EXHIBIT A
THE PHOTOGRAPHS

11.7 ASSIGNMENT OF ALL RIGHTS TO PHOTOGRAPH

This Assignment of All Rights to Photograph (the "Agreement") is made and effective [DATE],

BETWEEN:	**[YOUR COMPANY NAME]** (the "Photograph Owner"), a corporation organized and existing under the laws of the [State/Province] of [STATE/PROVINCE], with its head office located at:

[YOUR COMPLETE ADDRESS]

AND:	**[PURCHASER NAME]** (the "Purchaser"), a corporation organized and existing under the laws of the [State/Province] of [STATE/PROVINCE], with its head office located at:

[COMPLETE ADDRESS]

For good and valuable consideration received and paid in hand, the receipt and sufficiency of which is hereby acknowledges, the Photograph Owner hereby agrees as follows:

1. All right, title and interest in and to the photograph(s) taken by me, which are described in Exhibit "A" attached hereto ("Photographs") are hereby transferred, conveyed, bargained and assigned to Purchaser. The rights that are transferred and assigned hereunder shall include all of the exclusive rights granted to the owner of a copyright under the [COUNTRY] Copyright Laws, copyright laws of any and all countries and jurisdictions throughout the world, and all international conventions and treaties relative to copyright protection.

2. Upon execution hereof, I am transferring and delivering to the Purchaser all existing developed copies, digital copies and negative copies of the Photographs and represent and warrant that I have retained no such copies in my possession.

3. I represent and warrant that I am the creator of such Photographs and the sole owner thereof and that no other party has any right in and to the Photographs. I agree to execute any further document and take any further reasonable action requested by the Purchaser to convey all rights in and to the Photographs and to assist the Purchaser in registering for a copyright in and to such Photographs.

4. I represent and warrant that the Photographs have not been published as the term "published" is defined in the [COUNTRY] Copyright Act.

IN WITNESS WHEREOF, the parties have executed this Agreement on the dates set forth first above, with full knowledge of its content and significance and intending to be legally bound by the terms hereof.

PHOTOGRAPH OWNER   PURCHASER

_____   _____
Authorized Signature   Authorized Signature

_____   _____
Print Name and Title   Print Name and Title

EXHIBIT "A"
DESCRIPTION OF PHOTOGRAPHS

11.8 MUSIC LICENSE AGREEMENT

This Music License Agreement (the "Agreement") is made and effective [DATE],

BETWEEN: **[YOUR COMPANY NAME]** (the "Owner"), a corporation organized and existing under the laws of the [State/Province] of [STATE/PROVINCE], with its head office located at:

[YOUR COMPLETE ADDRESS]

AND: **[LICENSEE NAME]** (the "Licensee"), a corporation organized and existing under the laws of the [State/Province] of [STATE/PROVINCE], with its head office located at:

[COMPLETE ADDRESS]

WHEREAS, the Owner is the holder of the copyright to certain musical compositions identified herein and Licensee is the creator and owner of a certain site on the World Wide Web who wishes to integrate the musical compositions of Owner into said Website.

RECITALS

A. Owner represents and warrants to the Licensee that it is the sole and exclusive owner of certain musical compositions which are described in Exhibit "A" attached hereto and made a part hereof (hereinafter referred to as the "Compositions").

B. Owner represents and warrants that it has registered and obtained registration certificate from the [COUNTRY] Copyright Office with respect to the Compositions and that the registration numbers applicable to such Compositions are as set forth in Exhibit "A."

C. Licensee maintains a site accessible through the World Wide Web, which site is located at [ADDRESS].

D. Licensee wishes to obtain a license to use the Compositions in connection with its Website and Owner wishes to grant Licensee such a license subject to the terms and conditions set forth in this Agreement.

E. Owner represents and warrants that it has full and unrestricted power and authority to enter into this Agreement and to grant Licensee the license to use the Compositions as set forth in this Agreement.

NOW, THEREFORE, in consideration of the promises and agreements set forth herein, the receipt and sufficiency of which are hereby acknowledged by the parties, the parties, and for other good and valuable consideration, each intending to be legally bound hereby, do promise and agree as follows:

1. GRANT OF LICENSE

1.1   Owner hereby grants to the Licensee, the non-exclusive right and license to use the Compositions, or any portion of the Compositions, as the Licensee shall see fit, in connection with the Licensee's Website.

1.2   The license granted hereunder shall be a non-exclusive, worldwide, royalty free (subject only to the one time licensing fee set forth herein) right to use the Compositions, subject to the terms and conditions set forth herein.

1.3   The term of this license shall be perpetual, unless terminated pursuant to the terms hereof.

1.4   The license granted herein shall be limited to the right to integrate the Compositions into the Website of the Licensee. Licensee shall have no right to offer the Compositions for sale or otherwise distribute, publish, grant any sub-licenses, sell, rent, convey, offer for download or otherwise exploit the Compositions. Licensee shall not be permitted to create any derivative works based upon the Compositions.

1.5   Licensee shall be permitted to use portions, and not the entire Compositions, in connection with its Website without violating any rights of the Owner hereunder. The License granted herein includes the right to synchronize and integrate the Compositions into the Licensee's Website design and include the Compositions in connection with Flash presentations, applets, page loads, online video presentations, and any other use that integrates the Compositions into the design of the Licensee's Website.

1.6   It is acknowledged and agrees by the Owner that users who access the Licensee's Website will be permitted to hear the Compositions upon accessing the Licensee's Website and that such access by users shall be permitted pursuant to the terms hereof. It is further acknowledged by the Owner that the Licensee cannot prevent users from violating the copyrights and other proprietary rights of the Owner and that Licensee is not responsible for the infringing acts of users. Owner holds Licensee harmless from and against any acts of the users that may infringe upon the rights of the Owner, including but not limited to actions based upon contributory infringements or any theory based upon the Licensee providing users with the means and facilities through which copyright or other proprietary rights infringement may take place.

1.7   The License granted herein includes the right to adapt the Compositions to an appropriate file format for access through the World Wide Web, including WAV files, Mp3 format, or any other format which will permit integration into the Licensee's Website and access to the Compositions over the World Wide Web.

1.8   Owner hereby grants to the Licensee the right to use the name of the Owner and the composer and artists involved in the Compositions in connection with it's Website. Owner represents and warrants that it has the full right and permission to grant such licenses and permissions from all such individuals.

2. COMPENSATION FOR LICENSE

2.1   In consideration of the license granted herein, Licensee agrees to pay a one-time license fee to the Owner in an amount equal to [AMOUNT] ("License Fee").

2.2   Such License Fee shall be due and payable in full within [NUMBER] days following the execution of this Agreement. The right to use the Compositions pursuant to this Agreement shall not commence until such License Fee is paid in full.

3. TERM OF LICENSE

3.1   This License Agreement shall be effective upon execution by both parties; provided however, that the Licensee's right to use the Compositions shall not commence until the License Fee as set forth above is paid in full.

3.2   The license granted hereunder to use the Compositions within the scope and terms set forth herein shall be perpetual but may be terminated by the Owner upon a breach hereof by the Licensee.

3.3 Owner shall have the right to terminate this Agreement and the license granted herein upon written notice to the Licensee upon the occurrence of the following events:

    A. Licensee makes any use of the Compositions beyond the scope of the license granted herein.

    B. Licensee files a petitions in bankruptcy or an involuntary bankruptcy petition is filed against Licensee, Licensee is adjudicated to be insolvent, Licensee makes an assignment for the benefit of creditors, Licensee discontinues its business, or if a receiver is appointed over Licensee's business and is not discharged within [NUMBER] days following appointment.

    C. Licensee assigns or attempts to assign this License Agreement in violations of the terms hereof.

    D. Licensee engages in any activity which infringes upon any trademark, copyright, patent, or other proprietary right of the Owner.

3.4 Upon any termination of this Agreement, Licensee shall cease and desist from all use of the Compositions and shall immediately remove the Compositions from its Website.

4. REPRESENTATIONS AND WARRANTIES

Owner makes the following representations and warranties to the Licensee, which representations and warranties shall apply during the term of this Agreement and shall continue to apply following the terminations of this Agreement. Owner shall indemnify and hold the Licensee harmless from and against matters that arise relating to the representations and warranties of the Owner made herein.

4.1 Licensor (the Owner) is the sole and exclusive owner of the Compositions and the copyrights and other proprietary rights contained therein.

4.2 The Compositions do not infringe upon or violate the copyrights, trademarks, patents, or other proprietary rights of any other party.

4.3 Owner has the unrestricted right and power to enter into this Agreement and to license the Compositions to the Licensee as provided herein.

4.4 There are no other agreements, court orders or the provision of any law or administrative rule that interfere with the Owner's right to license the Compositions hereunder.

4.5 Owner has obtained all necessary consents, permissions, licenses and other documents from recording companies, composers, musicians, musician unions or other labor unions, copyright owners and others with any interest in the Composition or who performed on the Compositions, at Owner's sole cost and expense and will indemnify and hold Licensee harmless from and against any and all claims, suits, threats, demands, actions and causes of action brought directly or indirectly by any of these parties.

5. COPYRIGHT NOTICES/RETAINED RIGHTS

5.1 Licensee shall place on its website a notice of copyright relative to the Compositions and credits to the songwriter and artists performing in the Compositions. Such copyright notice shall be included on each page of the Website that includes the Compositions as the sound component of such page.

5.2 Owner shall retain the copyright to the Compositions and all right, title and interest in and to the Compositions, including the right to publish, distribute, publicly perform, modify, enhance, change and improve, and all other exclusive rights of the copyright owner, except only for the right of license granted to Licensee hereunder.

5.3 Licensee hereby agrees to and acknowledges the rights retained by the Owner hereunder and acknowledges that the Owner shall retain all exclusive rights of the owner and holder of a copyright. Licensee agrees that it shall not challenge or dispute any of Owner's exclusive rights or right, title and interest in and to the Compositions or the copyrights thereof.

5.4   Owner shall have the sole right to pursue any party that infringes upon the Owner's Copyright or other proprietary rights in and to the Compositions and shall shoulder all expenses of prosecuting such infringement actions against third parties.

6. RESPONSIBILITY FOR WEBSITE

Licensee shall be solely responsible for the content of its Website and for assuring compliance of such site with applicable laws. Licensee shall hold Owner harmless from and against any and all claims related to the content of the Licensee's Website.

7. MISCELLANEOUS PROVISIONS

7.1 Notices
Any notification or written communication required by or contemplated under the terms of this Agreement shall be in writing and shall deemed to be delivered if transmitted via Email at the Email addresses listed below, except for any notice of termination of this Agreement which shall be in writing and sent by Certified Mail, Return Receipt Requested and shall be deemed to have been delivered [NUMBER] business days after the date of mailing. Email addresses for such notices shall be:

> If To Owner: [EMAIL ADDRESS]

> If To Licensee: [EMAIL ADDRESS]

7.2 No Assignment
Neither this Agreement nor any right, interest, duty or obligation hereunder may be assigned by the parties hereto.

7.3 Governing law
In interpreting the terms of this Agreement, the parties agree that the laws of the State of [STATE/PROVINCE] shall be applicable. All suits permitted to be brought in any court shall be in [STATE/PROVINCE].

7.4 Entire agreement
This Agreement contains the entire agreement and understanding of the parties with respect to the subject matter hereof and supercedes and replaces all prior discussions, agreements, proposals, understandings, whether orally or in writing, between the parties related to the subject matter of this Agreement. This Agreement may be changed, modified or amended only in a written agreement that is duly executed by authorized representatives of the parties. If any provisions hereof is deemed to be illegal or unenforceable by a court of competent jurisdiction, the enforceability of effectiveness of the remainder of the Agreement shall not be effected and this Agreement shall be enforceable without reference to the unenforceable provision. No party's waiver of any breach or accommodation to the other party shall be deemed to be a waiver of any subsequent breach.

IN WITNESS WHEREOF, the parties have executed this Agreement on the dates set forth first above, with full knowledge of its content and significance and intending to be legally bound by the terms hereof.

OWNER   LICENSEE

_____   _____
Authorized Signature   Authorized Signature

_____   _____
Print Name and Title   Print Name and Title

EXHIBIT A
COMPOSITIONS

11.9 INFLUENCER MARKETING AGREEMENT

This Influencer Marketing Agreement (the "Agreement") is made and effective [DATE],

BETWEEN: **[YOUR COMPANY NAME]** (the "Company"), an individual with his main address located at: OR a company organized and existing under the laws of the [State/Province] of [STATE/PROVINCE], with its head office located at:

[COMPLETE ADDRESS]

AND: **[NAME OF INFLUENCER]** (the "Influencer"), a company organized and existing under the laws of the [State/Province] of [STATE/PROVINCE], with its head office located at:

[YOUR COMPLETE ADDRESS]

The Company and the Influencer may be referred to collectively as the "Parties."

In consideration of the foregoing and of the mutual promises set forth herein, and intending to be legally bound, the Parties hereto agree as follows:

1. ENGAGEMENT

1.1 The Company hereby engages the Influencer from the date of execution of this Agreement through and including the date(s) of performance ("the Term") for the limited purpose of promoting certain brands and brand content, through the Influencer's social media outlets. The nature of the brand content to be promoted and the specific details and requirements of the promotion are outlined in the attached Schedule A. During the Term, the Influencer agrees to be engaged for the purpose of promoting the brand content and to be bound by the guidelines as attached as Schedule B ("Guidelines"). The Company hereby appoints the Influencer as its representative on a non-exclusive, non-employee basis to endorse and promote its Services to the target audience.

2. TERM

2.1 This Agreement shall have an initial term of one year and shall automatically renew for additional one-year terms thereafter unless either Party provides 21 days' prior written notice of its intention of nonrenewal.

2.2 When this Agreement shall terminate, the Influencer's rights to use the brand name as described within this Agreement shall terminate as well.

2.3 Should the Influencer fail to perform and meet the Company's expectations, the Company can terminate this Agreement with 21 days' prior written notice.

3. DELIVERABLES

3.1 The Influencer will deliver the agreed number of posts on the agreed platforms on behalf of the Company as outlined in Schedule A. The Services shall conform to the specifications and instructions of the Company as outlined in Schedule B, abide by the rules of the relevant social media platforms, and are subject to the Company's acceptance and approval. The Company has a maximum of [No. of days] days to reject any deliverable in accordance with this Section and must notify the Influencer within [No. of days] days of receipt of work that additional revisions and/or amendments will be requested.

4. OWNERSHIP

4.1 The Influencer acknowledges and agrees that the Company, for the purpose of performing the Services under this Agreement. shall own, exclusively and in perpetuity, all rights of whatever kind and character, throughout the universe and in any and all languages, in and to the videos, photographs, text and/or all works of similar nature produced, developed, or created by the Influencer for this Agreement, and any and all intellectual property rights thereto, including trademarks, trade secrets, trade dress, design, mask work, copyrights, and patent rights (collectively, the "Content"), including the right to sublicense the Content to the Company's brand partners (the "Brand Affiliates"). Notwithstanding the foregoing, the Influencer may delete posts from his/her owned and/or controlled social media channels containing any Content after a period of ninety (90) days from post date.

5. USAGE

5.1 The Company shall cause the Influencer to grant to the Company and to the Brand Affiliates a limited, non-exclusive, royalty free, right and license to feature the Content generated by the Influencer as part of the Campaign (including the Influencer's name and likeness) on the Company's and Brand Affiliates' owned and controlled social media platforms and within third-party digital and broadcast platforms and print platforms, including but not limited to: ad networks, email marketing, paid search listings, television, radio, newspapers, magazines and brochures, Facebook, Instagram, Tik Tok, Twitter, YouTube, Pinterest, and website blogs during the term of this Agreement and for a period of twelve (12) months thereafter.

6. LICENSE

6.1 The Company grants to the Influencer a temporary license to use the Brand Affiliates' name and promotional materials as may be necessary to achieve the promotional purpose but only in compliance with the Guidelines and only to achieve the promotional purpose as described in Schedule A. The Influencer grants to the Company a perpetual license to use the Influencer's name and likeness in all media including the Company's website and the Brand Affiliates' website and on social media sites and in all formats of print and digital media advertising.

7. CANCELLATION

7.1 Either Party may terminate this Agreement upon fourteen (14) days' prior written notice if the other Party breaches this Agreement and does not cure such breach within such time period. In addition to any right or remedy that may be available to the Company under this Agreement or applicable law, in addition, in the event that the Influencer has breached this Agreement, the Company may (i) immediately suspend, limit or terminate the Influencer's access to any Company account and/or (ii) instruct the Influencer to cease all promotional activities or make clarifying statements, and the Influencer shall immediately comply. Either Party may terminate this Agreement at any time without cause upon thirty (30) days' prior written notice to the other Party.

8. CONFIDENTIALITY AND EXCLUSIVITY

8.1 During the course of the Influencer's performance of Services for the Company, the Influencer will receive, have access to and create documents, records and information of a confidential and proprietary nature to the Company and customers of the Company. The Influencer acknowledges and agrees that such information is an asset of the Company or its clients, is not generally known to the trade, is of a confidential nature, and, to preserve the goodwill of the Company and its clients, must be kept strictly confidential and used only in the performance of the Influencer's duties under this Agreement. The Influencer agrees that he/she will not use, disclose, communicate, copy or permit the use or disclosure of any such information to any third party in any manner whatsoever, except to the existing employees of the Company or as otherwise directed by the Company in the course of the Influencer's performance of Services under this Agreement, and thereafter only with the written permission of the Company. Upon termination of this Agreement or upon the request of the Company, the Influencer will return to the Company all of the confidential information, and all copies or reproductions thereof, which are in the Influencer's possession or control. The Influencer agrees that during the tenure of this contract, and for a three-month term afterward, the Influencer will not undertake influencer marketing for a competitor in the same vertical as the Company.

9. COMPENSATION

9.1 In full consideration of the Influencer's performance, his/her obligations and the rights granted herein, the Influencer shall be paid [THE AMOUNT AGREED UPON BETWEEN THE COMPANY AND THE INFLUENCER]. This includes any agreed bonus incentives, should the Influencer meet the agreed targets. The Influencer will otherwise perform the Services at his/her own expense and use his/her own resources and equipment. The Influencer acknowledges that the agreed upon compensation represents the Influencer's entire compensation with respect to this Agreement, and the Company shall have no other obligation for any other compensation to or expenses or costs incurred by the Influencer in connection with the performance of its obligations under this Agreement. If the Influencer has obtained employees or agents (the "Influencer Personnel"), the Influencer shall be solely responsible for all costs associated with Influencer Personnel.

10. PAYMENT TERMS

10.1 Payment can be made by [SPECIFY PAYMENT METHOD] to the address given by the Influencer. Payments will be due seven days after the agreed invoice date.

11. MATERIAL DISCLOSURES AND COMPLIANCE WITH GUIDELINES

11.1 When publishing posts/statuses about the Company's products or services, the Influencer must clearly disclose his/her "material connection" with the Company, including the fact that the Influencer was given any consideration, was provided with certain experiences or is being paid for a particular service. The above disclosure should be clear and prominent and made in close proximity to any statements that the Influencer makes about the Company or the Company's products or services. Please note that this disclosure is required, regardless of any space limitations of the medium (e.g. Twitter), where the disclosure can be made via hashtags, e.g. #sponsored. The Influencer's statements should always reflect the Influencer's honest and truthful opinions and actual experiences. The Influencer should only make factual statements about the Company or the Company's products which the Influencer knows for certain are true and can be verified.

12. FORCE MAJEURE

12.1 If either Party is unable to perform any of its obligations by reason of fire or other casualty, strike, act or order of public authority, act of God, or other cause beyond the control of such Party, then such Party shall be excused from such performance during the pendency of such cause.

13. INDEPENDENT CONTRACTOR

13.1 The Influencer is retained as an independent contractor of the Company. The Influencer acknowledges and agrees that (i) the Influencer is solely responsible for the manner and form by which the Influencer performs under this Agreement, and (ii) the Influencer is a self-employed individual, who performs Services similar to the Services outlined in Schedule A for various entities and individuals other than the Company. The Influencer is responsible for the withholding and payment of all taxes and other assessments arising out of the Influencer's performance of Services, and neither the Influencer nor any of the Influencer's employees or independent clients shall be entitled to participate in any employee benefit plans of the Company.

14.   REPRESENTATIONS AND WARRANTIES

14.1   Parties represent and warrant to each other that each is free to enter into this Agreement and that this engagement does not violate the terms of any agreement with any third party.

15.   GENERAL TERMS

15.1   If the scope of any of the provisions of the Agreement is too broad in any respect whatsoever to permit enforcement to its full extent, then such provisions shall be enforced to the maximum extent permitted by law, and the Parties hereto consent and agree that such scope may be judicially modified accordingly and that the whole of such provisions of this Agreement shall not thereby fail, but that the scope of such provisions shall be curtailed only to the extent necessary to conform to law.

15.2   This Agreement may not be assigned by either Party without the prior written consent of the other, and any such purported assignment shall be void.

15.3   This document is a complete and exclusive statement of the terms of this Agreement and may not be changed orally but only by writing signed by both Parties.

This Agreement shall be construed and enforced in accordance with the laws of the [State/Province] of [STATE/PROVINCE].

IN WITNESS WHEREOF, the Parties hereto have executed this Agreement as of the date first above written.

COMPANY   **INFLUENCER**

_____   _____
Authorized Signature   Authorized Signature

_____   _____
Print Name and Title   Print Name and Title

11.10 EMPLOYEE NON-COMPETE AGREEMENT

This Employee Non-Compete Agreement (the "Agreement") is made and effective this [DATE],

BETWEEN:	**[EMPLOYEE NAME]** (the "Employee"), an individual with his main address at:
	[COMPLETE ADDRESS]
AND:	**[YOUR COMPANY NAME]** (the "Company"), a corporation organized and existing under the laws of the [State/Province] of [STATE/PROVINCE], with its head office located at:
	[YOUR COMPLETE ADDRESS]

1. COVENANT NOT TO COMPETE

For good consideration and as an inducement for Company to employ Employee, if such employment is terminated for any cause, employee shall not, for a period of [TIME PERIOD] years after leaving the employment, engage directly or indirectly, either personally or as an employee, associate partner, partner, manager, agent, or otherwise, or by means of any corporate or other device, in the [TYPE OF ENTERPRISE] business within [GEOGRAPHICAL AREA] [if appropriate, add: nor shall employee for such period and in such localities solicit orders, directly or indirectly, from any customers of Company, or from any customers of its successor, for such products as are sold by Company or its successor, either for (himself or herself) or as an employee of any person, firm, or corporation].

2. DEFINITION OF THE TERMS

The term "not compete" as used herein shall mean that the Employee shall not own, manage, operate, consult or to be employed in a business substantially similar to, or competitive with, the present business of the Company or such other business activity in which the Company may substantially engage during the term of employment.

Competition means owning or working for a business of the following type: [SPECIFY TYPE OF BUSINESS EMPLOYEE MAY NOT ENGAGE IN].

3. TRADE SECRETS

The Employee acknowledges that the Company shall or may in reliance of this agreement provide Employee access to trade secrets, customers and other confidential data and good will. Employee agrees to retain said information as confidential and not to use said information on his or her won behalf or disclose same to any third party.

The Employee will take necessary actions to keep the Company's business secrets, including but not limited to customer, supplier, logistical, financial, research and development information, confidential and not to disclose the Company's business secrets to any third party during and after the term of the Employee's employment.

4. SPECIFIC ACCOUNT NON-COMPETITION CLAUSE

On the termination of the Employee's employment with the Company for any reason, the Employee will not solicit any customer of the Company that was a customer of the Company during the course of the Employee's employment with the Company, whether or not still a customer of the Company and whether or not knowledge of the customer is considered confidential information, or in any way aid and assist any other person to solicit any such customer for a period of [TIME PERIOD] from the date of termination of the Employee's employment.

5. INDEMNIFICATION

Employee agrees to pay liquidated damages in the amount of [DOLLAR AMOUNT] for any violation of the covenant not to compete contained in this Agreement.

6. BINDING AGREEMENT

If any part of these promises is void for any reason, the undersigned accepts that it may be severed without affecting the validity or enforceability of the balance of the promises.

This non-compete agreement shall extend only for [GEOGRAPHICAL AREA] and shall be in full force and effect for [NUMBER] years, commencing with the date of employment termination.

This agreement shall be binding upon and inure to the benefit of the parties, their successors, assigns, and personal representatives.

IN WITNESS WHEREOF, each party to this agreement has caused it to be executed at [PLACE OF EXECUTION] on the date indicated below.

COMPANY   EMPLOYEE

_____   _____
Authorized Signature   Authorized Signature

_____   _____
Print Name and Title   Print Name and Title

12. Checklists for Fashion Brands

12.1 Must Have E-Commerce Policies

The recent surge of the E-commerce business demonstrates that E-commerce has become an essential element of life. Consumers used to be hesitant to purchase online because they were concerned with the quality, their cash possibly misappropriated, or the product not being delivered on time. It has been found that a substantial portion of the public now trusts E-commerce websites for their everyday necessities. As a result, prepaid orders outnumber cash-on-delivery transactions in today's market. This is evidence of the overall majority's acknowledgement of E-commerce services, particularly during the COVID-19 pandemic when E-commerce consumption grew significantly.

To protect the interests of consumers, our laws are continuously creating new policies and procedures to cope with all of this huge transformation in the marketing strategy. To survive in this field, E-commerce enterprises must have a complete awareness of the law framework and the potential disputes that they may encounter, as well as a proper risk management technique.

It is of utmost importance for you to have these essential policies on your e-commerce website to stay safe legally and also deliver a satisfying customer experience. Below is the list of the crucial policies that you ought to have on an e-commerce website if you are an e-commerce business owner-

- **Shipping Policy Page:**

When an order is placed online, a shipping policy is succinct documentation that contains critical facts about shipment. It commonly contains data on delivery charges and procedures, as well as shipping timeframes and other facts. Some delivery rules are more comprehensive compared to others, but they should be straightforward, precise, and simple to grasp in general. Detailed data, such as a return and exchange policy, is commonly given, giving a full platform for buyers prior to their shopping. A clear e-commerce shipping policy has several advantages: It effectively educates your consumers prior to their purchase, assists in answering shipment inquiries, and enables the business to be effective when dealing with any shipment concerns that could emerge. The following has been explained in brief for your better understanding.

a) **Shipping methods and predicted delivery date/dates**

Whenever you provide one or more shipping options like regular, express delivery and overnight delivery; it must include them all on the website along with the predicted delivery date/dates after the order is placed. Keep your customer informed about the product leaving the warehouse and reaching the logistic services via texts and emails. This builds consumer trust and keeps the consumer well informed about the product's shipment journey till the final day of delivery.

b) International shipping

When you provide international shipping, you ought to include a disclaimer stating who is liable for customs and importation duties. Establish your foreign shipping policy by specifying which operator manages international shipments and who covers international tariffs, charges, as well as any expenses incurred.

c) Shipping charges & rates

Listing delivery charges enables your consumers to evaluate and estimate their entire expenses before shopping. Highlighting shipping prices is especially crucial for overseas consumers, who may not be eligible for certain deals available, such as free delivery. Often, international shipping rates differ dramatically across businesses pertaining to their response to growth in transportation rates, and hence you'll want to be precise.

d) Damaged, stolen and lost packages

There is indeed a plethora of reasons as to why a shipment is lost or becomes a shipment violation. In many such cases, it is beyond your reach to control these unfortunate circumstances. However, informing clients about the process to deal with if faced with such a situation when their product is lost, stolen or damaged gives them comfort and assurance. You can accomplish it all by prominently posting contact details as well as for instructions on how to submit a lost, stolen or damaged package's complaint.

- ### Return Policy Page:

Returns and exchanges may be changed from a loathed feature of e-commerce into a possibility that creates additional income for your business and enhances customer loyalty with a well-defined return policy and the appropriate system in place. If you're getting your first return request or attempting to restore a malfunctioning process, developing a strategy can help you instantly decrease the number of customer care hours spent on returns and exchanges. Even though return or exchange may not be profitable on the first purchase, an excellent customer experience is more likely to result in increased loyalty and long-term profitability.

The policy should cover the following essentials: What items can be returned, what items can be exchanged, what products are final sale, when things can be returned or exchanged, in what condition items can be returned, what products can be returned for, how to initiate a return or exchange, and how to initiate a return or exchange etc. The following has been explained in brief for your better understanding.

a) Set a time limit for returns

It's critical to inform your consumers about the timeframe in which they ought to return a purchased product. In particular, 15-30 days is common, while some businesses prefer 90 days. In either case, allowing returns after that time will be of no profit. Hence establish a clear instruction on the time limit of acceptance of returned goods.

b) Specify the expected return condition.

Accepting a return is one thing if the customer is instantly dissatisfied with a purchased product or if the product delivered turns out to be defective. Receiving a return if a product has already been used, damaged, or depreciated in any way by the consumer is completely a separate issue. Specify the conditions a product ought to be in before such a return can be accepted when you are developing your business' return policy. Consumers often seek to return products in difficult to sell state if you do not convey this knowledge. You will be obliged to suffer a loss in this scenario.

c) Specify return requirements

If there are any conditions that should be fulfilled before a return can be approved, you ought to inform consumers long in advance.

For eg- You may specify that all returns should be received undamaged and/or in their original packaging. You must also notify consumers if they require an identification code, delivery information, transaction receipt, or anything else. Whichever terms you select, make sure they are explicitly indicated for everybody to see.

A Return Merchandise Authorization (RMA) system is one straightforward approach to do the same. You can use this to obtain data and photos from the consumer. You provide approval if you chose to accept the return. If your company offers return shipping, you'll provide proof of delivery with approval.

d) Select either a refund or in-store credit.

Before they return a product, consumers want to know whether you intend to reimburse them. Most people will expect a complete refund, whereas others accept in-store credit. As an e-commerce entrepreneur, you must choose between the two.

It is mostly recommended to give consumers a complete refund on all returned products as long as it serves your return policy conditions. You can choose to grant store credit for specific types of returns at your convenience. If you decide to do this, make sure to include explicit details in your business policy. When used effectively, the store credit can serve to improve and optimize your returns procedure.

e) All expenses related to returns should be mentioned

Whenever a consumer wishes to return the product purchased online, who would bear the expenses of return shipping, repackaging, and so on? This sort of information should be explicitly mentioned in your return policy.

Nothing could be more frustrating for a buyer than receiving a product they don't like just to find out they have to pay to return it.

If you intend your consumers to bear financial responsibility for product returns, make it absolutely clear in your policy. Neglecting to do so will result in a swarm of irate consumers equipped with laptops and Twitter, Instagram, Facebook handles open to complain and write bad reviews.

- **Privacy Policy Page:**

A Privacy Policy explains how you will collect, store, use, and share personal information from your online consumers. A Privacy Policy for your e-commerce store is crucial for minimising accountability and guaranteeing compliance with local, state, federal, and international data protection laws. The content in your e-commerce store's Privacy Policy should be thorough, yet worded in such a way that the ordinary site visitor understands your policies and their rights. If you intend to share the details of your customers on a third-party website in the future then your Privacy Policy must include a paragraph identifying those third parties and how they acquire and use your consumer's data.

When developing an e-commerce store Privacy Policy, four crucial goals should be attained: Inform your store visitors about the private data you collect and manage, give your visitors the option to opt-in and opt-out, give your visitors access to the information you and third parties collect, inform your visitors of how you secure their data if you use remarketing technology, and so on.

The 8 crucial pointers to include in your Privacy Policy Checklist have been combined together and summarised for your better as well as easier understanding.

a) **Website Privacy Statement and laws**

According to the Information Technology Act, all enterprises must have a privacy policy that is available on their official website. The privacy policy must define all the data gathered, the objective for which the data will be used, to whom as well as how the data will be shared, and the appropriate security protocols that will be used to protect such personal information. You ought to state all the laws that govern your privacy policy. For eg: The IT Act 2000, GDPR guidelines, HIPAA guidelines etc.

Numerous sites have terms and conditions in addition to a privacy policy. The website Terms & Conditions is a legal document that outlines the terms and conditions that users ought to abide by when using the website. The terms and conditions agreement of your e-commerce business basically specifies the licence of the copyrights on the internet and incorporates a liability disclaimer, a permitted use clause, a variation clause, and a clause defining the pertinent laws as well as the jurisdiction and other legal information.

b) **Personal details**

Your policy must define that your website will collect and store personal details submitted by its visitors, such as their names, addresses, phone numbers, email addresses, and so on. This would also make it clear that the majority of data they disclose is entirely discretionary; yet, submitting lesser details may restrict a customer's privilege to utilize all of the website's services.

c) **Analytics and usage data**

Notify the consumers if your business' website acquires personal details in order to evaluate how users access and use the site. This information is beneficial to the business for a number of distinctive purposes, such as monitoring and enhancing the site's performance. Please be sure to declare, if relevant, that the data you collect may include the user's Internet service provider, kind of search engine or system software, IP address, visited sites, time and length of site visits, crash logs, and other website user activity.

d) **Cookies**

Whenever necessary, your privacy policy should explicitly state that your website uses cookies to achieve high performance. Well here's a basic provision pertaining to cookies preferences for users: Most web browsers are pre-configured to allow cookies. You may configure your web browser to refuse all cookies or to notify you when one is being sent. Please keep in mind, however, that deleting or disabling cookies may prevent certain aspects of the site from functioning properly. "Cookies from this website do not and cannot infiltrate a user's hard drive to collect any information stored on the hard drive."

e) **Providers of third-party services**

Personal customer information may be required by your business in connection with technical support, modifications, product updates, or analytics and data inspection or compilation. Your privacy policy must define clearly and unambiguously that your company will indeed be obliged to share user information with any third-party service providers and that they may recruit to help with all these activities. Consequently, your business may be required to share personal data with third-party promotion and advertising agencies. Your business, on the other hand, ought to be committed to ensuring that all these service providers adhere to security protocols concerning customer data.

f) **Privacy Policy Updates**

Inform the user that your business' privacy policy may alter over time and thus they should review the policy for any adjustments on a regular basis. Your business must also take the opportunity to inform customers of any policy changes or encourage users to agree on these modifications by ticking a box or clicking a link. In either scenario, visitors who actively engage with the website after the business' privacy policy is revised will be immediately compliant with the new terms and conditions.

g) **Warn the user of the importance of data protection**

Your privacy policy must notify users to properly secure the personal details they enter on the website, such as login credentials, usernames, geolocation, photos, and videos so that third-party service providers cannot hack/manipulate their accounts or claim their identities. Whenever your website enables users to communicate with each other or view other users' identities and perhaps other data, warn them never to reveal any critical data on that public domain.

h) **Providing contact details**

Always provide contact details in the document for consumers who might have a question or concern about your privacy policy (or simply tell them to ask questions through your Contact Us form).

When you write your own policy content, remember to include the following topics:

1. **Your website's copyright information**

Copyright must be used to safeguard your database, as well as trademarks for your company name, logo, domain name, and product name. Screen displays, computer-generated visuals, and websites can all be protected under industrial design law.

The underlying parts of a webpage, such as code, algorithms, technical scripts and descriptions, programming, logic flow charts, and databases information, can be safeguarded by copyright law under trade secrets if they are not revealed to the public and adequate measures are in place to keep them confidential. Registering your domain name as a trademark must be a priority too. Thereby, your business will have a legal remedy against anyone who seeks to promote identical services or products using the domain name. It also stops others from acquiring the same name as their trademark. It is mandatory that you register your website and any copyrighted material with the intellectual property office.

2. Your business's contact information and where your customers should direct any complaints

An email address provided on a contact us webpage does not have the same effect most of the time. The contact form can demonstrate to your customers that you are well-organized and have taken the trouble to get in contact with them in a more efficient manner. Having a contact form and strategically displaying it on your website to make it more accessible and approachable can optimize your website and demonstrate that you value a customers' opinion and your brand. This way even after the purchase the consumer can use the contact form to launch a complaint or feedback about a delivered product if they are not satisfied with your product/services. Several website owners utilize relevant hashtags on their social media pages to connect with consumers. You might then expect that consumers will contact you through your social media accounts.

If a consumer isn't active on social media or doesn't want to go to the trouble of contacting you there then it becomes troublesome and an unneeded burden for them. As a result, you will most likely lose a potential consumer to competitors. This is where the contact form is useful. It's a terrific and simple approach to let customers know that you can be reached immediately through your website's contact us form. An additional benefit of contact forms is that they offer the idea that you are always available to tend to their queries. Customers will be more likely to contact you instead of searching for a rival brand if they can immediately find your form and contact you without using their email or social media accounts.

3. Product and service warranties

Consumers arrive with preconceived notions about how long a product will function and what difficulties the company will tackle. Picture this scenario- A consumer calling in with a damaged product only to discover that their limited warranty has just ended or that their concern isn't protected. Establishing objectives does nothing but set the scene for bad client encounters.

Providing extended warranties allows the user to set standards about what is and isn't protected in the limited replacement warranty vs. a premium insurance policy. Since the coverage of any potential concern can be costly to serve, giving extended warranties can provide clients with the choice of getting the insurance they want and are prepared to pay for. Overall, providing warranties helps the consumer to set the guidelines while also delivering on services guarantees, resulting in consumer loyalty. Providing a protection policy can boost client confidence in your business by demonstrating your commitment to support your goods and stand by them in the long run.

Throughout businesses that are renowned for excellent product quality are more likely to provide a secure product guarantee and warranty services. This communicates to its consumers that they can be sure to invest in their goods and services.

4. Liability disclaimer

A Limitation of Liability disclaimer is one of the most critical disclaimers for any website. Because disclaimers are fundamentally intended to inform users of the boundaries or scope of a website's duty to them, having a Limitation of Liability is crucial. Generally, Limitations of Liability are stated identically, however you can incorporate particular limitations pertaining to your product or service if desired. A Limitation of Liability disclaimer is often found in the Terms of Service of a website. Another disclaimer that any website ought to have is displayed right beside the Limitation of Liabilities as well as in the Terms of Use.

A Disclaimer of Warranties is a disclaimer that informs consumers of what the website does not guarantee or warrant. This disclaimer is essential for e-commerce sites since it can safeguard you from probable product-related disputes.

5. Data and security information

In order to protect data and security information, you ought to have a privacy policy on the website. If you're taking the email of your customer or any visitor of your website then it needs to be mentioned in the privacy policy. Whatever information you're retaining of a potential customer or regular customer, what are the reasons and what you will do with that information needs to be explained. Credit card information- whether the credit card information is safe or not or consent for cookies, browser information for the way of collecting cookies etc. should all be mentioned in the privacy policy. There are various software available like you can use Shopify to create a website and take your brand online. The GDPR guidelines are available in European countries and HIPAA guidelines in the United States of America.

- **Obtain SSL (Secure Server Layer) Certificates**

One of the key advantages of SSL Certificates is that they encrypt sensitive data transmitted over the network. It assures that only the designated recipient collects the data. This is a vital stage since any transmitted data will be routed through multiple servers before reaching the destination server. Use efficient e-commerce software and plugins to block untrustworthy networks and govern website traffic input and outflow. They ought to have high selectivity, enabling only trustworthy traffic to pass through. Digital security refers to the policies that provide secure online transactions. It specifies the methods that protect those who sell and buy products and services online. You must acquire your clients' trust by implementing eCommerce security principles. These essentials include:

- Privacy

- Integrity

- Authentication

- Non-repudiation

6. **Applicable laws related to your industry enforced by your country, state, territory or local municipality**

Compliance is the necessary legal documentation that is required to run any organisation or business or trade. Always get legal assistance to be completely sure about your website abiding by the law and having all the necessary agreements, policies, contracts etc. Make sure it's in accordance with your respective country, state, territory or local municipality. This will ensure legal protection as well as enable you to have a legal remedy if faced with any disputes. For eg in India: The IT Act 2000, Payment and Settlements Systems Act 2007, Consumer Protection Act 2019 and so on.

7. **Partners and affiliations of your website**

Affiliate collaborations can expand beyond people and influencers to include large name brands or similar businesses. Many businesses use connections for affiliate marketing; for example, Sephora has an affiliate partnership programme. It's a winning scenario for all parties. While Consumer Search receives a fee on every purchase, Sephora increases visitor traffic and achieves powerful referrals. There will always be prospects for your business to form affiliate partnerships with well-known brands.

12.2 Website Privacy Policy (Template)

The Internet is an amazing tool. It has the power to change the way we live, and we're starting to see that potential today. With only a few mouse-clicks, you can follow the news, look up facts, buy goods and services, and communicate with others from around the world. It's important to [YOUR COMPANY NAME] to help our customers retain their privacy when they take advantage of all the Internet has to offer.

We believe your business is no one else's. Your privacy is important to you and to us. So we'll protect the information you share with us. To protect your privacy, [YOUR COMPANY NAME] follows different principles in accordance with worldwide practices for customer privacy and data protection.

- We won't sell or give away your name, mail address, phone number, email address or any other information to anyone.
- We'll use state-of-the-art security measures to protect your information from unauthorized users.

NOTICE

We will ask you when we need information that personally identifies you (personal information) or allows us to contact you. Generally, this information is requested when you create a Registration ID on the site or when you download free software, enter a contest, order email newsletters or join a limited-access premium site. We use your Personal Information for four primary purposes:

- To make the site easier for you to use by not having to enter information more than once.
- To help you quickly find software, services or information.
- To help us create content most relevant to you.
- To alert you to product upgrades, special offers, updated information and other new services from [YOUR COMPANY NAME].

CONSENT

If you choose not to register or provide personal information, you can still use most of [YOUR WEBSITE ADDRESS]. But you will not be able to access areas that require registration.

If you decide to register, you will be able to select the kinds of information you want to receive from us by subscribing to various services, like our electronic newsletters. If you do not want us to communicate with you about other offers regarding [YOUR COMPANY NAME] products, programs, events, or services by email, postal mail, or telephone, you may select the option stating that you do not wish to receive marketing messages from [YOUR COMPANY NAME].

[YOUR COMPANY NAME] occasionally allows other companies to offer our registered customers information about their products and services, using postal mail only. If you do not want to receive these offers, you may select the option stating that you do not wish to receive marketing materials from third parties.

ACCESS

We will provide you with the means to ensure that your personal information is correct and current. You may review and update this information at any time at the Visitor Center. There, you can:

- View and edit personal information you have already given us.
- Tell us whether you want us to send you marketing information, or whether you want third parties to send you their offers by postal mail.
- Sign up for electronic newsletters about our services and products.

- Register. Once you register, you won't need to do it again. Wherever you go on [YOUR WEBSITE ADDRESS], your information stays with you.

SECURITY

[YOUR COMPANY NAME] has taken strong measures to protect the security of your personal information and to ensure that your choices for its intended use are honored. We take strong precautions to protect your data from loss, misuse, unauthorized access or disclosure, alteration, or destruction.

We guarantee your e-commerce transactions to be 100% safe and secure. When you place orders or access your personal account information, you're utilizing secure server software SSL, which encrypts your personal information before it's sent over the Internet. SSL is one of the safest encryption technologies available.

In addition, your transactions are guaranteed under the Fair Credit Billing Act. This Act states that your bank cannot hold you liable for more than $50.00 in fraudulent credit card charges. If your bank does hold you liable for $50.00 or less, we'll cover your liability provided the unauthorized, fraudulent use of your credit card resulted through no fault of your own and from purchases made from us over our secure server. In the event of unauthorized use of your credit card, you must notify your credit card provider in accordance with its reporting rules and procedures.

[YOUR COMPANY NAME] strictly protects the security of your personal information and honors your choices for its intended use. We carefully protect your data from loss, misuse, unauthorized access or disclosure, alteration, or destruction.

Your personal information is never shared outside the company without your permission, except under conditions explained above. Inside the company, data is stored in password-controlled servers with limited access. Your information may be stored and processed in [YOUR COUNTRY] or any other country where [YOUR COMPANY NAME], its subsidiaries, affiliates or agents are located.

You also have a significant role in protecting your information. No one can see or edit your personal information without knowing your username and password, so do not share these with others.

NOTICE TO PARENTS

Parents or guardians: we want to help you guard your children's privacy. We encourage you to talk to your children about safe and responsible use of their Personal Information while using the Internet.

The [YOUR COMPANY NAME] site does not publish content that is targeted to children. However, if you are concerned about your children providing [YOUR COMPANY NAME] any personal information without your consent, [YOUR COMPANY NAME] offers a Kids account. It allows parents to give parental consent for the collection, use and sharing of children's (ages 12 and under) personal information online.

ENFORCEMENT

If for some reason you believe [YOUR COMPANY NAME] has not adhered to these principles, please notify us by email at privacy@email.com, and we will do our best to determine and correct the problem promptly. Be certain the words Privacy Policy are in the Subject line.

ELECTRONIC PRODUCT REGISTRATION

When you buy and install a new product, we may ask you to register your purchase electronically. When you do, we merge your registration information with any information you've already left with us (we call that information your personal profile). If you haven't previously registered with us, we create a personal profile for you from your product registration information. If you ever want to review or update that information, you can visit the Profile Center, click on Update Profile, and edit any of the Personal Information in your profile. If you haven't already created a Registration ID, we will ask you to do so. This ensures that only you can access your information.

CUSTOMER PROFILES

As mentioned above, every registered customer has a unique personal profile. Each profile is assigned a unique personal identification number, which helps us ensure that only you can access your profile.

When you register, we create your profile, assign a personal identification number, then send this personal identification number back to your hard drive in the form of a cookie, which is a very small bit of code. This code is uniquely yours. It is your passport to seamless travel across [WEBSITE], allowing you to download free software, order free newsletters, and visit premium sites without having to fill out registration forms with information you've already provided. Even if you switch computers, you won't have to re-register – just use your Registration ID to identify yourself.

WHAT WE DO WITH THE INFORMATION YOU SHARE

When you join us, you provide us with your contact information, including your email address. We use this information to send you updates about your order, questionnaires to measure your satisfaction with our service and announcements about new and exciting services that we offer. When you order from us, we ask for your credit card number and billing address. We use this information only to bill you for the product(s) you order at that time. For your convenience, we do save billing information in case you want to order from us again, but we don't use this information again without your permission.

We occasionally hire other companies to provide limited services on our behalf, including packaging, mailing and delivering purchases, answering customer questions about products or services, sending postal mail and processing event registration. We will only provide those companies the information they need to deliver the service, and they are prohibited from using that information for any other purpose.

[YOUR COMPANY NAME] will disclose your personal information, without notice, only if required to do so by law or in the good faith belief that such action is necessary to: (a) conform to the edicts of the law or comply with legal process served on [YOUR COMPANY NAME] or the site; (b) protect and defend the rights or property of [YOUR COMPANY NAME] and its family of Websites, and, (c) act in urgent circumstances to protect the personal safety of users of [YOUR COMPANY NAME], its Websites, or the public.

For Latest Fashion Law Insights and Industry Updates, visit: fashionlawjournal.com

Check out our Courses in Fashion Law at:

legaldesire.com/fashionlaw

Made in the USA
Las Vegas, NV
10 June 2023

73155267R00171